D1431992

Democracy and the Nature of American Influence in Iran, 1941–1979

Contemporary Issues in the Middle East
Mehran Kamrava, *Series Adviser*

Democracy
and the Nature of
American Influence
in Iran, 1941-1979

David R. Collier

Syracuse University Press

Copyright © 2017 by Syracuse University Press
Syracuse, New York 13244-5290

All Rights Reserved

First Edition 2017

17 18 19 20 21 22   6 5 4 3 2 1

∞ The paper used in this publication meets the minimum requirements
of the American National Standard for Information Sciences—Permanence
of Paper for Printed Library Materials, ANSI Z39.48-1992.

For a listing of books published and distributed by Syracuse University Press,
visit www.SyracuseUniversityPress.syr.edu.

ISBN: 978-0-8156-3497-3 (hardcover)
    978-0-8156-3512-3 (paperback)
    978-0-8156-5397-4 (e-book)

Library of Congress Cataloging-in-Publication Data

Names: Collier, David R., author.
Title: Democracy and the nature of American influence in Iran, 1941–1979 /
    David R. Collier.
Other titles: Contemporary issues in the Middle East.
Description: Syracuse, New York : Syracuse University Press, 2017. |
    Series: Contemporary issues in the Middle East | Includes bibliographical
    references and index.
Identifiers: LCCN 2017003758 (print) | LCCN 2017006776 (ebook) |
    ISBN 9780815634973 (hardcover : alk. paper) | ISBN 9780815635123
    (pbk. : alk. paper) | ISBN 9780815653974 (e-book)
Subjects: LCSH: United States—Foreign relations—Iran. | Iran—Foreign relations—
    United States. | Democracy—Iran. | Iran—Politics and government—20th century.
Classification: LCC E183.8.I55 C65 2017 (print) | LCC E183.8.I55 (ebook) |
    DDC 327.73055—dc23
LC record available at https://lccn.loc.gov/2017003758

Manufactured in the United States of America

Stop this extravagance, this reckless throwing of my country to the wind.
The grim-faced rising cloud, will grovel at the swamp's feet.

—Simin Behbahani, "Stop Throwing My
Country to the Wind"

Contents

Illustrations

Abbreviations

AIOC	Anglo-Iranian Oil Company
CIA	US Central Intelligence Agency
CIS	Center for International Studies at MIT
MEK	Mujahadeen-e-Khalq (People's Mujahideen of Iran)
NIP	Iran-e Novin (New Iran Party)
NRM	Nehzat-e Moghavemat-e Melli-ye Iran (National Resistance Movement of Iran)
NSC	US National Security Council
OCB	Operations Coordinating Board
OPEC	Organization of the Petroleum Exporting Countries
SAVAK	Sazeman-e Ettela'at va Amniyat-e Keshvar (Organization of Intelligence and National Security)
SOFA	Status of Forces Agreement
USAID	United States Agency for International Development

Democracy and the Nature of American Influence in Iran, 1941–1979

Introduction

The United States, Iran, and the Legacy of Democracy

On the evening of June 12, 2009, cities across Iran filled with hundreds and thousands of protesters disputing the reelection of President Mahmud Ahmadinejad. The protests were of such size and intensity that they dwarfed anything the country had seen since the Iranian Revolution some thirty years earlier. The movement rallied around the cry "Where is my vote?" as people angrily reacted to what they perceived were rigged elections.[1] Was this the downfall of an Islamic government deemed illegitimate by many in the West? Could it be the final victory of democracy over the forces of authoritarianism that had restricted the liberties of the Iranian people for more than one hundred years?

No. After months of protests, the regime was finally able to clear the streets, arrest key opposition figures, and overcome the crisis. Iran's struggle for democracy continues. The Green Movement, as it became known, was just the latest demonstration of the Iranian people's desire for more democratic governance. To understand modern Iran is to acknowledge and appreciate its history and in particular its fraught relationship with democracy. The experiences of past generations of Iranians served as the backdrop for the protests in 2009 and will do so again for the inevitable struggles to come. The Green Movement's congregation at Azadi Square in Tehran mirrored events thirty years earlier when the same square became the focal point for protests against the monarchy. *Azadi* means "freedom," and the square was named in recognition of the millions of people who took to the streets to finally overturn the shah's brutal dictatorship. Yet for many the search for freedom continued as the shah was replaced by an Islamic regime equally effective at quelling dissent and restricting liberty.

Tension has continued to simmer since the revolution, but the Islamic regime has kept the lid on this fractious society as stubbornly as the shah's regime before it. The occasional public outcry and subsequent crackdown form a pattern that dates back to the nineteenth century, a pattern to which external powers have contributed greatly. Iran's Constitutional Revolution of 1905–11, when the country first adopted a modern constitution and parliament (the Majles), was brought to its end by the intervention of Great Britain and Russia, which preferred the perpetuation of the monarchy. In 1941, foreign powers intervened to force the abdication of a powerful shah in favor of his weak and inexperienced young heir, which provided space for the return of constitutional politics. The removal of the democratically elected prime minister, Mohammad Mossadegh, in 1953 was masterminded by Britain and the United States, which welcomed the shah back to the center of power and assisted his subsequent crackdown on opposition with aid and moral support. Likewise, external events helped create the revolutionary situation in Iran in the late 1970s.

So entangled have foreign powers been in Iran's internal politics that they remain prime suspects in the outcome of all manner of events. In recent times, foreign agents have been blamed for both orchestrating the Green Movement as well as killing the protesters; for assassinating Iranian scientists; for being behind a string of acid attacks on women; and even for deliberately creating the terrorist group Islamic State, best known as ISIS.[2] Accusing domestic rivals of being beholden to foreign powers has long been a trope of Iranian politics. Even Ayatollah Ruhollah Khomeini, the founder of the Islamic Republic of Iran, was accused of being in the pay of the British.[3] According to Mohammad Reza Shah Pahlavi, among others, if you lifted Khomeini's beard, you would find a label reading "Made in England."[4] One expert has argued that belief in such conspiracies is deeply rooted in Iran's cultural heritage, which emphasizes a mythological mode of thought and "a propensity to poetic exaggeration."[5] But more importantly, there is also a rich vein of truth that flows through many of the stories of foreign action in Iran. Foreign governments have often been the decisive factor in changes of government, outbreaks of liberalization, and the resurgence of periods of authoritarianism.

And yet overemphasis on foreign control negates the importance of Iranian agency in deciding the future and has contributed to political malaise and a lack of rational responses to internal and external crises.[6] To address the true extent of external action in Iran, this book seeks to analyze the impact of the United States, the dominant foreign power during the reign of Mohammad Reza Shah Pahlavi. In particular, it will examine whether Iran's various movements between constitutionalism and authoritarianism between 1941 and 1979 were directed by the United States or can be better explained by internal factors. Was the shah in charge, or was he largely an empty vessel that followed the whimsical course set in Washington? Why was Iran's indigenous democracy movement unable to bring about change despite its popularity and persistence? This work is therefore the story of three forces—the United States, the shah, and the Iranians themselves. It analyzes what made American pressure at times effective while at other times ineffective and charts the evolution of the shah from an insecure and weak young king to the dominant, confident, and independent ruler he later became.

To understand how the United States was able to play an effective role in directing Iranian policy, I expand on the framework of linkage and leverage developed by Steven Levitsky and Lucan A. Way.[7] They define leverage as an "authoritarian government's vulnerability to external democratizing pressure," often exercised through sanctions, diplomacy, financial dependency, and military intervention.[8]

I adapt this definition slightly here to refer to *all* external pressure rather than merely to democratizing pressure because for much of the Cold War the United States preferred stable authoritarian allies rather than a potentially capricious and weak democratic regime. With a high degree of leverage over a country, the United States could exert top-down influence on the target state's leadership and push it toward policies that best achieved Western goals. For example, a leader with little internal support might look to the United States to support his regime through diplomacy or financial assistance and in return be open to following policies that best suited US priorities.

Linkage is defined as political, economic, and social cross-border flows of information.[9] These flows traverse not only from the authoritarian leadership but also from senior officials, politicians, the military, members of the opposition, and civil society in general. The more linkages a country has with the West, the more Western powers have knowledge of and influence over what happens within that country. Linkage is therefore a "multidimensional concept that encompasses the myriad networks of interdependence that connect individual polities, economies, and societies to Western democratic communities."[10] Through linkage, the West can identify authoritarian abuses or rising opposition, which allows for preparation and support for a change in regime. The West can also use linkage to send signals of acceptance or disapproval of movements toward authoritarianism.

Linkage can therefore be a means for an external actor to project power and influence inside another country through formal and informal ties to that country's political, social, and economic elites. During the 1940s, for example, the United States increased linkage with Iran by sending economic and military missions to help reorganize a country in disarray from World War II. These missions created strong ties that improved the effectiveness of American leverage as the more the Americans learned about the country, the more they knew what policies could best achieve their goals. The United States used its influential financial missions to ensure that certain economic reforms were put in place and specific officials were appointed to influential positions. These networks therefore act as transmitters of external influence.[11] Whereas leverage can be seen as top-down pressure to punish or reward a country for certain behavior, linkage looks to identify, strengthen, and support bottom-up pressures on the host government.

The vast majority of literature on US relations with the shah has focused on US support for authoritarianism, coups, and repression. However, the literature has largely ignored Iran's experiments with democracy.[12] This gap is illustrated by two recent books on the subject. In *The Quest for Democracy in Iran*, Fakhreddin Azimi devotes some time to the return of constitutional politics to Iran between 1941 and 1953 but thereafter emphasizes the shah's steady return to authoritarianism. Likewise, in *Democracy in Iran* Ali Gheissari and Vali Nasr devote a mere 21 pages of their 230-page book to democratization during the time of the shah.[13] Because of its absence in much of the literature, the shah's reign has been called "one of the less studied periods of modern Iranian history."[14]

This neglect has recently begun to be addressed as more works focus on aspects of the shah's reign.[15] However, most of them examine snapshots, such as the coup in 1953 or the buildup to the Islamic Revolution in 1979. This book takes on the ambitious task of analyzing the entirety of the shah's reign and Iran's relations with the United States. Through an all-encompassing approach, I examine in detail the shah's changing relationship with the United States, his move toward authoritarianism, Iran's resilient internal reform movement, and how all of these things were affected by US policy. Throughout this period, there were numerous movements between democracy and autocracy, and by using the framework of linkage and leverage, this book assesses the extent of the role played by the United States in influencing these movements.

It also challenges many popularly views held about US–Iranian relations during this period. The extent of American interference in Iran through linkage and leverage has largely been underestimated. So, too, have been American attempts to promote liberalism and constitutionalism, which I show here to be a constant, albeit not necessarily prioritized, goal for much of this time period.

The Importance of Iran and Its History

From the perspective of US foreign policy and peaceful global relations, Iran is a country of vital importance. Many of the issues faced during the shah's reign continue to be present today: reform, regional security, stability, terrorism, nuclear power and weapons, transitions from authoritarian rule, and the promotion of democracy. It is instructive to analyze such issues in the context of past events to better understand and respond to today's problems in Iran and elsewhere in the world. Having a sense of history is critical to sound policy making, and so this study aims to analyze history with a view to applying lessons learned from the past to more current relations between Iran and the United States.

To better understand what the future holds, it is essential to look backward. History matters, especially when that history is very much alive in the countries of the Middle East. Governments that ignore history have paid the price, one spectacular example being the administration of Jimmy Carter. During a press conference on the ongoing Iran hostage crisis in February 1980, President Carter refused to comment on whether American actions in removing Iran's democratic leader, Mohammad Mossadegh, in 1953 had been appropriate. "That's ancient history," he replied, "I don't think it's appropriate or helpful for me to go into the propriety of something that happened thirty years ago."[16] But ancient history it is not to Iranians, neither then nor now. Mossadegh's legacy remains relevant, as shown by demonstrators carrying his picture with pride in 1979 and again in 2009.

Iran is also an important country to study with regard to democracy in the Middle East. It has one of the longest histories of experimentation with political reform and civil society of all the countries in the region. The Constitutional Revolution of 1905–11 made Iran a regional pioneer in the establishment and codification of democratic rule.[17] Local grievances and protest were transformed into a national movement that the monarchy could no longer contain. The formation of a national assembly and the drafting of a modern constitution made Iran unique in the region.

Although much of this progress was ultimately reversed by a new shah with foreign support and then again by the Islamic regime, the country has continued to make occasional movements toward democracy.

These movements, which are failures when viewed in isolation, are important when viewed in aggregate because they create a "usable democratic legacy."[18] Very few transitions succeed initially, but what is past is prologue; having a history of democratic experimentation and democratic stock means Iran is in a better position than most other countries in the Middle East to experience a successful future transition.[19] Previous experience is no guarantee for success, but it provides instructive lessons for transition leaders as well as protection from xenophobic and nationalist claims that democracy is an alien import that must be resisted—an all too popular meme of the current Iranian regime.[20]

An Iranian Case Study

The history of US–Iranian relations has been covered in many books, but the extent of American involvement in Iran's movements to and from democracy remains largely absent from this literature. The United States first took a real interest in the country in 1941, but even before then it had gained a reputation as a friend of Iranian democracy. During the Constitutional Revolution, an American teacher working in Tabriz, Howard Baskerville, was killed while taking part in the protests. A martyr for the cause of Iranian democracy, he gained the nickname "the American Lafayette" after the French general who fought for the Americans during the American Revolutionary War.[21] His martyrdom shook the nation, and his memory lives on in numerous Iranian schools and streets named after him. A plaque was made in 1950 to commemorate his actions, and even during the dark years of US–Iranian relations in the 1980s and 1990s his tomb was always covered in fresh yellow roses.[22]

Another American hero to join the popular cause was William Morgan Shuster, appointed by the newly created Majles to become

Iran's treasurer-general in 1911. His economic reforms helped strengthen the burgeoning democracy in Iran but led to protests from Great Britain and Russia, who saw the reforms as American meddling in what they considered their interests. For decades, the two countries had competed for financial gain in Iran and had harvested lucrative concessions from the money-hungry ruling Qajar dynasty. After British and Russian complaints to the US government over Shuster's appointment, the State Department responded that the appointment was a contract between a sovereign country and an American citizen and so beyond US jurisdiction to intervene.[23] Nevertheless, after seven months of intense pressure by Britain and Russia, including invasion and the shelling of the Majles building, Shuster was forced to resign, yet he remained a popular figure in Iran.[24]

After such auspicious beginnings in the relationship between the United States and Iran, the United States largely failed to carry on Baskerville and Shuster's legacy. However, a close study of American action in Iran during the reign of Mohammad Reza Shah (1941–79) reveals many attempts to rekindle US interest in Iranian democracy. Based on detailed archival research at the National Archives in College Park, Maryland; the Library of Congress in Washington, DC; and various presidential libraries scattered across the country as well as on examination of many private paper collections and oral histories of government officials of the time, both Iranian and American, I conclude that American influence within Iran's domestic political system during much of the shah's reign was above and beyond that which has hitherto been documented.

Although the corresponding Iranian records of the shah's government remain largely inaccessible to historians, a number of Persian sources were referenced in the materials I did find, such as memoirs, diaries, interviews, and oral histories. The collections of the Iranian Oral History Project at Harvard University and the Foundation for Iranian Studies in Bethesda, Maryland, were especially useful in gaining insight into the view from Tehran.

The period of study for this case begins in 1941, when the United States first took an active interest in Iran's internal situation. From there, the book is arranged in chronological order to chart the changing relationship the United States had with Iran during the shah's reign through several US administrations. This arrangement is necessary to focus on what factors made American linkage and leverage at times determinative and at other times ineffective.

As James Bill writes in his history of US–Iranian relations, the story of this relationship "does not always make pleasant reading, since it documents many instances of the politics of greed, misunderstanding, oppression, and suffering."[25] The passing of time and the new information that has come to light since 1988, when Bill's book was published, has only made the story even more unpleasant. It is the story of a tragic evolution between three forces: the US government, the shah, and the popular Iranian democratic movement. All three had their own demands and wishes for Iran, and in the end all three lost. To understand why, we must delve deeply into this multidimensional story.

1 Roosevelt and the Return of Constitutionalism, 1941–1945

The general strode purposefully down the black-slate and white-marble corridors of the south wing of the Old State Department Building. Six foot two, lean, and straight-backed, he cut an impressive and imposing figure. His proclivity for cowboy hats and boots put him at odds with the architecture of his French Second Empire–style surroundings, not to mention with the other State Department officials scurrying between the offices. "Trouble," said one contemporary, "moved with him like a cloud of flies around a steer."[1] On that day in 1944, the general was in his early sixties but still boasted lethal speed on the draw honed in his days in the Old West. His reputation for belligerence and determination was aided by a national news magazine article that chronicled how as a young child he had once killed a fractious mule by "bashing its head with a two-by-four." Major General Patrick J. Hurley later joked, "I never killed a mule. I have not even killed a career diplomat."[2]

On that particular day, however, Hurley's quick march led him directly toward two diplomats, who perhaps feared a fate similar to that of the apocryphal mule: Assistant Secretary of State Dean Acheson and Eugene V. Rostow—the former soon to assume the position of secretary of state, the latter to become undersecretary of state for political affairs in the Johnson administration. For months, Hurley had been working on a program he hoped would turn Iran into a genuine democracy, a program that would serve as a model for the rest of the Middle East. However, a critical response written by Rostow and approved by Acheson lampooned the proposal as "hysterical Messianic globaloney."[3] It was this insult that precipitated the general's long and angry march to Acheson's office. Not one to hold his tongue, he immediately challenged Rostow to fight. "Come out in the hall and repeat what you said about my program!" he yelled, ignoring Acheson's frantic attempts to calm the situation. Fixing Rostow with a steely glare, Hurley scoffed and said Rostow was not "a real man" but another of the "stuffed-shirt diplomats in the State Department who were kowtowing to the British" in the Middle East. Before storming out, Hurley warned that it was high time for the United States "to fish or cut bait" in the Middle East and promised that if his report were sidelined, he would "take the issue to the country."[4]

These were the passions that enveloped the Franklin D. Roosevelt administration during early efforts to formulate a postwar strategy for the Middle East. The United States had first become involved in Iranian affairs just three years earlier, and yet in that short time emotions on the subject ran high. Hurley was fighting for a policy he felt would shape US–Iranian relations for decades to come and commit the United States to an extensive program of democracy promotion that could serve as a model for the rest of the developing world. Acheson and Rostow, meanwhile, embodied the realist contingent in the State Department. The conflict between these two camps—the idealists who wished to build a world in America's image and the realists who wished to deal with the world as it was—shaped US–Iranian relations for the next forty years. The ensuing battle swung both ways, with each camp having its chance to tackle the problems of the Middle East. The pendulum in the early 1940s had swung to the idealist camp, and the United States played an important role in allowing space for Iranian civil society to begin the process of democratic transition. Soon, however, the pendulum would swing the other way as the Roosevelt administration became increasingly interested in acquiring Iranian oil and preventing Soviet expansion into the country. Although figures such as Hurley would fight against this change in emphasis and demand that the United States hold firm in its support for democracy, Iran's strategic position and its oil wealth meant that by the end of Roosevelt's presidency the realists' view was dominant.

Roosevelt himself often walked a tightrope between the idealist and realist camps, leading some to label him a "practical idealist."[5] Before the United States entered World War II, there was a strong push for it to remain isolationist, but Roosevelt believed that security was best assured by the active defense and promotion of democracy across the globe.[6] By establishing the Reciprocal Trade Agreements Act of 1934 and later the Bretton Woods system in 1944, the United States had already begun to establish the foundations for the expansion of international commerce and cooperation for the postwar world. Democracy was seen as a vital political corollary of economic integration.[7]

Roosevelt articulated his idealist worldview in his State of the Union Address on January 6, 1941. He spoke of a world based on four democratic freedoms: freedom of speech, freedom of religion, freedom of economic liberty, and freedom of security. For Roosevelt, the promotion of these "Four Freedoms" would be "the very antithesis of the so-called new order of tyranny," of dictators seeking to expand authoritarianism. Moreover, he believed a world governed by these freedoms was "no vision of a distant millennium . . . [but] attainable in our own time and generation," albeit reliant upon the success of Great Britain and its allies over the Axis powers.[8] To this end, although unable to lead the United States into war against the wishes of Congress at this time, Roosevelt announced that the United States would instead become "the great arsenal for democracy," providing the munitions and materiel with which the democratic powers would defeat the common enemy.[9] It was clear before the events of Pearl Harbor in December 1941, therefore, that Roosevelt planned to help win not only the war but also the ensuing peace by promoting his vision of international trade and world democracy.[10]

In August 1941, Roosevelt signed a joint statement with Great Britain known as the Atlantic Charter. It proclaimed the two countries' shared war aims and aspirations as well as the ideas based on the "Four Freedoms" for a postwar world. It committed its signatories to respect and uphold territorial boundaries, restore self-government, and expand global cooperation to ensure freedom and better economic and social conditions for all.[11] Such a universal charter was felt necessary to realize Woodrow Wilson's desire of making the world "safe for democracy."[12] Desperate to lure America ever deeper into involvement in the war, British prime minister Winston Churchill conceded to much of Roosevelt's vision. Others in the British government recognized its more negative potential, however; Minister of Supply Baron Beaverbrook decried the emphasis on expanding democracy and damned the entire charter as a shameful betrayal of British overseas colonies, whose current subjugation would no longer be possible under the charter's conditions.[13] An ambitious and idealistic Roosevelt had therefore set a course for an active US role in ensuring global security through the promotion of freedom. To refine this vision, Roosevelt needed a country to experiment on, and Iran soon became his laboratory.

The next few years would see the United States become intimately involved in Iranian affairs in the hope of creating a model of fair dealing with the developing world. The tension between this idealist vision and the pragmatism of having to wage war and secure important natural resources would divide the administration and lead to confrontations like the one between the idealistic Hurley and the State Department realists such as Rostow and Acheson. The two groups that these men represented would clash repeatedly over policy toward Iran for the next three decades. At times, the idealists would hold sway and promote the cause of democracy in Iran; at other times, the realists would prioritize strategic and economic interests often at the expense of democracy. The result was a confused and muddled policy as the two groups competed for influence. In 1941, however, as relations between Iran and the United States began to form, the idealists held the upper hand and hopes were raised inside Iran of a return to constitutionalism.

Catching America's Eye: Iran Reaches Out to America

World War II was not kind to Iran. Home to an important supply route between the western and eastern fronts, the country was dominated by British and Soviet personnel who held more than a passing interest in its rich natural resources. Iranian oil had long been a source of conflict between the two imperialist powers, and Reza Pahlavi, the shah of Iran, feared they would soon usurp his country to claim this rich prize. Fearing an imminent loss of sovereignty, he looked for a third party to balance out their influence. His own peculiar political tendencies led him first to look to Hitler's Germany—a serious miscalculation. Rather than preventing the occupation of Iran, his outreach to Berlin provided a green light for the Soviet Union and Britain to occupy the country to secure the trade route. Realizing his error, Reza Shah turned quickly to the United States for assistance. President Roosevelt's statements on the need to protect developing nations against imperialism made him a far more suitable protector from the predatory intentions of Britain and the Soviet Union. The move was also welcomed by the Iranian people, who regarded the United States as that shining city upon a hill. Sattareh Farman-Farmaian, twenty years old at the time, recalled in her memoir how "a whole generation of educated Iranians . . . felt that 'Amrika' was the only Western country that was sincere and selfless, and that had truly supported our aspirations to be strong and respected by the world."[14]

A move toward the United States therefore gave succor to Iranian democrats who had seen their own aspirations dashed by the failure of the Constitutional Revolution decades earlier. Reza Shah began to talk about the importance of democracy in an attempt to reach out to the Americans. Following the publication of the Atlantic Charter in August 1941 and under the "principles of international justice and the rights of peoples to liberty," he wrote to President Roosevelt directly to ask for support against the encroachments of Great Britain and the Soviet Union.[15] The president cordially replied with a message of friendship, but time had slipped away. Despite the shah's last-minute appeal to Washington, the other Allied powers had already decided he could not be trusted to remain strong against the Nazi enemy. He was summarily ordered to surrender his throne to his eldest son.[16]

Real American involvement in Iran would therefore begin with a new monarch: the twenty-one-year old Mohammad Reza Shah Pahlavi (hereafter referred to as "the shah"). The new king had attended boarding school in Switzerland and then military academy in Tehran but did not see any actual fighting. His father, however, had risen up the ranks to become the first Iranian commanding officer of the Persian Cossack Brigade. He later forced himself to power through strength, ability, and determination, toppling the Qajars, who had ruled Iran since 1785, and establishing the Pahlavi dynasty in its place.

The shah was just six years old when his father, a man he called a "dominant" and "towering" figure, pushed his way to the throne.[17] He demanded respect and perfection and was known to tear the epaulettes off the shoulders of senior army officers and strike them in front of their subordinates for failing to meet his standards.[18] Although Mohammed Reza Shah would not say it, his sister, Princess Ashraf, recalled being terrified of their father's temper, writing that "even years later as a grown woman I can't remember a time when I wasn't afraid of him."[19] The shah therefore grew up in a strict household but amid luxury and the expectation that the Peacock Throne was his destiny. When he assumed the throne, he did so with a great feeling of inferiority, having done nothing to warrant his position and believing he would not live up to his father's reputation. According to one biographer, it later became a rule among members of the shah's royal court not to praise his father too profusely for fear of offending the insecure monarch.[20]

His deep inferiority complex would manifest itself in numerous ways throughout his reign, leading him to favor strong rule and military strength rather than compromise or democracy. It would also cloud his relationship with many of Iran's prominent intellectuals, generals, and political leaders of his time, who might potentially

outshine him. He distrusted men such as Ahmad Qavam, Mohammad Mossadegh, Ali Amini, Hassan Arsanjani, and General Ferey-
doun Djam and removed them from positions of power. Fear of
political rivals was a major factor in the thirty-two changes of prime
minister that occurred during his thirty-seven-year reign.[21] It would
also affect his relationship with American presidents, who often
treated him as a junior partner. In time, he would skillfully overcome the client–patron alliance with the United States that began
in 1941, but when the Islamic Revolution commenced in the late
1970s, he reverted at once to an almost son–father dependence on
American advice.

This dependency was at its greatest when the young shah first
took control of Iran in 1941. In awe at the ease with which the foreign powers had dispatched his father, he recognized the importance
of appealing to the West. To ensure that the United States would
look favorably upon his country, the shah positioned himself as a
committed supporter of democracy. He therefore immediately promised a constitutional government with full powers to be ceded to
the cabinet and Majles (Parliament). A wide program of reform was
unveiled that included the protection of individual rights and other
improvements known to appeal to the West.[22] Louis G. Dreyfus Jr.,
US minister plenipotentiary in Tehran, called it a "wise and active
beginning" by the young shah, who impressed diplomatic officers
and Iranians alike with his "apparent sincerity, direct approach and
democratic spirit."[23] As the cherry on top of his democratic credentials, the shah also signed on to the Atlantic Charter and wrote to
President Roosevelt that he hoped the United States would support a
future of peaceful democratic development in Iran.[24]

Thus commenced what Fakhreddin Azimi has called Iran's "most
important period of sustained experimentation with constitutionalism."[25] To the shah, however, democracy was just a means to an
end. Unsure and unstable on the throne, he lacked both international
and internal support, but he saw a chance to secure both by advo-
cating democracy. He moved quickly to prove his policy was one
of action rather than words. As well as giving more powers to the

cabinet and Majles, he returned property previously seized by his father to its original owners, bequeathed the large inheritance he had received to the nation, granted an amnesty to all political prisoners, and released more than twelve hundred dissidents from prison in the first few months of his reign. Taxation was reduced, habeas corpus introduced, censorship on book publications reduced, trade unions allowed to form, and freedom of mobility introduced by revoking the need for police permits for domestic travel.[26]

The new shah therefore seemed to want to distinguish his rule from that of his father's totalitarian leadership. He styled himself rather as an apolitical youth who aspired only to the role of constitutional monarch. Emphasizing his education in democratic Switzerland, the shah hoped to convince the West to see Iran as a vibrant, modernizing, and developing state. In an interview published shortly after his twenty-second birthday in October 1941, he denounced dictatorships and autocracies as disastrous and inherently short-lived and praised democracy as a system that allows for the pooling of ideas through checks and balances. In particular, he welcomed the growth of newspapers in his country, calling them the "safeguard to democracy" that "serve as mirrors and barometers in informing" the public.[27] The Constitutional Revolution was back on track.

The shah's policies had immediate effects. Civil society, which had been dormant since the Constitutional Revolution, sparked back into life; public debates, previously outlawed, were convened and frequented by the intelligentsia; and numerous associations and political parties were formed. Reporting on the formation of one such party, Azadi (Freedom), Minister Dreyfus approvingly stated it was one of the "first endeavors of responsible Iranians, since the dictatorial government of the former shah gave way to the present constitutional one, to get together in a democratic way to consider the solution of common problems."[28] Many of the newly released prisoners were allowed to continue their prior political activity, the most important of them being fifty-three men previously arrested for Communist activity, who formed the Tudeh (Masses) Party upon release, a Communist organization with strong links to the Soviet

Union. In addition, many notable politicians who had been kept out of politics during Reza Shah's reign, reappeared. Most famous were former prime minister Ahmad Qavam, who returned from Europe, and Mohammad Mossadegh, who had gained fame during the Constitutional Revolution but later retreated from politics in protest against the authoritarian rule of the shah's father.[29]

International factors were paramount in this sudden return of constitutional rule, but most of the literature covering the period has generally ignored their influence.[30] By removing Reza Shah and allowing his son to claim the throne, the Allied powers proved themselves both kingmakers and decision makers in Iran. The United States in particular held enormous leverage over the country. The new shah looked to Washington to help maintain Iran's independence and specifically to President Roosevelt for guidance and support. The shah's democratic journey was designed largely to convince the Americans to support and protect his rule at a time of severe peril. Insecure on his throne owing to Britain's and the Soviet Union's continued predations, the shah curried favor with the Americans in the hope that Roosevelt would limit these countries' actions.

The importance of the United States in the return of constitutionalism is even more apparent when the shah's true intentions are taken into account. From the moment he assumed the throne, his desire was not to create a democratic society or to be the enlightened monarch he espoused to be but to surpass his father's authoritarian leadership. Aware that overt authoritarianism ran counter to the global mood that would later be known as the second wave of democratization, the shah bided his time. Movement toward democracy was a short-term necessity at a time when his rule was weak and uncertain. In his biography of the shah, Abbas Milani notes that during the early years of his reign the shah would often say in private that true development was possible only under the reign of a strong king, not an enlightened and constitutionally restricted monarch.[31] His father's dynasty had been built on three pillars: the bureaucracy, court patronage, and control over the military.[32] All three had been decidedly weakened and undermined through war, occupation, and abdication. In the absence of these pillars, support from the United States was vital to protect the sovereignty of the shah's country. Mohammad Reza Shah did not want to be a puppet of foreign powers but understood that the return to royal dominance had to be a slow and gradual process, often demanding short-term concessions to internal and external demands. For now, the shah was willing to submit to American demands, but his ultimate goal, even at this early stage of his reign, was total dominance.[33]

The shah's youthful appearance hid a mature and capable political mind, and in time he would achieve his goal despite the incredible odds he faced as he assumed the throne. He set about the process of restoring royal authority even while outwardly remaining supportive of the democratic reforms he sanctioned and immediately went to work on restoring the three traditional pillars of Pahlavi support. Most important was rebuilding the military and gaining its trust and allegiance. Under the Iranian Constitution in the 1940s, the shah's only real power was executive control over the military.[34] He therefore quickly increased military salaries and showered the officer corps with so many promotions that within the first twenty months of his reign he created twice as many colonels and generals as his father had in the previous twenty years.[35]

Democracy returned to Iran, therefore, not as a natural transition but as a concession to the demands of the international environment as well as those of his people. This period of constitutionalism in the early 1940s could not have been achieved without external intervention because the shah's democratic entreaties were arguably more for foreign than domestic consumption. External forces had removed one shah from power and installed a new weaker king who understood the necessity of remaining on good terms with the United States. Had foreign powers not intervened in Iran, it is likely that both Reza Shah and his brand of authoritarianism would have remained intact. The importance of American support instead forced Mohammad Reza Shah to accept a movement he had no intention of tolerating for long. In this acceptance, however, the United States was given leverage over the shah's actions. How much he could stray from democratic principles would depend greatly on his need for American support, a need he would endeavor to remove in the years ahead as he continued to rebuild the pillars of Pahlavi dominance.

Linking the United States to Iran

The shah's dreams of returning to authoritarianism required patience and persistence; no such move could be made until his regime was stabilized both internally and externally. External stability, he hoped, had been achieved after his outreach to the United States proved fruitful. Finally entering the war in December 1941, America took an active role in the fighting and logistical aspects of the Allied effort. Iran was important as a vital supply route between the western and eastern fronts, so Roosevelt declared its defense essential to the national interest of the United States, thereby making it eligible for financial aid and support.[36]

Along with American aid, however, Roosevelt also sent American troops and advisers, who flooded the country and created a web of linkage between the United States and Iran. Their job was to ensure that Iran remained stable and did not internally combust owing to the pressures of wartime occupation. Chief among these efforts was a financial mission headed by the American economist Arthur C. Millspaugh, whom the Iranian government invited to take control of the country's finances, a task the US State Department urged him to accept.[37] He tackled corruption, reduced inflation, and improved the efficiency of the Iranian economy to ensure it remained a stable and viable part of the Iranian state. Toward the end of 1942, Millspaugh succeeded in passing a progressive income tax bill and in May 1943 was given additional powers to tackle food hoarders and control food prices and distribution. As a result of these powers, Americans soon controlled all important economic departments of the Iranian government.[38]

In addition to Millspaugh's mission, Brigadier General John Nesmith Greely was sent to reorganize the Iranian army, and a similar operation was formed to modernize the police force to better ensure internal stability. The latter mission was headed by Colonel H. Norman Schwarzkopf, former commander of the New Jersey State Police who had catapulted to national fame for his work on the Lindbergh kidnapping case a decade earlier. His work with the police and gendarmerie in Iran not only helped stabilize the country but also began to "create an elite corps of rural police that will be able to enforce the police powers of the central government through-out the rural and tribal areas of Persia."[39] American officials also took control of the Iranian Public Health Service and the Depart-ment of Supply and Transportation, so that by 1943 a total of six US missions and centers of US influence were linked to almost all aspects of the Iranian state.[40]

"An Unselfish Desire to Help": Early American Policy toward Iran

Initial US policy did not go far beyond wartime exigency and the desire for stability. Although American officials supported the shah's liberalization and welcomed his speeches on the virtue and neces-sity of democracy, they were wary of the impact of democratization on stability. The sudden departure of an authoritarian monarch and the rise of civil society had led to an increase in corruption, attacks on the government by newspapers, and the formation of many new political groups that competed for influence. As a result, the United States was in the awkward position of supporting democracy but only to the extent that democracy did not deleteriously affect the war effort. Without direction from an overall strategy, US relations with Iran were confused and contradictory. Praise for the shah's reforms was given concomitantly with actions that undermined those same reforms. For example, in August 1942, after welcoming a move toward constitutional rule, the United States joined with its allies to undermine that very process by forcing the resignation of Prime Minister Ali Soheily, whom they felt was an inefficient and lackadai-sical manager of Iran's wartime resources. The British Foreign Office was particularly blunt in its assessment: "No man who suddenly discovers that Tehran has less than one day's wheat supply really deserves any consideration from us and [we] do not think we need make any effort to keep Soheily in power."[41]

Democracy and sovereignty were clearly secondary considerations to the Allies' wider goals of successfully concluding the war. As instability in Iran increased, Dreyfus reported to the State Department that there was a strong need for the United States to take "more forceful action in [Iran's] internal matters."[42] The Allies moved quickly to ensure the replacement of Soheily with Ahmad Qavam, a man highly regarded in Moscow and London. Qavam himself regarded foreign support as "indispensable" to his attainment of office.[43] He most likely held this view because he had little support from the shah. More than forty years older than the young king, Qavam was an experienced and ambitious politician. He had been temporarily forced out of the country by the shah's father for implication in a coup and since his return was viewed with suspicion.[44] His elevation to the premiership over Soheily, despite the shah's misgivings, demonstrated that external powers not only were able to remove Iranian monarchs but also had great influence over the selection of prime minister as well.

Once installed, Qavam quickly did the Allied powers' bidding and arrested 150 pro-German officials, including high-profile figures such as the military governor of the Fars province.[45] This intervention into Iran's political system was an early example of how the United States outwardly advocated democracy but took nondemocratic action to ensure that stability was maintained. David Halberstam has called this dualism the "liberal contradiction"—the conflict between the desire to do good and the need to hold and use power effectively.[46] It is a contradiction that US policy makers have projected numerous times toward Iran and other such countries, with the need for stability routinely prioritized over democracy.

Even so, the Roosevelt administration's practical idealism did attempt to combine stability and progress in Iran, at least for a short while. A driving impetus in Washington at the time was a desire to promote the Western way of life and expand American reach as far as possible. Mark Lytle has tied this desire to promote democracy with the concept of American exceptionalism: the belief that the United States was uniquely placed to "transcend the histories of old world societies" and spread democracy across the globe.[47] This concept gave an ideological edge to America's early involvement in Iran and manifested itself in attempts to formulate a coherent policy to promote democracy in a stable fashion so as not to interfere with the war effort.

The first idealist to step forward was Wallace Murray, a senior official in the State Department's Division of Near Eastern Affairs who believed completely in the idea of American exceptionalism. Writing in support of bringing Qavam to power in replace of Soheily in November 1942, Murray wrote that the "present political crisis . . . is of such vital concern" to US interests that more should be done to control Iran's development. The "obvious fact," he stated, "is that we shall soon be in the position of actually 'running' Iran through an impressive body of American advisors."[48] Indeed, shortly after his appointment, the new prime minister secured passage of a parliamentary bill giving Millspaugh full control of Iran's finances. With such US power and influence over Iran, Murray thought it "odd" that the British and Soviets were dictating to Iran which men should be put into positions of power in the Iranian government "without prior consultation with our Legation." Murray encouraged the United States to embrace the role of running Iran, not for selfish imperialist reasons but out of an "unselfish desire to help" through the controlled promotion of Western democracy. This help, he felt, would be most welcomed by Iranians.[49]

In this regard, Murray was in agreement with one contemporary British official, who wrote that the Iranians "wrongly believe they can 'run their own show' properly without foreign advisors[;] [they cannot because] corruption, tyranny and inefficiency flourish."[50] Murray argued that because instability ran counter to both American and Iranian goals, the United States had a right to interfere and direct Iran's internal political system for the benefit of both. It was his opinion and that of his colleagues in the Near East Division that stability would be maintained and the lure of communism diminished if the United States guided Iran's development.[51]

Thus, by late 1942 US policy toward Iran had begun its transformation from passive acceptance of the shah's democracy program to active attempts to direct and control it. The State Department instructed Minister Dreyfus to coordinate the American advisers in Iran and press the Iranian government to take action in areas the State Department felt needed attention. By June, Dreyfus reported that during a frank discussion with Prime Minister Qavam, he had conveyed American disappointment at the Iranians' apparent lethargy in tackling both corruption and enacting reforms.[52] State Department telegrams instructed Dreyfus to convey to the Iranian government the Roosevelt administration's belief in the "supreme importance of insuring [sic] maximum cooperation with Millspaugh" and the other American missions.[53] In November, to strengthen the government Dreyfus was instructed to formally urge the prime minister to seek increased powers and stress the American desire that cabinet members selected would "cooperate fully with American advisors."[54] One specific example of America's new proactive policy was directions for Dreyfus to informally mention to Qavam that an American-trained Iranian official, Allah-Yar Saleh, should be appointed minister of finance in a new government.[55] Such demands were made not necessarily because the individuals promoted were the best men for the job but because they were the ones most likely to cooperate with US policy.

By 1943, therefore, US policy had quickly evolved from involvement in Iran solely to maintain an efficient and stable supply route to the Soviet Union to attempts to "run" Iran and ensure that necessary reforms were undertaken and stability maintained. However, the Roosevelt administration still did not have a clear and defined policy upon which to organize US efforts in Iran. Murray had provided an ideological foundation, but how to practically assist Iran's transition toward democracy remained unclear. To fill this gap, Murray and John Jernegan, a young Foreign Service official in the Division of Near Eastern Affairs, coauthored a report in January 1943.

They praised the more active role the United States was playing in Iranian affairs, which, they said, had "arisen primarily out of our participation in the war and natural concern that political matters in all theaters of war operations should develop favorably with respect to the United Nations." They argued that Iran constituted a "test case for the good faith of the United Nations" and that it was in America's "vital interests" to make sure the United Nations "live[d] up to the Atlantic Charter," the basis of which was Roosevelt's "Four Freedoms." The authors envisioned that with American guidance Iran could be made independent of both the Soviet Union and Great Britain, thereby reducing the possibility of its becoming a protectorate in the postwar era. Guidance, they wrote, should be in the form of economic aid and "disinterested American advisors" who would assist Iran's development and modernization. They felt it was the responsibility of the United States "to make Iran self-reliant and prosperous, open to the trade of all nations and a threat to none." US policy had been focused too much on winning the war and not enough on winning the ensuing peace. "If the principles of unselfish fair-dealing enunciated by the Atlantic Charter are ignored when it comes to Iran," the report concluded, "the foundations of our peace will begin to crumble immediately."[56]

Absent from the report, however, was any mention of Iran's indigenous reform movement, which had renewed its activities with gusto since 1941. The report was also criticized by the more traditional members of the State Department, who remained unconvinced by the crusader spirit. Undersecretary of State Sumner Welles clashed repeatedly with Murray, arguing that it was "preferable for us not to interfere" in internal Iranian politics owing to possible unforeseen circumstances, which could "in the long run . . . be disastrous."[57] He vehemently exclaimed that he was "not willing to sign the telegrams [advocating the United States thoroughly involve itself in Iran's internal political system] even though [they] must have been approved through all relevant channels."[58] Minister Dreyfus similarly replied to the State Department that although he would naturally follow all orders, he "felt it unwise and dangerous to meddle in internal affairs of this kind."[59] However, with President Roosevelt's support, Murray's report was sent to Dreyfus at the US Legation in Tehran, with the instruction that it was the "general policy to be followed by this Government with respect to Iran."[60] Eighteen months after formally taking an interest in the fortunes of Iran, the United States was able to use its linkage with and leverage over Iran to formally adopt a policy to control Iran's development along Western lines of democracy and stability. Influence over the shah would be used to keep him from playing an active role in the day-to-day politics, to strengthen the institutions of prime minister and parliament, and to demand authority be given to American advisers.

The United States therefore began to bring to office "young men of the right type," according to Murray.[61] They would be Iranians committed to American reform plans, and every effort was taken to promote them despite internal protests. The appointment of Allah-Yar Saleh, an American-trained economist, as minister of finance remained a top priority. The United States first suggested his appointment in November 1942. When the prime minister refused, alleging that Saleh was stubborn and uncooperative, the United States persisted.[62] The US Legation stressed that Saleh was the personal preference of the influential economist Arthur Millspaugh, who now wielded incredible authority over Iran's economic system. By February 1943, facing stubborn resistance, the State Department directed the US Legation to continue to push for Saleh and to ask for "any instructions [the] Department might send you which would be helpful in bringing about an understanding between Saleh and [the] Prime Minister."[63] Prime Minister Qavam's refusal to bend was one reason he lost US support and was soon forced to resign.

Internal elites soon looked to American support to propel their careers, and the jockeying began even before Qavam's resignation. Keen to return to the office of prime minister, Ali Soheily traveled to Washington to curry American favor to expedite his political return. This trip was successful, and once Qavam stepped down, Soheily was ushered back in with American support. Illustrating the quid pro quo of this arrangement, he quickly announced that Saleh would indeed become the new finance minister. Before an enthusiastic Majles, the new prime minister praised the US government and its people, who, he said, belonged "to those unselfish and liberal people and governments which never refused to give all assistance to others in trouble."[64] In addition to Saleh's appointment, one of Soheily's first acts was to express Iran's commitment to "the Atlantic Charter and democratic principles" and his certainty that the American government would "not take any action inconsistent with the independence and integrity of Iran."[65]

These were still the early days of US–Iranian relations, but it would later become clear that the United States would certainly take action inconsistent with the independence and integrity of Iran if doing so achieved US foreign-policy goals. For now, however, the United States was seen as a supporter of democracy in Iran. Its influence was so great that even the shah had little option but to yield. When, for example, he attempted to set up discreet meetings with the US Legation without the knowledge of the Iranian cabinet, he was quickly rebuked and informed that he must remain within the confines of the Constitution.[66]

Iranian newspapers fell for the beguiling and apparently selfless United States. The newspaper *Bakhtar* elegantly eulogized, "Oh, gentle breeze, thou art the most truthful and unbiased of messengers. Cross the oceans, kiss the Statue of Liberty and tell the brave people of that great land that their Iranian friends send them greetings."[67] American intervention was seen as promoting Iranian independence and to that end was welcomed and encouraged. Apparently unencumbered by any overriding strategic or economic interest in Iran, besides the continuation of stability, the United States made democracy promotion a priority for US policy toward Iran. As long as Iran remained stable, the Iranian democrats were relatively free to carry out any activity that did not hinder American plans. Little was expected in return other than continued alignment with the Allied cause, and so the United States was praised for its seeming beneficence.

Habib Ladjevardi has referred to these first few years of American involvement as the closest Iran came to becoming a functional constitutional monarchy.[68] The United States made the shah allow space for Iran's indigenous democratic forces to operate by forcing him to return to a constitutional position in return for US aid. The shah complied against his wishes owing to the weak nature of his rule at the time. His withdrawal from government life allowed the office of prime minister to become more influential and the elected Majles to grow in significance. The United States also successfully limited the British and Soviet efforts to undermine US policy. As a result, civil society blossomed, but little real connection was made between the United States and Iran's growing democratic movement. The United States had leverage, but it established linkage more with the elites than with the masses.

Democracy Flourishes

By 1943, the United States did begin to pay attention to Iranian democrats but saw them as an annoyance rather than as an ally. In April that year, Wallace Murray warned that the social awakening in Iran was occurring at such a rate that unless the Iranian government adopted a "really democratic and progressive policy, others will take matters into their own hands, perhaps by violence."[69] So great was the Iranian demand for democracy that it was outstripping the wishes of the United States, which held stability as the priority. By this time, Tehran alone boasted forty newspapers and twenty political parties, all contributing to a sense of social vibrancy and optimism for Iran's democratic future.[70] That year's elections for the Fourteenth Majles were the most competitive and democratic in modern Iran. One contemporary account explained that "under Reza Shah anyone who uttered the word 'party' risked imprisonment[;] now every politician with grandiose ambitions gathers together his personal clique and announces to the world the formation of a new political party. We should name these few years the 'age of party planning' (*partibazi*)."[71]

By the time of the election in November 1943, the number of political parties had more than doubled as passions for political participation and democracy surged.[72] Although the Americans became increasingly suspicious of Iran's ability to maintain internal cohesion amid such a frantic democratic opening, the shah came to fear the election of a popularly supported parliament with views counter to his own. He therefore suggested to the Allies that the elections be cancelled until the end of the war or later. Believing his aim was to reinstitute a military dictatorship, the Allied powers replied that the elections were an important safety valve for popular feeling and that the people looked forward to a meaningful election for a parliament that would be a "safeguard for their liberties."[73] Still keen to remain in the Allies' favor, the shah complied, and a move toward authoritarianism was averted.

The increasingly worried shah instead looked for constitutional protection by attempting to convene a second debating chamber similar to the US Senate. He could fill it with his own supporters and use it as a check upon the actions of the Majles. Although the formation of a senate was permitted under the Constitution, the Allies again intervened and disabused the shah of the idea, telling him that it would only add to parliamentary "obstructionism" and delays.[74] With the shah thus restricted by what foreign powers wanted, elections were free to proceed. Again the United States had proven to be the dominant authority in Iran, and again Iranian democrats benefited.

The subsequent elections returned a set of deputies with a range of views and from a range of competing political factions. Almost half were newly elected, which meant the caucus that had traditionally supported the shah, the Fraksiun-e Ittihad-e Melli (National Union Caucus) was no longer the dominant group. This change alone was a major setback for the royalists, but compounding the problem was the emergence of six additional large groupings hostile to royal authority. Their names reflected the mood in Iran: Fraksiun-e Demokrat (Democratic Caucus); Fraksiun-e Azadi (Freedom Caucus); Fraksiun-e Mustaqel (Independent Caucus); Fraksiun-e Mehan (Patriotic Caucus); Fraksiun-e Tudeh (Communist Tudeh Caucus); and Fraksiun-e Munfaradin (Individuals' Caucus). His worst fears realized, the shah moved to cancel the results but was again dissuaded by the Allied powers.[75]

With external support, the democratization of Iran continued. One of the many freshman elected to the Fourteenth Majles was Mohammad Mossadegh. As a cousin later recalled, with "his droopy, basset-hound eyes and high patrician forehead, [Mossadegh] did not look like a man to shake a nation."[76] However, not only would he shake Iran, but the memory of him would also go on to shape events on a global scale long after his death. His return to politics in 1943 gave Iran's burgeoning democratic movement an idealistic and committed leader. He ran as an independent with a manifesto based on three issues. First was the adoption of measures to combat what he saw as the deleterious influence of foreign powers in Iran. These measures included greater Iranian control over the country's natural resources, the adoption of a neutral foreign policy in place of the present pro-Western stance, and an end to the granting of major economic concessions to the Great Powers. For too long he had seen Iran's resources exploited by the Great Powers, and he felt strongly that a neutral foreign policy was the answer. To Mossadegh, if no power were granted economic concessions, then no rival power would feel left out, and they all would be more inclined to leave Iran alone.[77]

Second, to augment the nascent democracy, Mossadegh called for the armed forces to be placed under civilian control rather than remain the preserve of the king. He understood that the Pahlavi dynasty had been founded upon control of the military and so saw civilian control of the military as essential to ensure that democracy would have long-term security from future royalist action. Left in the king's hands, democracy would forever be in peril because a simple royal command would allow the army to quash the movement by force whenever the shah so desired. And third, Mossadegh promised to reform the electoral system in a way that would limit the powers of the landed gentry, which was a key immobilizer of any attempt to improve social progress, particularly among the Iranian peasantry.[78] Such appeals to antimilitarism, democracy, and political liberalism quickly endeared Mossadegh to the burgeoning middle classes in Tehran and ensured his position as an influential figure in Iranian politics. So great was his popular support that he was elected with more votes than any of the other eleven deputies elected in Tehran and so became known as first deputy for Tehran.[79] Such indigenous democracy leaders would seem like natural allies for the Roosevelt administration, yet Mossadegh's commitment to removing *all* foreign intervention in Iran was not in line with US national interest. If the United States wished to control the transition to democracy, democratic figures such as Mossadegh were ironically a hindrance rather than a help.

Nevertheless, Iranian progress continued remarkably well. The elections for the Fourteenth Majles were as free and open as any since the Constitutional Revolution, and the elected deputies, once installed, worked quickly to assert the Majles as a strong and independent democratic institution.[80] They prevented the shah from unilaterally naming his own cabinet and successfully forced the resignation, for a second time, of Prime Minister Soheily in April 1944 upon charges of corruption.[81] His replacement, a diplomat named Mohammad Sa'ed, was independent from the shah and worked to further increase the power of democratic bodies. Action was even taken to place the military under a more constitutional footing, despite the shah's opposition.[82]

The power of the Fourteenth Majles was further demonstrated during the premiership of Muhsin Sadr, in office from June to October 1945. Sadr had been a chief state prosecutor who gained fame for his rulings against the democratic leaders of the Constitutional Revolution. He later became a leading politician and ally of the authoritarian Reza Shah. His illiberal history meant he was unsuited to the role of prime minister at a time of heightened constitutional fervor. Opposition deputies worried for the future of the constitutional system in Iran with Sadr in power and took action to form a united democratic front to oppose his government. This movement, which numbered around thirty deputies, coalesced around Mohammad Mossadegh and obstructed Sadr by denying his cabinet the necessary quorum required for approval. Sadr initially ignored this legality and attempted to govern regardless of de jure authority. However, the minority continued to remove themselves from the chamber every time Sadr's government sought to introduce legislation to the Majles. With an inquorate Parliament, Sadr's government was unable to rule, and he eventually resigned after only a few months in power.[83] According to Fakhreddin Azimi, the Fourteenth Majles reestablished

> the existing rules of the game by challenging what they considered to be a violation of the formal or informal procedures necessary for the effective participation of the minority in the political process. This does not imply that political preferences were not important in demarcating the majority from the minority, but that the formation and persistence of the minority arose from a feeling of deliberate marginalization and exclusion from the process of the exercise of power and the allocation of political spoils.[84]

A more united Majles showed similar gumption in foreign affairs by successfully rejecting the Soviet Union's increasingly aggressive demands to secure oil concessions in northern Iran. The debates and civic action surrounding the elections for and actions of the Fourteenth Majles showed that democracy could thrive in Iran when devoid of an overbearing authoritarian ruler or an international system that rejected democratic rule. Iran's democratic aspirations had survived the failure of the Constitutional Revolution and had reemerged as soon as conditions allowed them. This democratic tendency continues today. When space becomes available in Iran, democracy reemerges whether it has been restricted by kings or by today's clerical leadership. In the early 1940s, this space was provided by the United States, a fact recognized by one Iranian official, who in 1944 praised the United States for providing this "stimulus of democratic government," which brought with it "freedom of thought and the establishment of a system encouraging initiative and stamping out evasion of responsibility and lawlessness."[85] However, as democratic competition increased and the Fourteenth Majles grew ever more fractious and assertive, the United States began to rethink the opening it had provided. Too much freedom threatened internal instability and American interests in Iran. But before US officials could address the problem, they first had to take action to protect Iran's international independence from Britain and the Soviet Union, whose forces still remained in occupation of Iran.

Having a Try at It: A Greater Role for the United States

President Roosevelt liked to work as his own secretary of state, often bypassing the official department, which he felt was too conservative, old-fashioned, and generally incompetent. During his long tenure in office, the State Department was "brought to its lowest status in the history of the republic."[86] In particular, he felt that his current secretary of state, Cordell Hull, lacked the necessary energy to lead the country's foreign policy at such an important crossroads in history. Hull's assistant secretary, Dean Acheson, also felt his boss to be too "slow, circuitous [and] cautious."[87] Hull's office meetings were, to Acheson, akin to cruel and unusual punishment as his deliberate pace and proclivity for heat left others "half-fainting" and feeling "detached" from their "own body."[88] At one meeting, when Acheson was hoping for relief by cracking a window or lowering the thermostat, Hull called over Joe, his assistant:

> When he [Joe] appeared, Mr. Hull would say, "Joe, look at that thermometer."
> "Joe" would do so, and report: "Eighty, Mr. Secretary."
> "I thought so," Mr. Hull would say. "Let's have some heat."[89]

A wilting and inefficient Hull is an apt analogy for how the president viewed him and the State Department. His appointment had largely been a political necessity owing to his stature as one of the well-respected southern Democrats, but he remained outside the president's inner circle. "Cordell Hull," Roosevelt once said to a reporter who questioned his appointment, "is the only member of the Cabinet who brings me any political strength that I don't have in my own right."[90] Although Roosevelt may have been forced to appoint

Hull, he was not under any obligation to consult or work with him. As a result, Hull became one of the least influential members of the administration, and he referred to the president as "that man across the street who never tells me anything."[91]

To bypass his secretary of state, Roosevelt relied on ad hoc agencies and individuals to perform specific tasks. His contempt for the traditional means of conducting foreign policy was illustrated by his response to questions about W. Averell Harriman's position in London in 1940. He had sent Harriman there to facilitate the Lend-Lease program and gave him the title "defense expeditor." When quizzed on what Harriman's relationship would be to the American ambassador in London, Roosevelt retorted, "I don't know, and I don't give a damn!" When another reporter asked to whom Harriman would report, he snapped again, "I don't know, and I don't care!"[92] Roosevelt's lack of attention to the merits of State Department procedure prompted a sick, tired, and frustrated Hull finally to tender his resignation in November 1944. Edward R. Stettinius Jr. was subsequently promoted to the position, but no change in the department's relationship with the president would ensue. Stettinius was instead chosen as someone who "would accept state department [sic] subservience."[93]

Roosevelt continued to bypass the State Department on matters relating to Iran. Becoming more interested in using the country as a demonstration of what the United States could achieve by promoting reform in the developing world, he first had to secure Iranian sovereignty from British and Soviet predations. The rambunctious Patrick J. Hurley was therefore sent to Iran in November 1943 as Roosevelt's personal representative with the rank of ambassador to arrange for a joint declaration on Iranian independence to be signed by the three powers at the upcoming Tehran Conference. Such a mission would normally be undertaken by the State Department, but Roosevelt wrote to his son, "I wish I had more men like Pat, on whom I could depend. The men in the State Department . . . half the time I can't tell whether I should believe them or not."[94]

With the president's backing, Hurley worked quickly and effectively, serving as majordomo and successfully cajoling both British foreign secretary Anthony Eden and Soviet premier Joseph Stalin to agree to the insertion of an "Iran Declaration" to the conference, in which all three powers would agree to respect Iranian sovereignty. This achievement was remarkable given how intense the competition between Britain and the Soviet Union was becoming in Iran.

A joint communiqué released at the conclusion of the Tehran Conference stated that it would be common policy to oppose tyranny and welcome countries "into a world family of democratic nations."[95] Never before had the three Great Powers of the world so devoted themselves to the promotion of freedom and independence in the developing world. On Iran specifically, the leaders pledged themselves to uphold the "independence, sovereignty, and territorial integrity of Iran" as well as the "principles of the Atlantic Charter."[96]

US minister Dreyfus heralded the declaration as a formal and public pledge that Iran would remain a free country and as "one more small stone in the foundation of international fair-dealing."[97] At a speech before the Royal Institute of International Affairs in London, Abdol Hossein Hamzavi, press attaché at the Iranian embassy, praised the transformative power of the declaration and stated that the "complete implementation of the facts and purposes of the Iran Declaration flood-lights any dark passages that may have existed in the former relations of Iran with the three Powers."[98] The *Washington Post* excitedly exclaimed that in Iran the "eternal conflict between hard political realities and moral principles has found a satisfactory solution."[99] Persian newspapers similarly lauded the declaration: the principal Iranian newspaper, *Iran*, extolled the gracious Allied powers, saying that as a result of their pledge "the hearts of the people of Iran became one with those of the Americans, the British and the Russians"; the newspaper *Mehr* similarly professed that the "feeling of gratification of the Iranian people resulting from the Allied Declaration on Iran is so deep-rooted that it not only affects the present generation but will also permeate the feeling of future generations"; and *Setareh Iran* simply cheered, "Long live Freedom and Justice!"[100]

Although American actions on the international stage pleased Iran's democrats, Roosevelt next turned to address the growing problem of instability and how the United States could ensure stable democratization. A series of meetings between Roosevelt and leading American advisers to Iran called for a more forceful US role to lead change rather than permit it to grow organically. Arthur Millspaugh, the US financial administrator in Iran, impressed upon Roosevelt the importance of US missions and called for their expansion. The system of advisers and missions were to Millspaugh a clinic demonstrating the practical execution of Roosevelt's international policies.[101] The missions' apparent success in Iran led Roosevelt to favor replicating the program in other problem areas of Asia.[102] At Tehran Airport, prior to boarding a flight to Cairo, President Roosevelt met again with his old friend General Hurley, the architect of the Iran Declaration. The two discussed a tentative outline of future US policy toward Iran to allow the country to serve as the pattern for US relations with the developing world. So pleased was Roosevelt with their discussion that he instructed Hurley to type it up, flesh it out, and submit it as a proposal for future policy.

Historian Warren Kimball has written that Roosevelt held the "consistent position that colonialism, not communism, was the -ism that most threatened postwar peace and stability," and Hurley and Roosevelt agreed that it should be replaced by democracy.[103] Iran was identified as a good model for how to promote democracy, and Hurley's subsequent report stated that America's goal should be to "assist in the creation in Iran of a government based upon the consent of the governed and of a system of free enterprise" that would "afford the Iranian people an opportunity to enjoy the rights of man as set forth in the Constitution of the United States." To achieve an independent and democratic Iran, Hurley proposed that the United States should furnish expert advisers in all fields of government to supervise and direct the Iranian government in making the right choices and in utilizing its resources in ways the United States believed to be the most effective. Previous US advisers had focused narrowly on economic and military matters, but the Iran report called for them to take over all facets of Iranian governance, including the political reform of the country, which had hitherto been left to Iranians themselves. These advisers would be "indoctrinated in the policy of our government toward Iran" and would make regular progress reports to ensure "a vital element of coordination which is essential to direction of our policy and protection of our interests." In short, the US government should personally manage every facet of Iran's development and ensure it progressed safely and democratically. Rather than focusing solely on institutional reform, American officials would be at the forefront of all democratization efforts from the ground up. Although the report referred to the "intelligent and patriotic leaders of Iran," Iran's own democrats were assigned a mere supporting role.[104]

Iran was therefore to be the blueprint for the American program of building associated free nations through highly intrusive micromanagement on all levels. This program would provide an alternative to the doctrine of imperialism as practiced by Great Britain and the ideology of communism offered by the Soviet Union: to expand the doctrine of democracy and "to bestow upon the world the benevolent principles of the Atlantic Charter and the Four Freedoms."[105] Roosevelt received the thirty-page report with unrestrained delight, exclaiming himself to be "rather thrilled with the idea of using Iran as an example of what we could do by an unselfish foreign policy. We could not take on a more difficult nation than Iran. I would like, however, to have a try at it."[106]

So thrilled was he that just a few weeks later the report was serving as the basis for active measures in US relations with Iran.[107] In February 1944, Secretary of State Stettinius reported to the president that "measures are being taken as rapidly as personnel can be found to implement your policy," and he informed Hurley that four of Hurley's specific recommendations were already in the process of being accomplished.[108] One of these recommendations was the raising of the US Legation in Iran to full embassy status in recognition of the close relationship between the two countries. Another was the enlargement of the US military mission, responsible primarily for the wartime supply of the Soviet Union, to include also the provision of technical assistance to the Iranian government.[109] More generally, efforts were taken to increase coordination between the US missions in order to provide more effective and efficient assistance to Iran.[110] Toward the end of March 1944, Roosevelt told Hurley that he felt certain that their policy toward Iran would be a tremendous success.[111]

By June 1944, the US Office of Strategic Services—predecessor to the Central Intelligence Agency (CIA)—confirmed that present policy was moving in the right direction to create an "independent, strong and progressive" state in Iran.[112] W. Averell Harriman, by now ambassador to the Soviet Union, recalled that "Roosevelt enjoyed thinking aloud on the tremendous changes he saw ahead—the end of colonial empires and the rise of newly independent nations across the sweep of Africa and Asia."[113] The president hoped by expanding the program, he could convert "the Iranian experiment into a workable design for the post-war world."[114]

The Curse of Instability

While the United States worked to bestow democracy upon the Iranians in a managed and controlled manner, Iranian democrats were wishing to be left alone. Hurley's report described a program more akin to democracy usurpation than to democracy promotion. Instead of indigenous forces working to create democracy organically, the United States sought to implant its own version among them. The populist Mohammad Mossadegh pointed to this discord, arguing that the "Iranian himself is the best person to manage his house."[115] Mossadegh and his followers specifically singled out Arthur Millspaugh, the powerful financial adviser, as the epitome of unwanted foreign interference. Mossadegh called for Millspaugh's immediate termination and the return of economic control to Iranian hands. Joining such criticism, albeit for very different reasons, were the privileged classes and landowners. Millspaugh's attempts to introduce progressive tax systems and other liberal reforms directly affected their personal wealth, and so they too called for his removal from office. Even the generally pro-American Prime Minister Sa'ed criticized Millspaugh's power and handling of Iran's finances.[116]

In the ensuing power struggle between the Majles and the Americans, the Americans won out: Sa'ed was forced to resign, and Millspaugh retained his position.[117] The affair, however, was but one of a growing number of disagreements between Iranian democrats and the United States. Although both had the same end goal—a democratic Iran—their strategies were widely different. One necessitated increased US intervention, control, and a slow pace, whereas the other demanded greater freedom and independence as well as immediate democratization. So different were the two sides' strategies, in fact, that the Roosevelt administration regarded Iran's democratic institutions as a nuisance that often blocked US reforms and contributed to growing instability. With seven major factions competing for authority in the Majles, intrigue and infighting were common. Within just two years of the Fourteenth Majles, Iran was subject to seven different premiers, the formation and collapse of nine cabinets, and the comings and goings of 110 cabinet ministers.[118] Such frequent disturbances to the political system undermined the Americans' hope for the stable progress of democracy in Iran.

From an Iranian point of view, unstable governments were a necessary by-product of democratic experimentation, and many have argued that, despite the instability, democracy in Iran was becoming stronger and more deeply engrained. Ervand Abrahamian contends that by early 1944 "most [Iranians] expected the deputies [of the Majles] to assert themselves over the shah and establish a genuine parliamentary democracy."[119] Bills were regularly introduced to the Majles and energetically debated before being voted upon in a healthy and democratic manner.[120] The democratic zeitgeist also encouraged labor disputes: disaffected mill workers in Esfahan went on strike, calling for "equality," and were quickly joined by members of the Communist Tudeh, resulting in violent clashes with the authorities. The situation in Esfahan alone was rumored to have produced more than six hundred fatalities and had major repercussions for Iran's national politics.[121] With the Tudeh taking advantage of the situation, a movement was set up almost as quickly to counter its influence, the Jebheh-e Isteqlal (Independence Front). After a few months, the anti-Tudeh movement controlled twenty-nine newspapers and journals and repeatedly decried the Communists' rise and influence. One newspaper breathlessly exclaimed that unless the government dismantled the Tudeh, the social unrest in Esfahan would soon spread into a national revolution.[122]

Such an event was precisely what the United States wished to avoid, still focused as it was on winning the war against the Axis powers. America eventually looked to the shah—a man it had previously prevented from taking a greater role in politics—to try and enforce some level of stability upon Iran's internal situation. Before Parliament, Mohammad Mossadegh pinpointed the inconsistency in the Western approach, asking, "If democracy is not desirable, why do they fully subscribe to it in their own countries?" Addressing the issue of instability, he continued that democracy was the answer, not the problem: "If there is only one captain," he implored, referring to the shah, "the boat would be in danger every time he is ill, and sink the minute he dies. But if captains were numerous, the illness and death of one individual would not alter the course of the boat."[123] The Allies, however, were unmoved. Although the Roosevelt administration supported in theory the promotion of democracy, the associated instability threatened the US national interest. With war still ravaging the international system, stability was more important than immediate democratic progress in Iran.

General Hurley was therefore shocked when on a visit to Iran toward the end of 1944 he saw little action being taken on the policy he had helped formulate. The views of the more traditionalist members of the State Department instead held sway. Fundamentally at odds with the Hurley plan, senior State Department officials chose to ignore many of its policy directives. Despite being generally ineffectual during Roosevelt's presidency, the department was still important in the implementation, or in this case the *non*implementation, of policy. Hurley had been aware that members of the State Department were against his plan, and it was this knowledge that led him to confront Eugene Rostow for dismissing it as "hysterical messianic globaloney." Assistant Secretary of State Dean Acheson, however, agreed with

Rostow and worked hard to undermine the program, despite its presidential approval. Acheson dismissed Hurley as an "Oklahoma cowboy" who sought "simplistic answers to complicated problems."[124]

Acheson wrote in a memo to the secretary of state that the continued application of such a disruptive plan would multiply risks, cause unrest, and have "dangerous and unforeseen consequences."[125] This comment drew out Hurley's supporters, such as Wallace Murray, who complained that Acheson's memo was a "frivolous and unwarranted interference in political matters" and that he should be rebuked for acting in "direct opposition to our political policy towards Iran."[126] However, Dean Acheson was a powerful figure in the State Department, and despite being in direct contradiction with presidential directives he made sure that Hurley's report was all but ignored. Utilizing his influential position, he corralled fellow senior members of the administration to report jointly to the president that "the course of events [in Iran] had made it unnecessary to carry out General Hurley's recommendations."[127]

In addition to pressure from his own administration and mounting instability in Iran, Roosevelt was also counseled by his British allies to ignore Hurley. When Prime Minister Winston Churchill received a copy of Hurley's report and its warnings of the dangers of British imperialism, he was incensed. In reply to Roosevelt, he remarked that Hurley "seems to have some ideas about British imperialism which I confess made me rub my eyes."[128] He went on to explain that "British imperialism has spread and is spreading democracy more widely than any other system of government since the beginning of time."[129] The press attaché at the Iranian embassy in London astutely remarked at the time that "political instability" caused by "turbid external influences . . . [is] one of the main reasons why no reforms have been carried out since the recent advent of democracy in Persia."[130] Events in Iran and the views of such senior officials and allies stayed Roosevelt's hand from pushing forward with Hurley's the plan, despite his prior approval of it.

Such events were music to the shah's ears. With the United States losing faith in the free expression of democratic rule, he was finally able to assume greater control. The Roosevelt administration welcomed this assumption, seeing the shah as a potential unifying force and strong hand that could restore stability and allow for controlled progress where possible. In December 1944, the president sent Averell Harriman to meet with the shah to discuss how best to move forward. Having sensed that the Americans were losing faith in the promotion of democracy, he no longer sang democracy's praises as he had previously. He explained to Harriman that Iran was not ready for democracy and that "until the people . . . acquired sufficient education to understand the principles of democratic government," it should not be forced upon them.[131] Harriman assured the shah that the president was in agreement and that closer cooperation between the royal court and the White House would be best for Iran at this time. The active policy of promoting democracy was therefore replaced by a more laissez-faire approach, focusing on the US financial, military, and police reform missions to maintain Iran as an effective wartime ally rather than on more wholesale democratic changes. Realism had quickly usurped idealism in America's early relations with Iran.

Unselfish No More: The Lure of Oil

Although Roosevelt wrote of his excitement for what an unselfish foreign policy could do for countries such as Iran, reality soon intervened. Efforts to promote Iran's development became secondary to the desire for stability and toward the end of Roosevelt's presidency, were also overtaken by America's growing interest in securing economic concessions from Iran. With war coming to an end, the Americans' attention increasingly turned toward their desire to assert global leadership and create an international liberal economic order. This meant that control over the production and supply of petroleum resources was vital.[132] As early as September 1943, Washington had given its approval for an American oil company to sound out concessions in Baluchistan, a province in southeastern Iran. The US minister in Iran, Louis Dreyfus, spoke out in opposition to the move, worrying that it could "cause [the] British and Soviets to suspect that our attitude toward Iran is not entirely disinterested and thus weaken our general position here."[133] Secretary of State Cordell Hull dismissed such concerns, informing Dreyfus that oil concessions were vital not only for "war purposes" but also to the "long-range viewpoint" of American priorities in the postwar era.[134]

This change in emphasis—from the unselfish promotion of democracy to the search for economic gain—had profound repercussions, all of which proved fateful for Iran's nascent democratic movement. When these secret oil discussions came to light toward the end of 1944, Iran was at once plunged back into chaos. The Majles decried the actions of Prime Minister Sa'ed for secretly organizing concessions without parliamentary approval.[135] Perhaps more aggrieved were the Soviets when it emerged that the United States had been negotiating not only for an oil concession in the Southeast but also for one in the North, an area that had historically been the Soviets' sole economic preserve. In response, the Soviets upped their efforts to force Iran to submit to their demands. They also launched a devastating propaganda campaign against Sa'ed, including the organization of a mass demonstration of thirty-five thousand people, who called for his resignation and were supported by armed Soviet troops.[136]

Like dogs fighting over a bone, the Allied powers—Great Britain, the Soviet Union, and the United States—quickly became locked in frantic competition with one another over Iran's resources. Although the United States was late to the contest, its involvement changed the dynamic almost instantly. In the words of Sir Claremont Skrine, the British consul in Mashhad, US efforts to ensure oil concessions north of Tehran "changed the Russians in Persia from hot-war allies into cold-war rivals" and marked the beginning of what was to become the Cold War.[137]

The president's goal of "having a try" at democratizing Iran deteriorated in step with his health. The benefactor of this deterioration was the shah, who was able to gradually assume greater control of Iranian politics.[138] In mid-April 1945, while sitting for a portrait at the Little White House in Warm Springs, Georgia,

President Roosevelt collapsed and died. Iranian democracy was left at a crossroads. With Roosevelt gone, would space for democratic experimentation return, or would his successor look to bring the shah back to the center of power?

Conclusion

It has been said that the United States fought World War II "without a well-defined, workable, and publicly articulated geopolitical strategy to guide its actions after its victory over the Axis powers."[139] Recent historians have argued that despite Roosevelt's rhetoric on democracy promotion, little attention was actually given to progress toward this goal.[140] In Iran, however, the promotion of democracy became a top priority, and it was hoped that the US program could become the blueprint for policy toward the wider developing world. By the time President Roosevelt passed away on April 12, 1945, however, his attempt to embark on an ambitious program of external democracy promotion had largely been replaced by the need for stability and an interest in extracting oil concessions from the still weak and vulnerable Iranian government. Using Hurley's design, Roosevelt had hoped to build a true showcase for the promotion of American democracy. After an early flurry, however, the efforts made in pursuit of this goal stalled and then regressed.

Roosevelt and General Hurley's plan failed for four main reasons. Prime among them was the lack of understanding and cooperation between American officials and Iran's own reformers. The Roosevelt administration felt it could successfully democratize Iran without any internal Iranian support; when doing so resulted in political and social instability, the administration lost its nerve and returned support to the shah. Had Roosevelt reached out to Iran's energetic democracy movement, led by such people as Mohammad Mossadegh, he could have coordinated a more successful and sustainable transition by working in unison for stability and democracy. Although Mossadegh was against foreign intervention, a truly selfless and supportive policy could have been viewed favorably even by the most staunch advocates of independence. The United States played a major role in creating the conditions that allowed democracy to flourish, and it is possible that some form of unity could have formed between Mossadegh and the United States. When the United States changed its tack—restricting democracy, inviting the shah back into politics, and involving itself in economic competition for Iran's resources—Iranians working for democratic reform lost the one country they thought supported their cause. Restriction of Iran's democratic transition begun by Western powers led to the rise in feelings of betrayal and the stirrings of nationalist sentiment.

Second, the lack of support for Roosevelt's democracy program among influential members of his own administration, State Department officials in particular, hampered its implementation. Orders passed to US officials in Iran were drastically watered down versions of what Roosevelt or Hurley originally intended. On his resignation from the government in November 1945, General Hurley railed against the discrepancies between what he called "our announced policies and our conduct of international relations," the latter of which, he argued, actually served to "undermine democracy."[141] With an implicit reference to the shah's actions in Iran, he chastised America for falling "prey to the nations that gave lip service to our ideals and principles in order to maintain our material support." What had begun as an effort to encourage and promote democracy, Hurley continued, had degraded to something akin to imperialism by the start of the Cold War. Hurley singled out Dean Acheson as chief architect of this change and before a Senate Foreign Relations Committee bluntly accused him of personally "defeating" and "destroying" US policy toward Iran.[142] Although Acheson rejected this accusation, it is true that the policy paper on Iran, written by Hurley and approved by the president, largely failed to be enacted thanks in part to Acheson's intervention.

The clamor for oil concessions that became an additional goal of US policy toward Iran by the end of Roosevelt's administration was a third reason why the administration moved away from the promotion of democracy. America had been invited to Iran to act as a counterbalance to the predatory policies of the Soviet Union and Great Britain but after a few short years ended up joining them. It would have been naïve to expect the United States to pursue selfless policies in countries such as Iran, but the speed and manner of the American U-turn drastically changed the perception of the United States in Iran. Instead of praising America as a friendly and enlightened ally, Iranian civil society turned inward and focused more on nationalism. The benefactor of this shift in view was Mohammad Mossadegh. His principled and consistent stand against foreign concessions and interference rapidly increased his popularity, making him the preeminent opposition figure in Iran. Such actions as his introduction of a bill on December 2, 1944, that banned the government from granting oil concessions to foreigners made him so popular that he became the embodiment of resurgent Iranian national aspirations and the symbol of a defiant stance against the machinations of Great Britain, the Soviet Union, and now the United States.[143] Whereas an indigenous democratic movement could have been a US ally under Hurley's plan, its transformation into a nationalist movement meant that it was now an ever-increasing problem and inhibitor of American goals to promote development from the top down. The United States had been welcomed to Iran in the early 1940s as the savior of Iranian independence and democracy. By 1945, many Iranians wished the United States would leave Iran alone.

Fourth, Roosevelt's democracy program in Iran coincided with the dawn of global Cold War politics. The promotion of democracy became increasingly at odds with hard diplomatic realities that the burgeoning war produced. One of Roosevelt's biographers concluded that his global vision of a postwar world that included American promotion of democracy "could not withstand the historical and contemporary forces ranged against them. . . . Russian expansion, Chinese strife, and colonial revolutions were beyond Roosevelt's power to prevent."[144] As a result, the practical idealist moved toward strong, stable leadership instead of immediate democracy. This shift ultimately led to what was to become US foreign policy in the Cold War era: emphasis on the need for stability and a focus on security and strategic concerns. In Iran, this meant less support and respect for democratic principles and instead embracing the shah's more active role in Iran's daily political life. For example, the United States backed the ousting of Prime Minister Morteza Bayat in May 1945 for becoming too close to the Tudeh, an organization that continued to grow amid widespread popular discontent and frustration.[145]

The movement toward realpolitik in the mid-1940s should not, however, cloud the fact that for a brief period in the early 1940s, when American goals and internal Iranian efforts were aligned, rapid progress toward democratization was made. Iran's period of constitutionalism would not have been possible without the existence of favorable external factors. During these few short years, the United States was not focused on economic gain. The Americans instead convinced their wartime allies to agree to the Iran Declaration during the Tehran Conference and made clear their intention to support an independent and democratizing Iran. These actions gave space free from British and Soviet intrigue for legitimate independent political associations to form, debate, and compete with other independent political groups. American linkage with and leverage over the shah ensured he did not act against democracy despite his desires for authoritarianism.

This active US policy was at work numerous times when the shah attempted to assert royal supremacy. In December 1942, for example, the shah attempted to force his prime minister to resign so he could appoint a military government but was prevented from doing so by Western intervention.[146] Similarly, in the run-up to the elections for the Fourteenth Majles, a nervous shah again asked if he could delay democracy and form a military government but was again denied. Had the shah been able to institute military government at this time, Iran's experiments with constitutionalism would have ended far sooner, and a return to authoritarianism would have been assured.[147]

The Americans' ability to influence Iran and the shah came from their strong positions of leverage and linkage, which accrued quickly after the United States became involved in the country in 1941. When the two were first applied to the benefit of democracy, democracy benefited; when they were used to encourage stability, democracy in Iran suffered. The Persian Spring chilled quickly as the Cold War began. It would fall to Roosevelt's successor, a man from a small middle-America town called Independence, to decide whether Iran would continue its own movement for independence and democracy or if the shah would be permitted to reassert royal authority.

2 A More Selfish Iran Policy, 1945–1951

Harry S. Truman's political career started late in his life.[1] By the age of thirty-eight, he had succeeded in little and aspired to not much more. Even his own in-laws considered him low on the order of the social hierarchy and far beneath their daughter.[2] His persistence to keep working hard despite failure as a haberdasher and later as an investor, however, eventually paid off.[3] By the time Truman finally arrived in Washington at the age of fifty, his soon-to-be contemporaries were already well established. Franklin D. Roosevelt had become the thirty-second president of the United States, while in Germany Adolf Hitler was looking to combine the offices of chancellor and president into the new position of führer. Joseph Stalin was meanwhile concluding the Great Purge, which consolidated his control over the Soviet Union, and Winston Churchill, having already been a leading political figure for almost forty years, was on the verge of becoming prime minister of Great Britain. Remarkably, the freshman from Missouri would soon be on par with such titans, dictating not only the success of the Allied war effort but also the shape of the postwar world.

Truman had become a senator thanks to the efforts of "Boss Tom" Pendergast, a leading political figure in his home state, Missouri.[4] Back-room deals and compromises also brought him the nomination for vice president in 1944 because leading party officials viewed him as someone least offensive to the general public who could best balance Roosevelt's ticket. The uninspiring nature of his appointment was reflected in its nickname, the "Second Missouri Compromise."[5] Despite being picked, he would remain removed from President Roosevelt, meeting with him only once prior to the campaign and being kept at distance once in office. Less than three months after inauguration, Roosevelt suffered a massive cerebral hemorrhage. Just two decades on from living on the farm, Harry S. Truman became the thirty-third president of the United States on April 12, 1945.

"Boys, If You Ever Pray, Pray for Me Now!": Truman, Iran, and the Start of the Cold War

In a wonderfully oxymoronic summation, Truman has been described as "the Average American, par excellence."[6] Rarely in history has an obscure middle-aged farmer risen to the highest office in the land and probably never in such a short period of time. With World War II raging on two continents and relations with the Soviet Union declining, Truman approached the assembled media on his first day and urged: "Boys, if you ever pray, pray for me now!"[7]

In Truman's relations with Iran, his qualities of patience, determination, and perseverance would be stretched to the fullest. As war faded and thoughts turned to reconstruction, Iran would grow in importance, further challenging the ability of the United States to maintain the unselfish foreign policy that Roosevelt had hoped to pursue. This move toward a more self-interested policy would continue under Truman as the Cold War and demands of securing Iranian oil for the West came increasingly to the fore.[8] The period 1945–51 would present the United States with a choice: maintain support for Iran's constitutional movement and its unsteady and unstable development or relegate democratization to a secondary consideration in favor of seeking stability through the promotion of a strong ruler. The former would allow the United States to remain the global champion of democracy but without the certainty that democratically elected governments would maintain a close strategic alliance with the West. The latter would ensure close relations and the possibility of some reform but would undermine the goals of Iran's people to rule themselves. America's linkage to the Iranian leadership and opposition remained strong throughout this period, but, as we shall see, its leverage would be highly dependent on the type of regime that held power in Iran.

The Truman administration would initially maintain support for Iranian independence from both the shah's attempts to claim personal control as well as external threats. The latter would present Truman with his first Iranian challenge. During the Azerbaijan Crisis of 1946, the United States resolutely defended Iranian independence and sovereignty from Soviet attempts to break off parts of its northwestern territories. Just a year after the war ended in Europe, Joseph Stalin had taken the stage at the Bolshoi Theater and argued that communism and capitalism could never live in peaceful coexistence and that confrontation was inevitable.[9] The chargé d'affaires in Moscow, George Kennan, warned Washington in his now famous "Long Telegram" that the Soviet Union was already in a state of perpetual war with capitalism and that it constituted "undoubtedly [the] greatest task our diplomacy has ever faced and probably [the] greatest it will ever have to face."[10]

The Azerbaijan Crisis was the first standoff in this soon-to-be-named Cold War as the Soviet Union refused to remove its troops from the region and instead began to foment unrest and uprisings in the Iranian provinces of Azerbaijan, Mazandaran, and Gorgan.[11] By January 1946, Soviet-backed political parties were formed that demanded autonomy from Iran, and a separatist government was even established under the control of Jafar Pishevari, an Iranian Communist with allegiance to Moscow.

In Washington, the new president was determined to look tough and hold firm against the Soviets and in support of Iranian independence. He supported Iran's complaint before the United Nations and later claimed to have given Stalin an ultimatum to leave Iran "at once." However, no evidence of this ultimatum exists in the historic record.[12] It *is* known that the Truman administration was decidedly frank in its messages to Moscow, stating that the United States would "not remain indifferent" to Iran's occupation and that it

wished very much that the Soviet Union withdraw "immediately all
. . . forces."[13] With echoes of Roosevelt before him, Truman hoped
to use the crisis to replicate what the Iranians themselves had made
famous 2,500 years earlier: the establishment of the rule of law in
the Middle East.[14]

Although the luster of America as that shining city on a hill had
started to fade owing to its increasingly selfish policy, Truman's
forceful support for Iranian independence returned a sparkle to his
country's reputation. For their part, the Iranian government still welcomed and even encouraged closer relations with the United States
so that, in the words of one Iranian politician at the time, the Americans would be "witnesses of the Soviet political encroachments and
by their presence act as deterrence for the more open violations of
our independence and interference in our internal affairs."[15]

America's interference in Iran's internal affairs was largely
unwanted, but its support to protect Iran internationally was vital.
The latter gave the administration a high degree of leverage with
which to control Iranian action. International condemnation and the
promise of an oil concession from Prime Minister Ahmad Qavam
finally persuaded the Soviets to withdraw, but when Qavam dithered
over sending in Iranian troops to reclaim the territory, the United
States used its leverage. The US ambassador was asked to make it
clear that such dallying "would be an excellent way to lose Iranian
independence" and that monetary assistance to Iran would continue
only if Qavam acted quickly and firmly.[16]

This was the first times the United States had placed conditions
on its aid to Iran, and the added pressure had the intended result.
Iranian troops moved in and efficiently routed the Communist
separatists, who had now been abandoned by Soviet troops. More
bad news for Moscow followed; when the Soviet oil concession
that Qavam promised was presented to the Majles for approval, it
was summarily dismissed without a single vote in its favor, leaving
Moscow not only red-faced but also empty-handed. Persian chica-
nery and strong, consistent American support effectively scuppered
Soviet plans to annex northern Iran. The United States was now

deeply entwined in Iranian affairs and would remain so for the next thirty years.

Changing Priorities

The growing Soviet menace meant that idealistic and unselfish goals regarding the developing world were increasingly unviable. Events in Iran and later in Greece and Turkey formed the basis of a new foreign-policy doctrine announced in March 1947, which became known as the Truman Doctrine. This was the foundation for what later became the "imperial presidency" as the United States increasingly projected its power in response to the growth of the Soviet Union.[17] The Azerbaijan Crisis had been the opening move of the Cold War, but it was the Truman Doctrine that created the playbook for American action. It held that the United States would use its economic and financial aid to promote stability and orderly political processes in countries facing subjugation by armed minorities or outside pressures seeking to impose upon them totalitarian Communist rule.[18] The doctrine was developed as a response to the rise of the Soviet Union and the British withdrawal from the position of dominant superpower after World War II. The changing and uncertain environment led Washington to prioritize the strengthening of friendly governments in strategic areas. Although Iran was not a priority for the United States at this time, military aid to it began in 1950 on an initial basis of $124 million over seven years.[19] It would later increase considerably as the Cold War warmed up, defining the US–Iranian alliance and moving attention away from democracy in preference for matters of military or strategic importance.

The Truman Doctrine focused American attention on ensuring stability among its allies, but in the Middle East the Americans also began to focus on securing oil agreements. In September 1945, a report by the State–War–Navy Coordinating Committee, a precursor to the National Security Council (NSC), concluded that as known US reserves declined, "the world oil center of gravity is shifting to the Middle East."[20]

The United States focused its efforts on securing oil concessions from Saudi Arabia but took an interest in Iran. Secretary of State James F. Byrnes cautioned the US ambassador in Iran to avoid the "impression that our determination to carry out our obligations under the [Atlantic] Charter and the Iran Declaration has been influenced . . . by a selfish interest on our part in Iranian petroleum."[21] However, such statements have been called a policy of mystification as US interest in Iran's oil resources nonetheless continued apace.[22] Loy Henderson, head of the Department of Near Eastern Affairs, noted that World War II "emphasized the strategic importance of the Near East . . . [and the] need for a stronger role of this Government in [the region] . . . especially in view of the oil reserves."[23] American aspirations to democratize Iran, which had been sidetracked by the exigencies of World War II, were now threatened by the onset of the Cold War and the growing American thirst for Iranian oil.

US Private Businesses and the Development of Iran

Outside of the Azerbaijan Crisis, Iran was not a major priority for the Truman administration in the mid-1940s. Whereas Greece and Turkey were promised $400 million and $350 million, respectively, as part of the Truman Doctrine, aid for Iran was not so generous. Aware that the United States could not pay to rebuild all countries damaged by the war, Washington looked instead to the private sector to rebuild Iran's economy and structure its development. In the late 1940s, the Iranian government was encouraged to sign contracts with the private American firms Morrison-Knudsen International and Overseas Consultants Inc., to conduct a study of Iran's future economic potential and how best to augment it.[24] This study would form the basis of what became known as the government's Seven-Year Plan.

Despite this approach, the Truman administration still wanted responsibility for development to be placed in American rather than Iranian hands, specifically those of Max Weston Thornburg. Thornburg was chosen as the intermediary between the companies and the US government, and he would become an important figure in Iran's politics during this time. An informal diplomat, Thornburg had experience in both government service and the business world. He had spent much of his early career in the oil industry, eventually rising to vice president of the Standard Oil Company of California in 1936. At the outbreak of World War II, Roosevelt's secretary of state, Cordell Hull, appointed Thornburg special consultant on international petroleum matters.[25] Following the cessation of fighting, Thornburg became a freelance "industrial consultant" for private companies and foreign governments. In a letter to his friend Henry Luce, he wrote that his life's ambition was to seek "the adaptation of our free enterprise system—at least as it operates abroad—to changing world conditions."[26]

The concept of using a businessman's approach to the Cold War gelled with the Truman administration's hopes for Iran. Together the administration and Thornburg formulated a plan to reform the country through a series of small-scale projects. These projects would gradually open up Iran's economy to American businesses, which would in turn inject increasing levels of foreign investment to bolster local productivity. It was hoped that using the American private sector to invest in and modernize Iran would help maintain stability and develop democracy without vast sums of official financial aid. To this end, Thornburg organized contracts with Morrison-Knudsen and Overseas Consultants and remained a paid consultant to the State Department. He was the ideal "chosen instrument" through which the Truman administration could promote reform, modernization, and, it was hoped, *stable* and gradual democratization in Iran, while administration officials focused more on the priorities of oil deals and security.[27] Again, as with the Roosevelt administration, no mention was made of working with Iran's own democratic movement.

However, while the Truman administration looked to pass responsibility for Iran to the private sector, the shah remained determined to return to the center of political life. He repeatedly made clear that the attainment of American goals in the region could best be ensured through US support for his personal rule, and he began to forge a close personal relationship with the new US ambassador, George V. Allen, in the hope that Allen would argue his case back in Washington. At top of his agenda were reclaiming powers lost to the prime minister and the Majles as well as securing improved military aid to strengthen the main guarantor of the Pahlavi dynasty, Iran's armed forces. The shah's efforts would test US commitment to democracy in Iran because his firm rule would likely best assure stability.

Democracy initially won out, and Truman continued Roosevelt's policy of pressuring the shah to remain removed from everyday political life. But the shah's persistence easily matched that of the American president, and he would constantly test the administration's resolve and commitment. In early 1947, he approached Ambassador Allen for permission to remove Prime Minister Qavam over allegations of corruption.[28] That he felt it necessary to secure US permission illustrates the extent to which external factors were essential to understanding Iran at this time. Keen to allow constitutional government to continue, however, providing it did not interfere with other American interests, Allen made clear his government's position that any decision to remove or renew a government should be made by democratic institutions, not by the shah.[29] Later that year the shah again approached Allen, this time with the idea of strengthening the royal court by reducing the constitutional powers of the office of prime minister.[30] Under orders from Washington, the ambassador remained firm, restating that the US policy was to support the growth of constitutional governance in Iran. Allen later wrote of his feelings that he "did not think a king should be meddling in politics" and "was not certain where [the shah] would stop if he did succeed in whatever actions he might attempt."[31]

Like his predecessor before him, Truman kept the shah largely out of day-to-day politics and thereby kept alive Iran's unsteady movement toward democracy. Without the consistent rejection of the shah's advances, it is likely that Iran's nascent democratic breakthrough would have been quashed almost as soon as it had begun. Although Washington remained wary of the potential for instability as a result of ongoing democratic experimentation, it was hoped that the partnership with private US companies would provide a solid foundation for a more stable evolution.

As America Turns: The Rise of Authoritarianism

While Thornburg was focused on assessing Iran's economy, Prime Minister Qavam continued full steam with his progressive agenda. A seasoned politician, Qavam had served as prime minister four times since first coming to power in 1921. Before that, he had worked as private secretary to the royal court during the Constitutional Revolution, where he supported and wrote the royal proclamation granting the Iranian Constitution.[32] Now back in power, Qavam was a powerful elder statesman of Persian politics and looked to restrict the powers of the shah while strengthening his own office.

In June 1947, Qavam formed the Hezb-e Demokrat (Democrat Party) in preparation for the upcoming elections to the Fifteenth Majles. "A constitutional system without a disciplined party," he later wrote, "is like a building without a roof."[33] The Democrat Party's manifesto, released in October, promised extensive economic, social, and administrative reforms to build upon the democratic gains made since 1941. He proposed women's suffrage, the formation of provincial assemblies, the reintroduction of village elections, and the construction of rural schools, clinics, and irrigation projects.[34] Most unsettling for the shah, the program also called for "a drastic revision of the country's security forces," which entailed reassessing the organization and management of the army, police, and gendarmerie.[35] Ensuring civilian control over the country's security forces was the key to preventing the shah from using the army to assert royal authority at a time of his choosing. The shah, however, depended on the military to support his return to personal leadership when the conditions allowed, and such moves by politicians concerned him greatly. He already distrusted Qavam and became only more determined to reclaim power after hearing of Qavam's progressive political agenda.

Conversely, the Truman administration seemed pleased that Iran's indigenous democratic forces were apparently developing in a more stable manner, despite a growth in nationalist sentiment. Ambassador Allen praised Qavam for his progressive reforms and urged their continuance, saying the United States was "anxious to see progressive measures taken."[36] All was not how it seemed, however, as fears grew inside Iran that Qavam intended only to strengthen his own position, not further the cause of democracy. Mohammad Mossadegh, for instance, argued against Qavam's reforms, believing them to be aimed solely at creating a one-party state.[37] The tension was exacerbated as Qavam controlled the parliamentary elections to ensure favorable results for his followers. His party won an overwhelming victory in elections called the most corrupt since the time of Reza Shah.[38] With American assistance, Qavam had successfully marginalized the shah, and now, with a Majles crammed with his supporters, he seemed "set for a long term of office."[39]

Ironically, however, Qavam's electoral triumph precipitated his downfall as his coalition, which consisted of a broad base of diverse elements, fractured and split soon after election.[40] The shah, sensing the weakening of a prime minister he so despised, joined the attacks on him through both press statements and conversations with the US ambassador.[41] An intense power struggle ensued between the monarch and his prime minister as the shah gradually reduced Qavam's parliamentary majority by siphoning off members of his coalition and coaxing them to his own side. His ability to dispense altogether with Qavam as prime minister, however, still rested on permission from external actors.

As political instability rose, Washington quickly lost faith in Qavam. By September 1947, the State Department informed Allen that the situation had become "intolerable and dangerous" for the maintenance of national unity, which was a prerequisite for ensuring stability and the successful resistance of Soviet expansion.[42] Furthermore, rumors abounded that Qavam, now desperate for support, had become closely aligned with the Communist Tudeh Party.[43] This turn of events rekindled conversation in Washington over whether

US interests would be best served by democratic institutions or by the shah's personal rule.

Loy Henderson, director of the Division of Near Eastern Affairs at the State Department, was particularly vocal in calling for a pivot away from Qavam in favor of the shah. He felt only the latter could provide the strong governance necessary to effectively resist Soviet domination and ensure stability.[44] John Jernegan, acting chief of the Division for Greek, Turkish, and Iranian Affairs, agreed in part, arguing that Iran was a "backward country . . . not fully prepared for democratic processes." However, he also warned that "the shah's record is not one to inspire confidence in the personal rule which would probably follow the constitutional change he has in mind."[45] Ambassador Allen, whose support the shah had long cultivated, also regarded the monarch as the best leader for Iran at this time. Instructed by the State Department to give all appropriate support to any government the shah selected to replace Qavam, Allen went as far as to advise the shah to force Qavam out and "make him leave the country or put him in jail if he caused trouble."[46] Again, any discussion of backing the forces coalesced around the increasingly popular Mohammad Mossadegh or any other Iranian leader was noticeable only by its absence.

With the United States finally joining Great Britain and the Soviet Union in support of the shah over Qavam, the shah finally felt free to make his move without fear of external opposition. His actions demonstrated that as early as 1947, just six years after assuming the throne, he had become a shrewd political operator. His first step was to force the resignation of Qavam's cabinet in order to leave the premier politically isolated.[47] Qavam's response was weak, appealing for a vote of confidence from the Majles and warning that his removal would be a "sorrowful tragedy" that would spell the end of constitutionalism in Iran.[48] However, with his party fractured, he had little support to fall back on. Majles deputies were instructed to reject Qavam's vote of confidence or face the shah's personal displeasure.[49] As well as threats, the shah used his twin sister, the cunning and devious Princess Ashraf, to turn any remaining

Qavam supporters against him. To gain the support of the powerful Speaker of the Majles, Sardar Fakher Hekmat, the shah reportedly paid off Hekmat's hefty gambling debts.[50] These efforts proved successful as Qavam's request for a vote of confidence was denied, and his rule came to an unceremonious end on December 18, 1947. A few days later Ambassador Allen, who had previously supported Iran's democratic institutions, explained US strategic thinking in rejecting Qavam:

> I have often been faced with the problem whether to continue to insist on democratic processes in Iran. One is frequently made aware here that Iran is not ready for full democracy and that, as a result of insisting on democratic processes in a country not ready for them, we often get more fraud, corruption, and self-seeking than we do good government. One is tempted by the thought that, although a dictatorship of the Reza Shah variety would be undesirable, perhaps a middle ground of a somewhat stronger government would be preferable to the chaotic and corrupt condition we now have.[51]

Allen felt that a more prominent role for the shah, in close cooperation with the United States, would best ensure a democracy "handed down gradually from above."[52] However, the nature of Qavam's removal has been called a "devastating blow to Iran's infant constitutional government."[53] It marked both the beginning of the end for constitutionalism in Iran and the beginning of the return of the king. Although Qavam had begun to deviate from democratic processes, he represented a far greater chance of an eventual consolidation of constitutionalism than that offered by the shah and his royalist supporters.[54] Although Americans remained confident in their ability to control events in Iran, the reality was changing. US leverage over the shah had weakened slightly thanks to his clever manipulation of officials such as Ambassador Allen. By working so effectively to oust Qavam, the shah now had an opportunity to assert his own rule and achieve his goal of becoming an able successor to his authoritarian father.

The Return of the King

Despite Allen's description of the new prime minister, Ebrahim Hakimi, as someone who "gave every evidence of his thorough devotion to democratic principles," democracy in Iran was on the decline.[55] The shah's policy of forming a close personal relationship with key American officials, especially Ambassador Allen, had paid off in removing Qavam, and he hoped to continue the growing relationship. In January 1948, Allen wrote to the State Department in support of the shah's attempts to acquire the ability to dissolve the Majles at times of his choosing.[56] With US assistance, the shah also strengthened the army, a key source of royal power, from 65,000 men in 1941 to 102,000 in 1946 and 120,000 by 1949.[57] Six years earlier the United States had restricted the size of the Iranian army to just 30,000 men, but as the situation changed, the United States increasingly sided with the shah.[58]

The shah grew in confidence. Hakimi's tenure as prime minister lasted only a few months, and upon his resignation a resurgent shah demonstrated his return to center stage by personally nominating Mohammad Sa'ed as Hakimi's replacement. This was a bold move; the nomination of prime minister had become a prerogative of the Majles since the return of democratic practices, but now the shah dared the deputies to stop him. A constitutional storm erupted as both the Iranian press and the majority of Majles deputies protested the erosion of parliamentary privilege.[59] Yet after a protracted conflict, the shah emerged victorious, and Sa'ed formed his government.

The shah's goal during this time was clear: to return Iran to an authoritarian state. The US goal, however, was still confused. Ideologically the Americans supported reform and democratization but had to balance these aims with the practical need for a stable and Western-oriented Iran. The Truman administration therefore backed the greater role played by the shah in the short-term but also continued its efforts to develop a long-term program to reform the country. By the late 1940s, Morrison-Knudsen International completed its economic study and recommended that Iran undertake development projects to the tune of $500 million over a seven-year period.[60] The necessary reforms included improved farming methods and production, the establishment of new factories and roads, enhanced health and education systems, and the more efficient utilization of its natural resources. The reforms would be paid for by Iranian oil revenue and would, the Americans hoped, create an economic foundation on top of which democracy could later grow. This notion was an early example of democratic sequentialism—achieving preconditions such as economic reforms, the rule of law, and a well-functioning state before embarking on true democratization.[61]

US leverage over Iran was therefore used to promote economic reform and measures to improve stability, such as the eradication of corruption and the continued reorganization of the gendarmerie, rather than to support democratization.[62] This focus was further sharpened after John C. Wiley became ambassador in February 1948. No expert on the Middle East—he once compared negotiating with the Iranians to "eating soup with a fork"[63]—he nevertheless feared the creep of Soviet gains in the region. In his subsequent telegrams to the State Department, Wiley immediately began to hype the Soviet threat to Iran and advocated measures to promote strong governance and political stability.[64]

By the end of the decade, the US government's stated aims were "to prevent [Iran's] domination . . . by the USSR" and to "strengthen [its] orientation toward the West."[65] Secondary measures included enhancing internal security, fostering an expanded economy, and promoting the central government. Far down on the list of objectives prepared by the State Department were measures to "improve democratic institutions and processes in Iran."[66] Yet even this secondary interest in democracy was removed when on February 4, 1949, the shah was shot in the face from point-blank range.

The shooting changed the situation almost instantly. Moments earlier, resplendent in full military dress uniform, the resurgent shah had arrived at the opening celebration of the Faculty of Law and Political Science at Tehran University. Stepping out of his black chauffeur-driven Rolls Royce, he waved happily toward the banks of reporters and photographers before turning to climb the stairs that led to the faculty entrance.[67] As he approached, one of these photographers, Nasser Fakhrarai, working for the newspaper *Parcham-e Islam* (Flag of Islam), moved to within a few feet, pulled a revolver from his camera case, and began to fire. Fakhrarai was not a trained marksman, so the first three bullets found only the shah's hat, but the fourth pierced the royal lip and cheek. The shah later described the scene as he stood within six feet of his would-be assassin, who still had two bullets in his pistol:

> I thought, "What should I do? Shall I jump on him? But if I approach him, I shall become a better target. Shall I run away? Then I shall be a perfect target to be shot in the back. So I suddenly started shadow-dancing or feinting. He fired again, wounding me in the shoulder. His last shot stuck in the gun. I had the queer and not unpleasant sensation of knowing that I was still alive.[68]

The shah was rushed to the hospital, where his wounds were found to be only superficial thanks to his impressive acrobatic evasion technique. Despite the pain and trauma, the attempt on his life was one of the most fortunate things to happen to the shah. A communiqué was released the same day in which the shah nobly claimed that "a few shots won't deter my duties to my beloved country."[69] The outpouring of support from Iranians for their indefatigable king was immediate. He had been without public backing since assuming the throne, but this one act gave him the internal support to more fully move against his political opposition.

Investigations into Fakhrarai's past found he paid dues to a journalists' union loosely affiliated with the pro-Tudeh labor movement. This connection was not evidence that the assassin was under orders by the Tudeh, but it was enough for the shah to launch an attack on his Communist detractors.[70] He immediately accused the Tudeh of spreading "revolutionary communist ideology among students and the young," which, he said, fomented unrest and threatened Iran's "several thousand years of independence." Martial law and a curfew were quickly imposed in Tehran, and the Tudeh was outlawed. The *New York Times* reported that "angry crowds wrecked Tudeh clubs" across Tehran in support of their heroic leader.[71]

The shah's legitimacy had previously rested upon foreign powers and rich landowners. Now the country seemed united behind him, and he could act without first seeking foreign permission. He was finally able to pursue his own agenda, and after successfully suppressing the Tudeh, he next moved against Iran's civil society, which had grown steadily since the democratic breakthrough of 1941. More than sixty newspapers were forcibly closed down on February 6 as the now military government arrested editors and writers.[72] The press law was quickly tightened to prevent any criticism of the government or of members of the royal family in any publication.[73] Later in February, the Iranian police announced the rather dubious claim that they had thwarted a Tudeh and Soviet Communist plot to overthrow the government.[74] Under this pretext, the shah claimed the authority to declare martial law as he saw fit, edging the country closer to royal authoritarianism. To further weaken democratic institutions and despite no provisions for amendment in the Constitution of 1906, on March 1 the shah issued a decree to elect a Constituent Assembly to make changes to the Constitution he had long desired. Specifically, he requested the power to dissolve Parliament when he wished and to create a Senate chamber, half of whose members he would appoint.[75]

In the words of Ervand Abrahamian, the shah's popular mandate allowed him to turn "the assassination attempt into a royalist coup d'état."[76] Whereas the Truman administration had once been able to ensure the shah's withdrawal from an active role, it was now forced to accept his "coup" as a fait accompli given the speed with which he took action and his new lack of dependence on the United States. The events were a warning to the Americans: should their position of leverage and control over the shah be lost, he would waste no time in pursuing his own agenda, even if it ran counter to Washington's wishes. That the shah was not the ally they thought him to be was a lesson the Americans would fail to learn.

A Brief Return

The shah's popular support was not the only reason the United States proved unable to prevent his power grab. A series of other events both further weakened American leverage and strengthened the shah. Most notable was the news of George Marshall's resignation as US secretary of state just a few weeks before the attempt on the shah's life. Marshall had repeatedly vetoed the shah's requests for greater military aid and blocked Iran from becoming a recipient of Marshall Plan financial assistance, much to the shah's bitter chagrin. Marshall's resignation was therefore to the shah a cause for celebration, but so too was the announcement that Marshall's replacement would be a man who shared many of the same fears and concerns as the shah. Truman considered many names for the position, including William O. Douglas, associate Supreme Court justice and advocate for democracy in Iran, but he eventually nominated the scourge of General Patrick Hurley and President Roosevelt's plan to build a democratic Iran, Dean Acheson. Acheson had long been concerned about Soviet expansion, and events such as the McCarthy hearings and the impending fall of Nationalist China served only "to sharpen an already acute anti-communist psychosis."[77]

The shah now had both US ambassador Wiley and the new secretary of state feeling that Iran needed better protection against the Soviet Union, and so he thought he was best positioned to provide it. His newfound popular support limited the objections of those who feared that his personal rule would lead to public unrest.[78]

Another factor that weakened American leverage was the lack of financial aid the United States had sent Iran. In the Iran Declaration of 1943, the United States had committed to provide economic assistance to help Iran rebuild after its wartime occupation. Shortly after its signing, an Iranian government official optimistically explained how once the "economic assistance promised by the Allies has materialized," Iran will be able to focus on "systems of local government, general education, health," and all other necessary reforms.[79] Over the next six years, the shah and successive Iranian prime ministers were careful not to antagonize Washington in case this economic assistance be delayed, reduced, or denied. Iran carefully waited and was willing to follow American instruction in order to speed up delivery of financial aid. But in 1949 Iran was still waiting. A direct petition was made to the United States requesting $100 million in Marshall Plan aid to help the country rebuild.[80] This request was rejected because the Americans prioritized the rebuilding of Europe. An urgent appeal for two hundred thousand tons of wheat to avert famine was also ignored.[81] In September 1948, Iran requested an economic grant of $147 million but was once again turned down by the State Department, which cited the impossibility of obtaining congressional authority for such an amount when Iran maintained a favorable foreign-exchange position.[82] The Truman administration instead expected Iran to follow the Seven-Year Plan, which would be financed not from foreign aid but from Iran's own oil revenues.

By the end of 1949, however, the Seven-Year Plan itself was in disarray; one US adviser concluded that it had approached a "state of bust" owing to corruption and mismanagement.[83] Its relatively modest goals had not been met; projects were not carried out; and corrupt officials embezzled funds for nonexistent programs. The Truman administration had no alternative to the Seven-Year Plan but remained unwilling to assist the program with direct US financial aid. Ambassador Wiley repeatedly sent telegrams requesting that grants or credit be sent, comparing the amount of aid for Iran to "a bag of peanuts."[84] But the Truman administration obstinately refused to deviate from its stated policy. By February 1950, Ambassador Wiley wrote directly to Dean Acheson, lambasting the administration's refusal of aid, which he said was "as weird as the Eleusinian Mysteries and as unintelligible as the Epic of Gilgamesh."[85] By 1949, Iranians began to fear aid would never come, and so US leverage over Iran weakened as a result.

The United States could therefore do little to prevent the shah's movement to a more central role in Iran's political system and was coming to see it as maybe a positive thing. Although the United States did not want to see a return to the authoritarianism of the shah's father, stronger governance by the shah did appeal as Iran's political institutions continued to fight among each other rather than govern effectively. Ambassador Wiley described the Iranian government as being in a state of "semi-anarchy" owing to a lack of competent and honest leaders.[86] On March 23, 1950, George McGhee, assistant secretary of state for Near Eastern affairs, despairingly listing the ongoing conflicts among top Iranian politicians: the "Taqizadeh–Ebtehaj conflict, Abdorreza versus Ebtehaj, Ebtehaj versus Sa'ed, almost everybody versus Mansur, Razmara verses Yazdanpanah etc., ad nauseam."[87] A month later McGhee warned the secretary of state that unless checked "by positive American action," political infighting and corruption "might well result in the collapse of the present political structure and its domination by the Soviet Union."[88] Ambassador Wiley warned that Iran was "crumbling away" in the absence of urgent US action and an alternative strategy for assisting Iran.[89] The increasing instability also saw a return of the Tudeh Party, which took advantage of widespread popular dissatisfaction at the lack of progress. The Truman administration's hope for a stable and progressive Iran was quickly fading.

A resurgent shah therefore offered some glimmer of hope for stability, and the Department of State called for reforms that would lead to an "increase of both [the] shah's influence and Majles responsibility," but it remained cautious that the shah avoid the "appearance of dictatorial methods."[90] With little leverage over the now popular king, American caution failed to distract him from his attempted royalist coup. But as soon as the shah had freed himself of American control, events in Iran turned against him, and he was forced to quickly turn back to the United States for support and direction.

The warm glow of being a national hero that had enveloped the shah since the assassination attempt quickly cooled as the Iranian public recoiled at the extent of his power grab. According to Ann Lambton, a highly respected Iran expert of the time, the monarchy was "no longer regarded with respect, but with fear, contempt and disgust."[91] With internal support petering away, the shah therefore looked again to the United States, but there was still no clear US plan for how to proceed in Iran. Officials in Washington had welcomed a stronger shah but worried about a return to dictatorship; they generally supported constitutionalism but feared the instability that came with it. James Bill describes the United States at this time as "baffled, uncomfortable, and confused."[92] Without a clear strategy directing policy, the United States had only one goal: to ensure the progress of the decaying Seven-Year Plan. Rather than provide additional financial aid, the United States focused instead on tackling the corruption and mismanagement that restricted the plan's progress. The shah was pressed to unveil an anticorruption campaign formulated by the US embassy. Ambassador Wiley reported to the State Department that embassy officials were throwing their full "weight in favor of effective measures . . . against the more pernicious forms of corruption."[93] In addition, the secretary of state gave the ambassador permission to intervene further, instructing Wiley to push for the appointment of "progressive officials" to key positions and to pass on the administration's dissatisfaction regarding the shah's appointment of Ali Mansur as prime minister in March 1950.[94]

Mansur was known as "notoriously corrupt," and, according to the Department of State, his selection by the shah "exasperated all reform-minded and progressive Iranians, as well as most foreign observers."[95] Moreover, the shah had refused to allow any formal parliamentary vote of inclination on the appointment and proceeded to fill Mansur's administration solely with members of the royalist faction, the first time since 1941 that all other groups had been excluded from government.[96] These steps would not have unduly concerned the Americans had the shah maintained public support, but without it they feared the shah's actions would lead to large protests against his rule. They therefore attempted to steer him away from autocracy and back to a focus on reform. Dean Acheson instructed the ambassador to pass on the State Department's regret that the shah's "recent attitude and actions" had given the impression he had "faltered in his previous determination to show his people [the] road to progress."[97]

The American position therefore oscillated between support for the shah and support for progress on reform. Too much in either direction resulted in instability, whether in protest at the shah's authoritarian rule or owing to the fragile or corrupt nature of Iran's political class. This balancing, middle-road act, however, was unsuitable to either side, and the time had come for the United States to formulate a more cohesive policy. With leverage returned, the United States was in a strong position to influence Iran's development and was determined to have a major say in who would become the next prime minister.

Choosing a Prime Minister: Mossadegh versus Razmara

The shah's failures by the spring of 1950 either to restore stability or to rule effectively convinced the Truman administration that he lacked the character, ability, or popularity to actively lead Iran.[98] If the shah were unable to balance public support with stability, then someone else must be found who could do so. Ambassador Wiley demanded bold action, saying that "we are in a game for high stakes. We must play for chips; not with declarations and implied promises."[99] The administration therefore looked to appoint a prime minister who could push through reform proposals while carrying enough public support to avert internal unrest. The return of leverage over the shah meant that the administration was in a position to select the next prime minister and force the shah's acquiescence. However, the act of choosing a reliable and responsible vehicle through which to realize US aims was not straightforward. Ambassador Wiley reported that while "surveying the heads of political life in Iran, one detects more dandruff than hair."[100] Two Iranians with fine figurative heads of hair were General Ali Razmara and Mohammad Mossadegh.[101]

After graduating from the French military academy, Ali Razmara had become an intelligent and capable leader of men. During the reign of Reza Shah, he excelled in suppressing revolts in the provinces of Gilan and Azerbaijan before returning to Tehran as deputy director of the city's newly created Military College.[102] He was promoted to general during World War II and commanded the First Brigade in Tehran before serving as joint chief of staff in the royal court.

During this time, he also wrote an eighteen-volume military geography of Iran, including information on the economic, social, political, and geographical nature of its provinces. His forward-thinking political outlook shone through in his work, where he focused on the importance of freeing the Iranian "peasant from the social and economic decadence in which he is embroiled, and embark[ing upon] . . . the highway of civilization."[103] Although these reforms would seem to echo the Truman administration's goal, for Razmara these reforms were meant to prevent chaos and backwardness rather than to promote democracy and freedom, two concepts that he held in distaste.[104]

Initially jealous of Razmara's success, the young shah eventually joined forces with him following the Azerbaijan Crisis, and the two worked together to force Qavam's resignation in December 1947. Thoroughly ambitious, Razmara made no secret of his desire to one day become prime minister. The State Department's character assessment of him in 1950 showed that the Truman administration was well aware of his ambitious streak, describing him as someone who as prime minister would do everything he could, both legal and illegal, to remain so "indefinitely."[105] The upside for the Americans, however, was that the appointment of a strong man such as Razmara would certainly enforce order while also making progress on "some desirable reforms."[106] To others, though, he was "a replica of Reza Shah, . . . intelligent, tough, bold, ruthless, single-minded and politically astute."[107]

If unnerved by the prospect of bringing another Reza Shah to power, the Americans had an alternative: the prodigal son of Iran's constitutional movement, Mohammad Mossadegh. James F. Goode has described him as someone who offered a sign of encouragement for a democratic Iran if only Westerners' "had the wit to see what he stood for."[108] Born in 1882, Mossadegh spent his childhood and young adult life during the years of Iran's great democratic awakening between the Tobacco Protest of 1890 and the Constitutional Revolution of 1905–11. These early experiences of constitutionalism had a great impact on his life and career, and he became committed to returning Iran to constitutionalism and democracy. A prodigy from an early age and with family connections to the Qajar dynasty, Mossadegh was appointed chief tax officer for his home province of Khorasan by the tender age of fifteen. He was mature before his time; a business associate at the time thought he was twenty-five and predicted that such "an impressive young man is bound to become one of the great ones."[109]

After pursuing his education in France and Switzerland, where he earned a doctorate in law, Mossadegh returned to Iran and was elected to the Majles in 1924. There he gained a reputation as a fierce and committed defender of the Constitution and democratic principles. Speaking out against Reza Khan's proposal in 1925 to abolish the Qajar dynasty and install himself as shah, Mossadegh made passionate counterarguments, saying that even "if they cut off my head and mutilate my body, I would never agree to such a decision."[110] When Reza Khan became Reza Shah, Mossadegh remained true to his word and refused to accept positions offered to him, even the office of prime minister. Upon reelection to the Majles in 1926, he refused to take the oath of office because it included a vow to respect the authority of a shah he felt illegitimate.[111] As Reza Shah ended hopes of democratic consolidation in Iran, Mossadegh faded from view, withdrawing to his country estate until the shah's forced abdication in 1941.

Mossadegh quickly returned to politics following the resumption of constitutionalism. Despite his years away from the spotlight, he had maintained public support and was easily returned to the Majles in 1944.[112] There, he reasserted himself as the country's leading spokesman for the freedom and independence movement, calling for an end to foreign interference and for democracy under a purely ceremonial monarchy.[113] Both demands were popularly supported, and Mossadegh played a significant role in denouncing Soviet aggression during the Azerbaijan Crisis as well as in speaking out against British and Soviet efforts during the subsequent scramble for oil concessions. A popular movement known as the Jebha-ye Melli-e Iran (National Front) emerged around him, a loose coalition of political groups that opposed all forms of foreign intervention and supported the formation of a lasting democracy.

Mossadegh continued his activist politics as the shah began his power grab following the attempt on his life, and he strongly condemned the shah's resumption of an active role in Iranian politics. In protest at ballot rigging during the elections for the Sixteenth Majles, Mossadegh led a peaceful sit-in for four days and nights in the gardens of the Kakh Marmar (Marble Palace) in October 1949. He was joined by thousands of supporters to pressure the shah into promising free and fair elections.[114] He also derided the shah's plans for the formation of a senate as "fake and illegitimate," without any legal basis under constitutional law. Mossadegh once again symbolized Iran's constitutional movement both with his fiery speeches before the Majles and in his own physical frailty, which endeared him even more to the people, who saw him as the embodiment of a weak and embattled but defiant Iran.[115]

By the spring of 1950, with public disorder and governmental corruption on the rise, the Department of State concluded that Iran's "time of collapse may not be far away."[116] The laissez-faire tactic of leaving Iran's development in the hands of private US companies and Iranian leaders had failed, and averting disaster now depended on strong leadership. Unwilling to support the shah's unpopular and ineffective foray toward authoritarianism, the United States was faced with the option of asking Mossadegh or Razmara to form a new government more suitable to US needs. So desperate was the situation that, as government documents from the time show, the Truman administration was determined to force the resignations of the current Iranian government and "name the Iranian official who it believes most effectively could meet [the administration's] requirements."[117]

Razmara represented strength and the chance to restore stability with the backing of the army; Mossadegh represented democracy with the backing of an overwhelming proportion of Iran's urban population. The decision of whom to support would illustrate whether the United States prioritized stability to best counter the Soviet threat and secure economic concessions for the West or democracy and progress. This question was finally answered on June 26, 1950, when General Ali Razmara was sworn in as the new prime minister. As Razmara appeared before the Majles for his confirmation, dressed in a civilian suit and asking to be called "Haji Ali Razmara" rather than "General Ali Razmara," Mossadegh excoriated him as "a fox dressed up as a cat!"[118]

Getting "Its Feet Wet": The United States and a Proactive Policy

A major reason why the United States supported Razmara was that Max Thornburg was a vocal supporter of him. Thornburg was a "chosen instrument" of the Truman administration, so his opinions of Iran's reform program carried great weight.[119] He believed that Iran had tried too much too soon in its movement toward democracy under Roosevelt and the first few years of Truman's presidency. A Mossadegh premiership would merely exacerbate these problems. In his view, instability was largely the result of conducting constitutional politics before adequate economic reforms had been implemented. Iran was too politically immature and strategically important to be allowed to control its own future.

To offset these perceived weaknesses, Thornburg advocated US support for a strong government that could in time gradually relinquish powers to democratic institutions when those institutions were better able to deal with internal pressures.[120] Thornburg saw Razmara as the perfect vehicle for providing strong governance and successfully implementing his Seven-Year Plan. So determined was he for Razmara to become the next prime minister that he became Razmara's de facto economic adviser, personally drafting a reform manifesto that would appeal to Washington.[121] Thornburg's lobbying for Razmara helped change the administration's perception of Razmara from a dictator-in-waiting who would "resist by every legal and illegal means any attempt to remove him" to a noble reformer who would carry out reform while ensuring stability.[122]

In pushing for Razmara's appointment, Thornburg was joined by Gerald Dooher, a political officer at the US embassy in Tehran. Dooher would regularly involve himself in Iran's internal politics and had a reputation as an intriguer, manipulator, and political adventurer.[123] The two successfully convinced Ambassador Wiley of Razmara's merits, and Wiley, in turn, convinced the State Department. Wiley reported that although democratic principles should constantly be preached in Iran, greater emphasis should be "placed on developments and procedures," beginning with economic reforms, that would "eventually lead to democracy."[124] Truman, like Thornburg, shared a belief in the policy of liberal developmentalism and also became convinced that Razmara was the best man for the job. Mossadegh had no such American support team and was overlooked.

Truman administration officials had convinced themselves that bringing to power the replica of Reza Shah was not only the most assured way of achieving stability but, perversely, also the best way to secure the long-term success of democracy in Iran. After impressing Washington, Thornburg next had to convince the shah to support Razmara. Just weeks before Razmara's appointment in June 1950, fearing the general's ambition and strength as a threat to his own position, the shah had stated that he would never agree to the appointment.[125] The shah's own father had once been an ambitious young officer who used the office of prime minister to force the removal of the ruling Qajar dynasty, and the shah did not wish to suffer a similar fate. A recent interview with General Razmara's brother reveals that Thornburg began to chair regular meetings between Razmara and the shah in an attempt to allay the latter's fears.[126] To further persuade the shah, the United States applied diplomatic pressure, making clear that his present government did not live up to US expectations, that more emphasis was needed to push through reforms and stamp out corruption, and that Razmara would make a most suitable prime minister.[127] The British were soon informed that Wiley had been instructed "to secure the dismissal of the Ali Mansur Government," and they, too, were convinced to support Razmara.[128]

Despite falling in line with US plans, Sir Francis Shepherd, the new British ambassador in Iran, remarked to the Foreign Office that he was "rather startled by the apparent willingness of the State Department to plunge into Cabinet-making in what appeared to be a clumsy and obvious manner."[129]

In his biography of the shah, Abbas Milani writes that the shah ultimately "had no choice but to agree to the appointment," and he quotes British and American officials demanding that the shah "go out of his way to demonstrate" his support for Razmara.[130] The shah had little option but to acquiesce owing to his recent loss of public support and the return of American leverage. After convincing the shah to support Razmara, the Americans informed him that unless the Mansur government were dismissed, there would be severe cuts in economic aid to his country.[131] As an extra sweetener, if the shah then appointed Razmara, the United States would provide a $25 million loan, increase military aid for fiscal year 1951, and consider ways to increase grant aid from $10 million to $25 million.[132]

The United States therefore maximized its leverage to ensure Razmara's appointment, and the shah made the appointment despite not approving of Razmara. American influence in Iran was supreme. Even the announcement of the appointment was timed to coincide with American priorities. Ambassador Wiley was at the end of his tour in Iran, and Henry Grady was due to take over the embassy reins. Anxious that a new chapter in Iran begin properly, the Americans timed Razmara's appointment to coincide with Grady's arrival. Therefore, the day before Wiley left Tehran, he informed the shah that the time was now right to promote his chief of staff, and on June 26, 1950, Razmara became the fifty-eighth prime minister of Iran.[133]

To the Americans, Razmara was important not only for their reform plans in Iran but also for the wider security of the Middle East. On the day of Razmara's appointment, as war raged against communism in Korea, Truman worried that Iran would be where the Communists "will start trouble if we aren't careful. . . . [I]f we just stand by, they'll move into Iran and they'll take over the whole Middle East. There's no telling what they'll do if we don't put up a fight now."[134] Razmara's reputation as a fighter therefore made him a far more attractive option than the more populist and left-leaning Mohammad Mossadegh.

The appointment of Razmara has been called the first time the United States really "got its feet wet in the world of political intrigue in Iran."[135] Although really not the first time—the United States had previously been instrumental in the downfall of Qavam—this instance demonstrated the incredible influence the Americans had in Iran. The shah both disliked and distrusted Razmara, yet American pressure ensured his appointment. But the nature of Razmara's appointment, despite its importance, is an episode missing from many accounts of the period. Although setting out to analyze the "impact of US–Iranian relations on Iran's domestic politics," Mark J. Gasiorowski skips entirely the US role in bringing Razmara to power and sustaining him while in office.[136] So have more recent studies such as Ali Ansari's *Modern Iran since 1921*, Ali Gheissari and Vali Nasr's *Democracy in Iran*, and Fakhreddin Azimi's *The Quest for Democracy in Iran*. Barry Rubin's comprehensive analysis of US–Iran relations, *Paved with Good Intentions*, actually rejects the notion that the United States played any role in the appointment.[137] A more thorough look at the evidence, however, shows the US role to be sizable and decisive and the appointment made possible only by American leverage over the shah.

No "Milky Way," No Leverage

Hours after his appointment, Razmara publicly announced as policy the reform program drawn up by Max Thornburg and agreed to by the Truman administration. It called for the decentralization of the government, the immediate creation of provincial assemblies, new and revised social and economic legislation, judiciary reforms, a realistic and rigorously controlled budget, a plan to reduce the cost of living and improve living conditions throughout Iran, and electoral reforms that would enable a more popular representation in the Majles.[138] More importantly for American interests, it also promised a sustained commitment to the Seven-Year Plan. Cabinet appointments had been drawn up in consultation with the British and American embassies, which favored well-educated professional administrators who would not succumb to the corruption and mismanagement that marred their predecessors.[139] One week after Razmara's appointment, American officials happily noted that he had stabilized the internal political situation and remarked that his young, progressive cabinet was a "refreshing change from the traditional Iranian cabinet minister."[140]

However, the Truman administration's feeling of accomplishment was short-lived. Razmara had been the administration's preference but not the people's or the shah's. Almost immediately, friction between Razmara and the shah became evident and hampered the new Iranian government's ability to make progress. On July 22, 1950, a month after Razmara's appointment, Dean Acheson instructed Ambassador Grady to use all his "influence with [the] shah as often as may be necessary to prevent his working against his government."[141] This Grady did and by September reported that relations between the shah and Razmara could now hardly be better.[142]

The US ability to maintain cordial relations between the two men depended largely on its leverage, and, unfortunately for Razmara, this leverage was decreasing again. The promise of substantial aid had convinced the shah to go along with American demands, but now, seven years after the signing of the Iran Declaration, the money had still not materialized, and the shah began to lose patience. In an interview with the Reuters news agency in November, he complained bitterly that America had reneged on its promises. In the shah's mind, the United States had provided only limited, outdated, and inadequate military supplies; the promise, but no more, of a $25 million Export-Import Bank loan that came with a very high level of interest; and a mere $500,000 of Point IV aid.[143] The Truman administration, for its part, maintained the slippery position that the Iran Declaration didn't "mention a specific form of assistance at any particular time" and only stipulated aid during wartime, not "to the then distant postwar period."[144] The US ambassador best summed up the disconnect between Iranian expectations and American plans in January 1950: the Iranians' view of their strategic importance was so great that they felt the United States was "literally over a barrel and obliged to give Iran the sun, the moon and the stars." Washington's intention, however, he continued, was not "even [to] provide a slice of the Milky Way."[145]

The shah's dreams for Iran had been built on expectations of assistance in the realm of $250 million, similar to the amounts given to Turkey and Greece.[146] Ambassador Wiley explained that the Iranians "see the American cornucopiae [sic] gushing to the right of them; they see the American cornucopiae gushing to the left of them, but the gallant Iranian light brigade hasn't even got a charge account with which to plunge into the Valley of the Debt."[147] Supreme Court justice William O. Douglas, freshly returned from a trip to Iran, beseeched the president that aid in the amount of $100 million was vital to support the Razmara government and prevent the Soviets from taking over. "If something is not done in the immediate future," he wrote, "the Razmara Government may fall—and then we shall be in a bad spot."[148]

As far as the administration was concerned, however, the US priority was the Marshall Plan and the quick reestablishment of Europe as a trading partner. It was not prepared to stretch its already limited resources to Iran, which it felt could be adequately assisted through other means, specifically strict adherence to the Seven-Year Plan. Less than three years later, in August 1953, fears for Iran's future would prompt a US-sponsored coup, but in late 1950 the Truman administration was content to invite chaos by continuing with the failing Seven-Year Plan rather than furnish large amounts of financial aid. Warnings from people such as Justice Douglas and Ambassador Wiley were therefore ignored. The United States instead continued with the Thornburg plan and its emphasis on the American private sector and strong men such as Razmara as proxies for US government financial assistance.

For years since the Iran Declaration, the United States had used the promise of financial aid as a means to strengthen its leverage over the shah and the actions of the Iranian government. The promise of a $25 million loan had been added as an extra sweetener to ensure the shah supported Razmara's appointment, but there was no sign that even this money would ever actually be sent to Iran. The newly installed ambassador to Iran, Henry Grady, derided the administration's position in assuming "that on the basis of a [$25 million] loan which is to be paid back and on which interest is to be charged, we can secure drastic measures from the Government here against the pressure of all the various lobbies."[149] Iranians also took umbrage and began to refer to a broken promise as "an American promise."[150] The US position in Iran was weakening as the economic situation continued to decline.

Disabused of the idea that US aid was forthcoming, the shah again began to follow his own policies rather than direction from Washington. In particular, he began to undermine Razmara's position in the hope that Razmara's failure to achieve progress would cause the Americans to withdraw their support of him. The shah was joined by the National Front, which accused Razmara of seeking to establish a military dictatorship and labeled his appointment a semi–coup d'état. Mossadegh stated that "as long as the members of the National Front live, we are going to fight this government."[151] In an early example of Godwin's Law, another National Front leader compared Razmara's rise to Hitler, claiming that just as "the American and British capitalists . . . paved the way for Hitler's success . . . Razmara has [similarly] been brought to power by America and the British."[152] Even powerful clerics such as Ayatollah Abol-Ghasem Kashani joined the movement against Razmara, saying that he had "come to power against the force of public opinion and in order to serve the foreigners."[153]

The strength of this opposition, encompassing not only the royalists but also the National Front and the Islamists, made Razmara's task of carrying out Thornburg's reform policy nigh on impossible. For instance, an innocent plan to establish provincial assemblies to allow for economic progress without the burden of economic and administrative overcentralization was quickly opposed, attacked as a plot to "dismantle Iran," and summarily defeated by a united and strident opposition.[154]

Ironically, Razmara found some internal support by reaching out to the Soviet-backed Tudeh and even made promises to legalize it as a political party. The Americans, desperate for support of their Razmara project, did not protest. The American-backed prime minister's pro-Soviet roots actually ran quite deep.[155] Razmara's wife was related to a highly prominent Tudeh member, and Razmara himself had been implicated in the prison break of ten Tudeh leaders in 1949.[156] Not satisfied with wooing Persian Communists, however, Razmara also agreed to a trade deal with the Soviet Union and refused to send troops to support the West in the Korean War. Unperturbed, the Americans remained supportive of their Razmara experiment. Despite Razmara's unpopularity among the people, the opposition political forces, the shah, and the shah's royalist allies, despite his associations with the Tudeh Party and his difficulty in enacting much of the reform program Thornburg had laid out for him, the United States continued to support him because it failed to see any other alternative.

In January 1951, a little more than six months after Razmara's appointment, Ambassador Grady complained that Razmara's opponents were "greasing the skids" in preparation for his removal but stated that there was still no alternative to the embattled former strong man. Grady again called for extending a $100 million loan to support him, but the proposal was rejected for being too much for Iran to absorb. In addition, the United States did not want to be seen as giving in to Iranian pressure for increased levels of aid.[157] The United States had brought Razmara to power but was unwilling to support him financially and, with its leverage reduced, subsequently proved unable to protect him from the shah and other opposition forces when he was in office. On March 7, Razmara's unsuccessful time in office was abruptly ended after he was assassinated by a member of an Islamic organization. The Truman administration's policy for Iran lay in ruins.

Reviewing this period of US–Iran relations, James Bill summarizes that Razmara was "the wrong man at the wrong time for the wrong job."[158] On paper, however, Razmara appeared to be an ideal leader for the Truman administration to achieve its dual aims of stability and reform. He was a strong and respected figure with support from the police and armed forces. He was also willing to work closely with Max Thornburg to institute badly needed structural reforms. However, the Americans failed to take into account Iran's own constitutional and Islamic movements, ignored the kiss of death that being a puppet of an increasingly unpopular foreign power was for an Iranian politician, and seemed unaware that without providing financial support the United States would be unable to control events. Razmara was therefore met with stern opposition from the outset, and his proposals were blocked by an enraged Majles. Such opposition may have been overcome if Razmara had the shah's support—indeed, the British and Americans floated the idea of dissolving the Majles to eradicate one source of opposition.[159] Although the shah had been susceptible to external pressure when it came to Razmara's appointment, the Americans' failure to provide financial aid meant that the shah no longer had to follow their direction, and so he refused to support the embattled prime minister.

Aid at the level requested by Ambassador Grady would have kept both the shah onside and given Razmara a greater chance to achieve some of his key reforms. In the words of Ambassador Grady, failure to maintain royal support "so weakened Razmara's position that he doubtless would shortly have fallen from power" had he not otherwise been removed.[160] America's first major foray into political intrigue in Iran therefore ended in failure—but lessons were learned for future policy, in particular the importance of financial aid for maintaining leverage and the necessity of ensuring the shah's support. This lesson would be put into practice by the next Democratic president, but for the remaining period of Truman's presidency another issue would preclude any attempts to promote democracy in Iran.

3 Mossadegh and the Anglo-Iranian Oil Crisis, 1951–1953

In 1941, the United States was welcomed to Iran as the defender of liberty and independence. A decade later many Iranians wished the Americans would just leave them alone. The United States had been a major factor in restricting the continued rise of constitutionalism, and as a result Iran became awash with feelings of nationalism and hopes to remain neutral in the Cold War between East and West. Even the Seven-Year Plan to develop and modernize Iran was viewed as an instrument of subjugation. One senior administration official called the plan a "disastrous thing for Iran" because it gave Iranians expectations they could never reach and served only to offend burgeoning nationalist sentiments.[1] This growing nationalist movement would become so popular that the already weakened state of American leverage would be reduced still further. The period 1951–53 therefore highlights the fragile nature of American influence and US government's waning ability to control an Iranian government that had strong and vocal public support. This period became the high point of Iranian independence from both the shah and the United States. But given the importance of Iranian oil and its position on the border of the Soviet Union, the United States could not allow Iran to remain independent for long. Numerous attempts would be made to rebuild leverage, but with nationalism reaching fever pitch during the premiership of the supremely popular Mohammad Mossadegh, these attempts would not only prove futile but also ultimately increase instability, the very thing the Americans had previously sought to avoid. The period 1951–53 would therefore be a seminal moment in Iran's development: a contest between the right of a people to govern themselves and the ability of powerful foreign countries to achieve their goals.

At the start of this period in 1951, the United States was becoming increasingly unpopular in Iran but was still much more highly regarded than the British—the Lesser Satan compared to the Great Satan. In Iranian eyes, Britain was a "a nation of satanically clever and shrewd maneuverers who acted to bring power and prosperity to the British Isles while smilingly and secretly planting seeds of decay and impotence elsewhere."[2] It was the actions of His Majesty's government that had truly led to the development of a powerful and angry nationalist movement in Iran. At the center of this movement was a dispute over who owned Iranian oil. Britain had been the beneficiary of an extremely one-sided oil concession granted by the Qajar monarchy in 1901. Despite numerous Iranian appeals to renegotiate the agreement, the Anglo-Iranian Oil Company (AIOC, renamed British Petroleum in 1954), which was part owned by the British government, maintained control and therefore a vast majority of the profits through a lease not set to expire until 1993.

Mohammad Mossadegh led the fight against the concession and before the Majles in 1944 successfully argued for a bill that would forbid all future governments from granting foreign oil concessions without parliamentary debate and approval. Furthermore, he argued that because the original concession had been granted before the Constitutional Revolution, it was signed by an illegitimate monarch and therefore invalid. Britain, however, refused to renegotiate. Iranian oil provided the British Treasury with £24 million a year in taxes and £92 million in foreign exchange, and it supplied 85 percent of the British naval fuel needs.[3] At a time of declining empire, London was more determined than ever to cling to such a valuable resource. To surrender to Iranian demands would be seen as a sign of continuing weakness and an insufferable betrayal of British strategic interests.[4]

By the late 1940s, the AIOC was the second-largest exporter of crude petroleum in the world, yet it paid Iran only a few cents per ton of crude oil.[5] In 1947, it was reported that the AIOC made an after-tax profit of £40 million, of which only £7 million was passed on to Iran.[6] While AIOC profits soared to £200 million by 1950, Iran's share actually declined.[7] Despite this already high profitability, Britain was determined to keep costs down and profits high, which meant wretched working conditions for the Iranian laborers the company employed.[8] Manucher Farmanfarmaian, who later became director of Iran's Petroleum Institute in 1949, described what he witnessed on a visit to the British oil refinery at the southern port of Abadan:

> Wages were fifty cents a day. There was no vacation pay, no sick leave, no disability compensation. The workers lived in a shanty town called Kaghazabad, or Paper City, without running water or electricity, let alone luxuries [such] as iceboxes or fans. In winter the earth flooded and became a flat, perspiring lake. The mud in town was knee-deep, and . . . when the rains subsided, clouds of nipping, small-winged flies rose from the stagnant water to fill the nostrils. . . .
>
> Summer was worse. . . . The heat was torrid . . . sticky and unrelenting—while the wind and sandstorms shipped off the desert hot as a blower. The dwellings of Kaghazabad, cobbled from rusted oil drums hammered flat, turned into sweltering ovens. . . . In every crevice hung the foul, sulfurous stench of burning oil—a pungent reminder that every day twenty thousand barrels, or one million tons a year, were being consumed indiscriminately for the functioning of the refinery, and AIOC never paid the government a cent for it.
>
> To the management of AIOC in their pressed ecru shirts and air-conditioned offices, the workers were faceless drones. . . . In the British section of Abadan there were lawns, rose beds, tennis courts, swimming pools and clubs, in Kaghazabad there was nothing—not a tea shop, not a bath, not a single tree. . . . The unpaved alleyways were emporiums for rats. The man in the grocery store sold his wares while sitting in a barrel of water to avoid the heat.[9]

A year later a British employee suggested to his superiors that it would behoove the company at least to clean up the filthy bazaar that lay adjacent to the refinery. The reply summed up the British mood when it came to dealing with the Iranians: "If we gave a little they would ask for more so it was best not to give at all."[10] When the workers at Abadan went on strike in 1946, the British anchored warships off the coast to force a quick settlement on their terms. Iranian oil was a matter of national interest for Great Britain and would be defended by force if necessary.

Accusation of unfair dealing by the British was made worse by US oil agreements elsewhere. In 1948, the United States and Venezuela signed a revolutionary fifty–fifty profit-sharing agreement, which the United States later duplicated with Saudi Arabia—terms far and away more equitable than between Iran and the AIOC. According to James Bill, such "external developments were well known and contagious"; if Britain did not act quickly and offer a more generous oil agreement to Iran, Iran would soon demand a deal similar to those being signed by the US government.[11]

Therefore, as the Americans stymied the advances of self-governance in Iran, the British continued to exploit Iran for its natural resources. Both acts fueled the people's anger at foreign interference, while a lack of economic and social progress added to the growing feelings of nationalism. Previously directed toward positive measures such as the building of democracy, Iranian activism now focused on resentment and hatred of outside influence. Without the actions of foreign powers, which served as a catalyst for this move away from democracy, Iran's history would certainly have been profoundly different, both economically and politically.

Iranian Oil for Iranian People

The AIOC remained blissfully unaware of the depth of this growing nationalist movement. Mostafa Fateh, the AIOC's highest-ranking Iranian employee, desperately tried to make his company face reality. After thirty years of loyal service, he felt it his duty to offer his employers some frank advice. He urged the AIOC to show a "breadth of vision, tolerance for other people's views and clear thinking to avoid disaster" by recognizing the "awakening nationalism and political consciousness of the people of Asia."[12] Not only would Fateh's advice go unheeded, but one British official also noted that the company should no longer trust Fateh, despite his long and loyal service.[13]

The company's own historian later described the refusal to renegotiate terms as "an error of judgment similar to the assessment by the Suez Canal Company of the competency of Egyptian pilots."[14] The Majles and its oil committee, headed by Mossadegh, routinely rejected token offers of small increases in revenue for Iran. A US State Department report noted that one Majles session on the matter in 1949 was "marked by emotional excesses" that showed that the "AIOC and the British are genuinely hated in Iran" and that any Iranian's cooperation with the AIOC would be "political suicide."[15]

For Prime Minister Razmara, who owed his position to foreign powers and was forced to support their action, cooperation with the AIOC would be more than just political suicide. The Majles angrily called the AIOC a rapacious monster and identified Razmara as its key lackey.[16] Mossadegh was relentless in his attacks on the prime minister, telling him that continued cooperation with the AIOC would be "a disgrace which you will never be able to wash away."[17] Nationalist supporters cheered in support of this view and slammed their desk tops until they splintered as Mossadegh continued: "I won't submit to this sort of person. . . . I will strike and I will be killed! If you are a soldier, I am more of a soldier!"[18]

In late December 1950, before a rally of twelve thousand cheering supporters in Tehran, Mossadegh and the National Front demanded the full nationalization of the AIOC and its holdings so as to finally end the exploitation of Iranian resources. Senior religious figures such as Ayatollah Abol-Ghasem Kashani also gave support and encouraged all "sincere Muslims and patriotic citizens to fight against the enemies of Islam and Iran by joining the nationalization struggle."[19] Whereas Razmara hoped for a compromise, the British government remained defiant and instructed the prime minister to continue arguing in Britain's favor before the Majles.[20] He was assassinated four days later, an act that precipitated public dancing and cheering on the streets of Tehran.[21] After a brief spell in jail, the assassin was released and heralded a hero.[22]

Unmoved even by this act of violence and the popular support of it, the British contemplated having the shah dissolve the Majles and impose martial law until, as Geoffrey Furlonge, head of the Foreign Office Eastern Department, put it, "tempers cool."[23] The belief that in a few months Iranian demands for a fair agreement that had been bubbling for fifty years would suddenly dissipate or that martial law would calm a people demanding constitutionalism illustrated how out of touch the British were in understanding Iranian nationalism. The British were also sanguine regarding the possibility that their policy would return Iran to dictatorship, with Furlonge stating that Iran had a "long acquaintance with dictatorship . . . [in] the most recent of which the country undoubtedly made considerable progress."[24]

The Americans, however, did not want to see Iran return to dictatorship or to instability and public protests. Rising nationalism and the British refusal to compromise threatened American policies, in particular the Seven-Year Plan, which depended on oil revenues to operate.[25] Assistant Secretary of State George McGhee, who had made his own fortune in the oil industry, attempted to soften the British position but was instead told that Iran would "take a mile . . . [if] given an inch."[26] Secretary of State Dean Acheson decried the "unusual and persistent stupidity" of the AIOC and the intransigent stubbornness of the British government.[27] Vaughan Ferguson and William Rountree of the Office of Greek, Turkish, and Iranian Affairs at the State Department, wrote that it seemed "incredible that the British would expect us to believe the nonsense [they] put forward."[28] An American journalist at the time noted that the AIOC's delay in responding to the growing political forces in Iran was like missing not just one bus "but a whole series of busses."[29] As Britain refused to budge, the Iranian Parliament unanimously passed the nationalization bill on March 15, 1951, amid what one prominent Iranian newspaper called the "most extraordinary scenes of pride and magnificence . . . [after] years and perhaps centuries of humiliation and revilement."[30]

Prime Minister Mossadegh

Events in Iran moved quickly. The US embassy in Tehran reported that the "passion for nationalism . . . reach[ed] a white heat" in the days leading up to the bill's passing and that any opposition was "in danger of being liquidated."[31] Although the British looked at ways to bring a new pro-British prime minister to power and contemplated dissolving the Majles, Mossadegh's oil committee quickly passed a measure detailing the nationalization process and authorizing the seizure of AIOC properties.[32] Interim prime minister Hossein 'Ala resigned in protest at not having been consulted in the process, and Mohammad Mossadegh was quietly selected prime minister during an evening parliamentary session on April 28, 1951.[33] He had been offered the position on numerous occasions but had always declined, once asking prophetically, "Would the 50 year intervention of the AIOC allow me and persons like me to form a government and succeed?"[34] His acceptance now would put this question to the test and demonstrate how far the British and Americans would go in support of oil at the expense of democracy.

Mohammad Mossadegh was the first prime minister under the shah to come to power as neither a foreign power's chosen instrument nor a royal supporter. His first act as premier was to revive the process of parliamentary approval of prime ministerial appointments that had been lost to a resurgent shah, and he was accordingly confirmed on the same night as his appointment. Soon after, he signed a law that officially revoked the AIOC's oil concession in Iran. According to Acheson, it was British folly that had brought about the current situation. In his words, it was their stubborn refusal to "graciously grant . . . [what they] no longer had the power to withhold" that lost them the ability to negotiate from strength and caused them instead to play catch-up with rapidly moving events. In a twist on the fateful words of Winston Churchill, Acheson later lamented that never "had so few lost so much so stupidly and so fast."[35] Iranian oil was the bedrock upon which the British Empire rested, and its loss severely threatened its status as a world power. In Iran and across the developing world, the frail-looking Mohammad Mossadegh was heralded as David to the British Goliath.

Mossadegh has been described as "undoubtedly one of the most fascinating and unique personalities in twentieth century politics."[36] Dean Acheson admitted he was "one of the most amazing characters I have ever seen."[37] By the time of his appointment, Mossadegh was sixty-eight years old and in fragile health. For most of his life, he had suffered from a nervous illness that emerged in severe forms during times of difficulty or stress.[38] His illness was never accurately diagnosed despite numerous examinations by both specialists in Iran and abroad. One apparent expert from State Hospital South in Blackfoot, Idaho, felt he had found the cause for Mossadegh's distress. Writing to President Truman, he advised that the Iranian leader's fainting spells were caused by laryngeal vertigo, for which a medication had recently been developed. Symbolizing the Americans' confusion over what to make of Mossadegh, the doctor inquired, "Should I offer it to him under Point Four or should we let him faint?"[39] Unfortunately for Mossadegh, the Truman administration chose not to reply because "there was a question as [to] whether the writer was a staff member or inmate of the hospital!"[40] Although undoubtedly in ill health, Mossadegh was not averse to hamming it up on occasion, possibly as a way to disarm his adversaries and curry favor with the public. In 1954, Dean Acheson would recall how he saw Mossadegh on one visit to Washington, DC, hobble down the platform at Union Station using a walking stick and leaning on his son for support. When he saw Acheson, however, "he gave the stick to someone, let go of his son and just came skipping down the platform to say hello."[41]

Mossadegh's eccentricity did not stop there. As prime minister, he did virtually all of his work from home—even meeting foreign officials and statesmen in his bedroom. Visitors would be led into a large room on the second floor of his residence that had once been two separate rooms. Situated under the archway that had previously divided the space was an old iron bedstead with khaki-colored blankets and white sheets. Beyond the bed were arrayed twelve chairs for cabinet meetings, each accompanied with little tables upon which

guests and officials would be served tea, a staple of all Iranian meetings. One visitor described the setup as the most "unique and color-
ful preparation for the conducting of an important nation's business
as I had ever witnessed."[42] Upon the bed, Mossadegh would often
be dressed in gray, woolen pajamas and over the course of conversation would scramble and crawl all over the bed, gesticulating as he
spoke.[43] His illness meant that he was more at ease in a horizontal
position, hence his preference for the bed, yet this setup seemed also
touched with a degree of eccentricity and possibly with the aim of
manipulating his guests' compassion.

Even on the rare occasion that Mossadegh utilized a chair, Acheson recalled that he did not sit like anyone else he had ever met. He
explained how in one meeting Mossadegh had "one leg under him
and the other pulled up over that," so that "there were no legs on
the floor. He looked like a fellow who had his legs amputated. . . .
[I]t was a strange sight."[44] His penchant for the dramatic extended
to his speech making, where he would revel in the emotional: breaking down in tears, cracking jokes, and chastising his opponents, all
within the space of a few minutes. However, his oratory was excellent, causing listeners to weep, laugh, and become angry with him.[45]

Despite these eccentricities, Mossadegh was committed to freedom, independence, modernization, the rule of law, and democracy.[46]
This commitment would seemingly have made him a natural ally of
the Truman administration, but the two camps differed wildly on
implementation and the role of foreign powers in Iran's development.
For Truman, Iran's best chance for a successful democratic transition
was strong leadership combined with a weak Majles to force through
the required economic reforms upon which democracy could later be
built. Mossadegh meanwhile prioritized independence as the starting
point of democratization and sought to eliminate from the outset all
forms of foreign interference and control. What the Americans saw
as instability, Mossadegh saw as the expression of the people's right-
ful and legitimate wishes and demands.

Mossadegh's position was unpopular in Washington for three
reasons. First, allowing Iran, a strategically important ally in the

Cold War, to experiment with democracy on its own would diminish America's role in Iranian affairs. The United States was of the opinion that Iran was simply too important a state to leave to Iranians to administer themselves, especially with the Soviet Union so close and determined to involve itself in their affairs. Second, Mossadegh was not as actively anti-Tudeh or pro-American as they desired. According to *Time* magazine, which heralded him as "man of the year" in 1951, Mossadegh might "not in any sense [be] pro-Russian," but he was sufficiently independent that many felt his policies could have the effect of leading "to control of Iran by the Kremlin."[47] Third, the "special relationship" between the United States and Great Britain meant that the former was unable to support a man in direct confrontation with its closest ally over the issue of oil nationalization, regardless of how well his beliefs or policies dovetailed with its own. The Americans sided with the British position in the burgeoning oil dispute and hoped Mossadegh would soon be brought to his senses before his actions could stir similar movements elsewhere and potentially threaten America's own oil markets.

But Mossadegh's appointment negated almost overnight the Truman administration's prior position of leverage over Iranian politics. As happened for the shah after the attempted assassination, Mossadegh ruled with overwhelming public support, which meant he did not rely on foreign support. He also did not rely on the shah's support because the shah was similarly fearful of attacking a leader so beloved by his people. The United States therefore had to rely on diplomacy to settle the oil dispute and return Iran to the Seven-Year Plan as soon as possible.

The Need for a Speedy Resolution

The ensuing battle between Mossadegh and the British pitted rising nationalism against both declining imperialism and US leverage. Finding common ground between the two diametrically opposed parties would be a Herculean task. Whereas Acheson recognized in Mossadegh the rational politician beneath the eccentric, the British saw only an unstable fanatic, a demagogue, and lunatic, a man impervious to reason who would "bring his country nothing but economic ruin, chaos and eventual communism."[48] Similarly, Mossadegh distrusted the British to his very core.

Although Washington hoped for a speedy resolution so Iran could be brought back onto the path of the Seven-Year Plan, it did not condone military action to bring Iran to heel. In late May 1951, one month after Mossadegh's appointment, however, Britain had already drawn up two military plans.[49] The Lord Fraser of North Cape, the Royal Navy's Admiral of the Fleet,[50] hoped to implement one or the other contingency not only to teach Iran a lesson but also to dispel the "dumps and doldrums" of postwar British life at home. Moreover, a firm response would show the world that Britain was still a superpower that would not be "pushed around by Persian pipsqueaks."[51] Foreign Secretary Herbert Morrison in particular viewed military action as the ideal means through which "to cow the insolent natives."[52] The British press was equally pugnacious, the *Daily Express* arguing that "the time is near when we give in to the Egyptians and hand to them the Suez Canal—and Sudan. If we bow to Tehran, we bow to Baghdad later."[53]

The Truman administration, however, feared that military action would potentially "split the free world, and might cause the Iranian Government to turn to the Soviet Union for help."[54] Moreover, it would likely compel Soviet troops to invade northern Iran in order to protect its own oil interests. The Americans hoped instead that through diplomacy and a close Anglo-American alliance, Mossadegh could be forced to compromise in a deal that would continue Western control over Iranian oil.[55] As one American official explained in early April 1951, the US position was not to "deny a country the right to nationalize" but to ensure that real control remained out of Iranian hands and, more important, out of Soviet hands.[56] Without leverage, however, the US ability to compel Mossadegh to settle would not be easy.

Events in Iran moved quickly but not toward resolution. Mossadegh pressed ahead with the implementation of the oil nationalization program and in July 1951 broke off negotiations rather than submit to British demands. The AIOC responded by withdrawing essential technicians from the massive Abadan refinery, grinding its production to a halt and starving the Iranian government of badly needed revenue. This withdrawal, the company warned, would be reversed only once the Iranians showed a willingness to be "more cooperative."[57] Fearing that the situation was spiraling out of control, President Truman sent Averell Harriman to Iran to restart negotiations and, it was hoped, reach an agreement. Harriman's economic experience as a former US secretary of commerce, his diplomatic experience as former US ambassador to the Soviet Union and Great Britain, and his personal interest in Iranian affairs and prior acquaintance with the shah made him the ideal candidate to negotiate a resolution on this delicate manner.

Harriman initially lived up to his reputation. Negotiations were restarted, but both sides still refused to compromise. The British delegation, headed by Sir Richard Stokes, was ordered to stick to an offer Mossadegh had already rejected in a previous round of talks. Stokes was told to "dress it up and present its main points in different order, together with trimmings or sweetenings as may be required" to make it appear to be a new good-faith offer.[58] However, Mossadegh's keen eye saw through the ploy and declined the British terms a second time. The British similarly rejected the Iranian counteroffer. With the two sides again at an impasse, Harriman dropped the pretense of honest broker and began to actively lobby for the British position. Rejection of Stokes's proposals, he warned the prime minister, would lead to the misery of the Iranian people and a negative view of Iran in the eyes of the world, including the United States, from which the Iranians were desperate to receive financial aid.[59] The United States had lost one form of leverage thanks to the Iranian leader's massive internal support, but American officials hoped that the offer of financial aid to a government now cut off from its main source of revenue would force the Iranians to reconsider. However, the Iranian prime minister remained steadfast and refused to be cowed by international pressure. Stokes returned home, and Harriman informed his superiors that Mossadegh was nothing but a demagogue with whom a settlement was impossible.[60] As officials at the British Ministry of Fuel and Power made clear in their private papers,

> If Dr. Mussadiq [sic] resigns or is replaced, it is possible that we shall be able to get away from outright nationalization. . . . It would certainly be dangerous to offer greater real control of oil operations [to the Iranians]. Although something might be done to put more of a Persian façade on the setup, we must not forget that the Persians are not so far wrong when they say that all our proposals are, in fact, merely dressing up AIOC control in other clothing. . . . Any real concession on this point is impossible. If we reached a settlement on Mussadiq's terms we would jeopardize not only British but also American oil interests throughout the world.[61]

Harriman's report on the breakdown in talks struck similar notes. Although blunt in his assessment of Stokes, a man he felt particularly unsuited to such negotiations, Harriman saw the Iranian position as unsustainable. On a tour of the Abadan oil refinery, he expressed dismay at the "lunacy of [the Iranians] thinking they could run this themselves."[62] Moreover, he felt that Mossadegh's counterproposals proved Mossadegh was living in a "dream world" regarding what Iran should reasonably expect to achieve.[63] He explained to the Department of State that in his view "it seemed utterly hopeless to get any sense out of Mosadeq [sic]" and that "there was little chance of making any arrangement with the Iranian government as long as [he] was in control."[64] The two powers were therefore in agreement that Mossadegh was the blockage and that perhaps only his removal would allow both sides to move past the issue.

"We Have to Fly Wing to Wing" to Take Down the Mussy Duck

US policy between 1941 and 1951 had moved almost 180 degrees. What began as efforts to promote democracy had morphed into ways to remove the most popularly supported Iranian prime minister in memory. All attempts to control Iranian action proved futile owing to Mossadegh's passionate popular support. American leverage proved ineffective, and the shah feared taking action that might turn the anger of Mossadegh's supporters against him. The United States instead joined its British allies in a war of attrition against Mossadegh, hoping that his government's failure to achieve progress would ultimately lead to a peaceful resignation. It also began to utilize covert action to increase its bargaining position by further destabilizing his position.

American covert activities in Iran had begun as early as 1948. Operation TP/BEDAMN was initially intended to counter the Soviet Union's own political activity in the region but quickly expanded in line with Iran's strategic importance. By 1951, the CIA had enough money and ammunition in Iran to support ten thousand tribal warriors for up to six months of warfare should the need arise.[65] Led by CIA station chief Roger Goiran, the United States devoted $1 million a year to the operation, a large portion of the CIA's annual budget for covert activities at the time.[66] Most of this money went to a propaganda and political action program run by two Iranians codenamed "Nerren" and "Cilley," later understood to be Ali Jalili and Farouk Keyvani.[67] TP/BEDAMN's propaganda arm would publish anti-Communist literature as articles or cartoons in the Iranian press, distribute leaflets denouncing the Tudeh, and spread rumors on the street that the Communists could not be trusted.[68] More sinister, however, was the operation's political arm, charged with turning Iranians against the Tudeh by hiring street gangs to break up Tudeh rallies, sending agents provocateurs into Tudeh demonstrations to wreak havoc, paying religious figures to denounce the Tudeh as anti-Islamic, and organizing attacks on mosques and public figures in the name of the Tudeh.[69]

As the oil crisis continued, these assets now began to undermine Iran's democratic leader. By weakening Mossadegh's base of support through propaganda and street violence, they hoped to split his internal support and make him more susceptible to American control. Efforts were therefore made to strip apart his loose coalition of nationalist forces through propaganda that depicted him as corrupt and immoral.[70] Bribes were given to influential Mossadegh supporters, such as Mozaffer Baqai, leader of the Hezb-e Zahmatkasan (Toiler's Party), in return for their public rejection of his leadership. In the autumn of 1952, a CIA agent approached Baqai and urged him to leave Mossadegh's coalition in return for money deposited in his account.[71]

However, these efforts were too slow for the British, who continued to call for military action. Despite a government currently controlled by the Labour Party, a traditional left-wing party that had previously nationalized many of Britain's own key industries, no common ground could be found between the British and the Iranians. Manny Shinwell, the minister of defense, who forty years earlier had been a leading member of the Scottish left-wing political activist group Red Clydeside, excoriated Iran's quest for nationalization and demanded that action be taken immediately to defeat its supposed comrades. At a meeting of the Joint Chiefs of Staff, he warned that "we must be prepared to show that our tail could not be twisted interminably."[72] Power politics quickly negated ideological kinship. After closing the Abadan refinery, the British sent the HMS *Mauritius* of the Fourth Cruiser Squadron to patrol the waters off Abadan's coast, along with other Royal Navy ships already in the area. They made for an impressive show of force. The Sixteenth Independent Parachute Brigade was also shipped from its base in Aldershot to a forward station in Cyprus, ready for quick deployment to Iran when necessary. As a further signal of British intent, three battalions of troops were moved to a nearby camp in Sheiba, Iraq.[73] It seemed the situation was escalating irrevocably toward military action. Discussions in London centered not on whether military action was the desired course but on what scale would be most effective.[74]

Prime Minister Clement Attlee and Chancellor of the Exchequer Hugh Gaitskell opposed such moves but formed a minority that also had to contend with the upcoming general election and fear of being perceived as weak. The British public would not welcome meekly losing such a key resource of the fading British Empire. As a result, Gaitskell was moved to write in his diaries that although military action would precipitate similar action by the Soviets in northern Iran and therefore effectively a portioning of Iran, "I think it might be the best ultimate solution."[75] The opposing Conservative Party was in little doubt that the situation demanded strong military action and that failure to take it would be akin to appeasement.[76] It was the Conservatives belief that, in the words of Thomas Carlyle, a "whiff of grapeshot" would be sufficient to bring the Iranians unceremoniously to their knees.[77] Writing to the *Daily Telegraph*, Sir Alfred Cooper railed, "We have only one moment to stretch out a terrible right arm and we should hear no more from Persia but the scampering of timid feet. . . . Sir, we have got to risk it. Let us have done with it."[78]

The Americans, however, would not abide by a new partition of Iran between British and Soviet troops. Dean Acheson informed the British in no uncertain terms that "an exchange of fire between British troops and the army of the shah [would have] disastrous political consequences" and stressed that the solution lay solely in the resumption of meaningful and peaceful negotiations.[79] The British deputy prime minister and secretary of state, Herbert Morrison, ironically a conscientious objector during World War I, argued furiously against American pacifism.[80] He accused Attlee of failing to protect "our" wells, rebuked him for being "too United Nations-y" in waiting for support from the international community, and demanded Britain fight alone if necessary.[81] Mossadegh was similarly bullish, announcing in September 1951 that all British staff must leave Iran within a week so that Iranian forces could move in and occupy the oil zones.[82] The status of British attack forces was accordingly elevated to "twenty-four hours' notice."[83]

American pressure proved decisive, and the British government did not resort to military action.[84] Instead of Mossadegh, it was Atlee who was replaced, defeated by Winston Churchill in the general election of October 1951. Anthony Eden, the new foreign secretary, remarked how Attlee's "temptation to intervene to reclaim the stolen property must have been strong, but pressure from the United

States was rigorous against any such action."[85] Secretary of State Dean Acheson recalled that had it not been for American intervention, the British would most certainly have landed troops to protect their interests in Abadan.[86] Despite Churchill's obdurate remark that had he been in power a few weeks earlier, there "might have been a splutter of musketry, but we would not have been kicked out of Iran," he was determined to maintain close relations with the Americans and did not rekindle the prospect of military action once he was in power.[87] A close alliance was also important for the Americans. As Dean Acheson remarked, "Great Britain is our greatest ally. We have to go just like pigeons—when one turns; the others do it too. We have to fly wing to wing."[88] Although the Americans decried their British cousins' outdated imperialist attitude, they informed them that there were no "important policy divisions between" the United States and Great Britain.[89] This included agreement on the need to see an end to Mossadegh's rule.

Churchill dismissively referred to his Iranian counterpart as "Mussy Duck" and saw him as little more than "an elderly lunatic bent on wrecking his country and handing it over to communism."[90] The United States was also desperate to force Mossadegh to submit or resign and attempted to use whatever forms of leverage it still had to achieve its goal. In particular, the Export-Import Bank of the United States was instructed to cancel the $25 million loan that had initially been promised as part of the agreement that had brought Razmara to power.[91] The Truman administration had previously felt that failure to conclude the loan would be seen as an implicit exertion of economic pressure in favor of Great Britain, a perception the administration wished to avoid. Now, however, in closer cooperation with the British and no longer having faith in Mossadegh's ability to reach a settlement, administration officials were happy to exert pressure to force his hand or remove him from power altogether.[92] As a note of caution, the CIA warned in October 1951 that if the United States continued to "side spectacularly with the British," anti-American feelings in Iran would become as strong as anti-British sentiment.[93]

Mossadegh felt the pinch but still refused to flinch. Popular support for his rule remained strong despite an increase in American propaganda. Nevertheless, with the embargo and lack of oil revenues crippling Iran's economy, the embattled prime minister was desperate for assistance and turned with hope to the Americans. On a visit to the United States in late 1951, Mossadegh used all his charm to solicit support from Truman and Acheson. "Mr. President," he began, leaning forward and adopting his signature old and pathetic countenance, "I am speaking for a very poor country—a country all desert—just sand, few camels, a few sheep." "Yes," interrupted Acheson, "and with your oil, rather like Texas!" Mossadegh burst into laughter at his failed gambit but was left with the clear impression that the Americans were unwilling to provide financial aid to a country so rich in natural resources. When Mossadegh directly broached the subject of financial assistance, Truman blankly refused, saying that US aid was not going to be used to fight a vendetta against the British and again urging Mossadegh to reach an agreement. Once an agreement was reached, Truman assured him, Iran would be able to exploit its own plentiful natural resources and receive assistance from the United States.[94]

Before leaving the United States, Mossadegh appealed once more in writing, explaining that Iranians were "both sorry and bewildered" by the lack of US financial support following the Iran Declaration. He requested immediate financial help and warned that without assistance his government would collapse, and "a serious internal crisis in Iran could have repercussions that might place the government of the United States in a difficult world position."[95] Playing on American fears of the Soviet Union still did not alter Truman's position, and Mossadegh departed with nothing.

On January 13, 1952, Mossadegh appealed again for $10 million a month to save Iran from imminent collapse and governmental takeover by the Tudeh.[96] Despite this very real threat, confirmed by US intelligence, he was refused again and told to seek settlement with Great Britain.[97] It is no coincidence that one week prior to this request the British prime minister had asked the United States to refuse all further financial aid to Iran lest the dispute never be resolved.[98] However, it is surprising that the United States obstinately refused to break from its British allies despite the rapid increase in Communist activities in Iran and in the face of the credible threat that Iran could indeed be lost. American attempts to use financial aid as leverage over Mossadegh proved successful only in promoting instability.

A Window of Opportunity

Throughout this crisis and in spite of British and American efforts, Mossadegh maintained massive public support. Even the shah was forced to respect the prime minister's authority, and the British and Americans' efforts to talk him into appointing a replacement were unsuccessful. The shah's fears were made evident in September 1951, when he asked the US ambassador in exasperation, "What can I do?" "[Any] attempt on my part [to] remove Mosadeq [sic] just now would give his friends and my enemies opportunity [to] convince [the] Iran[ian] public that [the] Crown has degenerated into [a] mere Brit[ish] tool and such prestige as [the] Crown has would disappear. [Similarly I am fully] aware that if [the] British turn against me personally, our Monarchical system . . . can collapse."[99]

Restricted in his movement, the shah tried to find a middle road and subtly worked to undermine Mossadegh, hoping that in time the prime minister's continued inability to settle the oil dispute would lead to his resignation.[100] This approach was likely more nuanced and practical, but the United States and Great Britain still hoped to be able to force him from office in a more direct way. Upon presenting his credentials to the shah, the new US ambassador, Loy Henderson, ominously mentioned that "Iran's position was growing daily more desperate and in [the] end it might be necessary [to] resort [to] desperate remedies."[101] The British, meanwhile, were more forthright: "We must force the shah to bring down Mussadiq [sic]," concluded one representative report.[102] Thoughts of a coup to remove Mossadegh began to percolate around the corridors of Foggy Bottom and Whitehall in late 1951 and early 1952.

Whereas the British favored forceful action against Mossadegh, the Americans remained cautious. Ambassador Henderson presciently confirmed that unless the prime minister moved Iran toward communism, American officials in Iran were "not convinced that general interference in Iran's internal affairs was likely in [the] long run to pay."[103] Until then, the Americans and British looked for alternative leadership to Mossadegh in the hope that continued pressure would eventually force him to resign. One name that came up frequently was that of erstwhile prime minister Ahmad Qavam. The days in which foreign pressure could remove and install prime ministers at whim, however, had disappeared owing to the massive public support Mossadegh maintained.

The upcoming elections for the Seventeenth Majles, scheduled to convene in early 1952, gave the British and Americans a new opportunity to weaken the prime minister. Mossadegh continued to champion democracy and independence, and his party, the National Front, was expected to dominate in Iran's urban precincts; the shah hoped to pick up support from the rural areas, where royalist control over the people and the ballot boxes was strong. Mossadegh had done much to ensure the elections would be as free as possible but held "few illusions as to his ability to prevent improper interventions."[104] Once electoral irregularities were reported, such as the herding of peasants to polling stations by their watchful landlords, Mossadegh suspended the elections as soon as a parliamentary quorum had been reached.[105]

Some commentators, such as Kenneth M. Pollack, argue that ending the election in this manner meant that Mossadegh had "resorted to undemocratic powers" to remain in office. He admits that the elections were "being corrupted by foreign agents" but fails to state that the Constitution explicitly allowed the prime minister to take such action under such circumstances.[106] Rather than resorting to undemocratic means, Mossadegh made full use of the powers granted to him. He was determined to maintain the legality of his government despite intense antidemocratic influence from foreign powers and the shah's royalist supporters.

The Seventeenth Majles therefore contained the smallest number of members allowed to form a parliament, consisting of thirty National Front and forty-nine royalist or pro-British deputies.[107] This makeup inevitably led to conflicts as the anti-Mossadegh faction accused the prime minister of caring only about urban areas of the country while ignoring the plight of the more populated countryside, and the pro-Mossadegh members called for the peasants to rise up against their landlords in order to achieve "social progress and national independence."[108] British agents and embassy staff, in particular Sam Falle, head of the MI6 station in Tehran, intensively lobbied Majles deputies to vote against Mossadegh's policies.[109]

In the midst of such political and social turmoil, Mossadegh eventually resigned, but not in the manner expected. In July 1952, Mossadegh surprised the shah by exercising a constitutional prerogative to nominate the minister of war. Control of the army was a jealously guarded prerogative of the shah, who, shocked, refused to sanction such an act, saying that if he gave up control of the army, he may as well pack his bags and leave the country. The prime minister in turn threatened his own resignation if the shah failed to submit to what was the prime minister's clear constitutional right.[110] Why Mossadegh suddenly made this request is unclear.[111] The prime minister knew that the army was key to the shah's power, but after facing intense internal pressure from the shah's supporters, Mossadegh possibly wished to prevent the military from being used against him. It was control of the army that empowered the shah and allowed him to act unconstitutionally when he so wished. It was also through the army that the shah disrupted elections and struck fear into those who hoped to challenge his rule. It may also be true that Mossadegh wished greater control over the army in case Western military plans came to fruition.

The manner of the shah's denial of Mossadegh's request adds farce to what was a seminal moment in Iran's history. In a meeting at the royal palace, the shah explained why he could not accept, after which Mossadegh calmly rose and walked toward the door to leave. So scared that the supremely popular prime minister would at once rally his forces to bring down the monarchy, the shah instinctively ran to the door and used his body to physically block the exit. Demanding the discussion continue, the shah faced a shocked Mossadegh in a dramatic standoff. It continued for a minute or two—Mossadegh attempting to leave and the shah blocking him—until the frail prime minister fainted and collapsed, either as a consequence of his condition or as a diplomatic maneuver intended to end an embarrassing deadlock.[112] The next day, July 16, 1952, while recovering in bed, Mohammad Mossadegh issued his resignation. Despite his supporters beginning to protest on the streets, the rejoicing in London "could probably have been heard in Tehran."[113] Less-raucous rejoicing probably also occurred in Washington as, with Mossadegh out of the way, a window of opportunity had emerged to settle the oil dispute and get the Seven-Year Plan back on track.

Qavam's Brief Return

Western leverage had little effect in forcing Mossadegh to resign, but with the popular prime minister now removed, effective leverage could be placed on the shah to nominate a replacement that fit external demands. The British, with American support, immediately pushed for Qavam to be selected successor, a man the shah had long disliked and distrusted. The shah was unmoved when he heard of Qavam's American support, scoffing, "I gather that he has managed to fool those idiotic Americans."[114] However, he was unable to withstand the pressure placed on him by the Western powers, members of his court, opposition politicians, and even his own family, and so Qavam began his fifth stint as prime minister the day after Mossadegh's resignation. Despite being forced into making the appointment, the shah remained fearful of popular outrage and sought to distance himself from the decision. He refused to offer Qavam his public backing and made clear to Mossadegh's supporters that he had made the appointment only under duress.[115]

Once in office, Qavam confidently pledged to solve the oil crisis and restore order. He gave a stern and somewhat unwise public warning to anyone who might obstruct his policies: "The period of transgression is over. The day has come to obey the government's orders."[116] He also, perhaps even more unwisely given his own lack of popular support, attacked his predecessor's policies, denouncing Mossadegh's failure to resolve the oil crisis and foolish launching of a "widespread campaign against a foreign state." Qavam's Iran would be different, he assured the Iranian people in a radio address: "this helmsman is on a different course," and anyone who attempted to alter his setting would be arrested and delivered into "the heartless and pitiless hands of the law."[117] A keen poker player forced to wear dark glasses owing to his eyes' sensitivity to sunlight, Qavam carried the aura of a James Bond villain. Threats to his opponents did little to change the perception that he was an enemy of the people.

The British had taken the lead in ensuring Qavam became prime minister, but once he was in office, they offered him very little support or guidance. William Roger Louis has called this approach the doctrine of "masterly inactivity" and explains how at the time of the change in government, the head of British intelligence in Iran was camping in the mountains on a trout-fishing vacation.[118] It was assumed that bringing Qavam to power was the hard part and that the rest of what the British wanted would now fall pleasingly into place. However, Qavam inherited the same problems Mossadegh had before him: without a resolution to the oil issue, the Iranian government had no money and could not function effectively. While the British waited patiently for the new Iranian government to submit a proposal to solve the oil crisis, protests against his rule erupted.

Masterly inaction was leading to disaster, so the Americans demanded immediate action. Taking control from the British in an attempt to secure Qavam's position, they publicly announced their support for the prime minister and his "rigorous and courageous program of taking strong action against people in the Majlis and others who were inciting riot."[119] In Washington on July 21, 1952, Dean Acheson called an emergency meeting with Truman to secure emergency financial assistance for the new government, something the administration had obstinately and repeatedly refused to give Mossadegh. Without immediate and sizeable financial backing or popular support, Qavam had little chance of lasting long in the face of rising protests and continued economic problems. Acheson rushed the plan through, hoping that by the end of the day there would still be "a government to which we can extend help."[120]

The result of Acheson's machinations was an immediate aid package of $26 million in grant assistance to prevent bankruptcy, while a more detailed plan was mapped out. Dependent on progress toward an oil settlement, the United States signaled its intent to provide even greater amounts of aid at even more favorable rates in the future.[121] In Iran, Ambassador Henderson worked hard to bolster Qavam's ailing position, meeting with him and convincing the shah's close confidantes, Ernest Perron and Hossein 'Ala, to strengthen royal support for the new prime minister. Henderson even supported Qavam's wish to dissolve the Majles, informing the shah that "the constitution was not meant to paralyze the executive in moments of extreme danger."[122] As would be repeated many times all over the world, security interests and respect for democracy during the Cold War were rarely aligned.

The British were not impressed by the Americans' rush to action. Upon hearing of Truman's attempt to offer immediate financial assistance, Sir Donald Fergusson, permanent undersecretary of the Ministry of Fuel and Power, blithely stated that the British were not opposed to it per se but hoped "that the sum be limited so as to encourage Qavam to feel the need for a settlement."[123] But Qavam was more concerned with the immediate problem of remaining in power rather than working toward a quick settlement. By midmorning on July 21, four days after Qavam's appointment, a general strike had begun, and protests overwhelmed the police efforts to maintain order. Mossadegh's ally, Ayatollah Kashani, declared Qavam a "traitor and a gangster" and called on the people to wage holy war against him.[124] A panicked king sent in military units to restore order, but after the death of seventeen protesters many of the soldiers mutinied and joined the opposition. To stop more soldiers from changing sides, the military commanders ordered the troops back to the barracks after five hours of battle.[125]

Tehran was now completely in the hands of Mossadegh supporters, and the shah lost his nerve. At 4:00 p.m. that evening, he asked for Qavam's resignation and called on Mossadegh once again to form a government. As with the Razmara episode, the Qavam interlude illustrated to the Americans that if they were intent on supporting a candidate for prime minister who did not hold popular support, the shah's full backing was essential. Qavam lasted four short days, and even before the events of July 21 the shah had contacted National Front leaders in an attempt to get rid of him.[126] Without support from either the people or the shah, no prime minister could last long in Iran, despite being put there by the West. People power had been restricted during the reign of Reza Shah, but since 1941 it had become an important force in Iranian politics that could no longer be ignored.

Qavam's brief stint as prime minister also reveals much about US policy in mid-1952, although it is an episode often overlooked in most analyses of the period.[127] Gone were attempts to promote reform or modernization. Embassy telegrams and governmental memos no longer mentioned the ambitious Seven-Year Plan, which had become obsolete owing to the lack of oil revenues. Talk of development had been suspended until settlement of the oil dispute was assured. US policy was therefore directed solely to achieving resolution of the dispute. By April 1952, the British ambassador in Washington believed that the United States was now "more opposed than we are to a continuance of the Musaddiq [sic] regime," seeing him as the main factor in preventing a settlement from being reached.[128] As soon as an alternative to Mossadegh was found, the Americans moved quickly to support him both diplomatically and financially. Illustrating the importance of Qavam's government, Dean Acheson later referred to it as an attempt at counterrevolution that sadly failed after the shah, nervous about increasing demonstrations, "walked out from under him [Qavam]."[129]

As much as the episode informs us of US policy in the run-up to Qavam's appointment, the fallout from his departure is even more instructive and illustrates an important shift in the US position toward Britain and Iran. Whereas the prospect of revolution in Iran panicked the shah, it focused the Americans' minds. With Qavam's failure and Mossadegh once again in power, the Truman administration understood that dealing with Mossadegh was now unavoidable. The Americans could not count on his removal again because it would only lead to public insurrection until he was returned to office. The Qavam affair therefore split the Anglo-American union that had heretofore sought either to force a settlement on Mossadegh or to force him from power. For a resolution to be found and Iranian oil to be guaranteed for the West, it was time for the Americans to take the initiative and agree to a deal with Mossadegh.

Renewed Democratization

Qavam's failure and Mossadegh's stubbornness amid intense pressure illustrated how important public opinion had become in Iran. Democratic aspirations had grown since 1941, and without a free and independent executive or legislative branch they could be realized only through spirited protests on the streets and in the press. Kenneth Pollack has argued that Mossadegh's conduct during the Seventeenth Majles election and his reliance on popular support proved that "the lifelong constitutional democrat had effectively made himself dictator of Iran."[130] However, Mossadegh had not asked for or supported the demonstrations that broke out spontaneously against foreign intrigue. When citizens have no course for redress through institutional means, their best option often is to take to the streets in public demonstration, a right that is an intrinsic part of the democratic fabric of Western liberal democracies. Although some of Mossadegh's actions during the elections ran counter to democratic principles, they were mitigated by the intense external and internal manipulation of the results. Likewise, the popular uprisings in support of Mossadegh were a valuable check on his enemies' antidemocratic actions.

With popular support, therefore, Mossadegh swept back into office more powerful than before. As part of the package to ensure

Mossadegh's return, the shah consented to his taking over the Ministry of War and even asked whether he, the shah, should remain monarch.[131] If, as Pollack argues, Mossadegh sought dictatorship, this surely was an offer he could not afford to reject. But Mossadegh declined. Despite what the Americans would later conclude, he was not a republican and instead replied that he wanted to see the shah submit to his constitutionally prescribed role of reigning but not ruling.[132] A shah who "cooperated with democratic and nationalist forces," he stated, would undoubtedly "go down in history."[133] To achieve a more ceremonial monarchy in line with the Constitution, Mossadegh used his new powers so that by May 1953 the shah's authority was reduced to what it had been in August 1941, when the shah had first assumed the throne. Although it is true that Mossadegh also declared martial law and received special emergency powers from the Majles, these moves are understandable given the grave situation in Iran at the time, a situation that the *New York Times* described in August 1952 as "near anarchy."[134]

Instead of using these powers for nefarious reasons, Mossadegh instead cut the military's budget by 15 percent, transferred fifteen thousand men from the army to the gendarmerie to restore order, and set up two commissions to investigate allegations of corruption in the armed services.[135] Moreover, with the United States shelving all plans for reform until an oil agreement was reached, Mossadegh secured the passage of his own nine-point reform program. This program covered important reforms to the electoral laws, the banking industry, employment laws, the judiciary, the press laws, rural government, administration and financial institutions, as well as education, health, and communications services.[136] Suffrage at the municipal level was extended to women; factory workers were given health care; and the peasantry's harvest share was increased by 15 percent.[137] Under Mossadegh, political parties and groups were free to operate; the courts were independent; and, according to Homa Katouzian, the "press was so free that, in part, it may be described as licentious."[138] Mossadegh was attempting to achieve what the United States had once professed to support: the development and democratization of Iran. The only thing dampening his hopes for the consolidation of democracy was the interference of foreign powers that prioritized an oil agreement above all else.

"Agog for Action": The Last Throes of Diplomacy

Many analyses of this period argue that throughout the oil dispute, the Americans toed the British line. Mary Ann Heiss writes that "British officials skillfully maneuvered their US counterparts into becoming ever more involved but always on terms that suited Whitehall's purposes." Similarly, James Bill contends that American officials were awed by "British experience and expertise in Iran." In a more recent and less-sanguine analysis, Ivan Pearson nevertheless argues that the British wielded "a decisive amount" of influence over the Truman administration during the crisis. Ervand Abrahamian asserts that British and American officials walked lockstep in agreement on how to approach Iran throughout the oil crisis and that as soon as Mossadegh regained the premiership, both sides joined together to conceive of plans to remove him from power permanently.[139] In fact, the opposite is true, and the two powers actually diverged on how to approach Iran after Mossadegh's return.

The Truman administration was under no illusion as to what motivated the British. "The cardinal purpose of Brit policy," Acheson wrote in November 1951, "is not to prevent Iran from going Commie . . . [but to] preserve what they [the British] believe to be the last remaining bulwark of British solvency"—control over Iranian oil. Whereas the British sought a deal that would humiliate Iran for their impudent actions, the Americans merely wanted for the situation to be resolved. To Acheson, "Iranian oil is not essential" for the British, as "with firm support from her [sic] friends, [Britain] can recover from this blow."[140] What was essential was that Iranian oil be kept away from Communist control. Acheson therefore was incensed that the British failed to take advantage of the Qavam opening, and he mocked Foreign Secretary Eden for thinking he knew everything there was to know about the Iranians and for assuming they were merely "rug dealers" and nothing else. Eden's guiding principle, Averell Harriman recounted, was that you "should never give in [because the Iranians] would always come around and make a deal with you if you just stayed firm." Harriman shared Acheson's opinion of the British foreign secretary, remarking that he thought Eden to be "utterly impossible," someone who "thought he knew it all about Iran . . . [when in fact] he knew less than almost anybody."[141] The window of opportunity offered by Qavam had been lost owing to British incompetency, and now Mossadegh, back stronger than ever, could not be ignored. Furthermore, Acheson worried that should Mossadegh lose power again, there would be a "far greater risk that he would be succeeded by a group further to the Left than by a more constructive group."[142]

The British drew a much different conclusion. Qavam had fallen owing to the shah's failure to remain strong, and so it was he, not they, who could no longer be relied on to defeat Mossadegh.[143] They therefore steeled themselves to take a more aggressive posture and lead the efforts to overthrow Mossadegh. As the British intelligence officer Sam Falle later wrote, from the moment Mossadegh was reappointed prime minister, the British began to think of "fair or foul means" to remove him from office. While the United States contemplated negotiating with Mossadegh unilaterally, the British War Office began at once to look at the possibility of instigating a coup. In particular, studies were commenced to identify suitable leaders within the Iranian armed forces for such an action.[144] Mossadegh's reign and the future of democracy in Iran depended on which policy, American or British, would most quickly achieve success.

For Washington, the time to sit and wait was over; action had to be taken. For Acheson, "further temporizing in the hope of a change of government for the better would run unwarranted risks for all of us in the Middle East when a feasible alternative seemed possible."[145] Lest Iran be lost to an uncontrollable revolution, an agreement with Mossadegh was the only viable alternative. To that end, officials in Washington quickly began to work on a deal to offer badly needed financial assistance to the Mossadegh government. On the morning of July 31, 1952, ten days after Mossadegh's return to power, Acheson met with President Truman to finalize the plan. It would involve immediately transmitting $10 million in grant assistance to Iran, convincing the British to buy all surplus oil presently stored in Iran, and persuading Mossadegh to agree to the formation of an international arbitration commission to decide the question of British compensation for the nationalization of its oil concession.[146] Although offering Mossadegh aid was an abrupt change in direction for the United States, the $10 million offer was still considerably less than the $26 million package the Truman administration had put together to assist the short-lived Qavam government. The offer demonstrates that although the administration felt there was no other option than Mossadegh, it still did not have full confidence in his abilities to find a solution to the crisis. Nevertheless, Truman immediately signed the proposal and had it forwarded to the British for their endorsement.

Unsurprisingly, the British did not receive the proposal well and returned it to Washington after a thorough editing by Foreign Secretary Eden. What Acheson received incensed the usually mild-mannered secretary of state, who complained that the only related and relevant content between it and his initial proposal was that "they were both written on paper with a typewriter."[147] Truman wrote directly to Churchill that unless the British softened their position and accepted the Iranian nationalization law, which had, he said, "become as sacred in Iranian eyes as [the] Koran," then Iran is going "down [the] communist drain." Truman made clear that the United States would not allow this to happen and would take unilateral action to settle the oil dispute even if such action threatened the British monopoly on Iranian oil.[148] The threat to take over Iranian oil soon made London appreciate the sense of urgency Washington felt. The British ambassador to the United States, Sir Oliver Franks, informed his superiors that the Americans were suddenly "agog for action."[149]

Faced with a new determined attitude from the United States, Britain relented. In a secret message to Truman, Churchill wrote, "I thought it might be good if we had a gallop together such as I often had with FDR," and agreed to the original proposal written by Acheson.[150] Mossadegh, however, immediately rejected the joint offer of monetary assistance, the first to be made to him. Britain was not the only party wishing to hold stubbornly to its position. The Iranian premier was determined that any equitable plan must first satisfy Iranian demands that the AIOC pay $49 million in back taxes and royalties before any discussion over a financial settlement could begin.[151] Moreover, he felt the US offer of just $10 million in grant assistance was so small that it "smacked of charity," which he would not accept.[152] Mossadegh's insistence on back taxes before negotiation hints at the dire state of Iran's economy owing to the Western boycott of Iranian oil. Unless Mossadegh could stabilize the economy, he would not enter into negotiation for fear that he could be held to ransom. The British in turn rejected his counterproposal and insisted it was Iran who should be paying compensation to the AIOC as a result of unilaterally ending the British oil concession.[153] An agreement seemed as far away as ever, with Churchill calling Mossadegh's counterproposal "the driveling of [an] old man in bed" and Mossadegh formally severing diplomatic relations with Britain on October 22, 1952.

The Americans had pulled up lame in their brief gallop with the British as both sides seemed unprepared to make the necessary compromises to reach a deal. With the American public electing Republican Dwight Eisenhower to the presidency less than two weeks later, the Truman administration's hopes of finding a solution to the crisis were ending in abject failure. In a meeting with the new president-elect later that month, Acheson made clear that Iran remained in critical condition and that both Iran and Britain were "wholly unreasonable."[154] If diplomacy could not affect the situation, other methods, along the lines of those being formulated in London, may well have to be considered.

Displaying his characteristic persistence, however, President Truman refused to admit defeat and ordered his administration to make one last-ditch effort in their final few days left in office, even if "it may impair our relations with the British."[155] Acheson quickly suggested a lump-sum settlement that could be couched in vague enough terms that each side could take it home and make a good case in its favor. Acheson immediately got presidential authority to put forward a plan involving a US advance of up to $100 million dollars in return for future delivery of Iranian oil, which US companies, either alone or in conjunction with the AIOC, if it agreed to participate, would purchase or send to market.[156] Desperation had finally brought the administration to the realization that something similar to what Ambassador Henry Grady had suggested almost two years earlier would be necessary to settle the situation in Iran effectively. Implicit was a warning that unless Britain agreed to the deal, its monopoly over Iranian oil would end, and American companies would sign their own deals with Iran.

The Americans also exhumed the $25 million Export-Import Bank loan that had first been promised to the Razmara government but had since been cancelled to increase pressure on Mossadegh. The Americans hoped that such a massive injection of money, along with a threat to the British that American oil companies would usurp their role, would be enough to force a settlement. Mossadegh welcomed the approach and appeared willing to forego back taxes and royalties in return for immediate payments from the United States.[157] Five days before Eisenhower's inauguration, the Truman administration submitted the plan and on its penultimate day in office held its last meeting on the matter.

According to Henry Byroade, assistant secretary of state for Near Eastern affairs at the time, a solution to the crisis was "80 to 90 percent worked out when the administration changed."[158] Similarly, Acheson sensed they were "very close" to an agreement, but he failed to get a reply from Mossadegh before the Truman administration was required to vacate the White House. "I packed my little suitcase and left the Department on the morning of the 20th [January 20, 1953], and I haven't the faintest idea what happened afterwards," he recalled somewhat disingenuously a year after leaving office.[159] What happened was Eden's eventual rejection of the plan and continued counterproposals from Mossadegh. Eden later explained that it remained British policy to look "for alternatives to Mussadiq rather

than trying to buy him off," and the British were already in negotiation with members of the incoming US administration to remove
Mossadegh from power.[160]

Conclusion: Oil before Democracy

The period of Truman's presidency demonstrates the importance
of internal support in understanding the effectiveness of external
influence on a country. Prime ministers and shahs who depended
on American support could be controlled, but leaders with massive
popular support were protected from external leverage. Therefore,
the United States could control the shah but not Mossadegh. Similarly, when the shah heroically survived the attempt on his life, he
briefly gained public support and was inoculated from foreign pressure. This period therefore shows that leverage is heavily dependent
on the extent of internal legitimacy.

The period also witnessed the unsteady rise of Iran's democratic
institutions. The Majles and the office of prime minister repeatedly
asserted themselves at the expense of royalist control, to the point
that by the early 1950s the shah refused to proceed with certain
policies unless he had the support of one or the other, preferably
both. Majles deputies prevented the shah from installing certain
prime ministers, removed pro-royal prime ministers they no longer
felt fit for office, and elected others who were not in favor with the
shah. Successive prime ministers similarly asserted themselves, in
particular Mossadegh, who forced the shah to surrender additional
powers to democratic institutions. Behind these institutions was the
democratic fervor of the Iranian population and civil society. Their
protests against policies that undermined constitutionalism gave the
United States pause when it wished the shah would resume a more
authoritarian role in Iranian politics. And their support gave Mossadegh leverage over the shah's and external powers' undemocratic
influence. In addition, Iran's press during this time was comparatively
free, the courts were independent, and government officials were
increasingly honest and responsible.[161] In Mohammad Mossadegh,

Iran had a prime minister whose declared aim was the establishment of constitutional order and democratic government, and, if not for external factors, democratic consolidation would have been likely if he had been allowed to remain in office.

This outcome should have been welcomed by Washington. Since the early 1940s, the United States had aided and protected Iran's return to constitutionalism. It had warned the shah numerous times not to assume personal control, and it had given Iran's political development the space to continue.[162] These approaches had allowed Prime Minister Qavam to continue his progressive policies in the 1940s, which would otherwise have been halted by the shah's desire to reclaim authority. However, as the 1950s began amid growing fears of the Soviet Union and concerns for control over Iranian oil, the country's democratization threatened its stability. To ensure Iran remained free of Soviet control, the Truman administration favored the application of the Seven-Year Plan and a strong pro-Western government, so Iran's own development was checked. As nationalism increased and coalesced around Mohammad Mossadegh, the United States found itself unable to control events and unwilling to support the prime minister in Iran's oil dispute with Great Britain. The result was stalemate as Iran's internal situation moved inexorably toward chaos.

4 The Overthrow of Democracy, 1953

The man to deal with this continued move toward chaos was Dwight D. Eisenhower, the first Republican to take office since the ousting of Reza Shah in 1941. As supreme commander of the Allied Forces in Europe during World War II, Eisenhower was globally respected and easily won election in November 1952. To many, he was the ideal presidential candidate. One biographer concluded that "no one who wore the uniform of the United States or Great Britain during the Second World War possessed the political acumen of Eisenhower."[1] Both parties wished he would represent them, and Truman even offered to step down from the Democratic ticket in Eisenhower's favor in 1948 and again in 1952.[2] But Eisenhower identified more as a Republican and announced his candidacy in early 1952, with the promise to clean up Truman's mistakes in the fight against communism.[3]

Advising him on foreign policy was John Foster Dulles, the Republican Party's leading international strategist, who had long called for a more activist policy against the Soviet Union. Six years earlier he had warned of a "Pax Sovietica" as the Soviets enveloped more and more countries behind the Iron Curtain.[4] Iran in particular was a country that Dulles felt the Soviets were making concerted efforts to increase their control over with the aim of full absorption.

Dulles painted a grim picture of the effectiveness of the Soviet Union in luring countries to its side, yet others felt him too melodramatic over the dangers the United States faced.[5] He believed strongly in American exceptionalism and felt a world without the firm US leadership would "not be worth living in." Indeed, he continued, displaying his penchant for hyperbole, such a world "would probably be [one] in which human beings cannot live."[6] For Dulles, Truman's containment policy was not enough; the United States had to pursue an activist foreign policy to combat the Soviet Union, which, Dulles said, wished nothing more than to "finish us off in quick order."[7]

The incoming administration therefore brought with it a strong desire to push back against communism and in Dulles a plan of action that it felt could achieve this goal. Key to Dulles's thinking was covert action. After Eisenhower invited him to draw up the foreign-policy program for his campaign, Dulles wrote that the United States had to be bold in support of liberation movements in countries that bordered the Soviet Union. He wanted the United States to force uprisings and create separation from Moscow. He predicted that with the correct leadership committed to what he called "freedom programs," "within two, five or ten years substantial parts of the present captive world can peacefully regain national independence. That," he concluded, "will mark the beginning of the end of Soviet despotism's attempt at world conquest."[8]

Dulles hoped to create a "freedom program" for Iran that would rid the country of Mossadegh and the Tudeh once and for all. However, contrary to popular interpretations of the period, Eisenhower preferred compromise. The first few months of his presidency would therefore be a contest between his preference for negotiation with Mossadegh and Dulles's hopes for a more forceful policy. Without leverage, however, attempts to force Mossadegh to concede would prove just as difficult as they had during the Truman years. His continued intransigence, matched only by that of the British, would eventually tip the scale in favor of policies advocated by Dulles.

Roosevelt and Truman had shown that external powers could have an influential role in promoting democracy in Iran. Eisenhower and Dulles would prove that the United States could also end democracy.

Eisenhower, Oil, and Covert Action

Once in office, Eisenhower appointed Dulles as secretary of state.[9] His brother, Allen Dulles, shared similar feelings toward the Soviets and became director of central intelligence—the first time in US history that leadership of both covert and overt foreign-policy apparatus was held by siblings. Despite this family monopoly, Eisenhower was determined to remain in charge and wished to use his bombastic secretary of state as a "stalking horse behind which [he could] maneuver."[10] Contemporary journalist Murray Kempton asserted that Eisenhower would not trust John Foster Dulles "with a stick of dynamite to blow up a duck pond" but found him useful in clearing minefields.[11] Despite Dulles's prominent position in the administration, Eisenhower was determined to keep him in check and maintain presidential control over international relations. He relied on two things in his administration's conduct of foreign policy: planning and delegation. The planning was carried out by the NSC, whose meetings, unlike during Truman's reign, the president personally chaired. Of the 343 NSC meetings held during Eisenhower's eight years, he chaired 319.[12]

The NSC would prepare for every eventuality through studies, policy papers, and discussions. However, decision making would remain Eisenhower's sole prerogative. He made clear that despite the high profile of people such as Dulles, he would not hesitate to "take a different course than that almost unanimously proposed" by his advisers.[13] Once a plan was given his clearance, it would be delegated to others for completion. This process, however, did not mean the delegator was given free rein; a member of the administration later recalled that "if you were delegated a task, you had to know what the bounds of policy were. . . . With Eisenhower, there was no deviation from policy without coming back for an additional hearing."[14] Eisenhower later said, "There was no one I kept in as close touch with as I did with Foster." He made certain that Dulles consult him "frequently . . . [and] insisted that every single decision be approved by [him] in advance," even Dulles's speeches, which would be allowed only after Eisenhower "had edited [them] down to the last word."[15] Eisenhower was clearly aware of Dulles's proclivity for sensationalism and brinksmanship.

Although Eisenhower brought great international experience to the White House, the Middle East was largely terra incognita for him.[16] His overriding concern in the region was not that communism would take it over but that its oil remain in Western control. Before entering the White House, Eisenhower discussed the Iranian oil crisis with an old friend and admitted he was "concerned primarily, and almost solely, in some scheme or plan that will permit [Iran's] oil to keep flowing to the westward. We cannot ignore the tremendous importance of 675,000 barrels of oil a day."[17] Who was to blame for the crisis was not as important as how the situation could be resolved, even if it meant working with Mossadegh. To this end, Eisenhower came to the White House with a mindset similar to that of the outgoing Truman administration, which had come close to pushing Mossadegh and the British together to a deal.

This fact has generally been dismissed in the literature on the period. It has instead been claimed that Eisenhower brought a new and instant determination to remove Mossadegh from power through a coup d'état. Andrew Scott Cooper argues that the arrival of the new president "led to a sea change toward Iran and oil nationalization." Stephen Kinzer has written that the "American attitude toward a possible coup in Iran changed radically after Dwight Eisenhower was elected." Mark Lytle concludes that the change in administration meant that Mossadegh was about to "receive a lesson in cold war politics, Republican style," and Mark Gasiorowski argues that the incoming administration was determined to act more "aggressively" than its predecessors. Mostafa Zahrani sees Eisenhower as a "fundamental change" from Truman, and Kenneth Pollack contends that Eisenhower brought with him a very different weltanschauung.[18]

Contrary to these conclusions, Eisenhower's weltanschauung in regards to Iran in early 1953 was almost identical to Truman's. In particular, he shared his predecessor's exasperation with the British position. Writing in his diary after a meeting with Winston Churchill on January 6, 1953, Eisenhower lamented that the prime minister was trying to relive the days of World War II, where "he and our president were sitting on some rather Olympian platform with respect to the rest of the world and directing world affairs from that point of vantage." Eisenhower saw British policy toward Iran as old-fashioned and paternalistic, encapsulated by Britain's aging prime minister. Despite his personal affection for Churchill, Eisenhower wished he would "turn over leadership of the British Conservative party to younger men" with new ideas based on respect and cooperation.[19]

Another misconception is that Truman and Eisenhower viewed covert action in distinct ways. Mary Ann Heiss has written that, "unlike their predecessors, Eisenhower and Dulles were ideologically predisposed to covert operations."[20] However, Truman was no shrinking violet when it came to ordering such action. It was under Truman's watch that the CIA was first formed, and he relied on its work both to combat Soviet expansion and to protect American oil resources. Just two months after the CIA's formation in 1947, Truman authorized NSC 4-A, which launched peacetime "covert psychological operations" to counter similar efforts by the Soviets.[21] In 1948, he gave the go-ahead for covert operations to prevent a Communist seizure of Italy and did the same for the Philippines a few years later.[22] In March 1949, the United States engineered a coup in Syria and installed a government more amenable to supporting the Trans-Arabian Pipeline—the means by which the Arabian-American Oil Company hoped to transport oil to the Mediterranean.[23] More infamously, from 1949 to 1952 the United States conducted joint covert paramilitary operations with the British Secret Intelligence Service that sought to destabilize Enver Hoxha's Communist government in Albania. To this day, Operation BGFIEND, as it was known, "remains the only known attempt by the CIA to overthrow a Soviet satellite by using a paramilitary force."[24] Truman created and then expanded CIA covert operations sixteen times during his presidency and began covert operations in Iran as early as the late 1940s.[25] Although it is true that Eisenhower favored covert action, the same can also be said of his predecessor.

The Dulles brothers also favored covert action in the fight against communism, and they held a special interest in the Middle East. Their work at the international law firm Sullivan & Cromwell meant both had a certain perspective on the ongoing oil dispute. Their clients included not only big American oil companies such as the Standard Oil Company of New Jersey and Mobil but also AIOC subsidiaries in the United States.[26] In 1949, Allen Dulles even visited Iran while representing one of these clients. The Dulles brothers' view was very much in line with the British opinion that Mossadegh was the main obstacle to a resolution to the oil issue in Iran. American leverage had so far failed to ensure his removal, so the brothers favored covert action to achieve their goal, and they worked tirelessly over the next few months to convince their boss of the sagacity of removing the fragile yet stubborn Iranian prime minister.

The difference between Eisenhower and Truman has therefore been overblown in studies of the period. The incoming president's views were almost identical to those of his predecessor, who had already shifted from the idealism of Roosevelt to the realism that came to characterize the Cold War period. The main difference came in Eisenhower's assistants, with the Dulles brothers already in negotiation with the British on how to remove Mossadegh from office. Their ability to convince Eisenhower to support such action would determine Iran's fate.

Giving America the BOOT

Since Mossadegh's return to the premiership in July 1952, the British had been solely concerned with removing him. Their expulsion from Iran, however, meant they needed American support to bring their plan to fruition. Shortly after Mossadegh's election victory in November 1952, a British agent approached Kermit "Kim" Roosevelt Jr., a senior CIA operative, while he was waiting for a connecting flight at Heathrow Airport. Grandson of Theodore Roosevelt and a distant cousin of Franklin D. Roosevelt, Kim was a bespectacled, wiry, and a generally circumspect man in his mid-forties whose demeanor mystified many.[27] Kim Philby, the notorious British double agent, had worked with him while in Washington and described him as a "courteous soft-spoken Easterner with impeccable social connections, well-educated rather than intellectual, pleasant and unassuming. He was the last person you would expect to be up to his neck in dirty tricks."[28] But dirty tricks were his forte.

At the impromptu airport meeting, the British agent informed Roosevelt that Her Majesty's government wished to overthrow Mossadegh and required American assistance. He was told that the plan, codenamed Operation BOOT, was already at an advanced level and that Foreign Secretary Anthony Eden and, with special vehemence, Prime Minister Churchill, were fully behind it.[29] Roosevelt was immediately in favor but explained to the British that "the project would require considerable clearance from [his] government and that [he] was not genuinely sure what the results would be." He also said that there was "no chance to win approval from the outgoing administration of Truman and Acheson,"[30] a statement that has mistakenly been used as evidence that the Democrats were intrinsically against such action.[31] Rather, because the meeting was held shortly after the Democrats had been defeated in the presidential race, there was simply no time for the Truman administration to prepare such action.

Roosevelt felt sure that his superiors at the CIA, Allen Dulles and Walter Bedell Smith, as well as John Foster Dulles would approve of the plan, and they did.[32] Work began on the project even before Eisenhower had been either informed or inaugurated. Bedell Smith, head of the CIA until Allen Dulles took over, chaired a series of meetings between the British and the Americans in Washington to review BOOT's operational details. Kermit Roosevelt told the eager Bedell Smith that work could commence as soon as Eisenhower was inaugurated, but Bedell Smith did not want to delay. He instead told Roosevelt to "pull up your socks and get going, young man."[33] Once Eisenhower entered the White House, Bedell Smith joined the State Department as deputy to John Foster Dulles, and Allen Dulles was promoted to director of the CIA. Thus, by the time Eisenhower entered the White House, the top position in the intelligence service and the top two in the State Department were actively working on an operation to remove Mossadegh. Eisenhower would not be informed of the plan for several more weeks because the conspirators were unsure whether he would be in favor of it. They instead hoped to slowly convince him of its necessity. John Foster Dulles in State and Allen Dulles in the CIA worked tirelessly on the plan, and just two weeks after coming to office they had agreed in principle on a deal with the British to topple Mossadegh.[34] All that was left was to secure authorization from the president.

Doing so would not be easy, however; as previously mentioned, Eisenhower was keen to settle the oil dispute through negotiation, not force. Nevertheless, the Dulles brothers were confident of their ability to persuade him. An example of their efforts came at an NSC meeting on February 18, 1953. After the president asked what obstacles stood before a resolution of the Anglo-Iranian dispute, Allen Dulles replied that compensation was the main sticking point but that Mossadegh "could not afford to reach any agreement with the British lest it cost him his political life."[35] John Foster Dulles immediately agreed, sowing the seeds in the president's mind that dealing with Mossadegh was a lost hope. In actuality, Mossadegh had previously shown a desire to reach an agreement on compensation, just not the astronomical amounts demanded by the British.

Unmoved by the Dulles brothers' arguments, Eisenhower remained intent on reaching a peaceful resolution and rather than adopt a new strategy looked to his predecessors for advice on how to proceed. In the final days of the Truman administration, Dean Acheson had come close to finding a diplomatic solution between the two camps. Eisenhower wished to continue this effort. Sensing a new opportunity from a change in presidency, Mossadegh wrote to the president-elect in early January, expressing hope that the new administration would "give most careful consideration to the Iranian case so that Iran would be able to attain its just aspirations." American assistance, he continued, would "strengthen the cause of world peace [and] renew confidence in the determination of the United States to support with all its power and prestige the principles of the charter of the United Nations."[36] Despite the plans being formed by Bedell Smith and the Dulleses, Eisenhower was keen to reciprocate and show good faith.

Worse news for the conspirators soon followed. Although the Dulleses warned that Iran was susceptible to a Communist take-over, intelligence reports consistently showed otherwise. A National Intelligence Estimate dated November 1952, for instance, stated it "probable that a National Front government will remain in power through 1953." Moreover, the estimate showed it unlikely that the Tudeh would be granted legal status, nor would it "develop suffi-cient strength to gain control of the government by parliamentary means or by force."[37] An updated version of this estimate in Janu-ary 1953 reiterated this belief, and the State Department's Office of Intelligence Research agreed.[38] Whereas those in favor of the coup preached doom and gloom in Iran, reports in early 1953 repeatedly showed that Mossadegh was containing rather than facilitating the spread of communism in Iran.

Despite his senior advisers' views, therefore, Eisenhower pressed forward with direct negotiations. On February 20, US ambassador to Iran Loy Henderson presented the Iranian prime minister with an updated version of the proposals made by the Truman administra-tion a month earlier. However, its revisions still failed to address Mossadegh's basic objection to the inclusion of an explicit claim by the AIOC for the loss of future profits. Mossadegh rightly feared that the British would use the agreement to legitimize an extortion-ate amount of compensation based not on the current value of the AIOC's oil installations but on projected revenue up until when the concession was due to expire in 1993.[39] According to Henderson, Mossadegh said that if he approved such an agreement, Iran would be put "under bondage for at least twenty years . . . [and] be in no better position than" before nationalization.[40]

Rather than return to the drawing board, Eisenhower remained firm on the offer, hoping that by doubling down and refusing to cave in to Mossadegh's demands, the United States could force his hand and pressure him to accept the deal. The US embassy in London supported this approach, writing, "The only tactic we have not tried with Mossadeq [*sic*] is sustained firmness."[41] Yet Mossadegh was unmoved. Although he did not officially reject the proposal, he informed Henderson that it was unlikely he would accept. Unbeknownst to the Iranian prime minister, this negative response lost him the support of another key US official, Ambassador Loy Henderson. Henderson later wrote that it was after this meeting that he "finally came to the conclusion that no settlement of the oil problem was possible so long as Mossadegh was in control of the country, and I made my views clear in this regard to the [State] Department."[42] Another influential official thus lent his support to a coup. The Dulleses were sure that events in Iran would continue to deteriorate in such a way that the president would eventually be forced to support their plan.

Mossadegh's Coup

Without financial aid or oil revenues, Mossadegh was largely powerless to prevent Iran's deterioration. The pressures and constraints of his position weighed heavily on his mind when Ambassador Henderson presented him the new settlement proposal in February 1953. The day before, while lying in bed at his residence, Mossadegh asked a royal representative to deliver a message to the shah. He wished the shah to know that he could no longer tolerate the unfriendly relationship that had developed between them and wished to tender his resignation once again. This resignation, the message continued, would be declared in a public announcement in which he would claim an inability to perform his governmental duties while the shah and royal court continued to intrigue against him. In particular, he would state that the shah was encouraging conspiracies that were intended to bring about his downfall.[43]

It is unlikely that Mossadegh was aware of the true extent of intrigue against him, but, according to Henderson, he did suspect British collusion in attempts to remove him from power.[44] It is possible that Mossadegh once again felt defeat was inevitable, and so, rather than face the ignominy of being overthrown, he preferred to return to his country estate in Ahmadabad. A more likely explanation is that Mossadegh's announcement was a power play intended to force the shah to submit more fully to his demands.[45] Ambassador Henderson believed the prime minister's announcement either came from mental instability or was a prelude to the complete elimination of the royal position.[46] Henderson was sure that Mossadegh, despite having previously refused the shah's offer to abdicate, now wished to publicly humiliate the shah and reduce him to a state of servile dependence on the prime minister and cabinet.[47]

Mossadegh must have been aware that he held leverage over the shah and that his resignation would spark a wave of public outrage on the streets of Tehran that would threaten his own position. It is likely, therefore, that he expected the shah's capitulation and the success of democratic institutions over authoritarianism. At no time, however, did the prime minister demand the elimination of the monarchy, as Henderson feared. The shah quickly rejected Mossadegh's resignation and instead offered to leave the country until Mossadegh requested his return, said he would "make it clear once and for all that officers [in the] armed forces must look to Mossadeq [sic] not the shah for instruction," and agreed not to meet with "persons known to be critical" of the prime minister.[48] Mossadegh's silent coup to position democracy over monarchy seemed destined for success. His long refrain that the shah must reign but not rule was about to become reality.

Mossadegh accepted the shah's proposal and hoped he would "leave [the] country as soon as possible and . . . remain abroad until [the] situation [in] Iran had become more stable."[49] The shah hastily agreed, and Minister of Court Hossein 'Ala considered him to be in an "almost hysterical state," frantic to leave the country rather than be accused of hindering the popular prime minister.[50] 'Ala informed Henderson that the king was nearing a nervous breakdown and, in his opinion, had agreed to terms that would be the "first step in [the] direction of [the] abolition of [the] monarchy."[51] The minister of court and begged the United States to intervene, and on February

28, the day of the shah's proposed departure, it did. The shah would play an important role in Operation BOOT, and it was essential he remain in Iran.

British and American linkage to key Iranian figures, not only to the shah, was essential in ensuring that the shah did not leave the country.[52] Of particular importance was the growing relationship between the Western countries and Ayatollah Abol-Ghasem Kashani, a one-time staunch defender of nationalism and Mossadegh who had now grown tired of the prime minister.[53] Motivated in part by fear of communism, Kashani was also driven by the desire to acquire personal power, having already worked himself up to the position of Speaker of the Majles, and he felt that uniting with the West would accelerate his political rise.[54] According to John Waller, who was based in Iran first as a member of the Office of Strategic Services and later with the CIA, Kashani was not an agent per se, but he did accept CIA money and assistance.[55] In this regard, Kashani joined a third of the Majles deputies, who were similarly in the pocket of either the CIA or MI6 or, if extremely canny, both.[56] By February 1953, Kashani had been suitably convinced to support a coup against the prime minister.

Kashani and other well-paid agents were therefore tasked with creating a disturbance that would convince the shah that his leadership was still required.[57] As Mossadegh wished the shah a fond farewell at the palace, the influential Kashani called on his many followers to take to the streets. The manufactured disturbance followed Mossadegh as he returned home to attend a meeting with Ambassador Henderson.[58] Mossadegh's residence was well protected, and the crowd was kept away from the building by a large fence, but as Henderson left the estate, a military Jeep swung out from the curb and crashed through the gates. It carried an army colonel and Shaban "the Brainless" Jafari, a big-bearded bear of a man, gang leader, and loyal follower of Ayatollah Kashani. To the watching Henderson, this act was a clear signal for the pro-Kashani crowd to start protesting, and they swarmed through the gap now made in the fence.[59] Mossadegh soon appeared on a balcony in an attempt to calm the demonstrators but retreated when faced with a most hostile reception. As the riots increased in ferocity, he was forced to flee for his life by escaping over the rear wall and into a waiting car, all the while still dressed in his pajamas.[60] Seeing Mossadegh on the run from public protests convinced the shah to stay in Tehran.

The protests continued throughout the day because all police officers tasked with protecting Mossadegh had been discharged, reportedly by the shah's brother, Hamid Reza Pahlavi.[61] Soon, however, the protestors were met by an even larger crowd of pro-Mossadegh supporters. The two groups clashed, forcing the military to move in and restore order. Mossadegh blamed "British agents" for the problems he was facing and told Ambassador Henderson that he believed Americans were also interfering in Iran's domestic affairs.[62] He even accused Henderson of being personally involved in the events against him. According to Mossadegh, Henderson had no pressing matters to discuss on that day and certainly no need to call for an urgent meeting that would drag Mossadegh away from the palace just as Kashani's protest had begun. Mossadegh felt that Henderson had baited him to return home at that precise time so he would be personally exposed to the mob. He feared that if not physically attacked he certainly could have been accosted and affronted by the braying crowds. With his dignity, pride, and public image affected by such an encounter, he wrote that he would have no choice but to resign.[63]

Although Henderson's precise role in the protests is not known, it is clear the events had been organized by the British and Americans in alliance with Kashani. There is similarly no doubt that Henderson's other actions at this time also had a profound effect on Iranian politics. Mossadegh complained that the ambassador's meetings at the royal court over the previous few days "might have been the primary factor in causing [the] shah to remain in [the] country."[64] This was true: Dulles had ordered the ambassador to keep the monarch in Iran and to tell the frightened shah that he should either reach an accommodation with Mossadegh or find a new government to replace him.[65] Henderson defended his actions, claiming that keeping the shah in the country was "the proper thing for the free world."[66]

Had events been allowed to continue without external interference, it is likely Mossadegh would have stood a better chance of surviving the Anglo-Iranian crisis and eventually consolidating democracy in Iran. Under pressure from external forces, he had hoped to use his leverage over the shah to force him to give greater support to Iran's democratic institutions. But it was the power of linkage with Asadollah Alam, Kashani, and other significant Iranian players that allowed the United States and Great Britain to overcome Mossadegh's power play. With the shah now remaining in Tehran and anti-Mossadegh protests on the street increasing, the prime minister was battered and bruised. His silent coup had failed, while the British and American plans to replace him were back on track. External factors had once again been influential in thwarting democratic progress in Iran.

Convincing a President

By the time of the protests against Mossadegh in February, Eisenhower had still not been informed of Operation BOOT and remained committed to finding a diplomatic solution. The protests, however, gave John Foster Dulles the opportunity to attack Mossadegh. He wrote to Ambassador Henderson to say that in his view events demonstrated that Mossadegh and the Tudeh were essentially united in an attempt to remove the shah from power, despite the fact that it was the prime minister who had been the main target of the disturbances. He warned that once the Tudeh had dealt with the shah, it would surely then turn against the prime minister and subsequently force itself to power.[67] The one positive note seemed to be what he called the "substantial and relatively courageous opposition group both within and outside [the] Majlis" that supported the shah. It is unknown whether Dulles was ignorant of the organized nature of the protests, actually believed his evaluation of events in Iran, or was purposely distorting the situation to fit his narrative.[68] In reply, Henderson was moved to point out to the secretary that there was no evidence that Mossadegh and the Tudeh were working together.[69]

Regardless, Dulles's synopsis of events was passed on to the president and used to convince him that removing Mossadegh was essential to defeat communism in Iran.

Refusing to let reality temper their efforts, the Dulles brothers worked quickly to build on what they felt was a moment of opportunity to attack Mossadegh. Days after the protests, Allen Dulles sent a memo to the president arguing that a Communist takeover of Iran was increasingly likely, a claim he made despite intelligence from the ground showing otherwise.[70] The real opportunity to drive the point home to the president came at the NSC meeting on March 4, the same day Eisenhower was informed of Stalin's debilitating stroke that would soon end his life. Dulles delivered a presentation that would initially strike fear into the hearts of the assembled audience before revealing the silver lining that events of the past few days offered. Rather than explain that the main US motivation behind the removal of a democratically elected leader was the preservation of Western oil concessions, Dulles emphasized the Communist threat. He asserted that because of recent events in the country, Iran would now be under the dictatorship of the prime minister, who would control Iran, albeit with diminished power and prestige. How Mossadegh could simultaneously be both empowered and enfeebled by the same set of events, Dulles did not say. He instead warned that Mossadegh and the Tudeh were forming an alliance that was purely tactical on the Communists' part. For evidence, he presented what he called "a broadcast of the secret communist radio in northern Iran," which attacked Mossadegh as a vile servant of the shah and warned that he must join them if he wanted to survive.[71] On the basis of this broadcast, the veracity and authority of which are unknown, Dulles concluded that Iran was but one step away from a full Communist takeover. Either Mossadegh would join with the Communists freely, or he would be assassinated and replaced by a Communist regime.[72]

American officials would later admit that the Tudeh was "really not very powerful" and that "higher-level US officials routinely exaggerated its strength."[73] Russian state archives have revealed that Moscow viewed the Tudeh as irrelevant and Mossadegh as a weak leader with pro-American sympathies and an enemy of "true Soviet–Iranian friendship."[74] At the time, in early March 1953, however, Dulles presented his argument as fact and concluded that a Communist takeover in Iran would be such a catastrophe that it might ultimately cost the United States victory in the Cold War. It was here that Dulles focused on what he knew was Eisenhower's main concern, Middle Eastern oil. Wrapping up, he cautioned that the loss of Iran would lead to the similar loss of other regional countries, and "in short order . . . the [whole] Middle East, with some 60 percent of the world's oil reserves, would fall into communist control."[75]

One can only imagine the collective intake of breath drawn by the members of the NSC in response to this apocalyptic vision. The bewildered president asked whether there was any feasible course of action that might possibly save the situation. Continuing his performance but keeping his hand hidden for now, Dulles dramatically replied that he had for some time now been unable to envision any situation that could prevent the loss of Iran to a determined Soviet Union. He therefore framed the issue as one of utter hopelessness that nothing so far considered by the NSC could avert. Most likely speaking for the rest of the gentlemen in the room that day, Secretary of the Treasury George Humphrey expressed his utter shock that the council was "contemplating the loss of Iran in this fashion."[76]

Aware of the secretary of state's penchant for the dramatic, the president remained determined to look for ways the United States could peacefully ensure a Western-oriented Iran. Cognizant of America's diminished leverage over Iranian actions, one member of the NSC suggested that if they were to somehow solve the Arab–Israeli question, the United States would possibly then be in a position of strength in the Middle East to force a quick resolution on a weakened Iranian prime minister. Eisenhower, no doubt with the same exasperation felt by all the presidents who followed him, admitted that resolving the Arab–Israeli crisis would indeed eliminate many of America's problems, but he also stated that such a resolution would take a long time to work out. "I'd pay a lot for this peace," he mused.[77]

Eisenhower instead wished to continue along the path laid by Truman and Acheson: increase American leverage over Mossadegh by promising large amounts of financial aid but with less conditions attached. If Eisenhower had $500 million to spend in secret, he remarked, he "would get $100 m[illion] of it to Iran right now." Harold E. Stassen, director of the Foreign Operations Administration, replied that the United States could send funds to Iran from the Mutual Security Administration, but the amount would be more in the vicinity of $40 million rather than $100 million.[78] The conspirators' opening gambit had failed. The president ordered Dulles to meet with the British to judge if the events of the past few days could finally convince them to "concede to us in this situation" or if they were going to continue being "stiff necked[.]"[79] Eisenhower repeated his preference for monetary assistance a few days later during a visit by Anthony Eden. Mossadegh, he explained to the British foreign secretary, was "the only hope for the West in Iran," and if financial aid could stabilize his position, there would be more time to find a diplomatic solution.[80]

The Dulles brothers' inability to influence Eisenhower reflected a growing rift between them and Eisenhower not only on Iran but also on many other important foreign-policy topics. When informed that Dulles had responded to the possibility of peace on the Korean Peninsula with the hope that the United States would first be able to give the Chinese "one hell of a licking," the president erupted. Visibly angry, he said, "If Mr. Dulles and all his sophisticated advisers really mean that they cannot talk peace seriously, then I am in the wrong pew. For if it's war we should be talking about, I know the people who should give me advice on that—and they're not in the State Department. Now either we cut out all this fooling around and make a serious bid for peace—or we forget the whole thing."[81] After forty years in the military, Eisenhower valued the promotion of peaceful measures and did not worry if his policies were similar to those of his Democrat predecessors. Of Dulles, Eisenhower later remarked that "sometimes Foster is just too worried about being accused of sounding like Truman and Acheson. I think he worries too much about it."[82]

Britain, however, focused solely on the plan to remove Mossadegh and rejected out of hand the president's suggestion of further monetary aid. Dulles remained confident that despite Eisenhower's preference for diplomacy, it was only a matter of time before he would be left with no other option but to remove Mossadegh by force. At a subsequent NSC meeting on March 11, Dulles reported with finality that the British position was immovable and that the United States "should not give Iran hope that they [the Americans] would help in this way or buy Iranian oil."[83] Meanwhile, Britain continued to send Mossadegh new offers for compromise but only in terms it knew he would find wholly unacceptable, a process Kermit Roosevelt later likened to "going through the routine for appearance's sake."[84]

However, more than just appearances, the narrowing of options by Dulles and the British, combined with Mossadegh's continued rejection of offers, slowly convinced Eisenhower that a deal may not be possible. On March 11, he confessed that even if the United States acted unilaterally and provided Iran with financial assistance, it was unlikely to "make a successful deal with Mossadegh."[85] It was not Dulles's Communist fear mongering that finally convinced the reticent president but rather the belief that failure to agree to a deal on Western terms would have "very grave effects on United States oil concessions in other parts of the world."[86] Oil, not fear of communism, remained the prime motivating factor for the president of the United States.

With Eisenhower slowly coming round, preparation for the coup sped up. Covert activities were increased as all of Operation BEDAMN's propaganda and political-action capabilities, once used against the Soviets, were now directed to manipulating public opinion and turning people away from support of Mossadegh. The rise in instability that ensued allowed Dulles to place the blame for it on Mossadegh. At a press conference, he expressed concern over increased chaos in Iran as US-financed street gangs fought pitched battles with Mossadegh supporters. He criticized the Iranian government for allowing such activity to continue and questioned the sustainability of Mossadegh in a way that became a self-fulfilling prophecy: Iran was descending into ruin because Mossadegh could not control a situation in which the United States was promoting chaos by funding street protests and unrest.[87]

Stephen Ambrose has argued that Eisenhower's official acceptance of the coup came about over an evening of cocktails with John Foster Dulles.[88] The two men would often enjoy drinks of an evening, when, in Eisenhower's words, they would "try to analyze the broader aspects of the world drama we saw unfolding."[89] However, there is no evidence for the theory of a cocktail-fueled acceptance of the coup by Eisenhower, and it remains a mystery how or when Eisenhower finally learned of the coup plans.[90] Nevertheless, it seems likely that his approval came around mid-March 1953. By distorting and manipulating events, Dulles and his British allies had successfully presented Iran as unsalvageable and on the verge of a Communist takeover that all policy suggestions made earlier could not prevent. While emphasizing the potential loss of Middle Eastern oil, Dulles also hyped the apparent increase in internal support for the shah, demonstrated by the protests in February, while failing to mention the US role in financing many of these groups.

The plan worked. By March 18, Eisenhower gave the CIA authorization to discuss tactical details of the plan with the British and gave another presidential confirmation of the plan in mid-April.[91] Meanwhile, Allen Dulles approved a provisional $1 million budget for the CIA to use "in any way that would bring about the fall of Mossadegh."[92] The operation to topple Mossadegh had begun, and over the next few weeks Iran would decline further into manufactured chaos. With oil foremost in American officials' minds, the United States had moved from cultivators of democracy in Iran to agents of disruption and intrigue in the space of a decade.

"Let's Get Going:" The Coup and an End to Democracy

The date June 25, 1953, was a decisive day for US–Iranian relations. A muggy Thursday morning in Washington soon turned to rain as a number of senior government officials gathered in John

Foster Dulles's office. The discussion centered on what had by now become a twenty-two-page report detailing Operation BOOT, or, as the Americans named it, Operation AJAX. At the head of a long table, his brother Allen to his right and the report's author, Kermit Roosevelt, to his left, John Foster Dulles picked it up and growled, "So this is how we get rid of that madman Mossadegh."[93] Roosevelt recalled how the comment was "met with silence and, in some cases, barely concealed flinching" by the gentlemen in the room.[94] Although the CIA was strongly in favor of the plan, many members of the State Department had their doubts regarding the morality and efficacy of removing an elected leader of a sovereign country. These doubters included Assistant Secretary of State for Near Eastern Affairs Henry Byroade; Deputy Undersecretary of State H. Freeman Matthews; Robert R. Bowie, director of the State Department Policy Planning staff; and Ambassador Robert D. Murphy, deputy undersecretary of state for political affairs. However, John Foster and his irascible deputy, Walter Bedell Smith, had already overruled the doubters' opposition, and in the smoke-filled confines of Dulles's office these four men now sat in stony silence as Kermit Roosevelt presented the operation's main points. Allen Dulles would replace other doubters, such as the CIA station chief in Iran, Roger Goiran, with "team players" in the weeks leading up to the operation.[95] No dissension was permitted.

Once the presentation was concluded, Roosevelt recalled that "most people simply grunted, signifying consent with the least possible commitment," knowing that reiterating their objections would serve only to lose them their jobs.[96] The preservation of democratic principles was clearly not enough to cause them to fall on their swords. To assuage their fears, however, Ambassador Loy Henderson had returned to Washington and added some much needed gravitas to the coup plans. He had long regarded Mossadegh as the main obstacle to a successful conclusion of the oil crisis and had lamented as early as July 1952 that he had become "discouraged at the thought that a person so lacking in stability and so clearly dominated by emotions and prejudices should represent the only bulwark left between

Iran and communism." Like John Foster Dulles, he even admitted he "had the feeling at times that . . . [Mossadegh] was not quite sane."[97] A year later, his opinion had only hardened as the prime minister continued to reject Western proposals to end the oil dispute. Called upon to speak, he labeled Mossadegh as nothing but a "madman" and asserted that the United States had "no choice but to proceed with this undertaking."[98] When Allen Dulles blithely asked about the "flap potential"—the possibility that the plan might go awry— Kermit Roosevelt confidently replied, "I see no prospect of failure." "That's that, then," declared John Foster Dulles, drawing the meeting to a close; "let's get going."[99]

Eisenhower gave his final approval for the plan in mid-July after six months of attempting to reach agreement between Iran and the British. Without leverage to force Mossadegh to succumb, Eisenhower finally agreed to take advantage of American linkages with the shah and other authoritative figures in Iran who were in opposition to Mossadegh or could be convinced to be in opposition in return for US dollars. The coup was presented as the final option after years of failed US policy toward Iran: failure to provide promised monetary assistance, failure to maintain a position removed from the selfish British and Soviet demands, and failure to build linkages with Iran's democratic movement that now held power in Iran. Cold War exigencies and a lack of faith in the prime minister as someone able to come to a reasonable conclusion to the oil dispute had finally made up the president's mind. Flap potential, both immediate and long term, was ignored.

The coup plan was relatively simple. For months, Operation BEDAMN had prepared the grounds to remove Mossadegh through propaganda and a series of attacks and staged bombings that were blamed on the Tudeh Party.[100] Payments were made to General Fazlollah Zahedi, the man whom the British and Americans had identified to take over from Mossadegh and restore stability, so that he could bribe as many generals and Majles deputies as possible to support him. On the day of the actual coup, thousands of paid demonstrators would stage a massive anti-Mossadegh rally, and papers signed by the shah ordering the prime minister's dismissal would be delivered to Mossadegh, who if he resisted would be placed under arrest by army units under Zahedi's control.[101]

In Washington, most of the final arrangements were made privately within the confines of the CIA, a fact that unsettled an increasingly twitchy John Foster Dulles. Eager for the final operation to get under way, he panicked when at an NSC meeting on July 23 his brother failed to make mention of Operation AJAX. He nervously telephoned Allen the next day, inquiring, "The other thing, is it off?" Calming his elder sibling, Allen Dulles replied that he would not talk about the matter but assured him, "It was cleared directly with the president and is still active."[102] Indeed, Allen Dulles had briefed the president on AJAX's specific details one week earlier, although Kermit Roosevelt believes Eisenhower received only a "broad brush outline of what was proposed."[103] Nonetheless, D-Day was set for August 15, 1953.

The coup would be the pinnacle of US intervention in Iranian affairs. Since 1941, the United States had been a consistent and influential exogenous force, but Operation AJAX would eclipse all previous interventions, including the Allied decision to dispense of Reza Shah in favor of his son. The extent of US interference was remarkable. In his memoirs, Kermit Roosevelt relays the tremendous lengths the Americans had to go to just to convince the unwilling shah to support the plan. Amazingly, it was not until a few days before the coup's start that the shah was finally convinced. The extensive lobbying efforts included secretly flying in Princess Ashraf, the shah's twin sister, whom Mossadegh had forced into exile. She was a strong source of influence over her brother and was described in AJAX's operational plan as "forceful and scheming," qualities that Roosevelt hoped would successfully turn the shah.[104] Mossadegh quickly learned of the princess's return and re-exiled her, but not before she delivered the message to her brother.

This tactic was still not enough to convince the shah. Throughout his reign, he would shy away from making important decisions, often preferring to hope that the situation would resolve itself. This would be his strategy during a religious uprising in 1963 and again in the buildup to the revolution in 1979.[105] The Americans, however, would not allow any delay. On August 3, 1953, less than two weeks before the coup was scheduled to begin, the shah informed Roosevelt that he was "not an adventurer."[106] For the next five nights, Roosevelt met with him at midnight to personally assuage his fears, smuggling himself into the palace wrapped in a blanket and hidden in the backseat of a car to keep his comings and goings secret. To prove he spoke for the president of the United States, Roosevelt asked Eisenhower to insert a specific phrase into a speech he was about to deliver in San Francisco. Similarly, to show he was the emissary of Great Britain, he arranged for the BBC to issue a code word at the close of one of its daily broadcasts. Instead of the announcer saying, "It is now midnight," he would say, "It is now *exactly* midnight."[107] Each meeting eroded the shah's misgivings, until barely a week before D-Day he finally relented and signed the necessary orders to remove Mossadegh from power. That such efforts to convince the shah were necessary illustrates how truly external the coup was, including, as it did, provisions to proceed even if the shah failed to agree.[108]

With the coup about to begin, the shah left Tehran for his hunting lodge on the Caspian Sea, ready to fly to Baghdad at the first sign of blowback. Similarly absent was Ambassador Henderson, one of the leading proponents of the plan to evict Mossadegh from office. Ostensibly out of the country for vacation, he confided many years later that he wanted to separate himself from what was about to unfold. Almost thirty years later he wrote in a letter to Roy Melbourne, a friend and fellow member of the Foreign Service, that despite championing the plan in Washington "I could not bring myself to . . . carry on conversation with [Mossadegh] while I knew that plans were being carried out behind his back for his overthrow."[109]

After months of propaganda and bribery attacks, the coup finally began. It failed almost immediately. Although US-backed protests broke out as planned, Colonel Nematollah Nasiri, the man tasked with informing Mossadegh of his removal from office, met with resistance. As Nasiri and a small contingent of troops marched toward

Mossadegh's residence, General Taqi Riahi, the military chief of staff, had somehow learned of the coup and ordered Colonel Ezatollah Momtaz of the Second Mountain Brigade to march his own military detachment to defend the prime minister. "The future of constitutional rule in Iran," one historian writes, "depended on which column of soldiers reached Mossadegh's house first."[110] When Nasiri arrived at the residence, he was greeted by Momtaz and soldiers loyal to the government. Mossadegh rejected both the legality and authenticity of the royal decree and had Nasiri arrested and stripped of his uniform. That morning, as Kermit Roosevelt awaited news of Mossadegh's overthrow on the radio, he was surprised to hear the voice of the prime minister triumphantly declare victory over what he called efforts by the shah and certain "foreign elements" to overthrow him. By 10:15 a.m., a frightened and despondent shah was already in Baghdad, where he informed the US ambassador that he hoped to go on to America, where he "would be looking for work shortly as he has a large family and very small means outside of Iran."[111] Similarly, General Fazlollah Zahedi, the man chosen to replace Mossadegh as prime minister, went into hiding as the people, including Tudeh supporters, took to the streets, declaring "Victory to the Nation!" and "Mossadegh has won!"[112] Bedell Smith advised the president that to salvage anything from the situation the administration would "probably have to snuggle up to Mosadeq [*sic*]."[113]

Yet others were less willing to accept defeat, and Roosevelt and Ambassador Henderson continued to work for victory. Upon news of the coup's failure, Henderson immediately returned to Iran and after discussion with Roosevelt met with Mossadegh on August 18. This meeting was to prove vital to the coup's resurrection. Henderson complained that a number of American citizens had been attacked in the demonstrations and warned that if nothing were done to restore order, all Americans would leave Iran, including those working in the important American aid missions.[114] Deputy Chief of Mission William Rountree has said that this comment was "one of the reasons for the relatively easy success" of the coup.[115] Not wishing to antagonize the Americans, Mossadegh ordered the chief of police to break up the roving street gangs and restore order, a move that has been called a "fatal mistake."[116] After the army and police violently forced Tudeh protestors off the streets, the party's central committee proclaimed, "No more aid to Mossadegh, who is a compromising traitor."[117] Mossadegh had lost a powerful source of support and had unwittingly cleared the streets for Roosevelt to have a second go.

Making use of his Iranian contacts and CIA money, Roosevelt paid mobs to reclaim the streets on August 19 in the name of the shah. In fact, so many US dollars were spent during this time that its value on the black market reportedly dropped dramatically in favor of the rial.[118] Pro-shah sympathizers joined the CIA-paid thugs, and after much confusion and sporadic street battles, in which at least three hundred people died, Mossadegh fled his residence and was later arrested.[119] Throughout these events, the CIA also had the help of American journalists working in Iran, in particular Kennett Love of the *New York Times*. American reporters played key roles in supporting the coup, whether as informed agents of the CIA or out of a sense of what Love later called "misguided patriotism."[120] Not only did they fail to report the US role in the events, but they also disseminated material and propaganda from the CIA to their wide audience.[121] During the coup itself, Love even convinced some idle tanks to move toward Mossadegh's residence to disburse his supporters. Love later recalled that in doing so he was "responsible . . . for speeding the final victory of the royalists."[122] Thanks to the efforts by the CIA, royalist supporters, and members of the American press, the coup eventually triumphed. Mossadegh was defeated and held pending trial, and Zahedi emerged from hiding to be declared the new prime minister.

Conclusion: Uprooting the Plant of Freedom

Iran's democracy movement had stubbornly endured throughout the traumas of the shah's efforts to reclaim authoritarianism and Westerners' attempts to force Iran's submission over the oil issue, but it was finally defeated by the coup of August 1953. US policy toward Iran had changed markedly since the two countries had first established relations a little more than ten years earlier. With the Cold War now dominating the American mindset, oil and stability triumphed over the protection of constitutionalism. The coup was a double success for the Americans. Not only could action now be taken to settle the oil dispute without blockage by Mossadegh, but American leverage over Iran would also once again be determinative with the shah back to the center of power. As the international environment became increasingly unstable, Washington officials were thrilled that in Iran at least they could once again control the situation and ensure a close alliance with the West.

However, the relationship between the United States and the people of Iran, who had once lauded America as a land of virtue and fair dealing, was broken. Mossadegh had been the leader of the people, not the puppet of a foreign power or of the shah. Although his adherence to democracy grew strained toward the end of his time in office, that strain was a reaction to the intense illiberal pressure coming from both within the country and without. Not least, he was subject to the efforts of multiple CIA operations to unsettle and unseat him by fomenting instability and bribing officials who had once been allied to his cause.[123] Fakhreddin Azimi has shown that this war of attrition began as soon as Mossadegh accepted the position of prime minister in April 1951.[124] Expanding democratic rule in the face of such illiberal influences was an impossible task.

Following Mossadegh's arrest, it was made illegal to pay homage to his legacy, but as soon as the restrictions were lifted following the revolution in 1979, more than a million people converged on his Ahmadabad estate to remember their fallen leader.[125] The passing of time had not weakened their admiration for him. Had Mossadegh been allowed to govern without the constraints of the oil crisis and the interference of Great Britain and the United States, it is likely the consolidation of democracy in Iran would have been achieved. As Christopher de Bellaigue attests, Mossadegh's Iran

would have been democratic to a degree unthinkable in any Middle Eastern country of the time except Israel—a constitutional

monarchy in a world of dictatorships, dependencies and unin-
formed neo-democracies. The broad strokes of his government
would have been egalitarian and redistributive. . . . In social affairs,
secularism and personal liberty would have been the lodestones,
and the hejab and alcohol a matter for personal conscience.[126]

Mossadegh's personal probity in a country beset by corruption at
the highest levels was legendary. When his wife once tried to use the
Mossadegh name to escape punishment for violating a traffic law,
the prime minister rewarded the policeman who issued the citation
with a promotion for his strict adherence to the rules.[127] Similarly,
he instructed the chief of police to break convention and not clamp
down on newspapers that criticized the prime minister's office, saying that they can "write what they want!" An ally claimed him to
be "unparalleled in the history of Iran . . . [thanks to his] degree of
popular trust and faith" and said that from "the farthest point on
the Gulf of Oman to the Caspian, all the people of this country have
fixed their eyes on him so that he may heal their wounds."[128] The
formation of a stable democratic Iran would have become a source of
inspiration for people throughout the Middle East, potentially leading to similar movements in neighboring countries. The region's long
history of authoritarian leadership could have been replaced with
democratic governance according to the example of a democratic
and representative Iran.[129]

Instead, however, Western powers more concerned with the res-
toration of Iranian oil to fuel their armies and economic development sacrificed Iranian democracy. Alongside the shah, these powers
became the enemies of Iranian independence. Even six months after
the coup, intelligence sources in Iran reported that there "seems little
doubt . . . [that] the majority of the people still favour Dr. Mussadiq"
and that the replacement government installed by the British and
Americans "lacks any popular following."[130]

The feeling among Iran's opposition groups was summed up in
a note that the General Committee of the Nehzat-e Moghavemat-
e Melli-ye Iran (National Resistance Movement, NRM), a small

underground group of former low-ranking National Front members, wrote to the US embassy. Writing on the occasion of Selden Chapin's appointment as US ambassador to Iran in 1955, the NRM denounced US policy for having caused "the plant of freedom to be uprooted in our country." The committee argued that after the coup Iranians at once turned against the United States, accusing its government of having "destroyed our freedoms and national independence." According to the NRM, Iranians now hated "American policy more than we mistrust the Russian regime."[131] George McGhee, assistant secretary of state for Near Eastern affairs under Truman and later US ambassador to Turkey, believed that in addition to damaging America's reputation among Iranians, the coup resulted "in a great loss of confidence in us by other nations," especially those struggling for their own freedom and independence.[132] Justice William O. Douglas, who had almost become Franklin Roosevelt's running mate in 1944 and had since traveled to Iran several times, remembered Mossadegh as a true "democrat" and observed that "we united with the British to destroy him; we succeeded and ever since our name has not been an honored one in the Middle East."[133] To Douglas, Mossadegh was a man "who first brought democracy to Persia's villages and who strived to get a constitutional monarchy [in Iran]."[134]

There has been a trend in recent examinations of the coup to focus more on internal than external causes. These examinations are instructive because it is without doubt that Kermit Roosevelt's plans would have failed without the necessary support from government officials and religious circles such as those led by Ayatollahs Abol-Ghasem Kashani and Mohammad Hossein Boroujerdi as well as without the strategic mistake made by Mossadegh himself, who lost Tudeh support at a time he could least afford to do so.[135] Too heavy a focus on internal Iranian causes, however, ignores the leading role that external forces played in the organization and management of the coup events. According to the CIA's uncensored version of the events, recently made available to the public, the uprising on August 19, 1953, that ultimately removed Mossadegh was far from a spontaneous uprising but rather a protest planned by the Americans and the Iranian religious leaders. The mullahs had originally wished to hold the demonstration two days later so it would fall during a religious festival, but the Americans insisted the operation could not be delayed.[136] Simply put, without British and American organization, money, and preparation, the coup would never have happened when it did. In concert with internal forces, the United States and Great Britain successfully brought to an end Iran's experiment with democracy, which had lasted, albeit fitfully, since 1941. In its place returned the shah's rule, but his reliance in American and British action meant that for the next twenty-five years he would be seen as a puppet of the West rather than as part of the noble and honored institution that had ruled Iran for twenty-five hundred years.

The events surrounding the oil crisis and eventual coup are instructive to our understanding of external leverage. Although the United States was able to dismiss and appoint prime ministers with relative ease during the 1940s, the emergence of a popularly supported leader undermined external influence. Cutting aid and increasing diplomatic pressure failed to compel a determined and often obstinate prime minister who was able to balance external pressure with massive public support. External ability to influence a country is therefore conditioned by various internal forces, which can negate its efficacy. Understanding internal forces is essential to understanding when external pressure will and will not be effective. Even more recently, US attempts to use leverage to halt Iran's nuclear program failed in large part owing to its overwhelming popular support.[137] Indeed, the argument that a civilian nuclear program is a sovereign right being denied to Iran by external powers mirrors the debate over control of its natural resources in the early 1950s.

1. Patrick J. Hurley in his characteristic straight-backed stance, 1929. Photograph number LC-DIG-npcc-17834, Prints and Photographs Division, Library of Congress, Washington, DC.

2. Ahmad Qavam, the twenty-ninth, thirty-second, forty-fourth, fifty-first, and sixty-first prime minister of Iran, late 1940s or early 1950s. New York World-Telegram and Sun Newspaper Photograph Collection, Prints and Photographs Division, Library of Congress, Washington, DC.

3. Prime Minister Mohammad Mossadegh of Iran (*right*) speaking with Secretary of State Dean Acheson, October 24, 1951. Accession Number 66-8008, US Department of State, Harry S. Truman Library and Museum, Independence, MO.

4. Kermit Roosevelt Jr., who implemented the coup plans in August 1953, photographed in the 1950s. Photograph number LC-USZ62-115937, New York World-Telegram and Sun Newspaper Photograph Collection, Prints and Photographs Division, Library of Congress, Washington, DC.

5. Blowing out the flames of democracy: John Foster Dulles celebrates his seventieth birthday alongside former ambassador to Iran Loy Henderson and current ambassador Edward T. Wailes, February 25, 1958. Photograph number VS 247-3-58, US Department of State Photograph, National Archives and Records Administration, Washington, DC.

6. Secretary of State Dean Rusk (*center*) chats with Iranian prime minister Ali Amini (*left*) as US Russian adviser Charles Bohlen takes notes, March 13, 1962. Photograph number LC-DIG-ds-09277, New York World-Telegram and Sun Newspaper Photograph Collection, Prints and Photographs Division, Library of Congress, Washington, DC.

7. Women voting for the first time in Iran's parliamentary election, September 17, 1963. Photograph number L6427-NY14, New York World-Telegram and Sun Newspaper Photograph Collection, Prints and Photographs Division, Library of Congress, Washington, DC.

8. Robert Komer (*left*), photographed here in 1967, focused heavily on Iran while he was a member of Kennedy's National Security Council, but attention began to drift to other areas during the Johnson years. Photograph number 192537, White House Photo Office Collection, November 22, 1963, to January 20, 1969, National Archives and Records Administration, Washington, DC.

9. In happier times: President Richard Nixon and the shah of Iran shortly before the oil crisis, July 24, 1973. Photograph number 194536, White House Photo Office Collection (Nixon Administration), January 20, 1969, to August 9, 1974, National Archives and Records Administration, Washington, DC.

۳۳ بهمن رهبری امام مبارزهٔ امت انقلاب اسلامی

کانون فرهنگی شمیران

10. Poster celebrating the Islamic Revolution, c. 1980. The text at the bottom of the poster says, "22nd Bahman [February 11], the leadership of the Imam, the struggle of the Umma, the Islamic Revolution," and the flag says "Independence, Freedom, and the Islamic Republic." The Iranian people finally rose up to remove the shah in 1979. Ayatollah Ruhollah Khomeini is shown bursting through a tattered US flag, symbolizing Iran breaking free of US influence. Poster 59, Special Collections Research Center, Box 2, University of Chicago Library.

5 US Policy after Mossadegh, 1954–1960

John Foster Dulles marveled at the success of the coup. At an NSC meeting on August 27, 1953, he praised what he called the "spontaneous" events that had given the United States a "second chance" in Iran when all hope of avoiding a Communist takeover seemed to have vanished.[1] The coup also returned the United States to a position of leverage over the shah's new government, meaning that Washington could once again control Iran's actions. But rather than return to the policy of promoting reform and development followed before the oil dispute, the priority for the Eisenhower administration was stability and a strong, pro-Western leadership that would allow Iran to play a significant role in preventing the spread of communism. However, the Eisenhower administration would soon learn that without political reform Iran would never be stable. By the end of the 1950s, it would also learn how the rise of a competing superpower undermines leverage over countries such as Iran.

Although this period begins with the United States in supreme control of Iran, by the time Eisenhower leaves office, this control has evaporated. The period therefore tells us more about what makes leverage effective and demonstrates how easily it can be lost.

Stability Rather Than Democracy

In the afterglow of Mossadegh's removal, the Americans' hopes for Iran were the same as the shah's: firm, stable leadership and a quick resolution of the oil dispute. US financial assistance flooded into the country to bring it back from the edge to which it had been pushed. The United States sent $35 million in immediate aid, an amount that soon rose to $100 million. Ambassador Henderson advocated that the United States focus on social and economic reforms, without which "the country will not be able to enjoy political stability for more than brief periods."[2] It is important to note that he referred to political stability, *not* to political development; any mention of political development was noticeable only by its absence. Henderson was instead instructed to impress upon the new prime minister, Fazlollah Zahedi, the importance of proceeding rapidly with financial reforms such as taxation and changes to the fiscal system "in order to prevent the country from drifting over [the] precipice."[3]

Iran's reliance on financial aid further increased American leverage. By September 1954, the NSC reported that the Iranian government looked to the United States for help and guidance and was willing to carry out any reforms the Americans felt necessary.[4] With Washington demanding stability, the shah instigated a brutal and repressive crackdown on all opposition. To prevent pro-Mossadegh demonstrations, a curfew was declared, tanks were quickly moved into positions around the city, and opposition leaders and political activists were rounded up and detained en masse.[5] Freedom of the press became a thing of the past as publications were closed down and journalists incarcerated.[6] The speed of the crackdown after the coup hints of its being planned as part of the coup operation. Less than two months after Mossadegh's removal, reports estimated that thirteen thousand opposition figures had been jailed, mostly Tudeh and National Front supporters.[7] The police and military quickly crushed the few sporadic demonstrations that did break out. When students threatened to protest Vice President Richard Nixon's visit in December 1953, the security forces stormed Tehran University so violently that three students lost their lives.[8]

Those arrested by the regime faced military tribunals, long prison sentences, and even executions. An obscure decree against "collectivist ideology" enacted in 1931 was resurrected and followed with renewed vigor to crush both the Tudeh and Mossadegh's National Front.[9] Many rank-and-file members of the National Front, a legitimate political movement with no links to the Soviet Union, were imprisoned, albeit mostly for only a few months. Its leaders, however, were incarcerated on five-year sentences, and Hossein Fatemi, Mossadegh's close ally, was executed. Mossadegh himself was publicly tried and sentenced to three years solitary confinement in a military prison and then transferred to house arrest until his death in 1967.

The Tudeh bore the brunt of the repression. Forty of its leading members were executed by firing squad, fourteen tortured to death, and another two hundred sentenced to life imprisonment. Even regular members of the party lost their jobs or were given lengthy prison sentences of several years.[10] By the mid-1950s, the active body of the Tudeh had been forced outside Iran, with only a small and clandestine presence remaining in the country.[11] Tudeh membership, which had been around fifty thousand before the coup, was decimated, and those members who remained in Iran were either imprisoned or driven into hiding.[12] Furthermore, laws such as the Subversive Activities Control Act of 1954 and a new press law in 1956 gave the Ministry of Justice extensive powers to stifle any opposition.[13]

With the Tudeh effectively demolished and the National Front badly crippled, the shah also made efforts to strengthen his alliance with the clerical elite. During the oil nationalization crisis, many influential clerics had entered into a tactical alliance with Mohammad Mossadegh to protest against the imperial policies of the British, the most outspoken of them being Ayatollah Kashani. Although some clerics (including Kashani) had been turned with assistance from the CIA, the shah attempted to ostracize those who remained in opposition while drawing into a close alliance with the more supportive clerics. After the coup, Kashani slowly slipped into political obscurity, but the shah reached out to influential quietists such as Sayyid Hassan Imami, the *imam jum'ah* of Tehran, and Grand Ayatollah Mohammad Hossein Boroujerdi. Between the shah and these clerics there developed a modus vivendi in which the clerics refused to participate in politics in return for the maintenance of the sanctity of Shi'ism.[14] The shah would frequently emphasize his own Islamic faith and made sure his attendance at mosques and holy shrines was well publicized.[15] With the clerics' support, he was free to target more radical Islamists who were arrested with very little protest.[16]

The United States supported and funded the shah's efforts to centralize power and took action to protect his reign from other possible threats. For instance, to prevent tribal elements from taking advantage of the moment of chaos caused by the coup, the CIA station chief in Tehran traveled to the Qashqai region, home to the most powerful of Iran's tribes, to personally dissuade the Qashqai from making any move. In response to their attacks on an army barracks in the south, the United States warned that it would "crush" them if they continued to agitate.[17] The Operation BEDAMN propaganda network was also used to distribute books, articles, and other documents attacking the Tudeh Party and praising the government's crackdown.[18] The goal was to make nationalists and Communists appear anti-Iranian so as to align public sentiment against them. The Tudeh was therefore called a "Trojan horse" for Soviet imperialism and attacked for supporting Stalin's demands for a northern oil concession in 1944–47 as well as for trying to splinter Iran during the Azerbaijan Crisis.[19] The CIA also broke up planned Tudeh demonstrations and gave $1 million in unspent coup funds to the new government to help cover the immediate expenses of the crackdown while the larger amounts of US aid were finalized.[20]

Immediately following the coup, therefore, the United States and the new Iranian government worked in unison to decimate the opposition and stabilize the new regime. American officials repeatedly praised the brutal tactics being deployed in Iran. Even a year after the coup, President Eisenhower praised the shah, on vacation in the United States at the time, for the "resolute attitude" he was taking "vis-à-vis Communists."[21] US aid and coordination were essential; progress reports stated that without US support "the shah and the Zahedi Government would not have been able to maintain internal stability."[22] With US support, the new Iranian government proved extremely effective. A year after the coup, the NSC reported that the Tudeh's "operations have been almost totally obstructed."[23] Iran quickly became a sea of tranquility as the number of major industrial strikes fell sharply from seventy-nine in 1953 to seven in 1954 and then to just three from 1955 to 1957.[24] Its economy was also rebounding thanks to the resumption of oil revenues and US financial aid. At the center of these developments was the shah, a man whom previous US administrations had marginalized in favor of democratic institutions but who was now welcomed to center stage as the best chance for a quick return to stability.

Although an NSC report issued in May 1955 foreshadowed danger should American influence over the shah decline and predicted a return to instability if the United States reduced its support,[25] the immediate situation was stabilized, and so the United States and Great Britain could now turn their attentions to finally settling the long-running oil dispute.

Settling the Oil Dispute

Up to the coup, President Eisenhower's Iran policy was largely a continuation of his predecessor's, and it is likely that had Truman remained in power in 1953, he also would have consented to Mossadegh's forced removal. The real difference between the two administrations came after Mossadegh's ousting. Whereas the Truman administration restricted the shah's influence over day-to-day governance, the Eisenhower administration encouraged his personal assumption of power. At an NSC meeting on September 17, 1953, Allen Dulles said the shah's personal rule was a "favorable and stabilizing change."[26] The following day Ambassador Loy Henderson informed the shah that the United States would support "an undemocratic independent Iran" rather than risk elections that might return nationalist forces to power.[27]

With American support, the shah was finally realizing his dream of personal rule.[28] Although Zahedi was prime minister and had backing from the United States and Great Britain, the shah would undermine and soon dispense with him for someone more pliable.

However, foreign support for the shah depended on his ability to conclude a quick and favorable conclusion to the oil dispute. Eisenhower again continued the Truman administration's policy and presented a settlement very similar to the consortium arrangement devised by Dean Acheson in December 1952. In a twist of fate, just as one relative of a US president helped overthrow Mossadegh, another came forward to conclude the long-running oil crisis. In December 1953, Herbert Hoover Jr. brought all concerned parties together in London—symbolically at AIOC headquarters. Although Iran's act of nationalizing its oil industry was recognized, an international consortium was formed to buy the oil at rates favorable to the West. As recognition for the international effort to remove Mossadegh, what had once been AIOC's monopoly was now shared with American oil companies Esso, Chevron, Texaco, Mobil, and Gulf as well as with two European companies, which together formed the new oil consortium.

For the West, it was paramount that the oil crisis be resolved quickly and that the flow of oil resumed. To increase pressure on the shah, US emergency aid dropped dramatically in the run-up to the talks.[29] The Iranian negotiating team, led by Dr. Ali Amini, a French-educated economist, was forced to concede. Oil nationalization was officially recognized, but de facto control was held by the international consortium, which would sell and manage the oil on the international markets. Iran was also required to pay the AIOC, which became British Petroleum in 1954, the compensation for lost earnings, a concession that Mossadegh had strongly resisted.

Ali Amini later grumbled that the deal was neither what Iran needed nor what it deserved given the intensity of the nationalist movement over the previous four years.[30] Fatollah Naficy, another member of the Iranian delegation during the talks, conceded that it was the best deal Iran could have achieved given the circumstances. "Iran had to choose between the devil and the deep blue sea," he later recalled, "between chaos and humiliation. What happened is they [sic] chose humiliation rather than chaos, leading possibly to communism."[31] The British meanwhile heralded the agreement, and

Sir William Fraser, chairman of the AIOC since 1941, was praised for his conduct and persistence in securing a favorable settlement.[32] In recognition, he was awarded the grandiose title "First Baron Strathalmond of Pumpherstone," although a fellow oil magnate quipped a more appropriate title would have been "Lord Crude of Abadan."[33]

The Americans were also satisfied with the outcome. Not only had their adventurous policy prevented the loss of the country and its oil, but six American oil companies also now shared what had once been a lucrative British concession. With such a US financial interest in the country, the days of being able to pursue an unselfish foreign policy were well and truly over. Moreover, with the oil crisis ended, Iran could once again be stabilized with the help of US aid and Iranian oil revenue. As oil flowed to the West, dollars flowed just as quickly to Tehran. Oil returns increased rapidly from $10 million in 1954 to $91 million the following year and then to $285 million by 1960, and US aid reached $400 million by 1956.[34] That such amounts were necessary to stabilize Iran illustrates the dire straits to which it had been pushed during the oil crisis. Nevertheless, with the Iranian government now dependent on external rather than internal support, American diplomatic and financial pressure had ensured both a quick resolution to the oil dispute and a greater focus on restoring internal stability.

Iran's International Importance

US action in Iran became a source of pride in Washington. A country on the border of the Soviet Union and on the brink of collapse had been rescued and turned into a dependable international ally. The Eisenhower administration had little interest in promoting political development of the shah's regime but very much desired Iranian support in the containment of communism and the maintenance of regional security. Iran's role became even more important as the dispute between Britain and Egypt threatened to destabilize the region. The British Empire was in retreat following World War II, having consented to Indian independence and withdrawn from its role in Asia and parts of Europe.

Britain had controlled the Suez Canal since 1875 and saw it as a vital link for trade between Europe and the Middle East and Asia. Without free access through the canal, British merchant ships would be forced to sail around the Horn of Africa, an additional journey of 5,500 miles. It was therefore a lifeline for the fading British Empire and, with seventy thousand troops housed there, not something the British government would willingly surrender. However, a surge of nationalism in Egypt and the British role in the creation of Israel soured relations between the British and their hosts in the Suez. Just as the Iranians unilaterally overturned the British oil concession, in October 1951 the Egyptians cancelled the agreement that had granted Britain a lease over the Suez base. Also as in Iran, Britain refused both to recognize the revocation and to leave.

The crisis over the Suez concerned the Americans, who hoped to stabilize the region to prevent any Communist advance. The success of the operation in Iran therefore offered the administration some badly needed support. Almost as soon as the shah was reinstalled to power, talks began over Iran's role in US strategic defense plans. The first step came in late 1954 when the shah announced an end to his country's neutrality in the Cold War and declared Iran to be an open and active ally of the West.[35] Whereas Truman had favored a general containment policy, Eisenhower incorporated a series of collective-security agreements that functioned independently but under the auspices of the United States. With Iran stabilized and hostilities in Korea ended by an armistice along the thirty-ninth parallel in July 1953, Eisenhower was free to move forward with his vision.

That vision became known as the "New Look" and involved maintaining Truman's perimeter-defense containment strategy, but rather than the United States providing security, US allies would be responsible for conventional containment through a series of regional alliances operating under the principle that an attack on one would be an attack on all. Underwriting these alliances would be the US nuclear arsenal. A united umbrella would therefore encircle the Soviet Union, and any aggression would be met by overwhelming force in ways that would be less of a drain on US resources.

The Eisenhower administration felt that sharing the cost of containment—a policy referred to derisively as "brinksmanship" or "pactomania"—would be a more efficient way to protect US interests while avoiding a repeat of the situation in Korea. A regional version of the North Atlantic Treaty Organization was deemed particularly important for the protection of US interests in the Middle East. According to one diplomat stationed in the region, "there was really a definite fear of hostilities, of an active Russian occupation of the Middle East physically, and you could practically hear the Russian boots clumping down over the hot desert sands."[36] To defend the region, Washington envisioned a Middle East Defense Organization centered around Egypt, a country US officials called "the key" to regional security.[37]

But Egypt remained in dispute with US ally Great Britain. To coax Egypt into a strategic treaty, the Eisenhower administration attempted to mediate this dispute and offered economic aid if Egypt accepted membership in the Middle East Defense Organization.[38] Rising Arab nationalism, differences over Israel, and continuing tension with the British meant that an agreement could not be reached, and Eisenhower and Dulles were forced to anchor their strategic vision elsewhere.

The substitute was a defense perimeter based on a northern tier of states, which began with an alliance between Turkey and Pakistan in April 1954. With American prodding, Iraq and Britain also joined the alliance, which left just Iran as the final key piece. A memorandum by the Joint Chiefs of Staff Intelligence Committee in April 1955 explained Iran's importance to the security treaty:

> From the viewpoint of attaining US military objectives in the Middle East, the natural defensive barrier provided by the Zagros Mountains must be retained under Allied control indefinitely. Because Western Iran includes the Zagros Mountain buffer, geographically, Iran is the most important country in the Middle East,

excluding Turkey. Iranian participation in a regional defense organization would permit the member countries to take full advantage collectively of the natural barrier in Western Iran and would permit utilization of logistical facilities of the area. The relative importance of Iran in relation to other countries of the Middle East would be significantly increased if she [sic] became a partner in a regional defense organization which included Turkey, Iraq, and Pakistan.[39]

The shah was not thrilled with the Americans' plan, preferring instead that Iran be the regional powerhouse. The end of Iran's position of neutrality was also unpopular, having been a source of pride during the Mossadegh years. But American leverage proved too strong. According to the US embassy, the shah, after strong words from Washington, "allowed his last hesitation to be swept away," and Iran joined what became known as the Baghdad Pact on October 11, 1955.[40] President Eisenhower praised the pact as "a constructive step toward the broadening of the base of the collective strength of the free world," whereas the Soviet Union bitterly attacked "the forming of military blocs" that directly affected its security.[41]

This was the extent of the Eisenhower's plan for Iran: internal stability to allow for its effective membership in what was seen as an essential regional security pact. When visiting Iran in the fall of 1955, members of a congressional delegation were concerned by the denial of democracy and strong popular opposition to the shah's end to the policy of neutrality. The delegation reported that the shah had "staked his own life as well as that of his country in making this choice."[42] Sensing that continued unpopular activities might lead to the return of popular protests, the Eisenhower administration looked not to mollify the people's concerns but to increase the efficacy of the shah's repressive system. Military aid was increased, and plans were begun to form an Iranian security and intelligence agency to monitor potential opposition. Since the coup, the CIA had trained and advised the shah on internal intelligence and in 1955 installed a permanent group of officers to increase the production of Iranian intelligence officers.[43] A bill was put to the Majles in December 1956 that eventually codified this group as the Sazeman-e Ettela'at va Amni-yat-e Keshvar (SAVAK, Organization of Intelligence and National Security). In the shah's hands, SAVAK became a brutal tool to monitor and crush indigenous opposition and strengthen his rule for the next three decades. American specialists trained virtually the entire first generation of recruits, who effectively and mercilessly restricted all forms of internal opposition.[44] A decade after the United States had supported the growth of Iranian civil society, it was now helping to dismantle and undermine all forms of popular association that opposed the shah.

A Royal Dictatorship with American Consent

With American support and assistance finally achieved, the shah was determined to prove himself an effective leader. He was undoubtedly a shrewd political operator, as he had shown in 1947 when he efficiently dispatched Ahmad Qavam, but he still had to prove himself capable of ruling his country. So long as stability was maintained, the Eisenhower administration made clear that the shah could rule as he wished. This meant undermining all the democratic gains made in the previous decade. The elections of 1954 were heavily rigged through the use of the same violent street mobs that had helped overthrow Mossadegh the previous year.[45] Shaban "the Brainless" Jafari, a 250-pound former athlete, was most effective in his efforts to ensure people voted the correct way. As reward for his action in leading the street battles for the royalists during the coup, the shah had given him a bright-yellow Cadillac convertible, which became a frequent sight on the streets of Tehran. On election day in 1954, he cruised the streets in his Cadillac, searching for suspected antigovernment voters standing in lines at polling stations. He attacked with fists or knives those he found until they were unable or unwilling to cast their votes.[46] Another vote-rigging technique involved confiscating Mossadegh supporters' identity cards and giving them, along with completed ballots, to voters who were specially bussed to the polls in overflowing vehicles.

Even if genuine Mossadegh supporters did manage to vote, their votes were unlikely to make any difference given the regime's control of the counting procedure. One such lucky voter was later seen bowing in reverence to the ballot box shortly after casting his vote. When asked why, he replied, "I am merely making my obeisance to the magic box. When one drops a ballot in for [Mossadegh], lo, when the box is opened it is transformed into a vote for [Prime Minister Zahedi]."[47] Conduct during the elections two years later was even worse. Disillusioned with the decay of democracy, turnout plummeted to only ten to fifteen thousand people in Tehran, a city of more than a million people. Despite "organized multiple voting by government employees and simple ballot box stuffing," the total ballots still only reached less than ninety thousand.[48] The same pattern was repeated in the provinces and resulted in a very servile parliamentary cohort that effectively had been chosen by the shah and his advisers. One deputy complained to the US embassy that his new colleagues were "no better than [the shah's] personal servants" and that if "any of these men cease to be loyal servants and bootlickers, they will leave the Government."[49] During the early 1950s, the Majles had become an effective check on the shah's powers, but by the mid-1950s the shah was able to dictate and force through his policies with little objection.[50] In conversation with the British ambassador, the shah dismissively referred to the once influential Majles as a "relatively insignificant body" that he could easily "deal with."[51]

With the opposition and the Majles brought to heel, the shah next worked to replace Prime Minister Zahedi. Britain and the United States had favored Zahedi for being able to rally the army during the coup and saw him as essential to successfully concluding the oil dispute.[52] The shah had always been wary of potential challengers to his authority, and he instead viewed with suspicion and jealousy those figures such as Zahedi who garnered substantial international as well as internal support. According to the shah's wife, the shah "was afraid of General Zahedi's huge popularity. What if one day he tried to topple him from the Iranian throne to have himself proclaimed the Shah of Shah, the sort of thing Nasser had done with Farouk of Egypt? Persecution mania."[53] With the oil dispute now settled, the shah felt confident that Zahedi's international backers would not prevent his dismissal, and so he appointed the elderly Hossein 'Ala prime minister, a man widely seen as no more than an extension of the shah himself.[54] The British embassy reported that 'Ala was "the almost perfect" tool through which the shah could take "a direct and major part in governing the country."[55] Ageing rapidly, 'Ala had to leave Iran for medical treatment in Europe immediately after his appointment, and on his return he was able to work only one or two hours a day.[56] The once powerful position of prime minister had been reduced to that of "the shah's executive assistant."[57]

An NSC progress report in May 1955 found that "more than ever the stability of Iran depends on [the shah]."[58] In the years immediately following the coup, the shah centralized power, bolstered the military, and packed the cabinet and Majles with his own supporters.[59] With political institutions under his control and the once vibrant popular opposition successfully broken up, the shah ruled supreme. In March 1956, US ambassador Selden Chapin reported that "not since the time of Reza Shah has it been evident to most Iranians that government policy was being made and administered under the personal direction of the monarch."[60] The shah reveled in his new position, calling himself "the fountainhead of all authority" in Iran.[61]

The Americans could not be more pleased with Iran's progression since the coup. The country team at the US embassy happily reported that the shah was now the "chief bulwark of internal security" and gushed that since his crackdown on the opposition he now had the "confidence of the people and the loyalty of the Army."[62] To show their appreciation for his stable rule and cooperation on the international scene, the Americans sent an additional $160 million in financial aid to Iran in 1955–56, finally meeting the shah's expectations of financial aid since the Iran Declaration in 1943.[63] Most illustrative of all, however, was the sharp increase in military aid. The United States provided more than $130 million in direct military aid between 1953 and 1957 as well as $224 million over the next four years.[64] So long as stability was maintained and Iran remained an effective international ally, this cornucopia would continue to overflow. But repression alone would not quiet the popular desire for reform. Public unrest would soon return, and a new approach would have to be adopted. American linkage and leverage would again be tested.

The Return to Democratization

By 1956, Iran was an unrivaled success story for US intervention. Its oil had been saved; massive popular insurrection had been avoided; its economy had been rescued from the brink; and it had become a valuable and effective strategic ally. In December that year, the *New York Times* declared Iran to be the "the calmest country in the troubled Middle East today."[65] Like later statements on Iran's relative tranquility, however, this assessment was inaccurate. Closer inspection showed increasing unrest that threatened to plunge Iran back into instability. Although authoritarian regimes can be successful for a period of time in ensuring stability through repressive control, their reliance on rigid ideologies or illegitimate systems of government ensures that discontent eventually returns. This is the great irony of historical US support for dictatorship during the Cold War: supporting authoritarianism as a means to secure stability ultimately resulted in the very instability the United States was trying to avoid. Iran was quickly becoming proof of this pattern.

Although US support and aid to the shah was designed to bolster his position, it formed in the minds of many Iranians the view that the shah was merely a puppet of the West rather than a legitimate leader. The full consequences of this view would not be felt for another twenty years, but the shah's repressive rule and restriction of popular participation soon began to threaten stability, the one thing the Americans demanded. Senior administration officials, however, did not predict trouble in Iran, despite having discussed similar patterns in other countries as early as February 1955. During an NSC meeting that month on the issue of combating communism in Latin America, for instance, the president argued that although dictators might effectively deter communism in the short run, long-term US policy must be to encourage the growth of democracy because it offered the best means through which to ultimately defeat the enemy.[66]

Rising unrest would slowly force Washington to reconsider its policy in Iran. A report by the Interdepartmental Committee on Certain US Aid Programs in July 1956 concluded that even with large injections of US money over the previous three years, "Iran has been unable to cope with a chronic and increasing budgetary deficit." Furthermore, it predicted Iran would likely run an annual deficit of roughly $70 million through fiscal year 1960.[67] Resentment and a feeling of helplessness spread across the Iranian population as the situation deteriorated. Civil disturbances broke out when the price of sugar and tobacco increased and inflation rose precipitously. The shah's lack of action on this problem demonstrated once again that he was not an effective leader. A British report concluded that "Persia is drifting" amid the shah's inability to govern and his refusal to "let anyone else do it." He was, the report concluded, "a dictator who cannot dictate."[68]

US reports generally agreed with the British assessment. The Operations Coordinating Board (OCB), tasked with formulating NSC reports, saw rising public tension in Iran as the result not only of economic problems but also of the mounting "opposition to the shah's dictatorial powers."[69] By centralizing power in Iran, the shah ensured that all dissatisfaction focused on him. As these problems began to mount, his position became ever more insecure. He still had very little popular support and no political backing outside of the royal court. Even the armed forces, upon which he had built his regime since 1941, remained fragile, with 20 percent of its personnel reporting dissatisfaction, according to an NSC report.[70] Such news unnerved US policy makers. In March 1956, Ambassador Chapin asked of Washington the key question: "Should the United States rely entirely on the shah's government, if danger signs are already appearing that it might not last?"[71]

The Eisenhower administration had reached a crossroads in Iran: despite early promise and hundreds of millions of dollars in aid, the shah had failed, despite appearances to the contrary, to provide the required stability owing to a lack of internal support and ability to govern. Perhaps the United States should find someone with more ability. One option was to support a government with popular support and move the country back toward democracy as a means of pacifying internal demands. The time, money, and effort taken to remove the most recent populist leader, however, made this option most unattractive. As Mossadegh had shown them, popular leaders could be unstable and capricious to the people's changing demands, could fall victim to demagoguery, and, given the anti-Western sentiment in Iran, would inevitably threaten Iran's membership in the Baghdad Pact and continued westward orientation. Moreover, a powerful and popularly supported leader would limit the effectiveness of external leverage.

Therefore, instead of promoting a more popular government, the Eisenhower administration decided to double down on the shah and attempt to mold him into a more representative authoritarian leader. The US embassy in Tehran was instructed to take measures to "popularize the shah as a living symbol of patriotism and progress" in order to increase his support among Iranians, who were becoming increasingly resentful of his autocratic rule.[72] Furthermore, the NSC agreed to take a greater role in Iran's internal system and embarked on a more rigorous policy of exercising influence and indirect pressure on the shah to encourage more rational leadership. This policy would include developing populist policies to appeal to the Iranian population and persuading the shah to withdraw from certain areas of governance to prevent him from being the sole focus of popular discontent.[73]

The Americans identified land reform as key to improving the shah's base of support and to reaching out to Iran's sizable rural population. The shah had previously attempted to institute land reform, most notably its redistribution in 1954, but the strong reaction from the powerful landlords had forced him to back down.[74] However, the Eisenhower administration felt it essential that Iran, in the words of one member of the US Operating Mission, be "put through the industrial reform wringer."[75] Thus, a second Seven-Year Plan (1956–62) was adopted, supported by the United States and a $920 million budget, and tasked with rejuvenating Iran's economy in such a way that Iranian citizens would directly benefit and more greatly appreciate the shah's regime.[76]

By late 1956, therefore, the Eisenhower administration began to play a more active role in Iran's internal situation while also prodding the shah to limit his personal role in government—a return to Truman's prenationalization crisis policy. With favorable degrees of linkage and leverage, the Americans began to reapply pressure on the shah to give more space for free expression. As well as utilizing leverage from US financial assistance programs and linkage from American officials' close contacts with Iranian officials, Eisenhower also resorted to covert pressure to ensure the shah made the right moves. One such operation involved a CIA officer planting stories in Iranian newspapers that promoted US-favored reforms. That same officer also introduced *New York Times* reporter Sam Pope Brewer to opposition groups such as the NRM and the National Front, encouraging him to write articles about them and the growing unrest in Iran.[77] These articles were duly printed and claimed that unrest had become so extensive that it was now "dangerous to [Iran's] internal security and to the stability of the Middle East."[78] The CIA made sure the shah knew it was behind Brewer's articles and, by showing him that it was conscious of growing opposition, hoped he would take corrective action.[79]

The shah took the hint and in early 1957 began political reforms to satisfy the Americans, but doing so only in a way that would not threaten his grip on power. It had taken more than ten years for him to finally gain personal control of Iran, and he was not willing to relinquish that position. The shah's reforms were therefore designed to give a sense of liberalization without threatening his power. For example, he introduced an official political party system, proudly announcing that Iran was now ready "to enjoy the blessings of a democratic system of government."[80] Most other democratic countries had a two-party system, so he felt Iran should follow suit. One party would be conservative, the other "radical"; toward both, he assured his skeptical audience, he would remain neutral. Next, the shah announced the termination of martial law, which had lasted since World War II and had been used repeatedly to clamp down on opposition activities. As a result, Ambassador Chapin reported to the State Department in April 1957 that many groups in Iran were stirring back into action to test the waters.[81] The shah also announced his intention to permit a limited amount of press freedom, which had remained under severe restriction since the coup. Shuttered publications reopened, and Chapin again reported that almost immediately articles appeared in newspapers that "no editor would have dared to run two months ago."[82] A test of the shah's more relaxed position vis-à-vis opposition groups came early that summer. A small nationalist group known as the Toiler's Party celebrated its seventh anniversary with an audacious open meeting in Tehran. The meeting was allowed to go ahead and passed without disturbance, thus proving that the era of repression was coming to an end.[83] Thanks to pressure from the Americans, liberalization was again returning to Iran as the shah was forced to comply with their demands in order to maintain US aid and support for his regime.

Three months after the shah announced the new party system, the two official parties became a reality. The first, Mardom (People's Party), was established on a platform of agricultural improvement, land redistribution, increased aid to farmers, and women's rights. The second, Melliun (Nationalist Party), was designed to appeal to conservatives, landlords, and some of the leading Muslim clerics. Although the shah would closely monitor both parties, the US embassy reported that if he "plays his cards carefully and forces himself to disengage gradually from the day-to-day business of government, he might, over a period of years, be able to build up something resembling a real two-party system in Iran."[84] A busy summer in Iran's democratic history concluded with the establishment of a third party called the Anjoman-e Azadi (Freedom Society), which, surprisingly, was permitted to form independently.[85] Made up of energetic leftists and members hostile to the shah, it was reluctantly given permission to form despite being seen as merely a vehicle to propel the Iranian politician and diplomat Ali Amini to the premiership. In return for this permission, although the Freedom Society campaigned for political and socioeconomic reforms, it was careful not to offend the shah or his leadership. Because Amini and the party's leader, Hassan Arsanjani, had once been close allies of Ahmad Qavam, a politician whom the shah had long disliked, the suspicious shah ordered three loyal Majles members to join the party and keep him briefed on its developments and goals.[86] Although the shah had been pressed to open up the political system, he was determined not to allow another Qavam or Mossadegh.

Thus, the two-plus-one party system was created. Although far from a democracy, its emergence, combined with a reduction in the shah's oppressive internal policies, raised expectations that a more competitive political system might soon be allowed to develop. The US decision to reapply pressure for reform had an immediate impact and created political space, which was quickly filled by Iran's indomitable democratic forces. It demonstrated the power of American leverage as well as the continued strength, patience, and desire of Iran's indigenous democratic movement. After almost five years of heavy repression, hopes for democracy were raised once more. The shah, however, had other ideas.

Dropping Like Kings

Two events occurred in 1958 that hardened the Americans' resolve to push the shah toward greater liberalization. The first happened in Iran, the second outside it. The internal event centered on the commander of the Iranian army's intelligence staff, General Valiollah Qarani. Although the Americans supported and protected the shah as the best means to ensure their goals, this did not prevent them from sounding out potential alternative leaders, especially because the shah was failing to maintain stability. As early as the mid-1950s, prominent Iranians had been in contact with US officials to share their ideas on alternatives to the shah. Supreme Court justice

William O. Douglas also repeatedly tried to interest the administration in supporting his friends, the Qashqai tribe, and introduced its leaders to US officials on numerous occasions.[87] Similarly, members of the US embassy kept in contact with opposition groups such as the NRM to hear their views on how best to reform the country.[88]

Therefore, it was not unusual that General Qarani had meetings with high-level US officials. What was surprising, however, was that Qarani met with them to speak about the possibility of a coup to replace the shah. Even more shocking was that the officials chose not to inform the shah of these intrigues against him. Qarani had face-to-face meetings with Foreign Service officer John W. Bowling; Fraser Wilkins, the embassy's second-highest-ranking member; and even Assistant Secretary of State William Rountree.[89] John Foster Dulles was also in Iran at this time, although it is not clear whether he met personally with Qarani or any of his supporters. Rountree, however, also traveled to Athens and met with another of Qarani's associates, Esfandiar Bozorgmehr, who complained of the lack of freedom in Iran and warned that public opinion had swung heavily away from the shah.[90] In these meetings, Qarani and his co-conspirators argued that just as the United States had returned the shah to power in 1953, it could force him to withdraw from an active political role and cede power to a reform-minded government, potentially led by Ali Amini, now serving as ambassador to the United States. If the shah resisted, the plotters planned either to force his abdication or to remove him.[91]

The Americans' refusal to inform the shah of such a plot has been called a "startling omission," considering their close relations.[92] It hints at the administration's increased displeasure at the shah's inability to maintain stability in Iran and its willingness to remove him should a viable alternative present itself. Qarani's plot was also a manifestation of the increased dissatisfaction within the Iranian army. When SAVAK discovered the plot in early 1958 and reported it to the shah, he angrily demanded the Americans explain themselves. After Qarani's arrest, the shah met with Ambassador Chapin and "with a great show of indignation" excoriated the Americans for having kept the plot secret from him.[93] The ambassador informed the shah that the United States kept in contact with all kinds of opposition but claimed not to know that officials were being "exposed to hearing non-constitutional means of opposition."[94] Hardly comforting words for an insecure monarch whose position depended on US support. Rather, this response was a clear warning that the United States would not back the shah indefinitely and that he must pay greater attention to fulfilling US demands for stability through reform.

The Qarani affair again highlighted the growing dissatisfaction with the shah's reign among members of the military, which greatly worried the Americans. It also shows that the shah's relationship with the Eisenhower administration was more ambiguous than commonly thought.[95] Indeed, the OCB had agreed as early as August 1956 to make contingency plans should the shah be removed from office.[96] The shah's response to the Qarani affair was to double down on surveillance activities; he instructed SAVAK to be more vigilant in monitoring the spread of oppositional ideologies within the military and to more actively break up political cliques.[97] As for the Americans, not seeing any viable alternative to the shah, they increased their determination to pressure him to make essential reforms to ameliorate the opposition.

The second shock of 1958 came in neighboring Iraq and foreshadowed what the Americans feared in Iran. On July 14, King Faisal II and his prime minister, Nuri al-Said, were toppled in a coup by leading military officers. Iraq was a founding member of the eponymous Baghdad Pact, the US collective-security arrangement for the Middle East.[98] The ousted regime had supported Western powers during the Suez Crisis two years earlier and had been a vital ally in fighting the spread of communism in the Middle East. So its sudden loss amid joyous scenes on the streets of Baghdad blindsided Washington, and the *New York Times* called the coup "a stunning blow to the Western democracies" in general.[99] The new regime quickly formed close ties to Moscow, accepted Soviet aid, and brought Communists into the government, forcing CIA director Allen Dulles to note that "Iraq is now the most dangerous spot on earth."[100] The United States had been given a taste of what to expect in Iran unless vital reforms were carried out quickly. One month after the Iraq coup, newly appointed ambassador to Iran Edward T. Wailes reported that the contagion effects were already spreading to Iran:

> Mosadeq-type [sic] individuals and small opposition groups in Tehran are markedly more confident and ubiquitous than before the coup. It is not uncommon to hear casual mention [of the] possible assassination [of the] shah among otherwise sober middle-class civilians. . . . There can be no doubt that criticism of [the] regime and preliminary discussions of ways and means of action against it are spreading among [the] officer corps. . . . [The] shah was apparently depressed and somewhat frightened on his return to Tehran [a] few days after the Baghdad coup.[101]

King Farouk of Egypt said shortly before his own ousting in 1952 that "soon there will be only five Kings left—the King of England, the King of Spades, the King of Clubs, the King of Hearts, and the King of Diamonds."[102] The removal of another close friend, King Faisal II, was not only a reminder to the shah of this prediction but also a grave warning to the Americans. Allen Dulles fully appreciated the coming expiration of the time of kings and informed the NSC in mid-August 1958 that without drastic reform the shah's "days will be numbered."[103] It was clear that a new, more forcefully interventionist policy had to be adopted to overt another similar disaster.

A More Determined US Policy

The Americans' anxiety was not confined to Iran; by the late 1950s, the Soviet Union appeared on the ascendency and had increased its influence within developing countries. After concluding a large technical assistance program with India, Nikita Khrushchev taunted the Americans: "Perhaps you wish to compete with us in establishing friendship with Indians? Let us compete."[104] A series of high-profile congressional hearings were held to address the issue of apparent

Soviet supremacy and the efficacy of Eisenhower's New Look policy. Six separate administration and congressional studies advocated a refocus of the US financial aid program toward longer-term planning rather than short-term security concerns. Former president Harry Truman summed up the new belief before a conference on development assistance: "The only thing we can do with [military aid] is to buy time. . . . One of our best hopes [to obtain peace] is economic assistance for other nations."[105]

This change to more long-term strategic thinking came at the same time as major changes within the administration itself. The old coup conspirators were moving out: Walter Bedell Smith resigned in 1954, and health problems forced John Foster Dulles to spend a great deal of time away from his desk. Eisenhower was therefore leaning more heavily on subordinates, such as Undersecretary Herbert Hoover Jr. and Deputy Undersecretary Robert Murphy, who focused on addressing congressional concerns and questioned the policy of support for dictators rather than reform for long-term stability. In Latin America, for instance, the administration worried about the sustainability of Cuban dictator Fulgencio Batista and even considered covert action to displace Dominican dictator Rafael Trujillo.[106]

The shah's rule in Iran therefore came under fresh scrutiny following the twin shocks of 1958.[107] The question was specifically addressed at an NSC meeting on August 15, 1958, five years to the day after the beginning of the coup that returned the shah to power. Gentle pressure had coaxed him to permit limited liberalization but had failed to quell the unrest. CIA director Allen Dulles felt the situation warranted even greater "pressure on the shah to carry out some of the most needed reforms, especially in land tenure and taxation."[108] The OCB agreed, favoring the use of "military and economic aid as levers" to force him to adopt urgent reforms.[109] For disaster to be avoided, it was agreed that a greater use of the US position of leverage was urgently required.

Setting conditions of reform on aid was immediately adopted as policy, and by early October 1958 the OCB was able to report that "US economic programs have had some small success in laying the groundwork for financial and administrative reforms."[110] However, it was feared that these reforms would be too little too late: US intelligence reports stated that Iran was "increasingly endangered."[111] An NSC study in November found that

> current dissatisfaction is based in part on awakening popular expectations for reform of Iran's archaic social, economic and political structure and a concomitant disillusionment with the shah's limited efforts to date to move in this direction with resolution and speed. . . . While this dissatisfaction has not yet coalesced into a vigorous, coherent opposition to the shah's regime, it is increasingly close to the surface and could lead to violence or attempted coups.[112]

Despite this high degree of dissatisfaction, the shah continued to drag his heels on reform, refusing to accept the Americans' fears that his regime was in danger. The NSC report questioned his willingness to "take sufficiently dramatic and effective steps to insure [sic] his position and syphon off the growing discontent" and argued that the United States had to modify the shah's "present dictatorial role to allow some scope for the expression of opposition sentiment."[113] A newly declassified briefing note from November 1958 contended that unless "meaningful steps towards reform" were taken, "the regime is in danger of an early overthrow."[114] Immediately following the coup, the shah's goals had aligned with American interests, but now they were drifting apart. This separation would test the ability of the United States to control the shah's actions.

The Failure of Exogenous Pressure

Officials in the Eisenhower administration agreed that more had to be done in Iran to avert danger, but they split on how best to convince the shah to take action. It was clear he did not share their fears, and so they knew pressure had to be applied, but many were concerned that too much pressure might push him away from an alliance with the West. Now that the Soviet Union was making a play to capture support among the world's developing countries, the United States had to be careful not to anger its important ally, the shah. If the United States began to place firm conditions on financial aid to force him to take action against his will, but Moscow offered unconditional support, he might not be an American ally for long. As Undersecretary of State Christian Herter cautioned, if "[we] really put the heat on him, he might very well tell us to go to hell and proceed to play ball with the other side."[115]

But failure to press the shah to act on reform would also lead to disaster. The CIA reported at the time that without drastic action the shah would be overthrown "within a year or so."[116] Eisenhower was therefore faced with the choice of either doing nothing and potentially losing Iran to revolution or doing something and possibly losing Iran to the Soviets. Neither option held much appeal, so US officials settled on a middle path: gentle but persistent pressure. A subsequent policy statement called for American officials to, "where appropriate, press the shah to initiate prompt, meaningful political, social and economic reforms designed to increase popular support for his regime."[117] The shah had so far been receptive to some measure of reform, and the administration hoped his receptivity would continue. Priority was given to three areas: the gradual elimination of corruption, social and economic reforms, and modification of the shah's present dictatorial role to allow scope for the expression of opposition sentiment. So as not to anger him, US diplomats were instructed to avoid ultimatums or threats to withhold aid. In other words, although the United States was in a strong position to promote change in Iran, the rise of the Soviet Union on the world stage meant it had to tread lightly.

The problem with this approach, however, is that gentle persuasion often does not lead to dramatic and responsive action. Nevertheless, the US ambassador was instructed to make only delicate "suggestions for reforms and encourage [the shah] in his efforts to achieve them."[118] After a long meeting with new ambassador Edward T. Wailes, the shah initially responded positively to this approach.

The essential issue of tackling corruption was addressed by the passing of the Whence Your Fortune Law, which investigated the income of high-ranking military officers and the political elite. By 1960, the government was able to announce that it had "fired, suspended, jailed, or brought before the court 4,272 officials" on corruption charges.[119] The shah, to prove he was committed to reform, ordered his officials to "serve" the heads of three officials guilty of corruption "on a platter" each month.[120] In late 1958, after Wailes suggested the shah conduct a series of "fireside chats" to improve his connection to the people, the shah introduced Iran's first ever press conference.[121]

However, budget constraints meant that increased pressure on the shah did not come with a concomitant increase in aid. This frustrated the shah greatly, and with the Soviet Union offering lucrative inducements, he soon became disgruntled. The bipolar nature of the international environment undercut the effectiveness of American leverage. By January 1959, Secretary of State Dulles remarked that he was "increasingly disturbed . . . [by the] shah's current attitude towards relations with the US" and feared a potential alliance between Iran and the Soviet Union.[122] As if to drive the point home, the shah soon entertained a Soviet delegation headed by Deputy Foreign Minister Vladimir Semyonov to discuss terms of a potential Soviet–Iranian nonaggression pact. Sir Roger Stevens, who served as British ambassador to Iran until November 1958, commented that the shah's goal was not neutrality but "a fat cheque from the Americans."[123]

In playing the United States off against the Soviet Union, the shah was now utilizing leverage of his own. He did not share Washington's fears of revolution and knew that the Americans would not push him hard for fear of losing him to the Soviet Union. Confident that he could deflect gentle pressure, he made only cosmetic reforms at this time rather than provide solutions to popular dissatisfaction. By April 1959, US officials reported that "few tangible results" had followed the shah's professed return to reform, and the programs he had announced with much fanfare were "little more than an excess of propaganda."[124] They derided the much heralded

Whence Your Fortune Law," for instance, for punishing only "small fry" rather than the serial and influential offenders who had close ties to the royal family.[125] An attempt to kick-start the land-reform program also failed as large land owners successfully watered down any reform-minded legislation, and the shah was not prepared to confront them.[126]

The clearest illustration of the shah's lack of interest in reform was the follow-up to his formation of official political parties. Although the parties were seen as an important release valve for popular discontent, the shah refused to allow them any semblance of independence. The British ambassador reported on a conversation he had with the shah in which the Iranian leader gloated that his "party arrangement is a mockery and that he has no intention of permitting any breath of fresh air of reality to enter into it. All he wants is two parties engaged in a shadow battle, both dependent on himself, both indeed taking their orders from him, neither representing any real principle or policy."[127] But as the shah continued discussions with the Soviets regarding a nonaggression agreement, the Americans were in no position to complain about the lack of action.

The shah was again proving himself a shrewd political operator. He understood the weakened US position and the opportunity he had to limit the Americans' interference. John Foster Dulles saw the situation for what it was and knew that the shah's outreach to the Soviets was merely "blackmail tactics" to undermine US pressure for reform and to secure greater financial aid from the United States.[128] Eisenhower agreed. Not wishing to risk losing Iran, the administration scaled back its attempts to push for reform and began the process of increasing aid to Iran in order to preserve its alliance with the West.[129] The United States was over a barrel in its relations with Iran, and the shah knew it. In March, he signed a generous new defense pact with the United States that gave Iran a military commitment comparable to ones given to Turkey and Pakistan. As was said at the time, "No longer would America treat Turkey as a wife and Iran as a concubine" when it came to military aid, the shah's top priority.[130]

Whereas the shah no doubt celebrated his ability to control the United States, the Soviets were angered at what they called his "two-faced insincere policy."[131] In retaliation, they launched a massive propaganda campaign aimed at fomenting even greater unrest and anger at the shah's rule.[132] Soviet broadcasts soon became required listening among Iranians already angry at the shah's authoritarian leadership. Of Soviet propaganda, the British ambassador reported back to London that Iranians "listen avidly to the strident repetition of criticisms which they have been muttering amongst themselves" and believe it to be "the truth boldly spoken."[133] Nikita Khrushchev himself spoke of his anger at the shah, warning that the shah would soon suffer the same fate as the Iraqi royal family and that "neither the Baghdad Pact nor the Dulles–Eisenhower doctrine could help."[134]

Although pleased that the shah remained on their side, the Americans despaired that his already precarious grip on power was now exacerbated by Soviet propaganda. A National Intelligence Estimate in March 1959 predicted that the likelihood of the shah's remaining in power over the next two years was "little more than fifty–fifty."[135] From its zenith of being able to control Iran following the coup just a few years earlier, US policy in Iran now approached its nadir. Instead of dictating to the shah, the Americans were forced to concede to his demands out of their fear of a resurgent Soviet Union and could do little to prevent growing insurrection in Iran. A rising Soviet Union greatly affected US leverage, and the shah was able to continue his authoritarian rule with greater aid than before and little pressure to undertake reforms.

Chaos in Iran

Chaos spread in Iran, and the Eisenhower administration, unable to affect the shah, floated the idea of alternatives to his personal leadership. One name that repeatedly cropped up in government dispatches and memos was Ali Amini, a former finance minister and recently ambassador to the United States. He had first drawn the Americans' attention in May 1953 when he asked the US embassy to support his claim to replace Mossadegh as prime minister. At the time, Ambassador Henderson cautioned Washington that Amini was someone who had "not yet proved his trustworthiness" and, presumably without irony, replied to Amini that the United States could not help him attain office as it "does not intervene in Iranian internal affairs."[136] From that point on, Amini looked to prove himself to the Americans.

Amini's stock rose precipitously after he led the Iranian delegation that finalized the oil consortium agreement in 1954. So pleased were the Americans that they reportedly told Prime Minister Zahedi that in return for US monetary assistance he "must include Amini in the government."[137] A few years later, while living in Washington as ambassador to the United States, Amini further ingratiated himself with administration officials and other influential American figures. It was at this time in 1958 that he became implicated in the Qarani plot to depose the shah, which included installing him as prime minister. Although the United States favored Amini's premiership, the shah was enraged by it and ordered him to resign his position as ambassador.

Once Amini was back in Iran, he maintained close links with the Americans and by February 1959 had sufficiently charmed John Bowling, chief political officer at the embassy, who reported that Amini was someone both "engaging and intelligent . . . [who] seemed tolerant and broad minded . . . [and] should be heard from in the future."[138] In July, Amini publicly announced his intention to seek the position of prime minister and openly courted American support. In an interview with one American reporter, he declared he would "certainly . . . take the necessary steps for bringing reforms in the country."[139] The US embassy sent its endorsement of Amini to the State Department and praised him as a "strong, energetic and independent type leader."[140] If the administration were serious about looking for alternatives to the shah's personal leadership, Ali Amini was quickly becoming the outstanding candidate.

However, the weak position of US leverage meant that the Americans were unwilling and unable to force the shah to appoint as prime minister someone who was independent of his control and, perhaps just as important, someone he already disliked. The US position was no longer what it was when the Americans had forced the shah to accept Razmara as prime minister. With no other viable alternative, US policy toward Iran stagnated, and Iran drifted ever deeper into chaos. As the new decade began, CIA director Allen Dulles opened an NSC meeting with a gloomy analysis of Iran's current trajectory.[141] The Soviet Union in particular was making the most out of Iran's decline into instability by continuing its propaganda campaign, warning of imminent coups against the shah's reign while calling for Iran's Communists to revive the Tudeh.[142]

Communism was not the only threat: continued dissatisfaction within the Iranian army also threatened the shah's position. The fall of the pro-Western Turkish government by a military coup in May 1960 highlighted the danger, while growing inflation and financial difficulties exacerbated an increasingly critical situation. Eisenhower despaired. After almost eight years in office, having intervened more and sent more financial aid than any of his predecessors, a forlorn Eisenhower was forced to admit that Iran was no more stable than when he took office. He mourned that "the situation in Iran sounded rather hopeless."[143] In a reflective mood shortly before leaving office, he questioned whether the United States should have ever supported the shah. At an NSC meeting, he despondently stated that he had heard "from some of our South American friends that our aid merely perpetuates the ruling class . . . and intensifies the tremendous differences between the rich and the poor."[144] He continued to muse that maybe US policy had been "stupid" for failing to use aid conditionally to ensure liberal reforms in Iran while it still held leverage because the situation now was "almost as difficult . . . as it had been during the time of Mossadegh." John Foster Dulles's replacement, Christian Herter, concurred and, epitomizing the evolution in thinking within the Eisenhower administration since 1953, questioned whether removing Mossadegh had indeed been the right call.[145] Although the coup had maintained Western control over Iranian oil in the short term, it had proven less successful in ensuring sustained stability and security. As the Americans lamented over the past, the present continued to spiral out of control.

Election Fiasco

By 1960, Iran was on the verge of collapse. An NSC report concluded that without reform "the monarchy is likely to be overthrown," and in such an event "the Tudeh Party, largely ineffectual at present, would find a golden opportunity to add to disorder and perhaps to participate in a successor regime."[146] However, Eisenhower had one final opportunity to salvage the situation before departing the White House. Like Truman before him, he hoped that an audacious final attempt to resolve the crisis would stabilize Iran before the handover. With parliamentary elections set for August 1960, the administration hoped that if the shah could be prevented from hand picking the winners and instead would allow a free vote, popular dissatisfaction might be reduced and disaster potentially avoided.[147]

Perhaps sensing American desperation, the shah assured them "categorically that [the] elections would be fair and honest" and made similar claims before the Iranian people, openly placing his own prestige behind the promise.[148] He had further angered the Soviets by refusing their offer of a nonaggression pact, so American leverage was stronger than before, and Washington could press him more firmly with less fear that he would move closer to the Soviet Union. American leverage could once again be effective, and in the run-up to the election open opposition was permitted in speech and in the press for the first time since the Mossadegh era. Fierce public attacks on the government ensued, and at one rally the shah's government was denounced as full of "crooks" and guilty of "treachery," words that the *New York Times* noted had been spoken only behind closed doors just a few months earlier.[149] Opposition forces took full advantage of the shah's liberalization and expected to make significant gains through a fair ballot box.[150] Moreover, public criticism of the shah from both Eisenhower and presidential hopeful Senator John F. Kennedy gave Iranians hope that pressure for democracy would be maintained, whoever won the upcoming contest in America.[151] Even the National Front, the political group headed by Mossadegh before the coup in 1953, was allowed to reconstitute, with many of the same leaders who had previously challenged the shah so effectively. Expectations were piqued for the first competitive elections in Iran since 1952.

These expectations were soon dashed, however. The shah was willing to permit greater freedom of expression, but actually allowing a free election that could possibly limit his power was something else.[152] He had patiently built up power since 1941, overcoming US pressure for democracy as well as challenges to his rule from the nationalists. Now finally he had attained the authoritarian position he had long craved, and he was not willing to share power with the country's political institutions.

The first sign of the shah's insincerity came on the eve of the election during a speech by Prime Minister Manoucher Eqbal. Eqbal's announcement that Mossadeghists would not be allowed to compete and that the new National Front would not be allowed to field any candidates set the tone for another disappointment for Iran's democratic movement.[153] Apart from a few independents, only the two official parties were given authority to put forward candidates.[154] One of these independents, however, was Ali Amini, whom the shah allowed to run possibly as a peace offering to the Americans. Amini's campaign received as much publicity as, if not more than, any candidate of the two official parties, and he quickly became a more dynamic opposition force than the National Front.[155] His clear, well-defined agenda of reform appealed to many Iranians, and the election in Tehran developed into a contest between Amini and Prime Minister Eqbal.

But permission to allow Amini to run did not extend to permission to challenge the establishment on a level playing field. On election day, the shah's vote-rigging program swung into operation, as it had done consistently since the coup. This time was different, however; popular expectation and the simmering unrest suddenly exploded in opposition to the shah's meddling. Amini's supporters were quick to show evidence of wrongdoing, such as villagers being forced onto buses and transported from the countryside to the cities to vote illegally. Other documentation alleged that hundreds of people had been allowed to vote numerous times.[156] One election official was seen falling from his bike outside a Tehran voting station and scattering across the sidewalk forty personal-identity cards that were to be used in fraudulent voting. When candidates favored by the shah seemed certain to lose, election officials simply stayed home "ill" rather than sanction the result.[157]

Despite pledges to both the Americans and his fellow Iranians, the shah remained content with maintaining only the facade of democracy. But he had overplayed his hand in making promises to his people that he did not fulfill, and public outrage swept across Iran in scenes that would be repeated in the protests after the election in 2009.[158] Numerous lives were lost as the shah attempted to crack down on opposition.[159] At its annual meeting in late August 1960, the National Front formally called for a revolution to remove feudalism and imperialism and to replace the current regime with a truly democratic government.[160] Unable to quell the protests, the shah backed down and cancelled the election, proclaiming that "it seems that the interest of the nation requires the mass resignation of all Deputies in order that new elections may take place."[161]

The size and extent of public reaction to the shah's management of the elections shocked and discredited him. Seeking a fall guy to take the blame, he turned to his faithful prime minister. Manoucher Eqbal, a man so subservient that he signed letters to the shah "Your House-Born Slave" (*gholam-e khaneh-zad*), publicly claimed responsibility for the vote rigging and resigned.[162] This admission in itself was extraordinary and demonstrated that the shah might finally have appreciated the severity of the situation. Government interference in the electoral process had become standard practice since the coup, but never before had it threatened or necessitated the resignation of a prime minister. However, the shah and his American allies had created a passionate and expectant electorate. The announcement of new elections in December temporarily calmed the situation, but the shah could not afford to give in to democratic demands for fear of being replaced. The new elections were therefore similarly controlled, resulting in a new wave of protests. Iran was spiraling out of control as Eisenhower prepared to hand the executive office over to the incoming Kennedy administration. A position paper by the CIA in early 1961 concluded that "the rigged elections produced a better organized and longer sustained opposition activity than has been seen in Iran since the ousting of Mossadegh in 1953."[163]

Ironically, however, the chaos was a blessing in disguise for the Americans. With a now chastened shah no longer able to reach out to the Soviets, US leverage over his actions returned. Whether there was still time for reform to save Iran would be a question for John F. Kennedy.

Conclusion

The Eisenhower period reflects the changing nature of American linkage and leverage during the Cold War. US pressure was effective in convincing an uncertain shah to support a coup against the popularly supported Mossadegh but ineffective in coaxing him to undertake the reforms necessary to avert chaos in the late 1950s. What changed between those two events tells us much about the nature of external influence.

The Truman administration had demonstrated that leverage was ineffective against a leader who had overwhelming public support. The Eisenhower period proved that leverage was also ineffective against a leader who could play one Great Power off against another. A bipolar world gave the shah an alternative to American largesse and the demands that often came with that financial aid. The shah's movement toward Moscow at a time when Washington was already reeling from the loss of Iraq ensured that American pressure was watered down. Although the shah was dependent on US support, the unstable international environment and the loss of Iraq as an ally meant that the United States depended on the shah for anchoring its regional security regime and ensuring that oil continued to flow to the West. When the shah came under pressure, he skillfully threatened the West with a move toward the Soviets, which ensured he was not victim to the type of invasive intervention that the United States had conducted during the presidencies of Roosevelt and Truman. Fear of losing Iran to the Soviets made US pressure ineffectual. This fear stymied the use of conditional foreign aid or overt pressure to push the shah back toward reform. The shah, just as he had done following the attempt on his life in 1949, showed a determination to act independently of the Americans' wishes when confident in his ability to do so. This was another warning sign to American policy makers that without leverage the shah would not think twice about following a policy contrary to US interests.

Throughout the Eisenhower period, US linkage with the shah and Iranian government remained strong and, when coupled with leverage, ensured that US pressure was effective. Linkage was essential to organize the coup that displaced Mossadegh, and the close relationship between the Americans and the shah after the coup ensured close cooperation during the crackdown on opposition and Iran's entrance into the Baghdad Pact. Close monitoring of opposition forces also enabled the Americans to identify the growing internal unrest in Iran during the late 1950s, which was unleashed in earnest following the shah's corruption of the electoral process in 1960.

Finally, the Eisenhower period also reflects a change in priorities: from creating the conditions for future democracy that had underpinned Truman's presidency to establishing a policy of contentment with authoritarianism so long as stability was maintained.[164] The return of the Democrat Party to the White House in January 1961, however, meant also the return of greater interest in promoting democracy in Iran. With the shah reeling from internal chaos and once again vulnerable to external pressure, the stage was set for a new opportunity for the Americans to control events and push Iran toward greater development and democracy.

6 Kennedy's Experiment, 1961–1963

John F. Kennedy represented a new generation: the first president born in the twentieth century taking over from the oldest man to have occupied the White House.[1] He encapsulated a new, vibrant, and idealistic spirit and immediately sought to challenge conventional wisdom and traditional politics.[2] To win the Cold War, he emphasized not the perceived arms race with the Soviet Union but the importance of addressing the economic gap between developed and underdeveloped countries, a disparity he called a "clear and present danger to our security."[3] In place of Eisenhower's military emphasis, Kennedy championed modernization and linking developing countries into the Western political and economic system to prevent their turning to communism. Once they were linked to the West, democracy would surely follow.

Although Kennedy represented change, his policy in Iran was largely a continuation of what Eisenhower had been trying to do for the last two years of his presidency: increase pressure on the shah to loosen his authoritarian rule in order to overt catastrophe. Whereas Eisenhower lacked the necessary leverage to convince the shah to truly change his ways, Kennedy came to power with leverage in

This chapter is adapted from David R. Collier, "To Prevent a Revolution: John F. Kennedy and the Promotion of Democracy in Iran," *Diplomacy and Statecraft* 24, no. 3 (2013): 456–75.

abundance. The shah's dalliance with the Soviets had ended, and the spike in protests on the streets of Iran made him more reliant on American support and therefore amenable to instruction. This factor, together with potentially more financial aid to assist in Iran's modernization, meant that the incoming administration had the potential to push the shah against his wishes in ways not seen since the years before the rise of Mossadegh. The Kennedy period therefore brought about an "interlude of reform" through a combination of an activist foreign policy and a strong position of linkage and leverage.[4]

When Rostow Met Kennedy

Kennedy's desire to promote modernization in the developing world had grown over time. At a garden party thrown by Arthur Schlesinger Jr. in 1956, he met a young professor of economics named Walt Whitman Rostow. An intellectual prodigy, Rostow was admitted to Yale at age fifteen and became a Rhodes Scholar just five years later, attending Balliol College, Oxford. Another five years later he completed his PhD at Yale and was determined to make his mark on the academic world.[5] As early as his sophomore year, Rostow committed his life to solving two problems. As he later recalled, "One was economic history and the other was Karl Marx. Marx raised some interesting questions but gave some bloody bad answers. I would do [sic] an answer one day to Marx's theory of history."[6]

A clear intellectual refutation of Marxism in favor of capitalism was of interest not only to academics but also to policy makers struggling to maintain parity with the Soviet Union. Rostow joined the MIT faculty in 1950 and became a leading light in its new Center for International Studies (CIS), formed in partnership with the CIA to offer analysis on the Cold War.[7] Kennedy was already interested in applying social science research to real-world events and found Rostow's research fascinating.

Rostow argued that US foreign-policy goals could best be met by a massive expansion of assistance programs for the developing world.[8] This expansion would lead to two major benefits. First, in an uncertain and dangerous Cold War environment, the United States would appear sympathetic and charitable, which would draw in countries that may otherwise drift toward communism. Second, Rostow believed that by attaching conditions that aid be used for specific reforms that would best assure development, the United States could create "energetic and confident democratic societies throughout the Free World."[9] This proposal's simplicity and clear order of operation appealed greatly to Kennedy.

US financial aid had long sought to promote modernity, such as the reconstruction of the Philippines in the early 1900s and the formation of the Tennessee Valley Authority, which transformed the American South in the 1930s and served as the blueprint for Truman's Point Four program in 1949.[10] However, previous programs had focused on banausic details of social and economic development rather than on any overt political dimension. During the 1950s, for example, US financial assistance emphasized economic planning and rational leadership but paid little attention to political development except for its condition that the recipient remain anti-Communist. Truman's Iran policy fell victim to this oversight: the Seven-Year Plan had been formed to provide a foundation for eventual democracy, but little detail was given on how economic development would lead to political development. Rostow provided this missing link.

Rostow and many of the other academics at CIS were at the leading edge of a new paradigm in the social sciences called modernization theory. A revolution in the history of social science had occurred in the 1950s.[11] In response to the wave of new state formation following World War II, academics attempted to understand the process of development and how best these new states could be incorporated into the global system. Modernization theory straddled the disciplines of anthropology, economics, and sociology and argued that "traditional" and "modern" states are merely different positions on a shared linear path, separated only by different levels of economic, political, and social values. Those states on the underdeveloped end of the path, the theory predicted, would advance toward modernity as they reached certain levels of economic organization, political structure, and social value.

Rostow argued that with American guidance and financial support, what took hundreds of years for the West to achieve on its own could be achieved far more quickly in the developing world if the United States provided assistance.[12] The end goal of this development would be self-sustaining democracy. Policy makers had long struggled with the problem of how to ensure that financial aid would encourage states to remain pro-Western, but as the sociologist Edward Shills said in 1959, "Modernity entails democracy."[13] The end point of modernization would be democracy, which in turn would make countries natural US allies in the fight against communism.[14] By the late 1950s and early 1960s, these academics and their theories of how best to win the Cold War became increasingly popular visitors to Washington, DC.

Nils Gilman has written of the certainty that modernization theorists such as Rostow held in the belief that history was on their side and that transition to democratic modernity was a natural progression. This unerring confidence, he writes, "helps explain why modernization theory would become so useful to policymakers groping for an explanation of the United States' place" in the postwar world.[15] It provided a clear and systematic blueprint for policy makers, and Rostow was particularly keen to bring his research to reality. In the mid-1950s, he had reached out to President Eisenhower but found little enthusiasm for massively increasing the financial aid program while the United States was suffering through a recession of its own.[16] Meeting Kennedy at the garden party was therefore a most auspicious moment.

The two men quickly formed a close bond, and Kennedy would write how he had "enjoyed and profited from Walt's advice" on how best to formulate a policy toward the developing world.[17] Unlike other academics' written work, Rostow's appealed for the style as much as for the content because he was able to present complex economic arguments in ways that were easily digested in Washington.[18] His explanation of development focused on a number of stages—at first three but later expanded to five—that he said all countries traverse in the march toward self-sustaining growth and modernity. The US government's task would be to give assurances to countries going through these modernizing stages that it would provide "as much capital as [each country] can use productively in accordance with a strict criteria of productivity."[19] As a CIS report to the Senate put it in 1956, "Launching a country into self-sustained growth is a little like getting an airplane off the ground. There is a critical speed which must be passed before the craft can become airborne; to taxi up and down the runway at lower speeds is a waste of gasoline."[20]

To Rostow, speeding up development was essential to defeat communism because it would enable the swift "development of stable, effective societies moving in a democratic [and therefore anti-Communist] direction."[21] Kennedy was convinced, and they worked closely to develop a plan for US aid to India, with Rostow invited to speak before the Senate Foreign Relations Committee and later to write two speeches for the young senator, both of which rebuked the Eisenhower administration for failing to demonstrate how liberal democratic capitalism could transform the developing world.[22] Their work resulted in the Kennedy–Cooper Resolution, which proposed the United States send $150 million to India in exchange credits from the Export-Import Bank and $75 million from the newly founded Development Loan Fund.[23] Although the resolution eventually died in the Senate, it showed Kennedy to be a growing force in the Democratic Party.

A Reliance on Social Science

Rostow continued to refine his theory and became more active in the political debate by critiquing President Eisenhower's policies. In *A Proposal: Key to an Effective Foreign Policy*, published in 1957, Rostow and CIS colleague Max Millikan provided what they called the intellectual foundation for a policy of developing "viable, energetic, and confident democratic societies through the Free World."[24] They argued not only that the United States *could* promote development worldwide but also that it was in the US national interest to do so. The Eisenhower administration had lost the initiative in the Cold War to the Soviets by placing "too much emphasis on pacts, treaties, negotiation, and international diplomacy, and too little on measures to promote the evolution of stable, effective, and democratic societies abroad."[25]

Rostow expanded this latter point in *The Stages of Economic Growth: A Non-Communist Manifesto*, published in 1960 no doubt to coincide with the presidential campaign season. The Cold War would be won, Rostow argued, by offering underdeveloped countries the intellectual, economic, and technological incentives necessary to undertake democratic reforms and form a part of the Western democratic system.[26] The most important reforms that the United States should encourage were land and tax reform, the expansion of civil society, and greater political participation. By following Rostow's program, countries would develop and modernize in such a manner that their economies would become reliant upon the Western international system, their political system would become democratic, and the countries would therefore become allied to the West.

Rostow would later write that Kennedy requested his "regular support as he sought the Democratic nomination and the presidency" and, upon entering the White House in January 1961, named him deputy special assistant for national security affairs.[27] Other modernization theorists joined Rostow as the new administration showed a strong commitment to social science. Max Millikan, director of the CIS and frequent collaborator with Rostow, joined the president's Task Force on Foreign Aid. Harvard economist Lincoln Gordon joined the president's Latin American Task Force and later became the US ambassador to Brazil. Lucian Pye was drafted from MIT to advise the State Department and the NSC, providing much of the intellectual backbone of the new US Agency for International Development (USAID). Eugene Stanley left Stanford to head a development mission to Vietnam. Other academics in the new administration included John Kenneth Galbraith, appointed to the Foreign Economic Policy Task Force, and McGeorge Bundy, a professor of government and dean of the Faculty of Arts and Sciences at Harvard, who became Kennedy's national security adviser.

One official noted that the "professors swarming into Washington talked tendentiously of 'self-sustaining growth,' 'social development,' [and] 'the search for nationhood,'"[28] but Rostow described them as "academics interested in public policy who were purposefully recruited by Kennedy. We were about the same age. Our outlook on affairs was similar . . . [and] we were greatly concerned with the dangers to both America and the wider cause of stable peace on the world scene."[29] In *Stages of Economic Growth*, Rostow coined the name "New Frontier," which Kennedy soon adopted to encapsulate his vision of change and hope for a new beginning.[30] These academics and policy makers became known as the "New Frontiersmen." They were typically "about 46 years old, highly energetic, distinctly articulate and refreshingly idealistic," and as Franklin Roosevelt's Brain Trust had done before them, they came to government with the express desire to roll up their sleeves and make America over.[31]

Their reliance on social science was so great that modernization theory has been called the ultimate "theoretical source for Kennedy administration policy design."[32] This was evident from the outset. In early March 1961, a few weeks after his inauguration, the president received a memo from Rostow saying that the time was right to move his plans from theory to reality by immediately launching the "Economic Development Decade."[33] On March 13, Kennedy duly unveiled the Alliance for Progress, an ambitious new program to realize Latin America's "unfulfilled task" and to "demonstrate to the entire world that man's unsatisfied aspiration for economic progress and social justice can best be achieved by free men working within a framework of democratic institutions." Kennedy explained that the program was to be a "vast cooperative effort, unparalleled in magnitude and nobility of purpose, to satisfy the basic needs of the [Latin] American people for homes, work and land, health and school."[34] Fear of the spread of communism in the region had heightened after the Cuban Revolution in 1959, but with Rostow's modernization theory and a well-funded economic aid program, Kennedy believed he had the perfect weapon to counter its pull.

Backed by scholars of modernization theory, the Alliance for Progress was designed to push states toward modernity both to ensure security in a region and to show the United States to be that shining city on the hill, committed to providing large amounts of aid to the developing world.[35] As Lincoln Gordon concludes, the Alliance for Progress can be understood only in this dual sense: not only as a measure to stem the spread of communism "but also, in the famous phrase of the inaugural address, 'because it is right'" and beneficial to American interests.[36] In addition to the Alliance for Progress, Kennedy launched USAID a few months later, and so Rostow's planned Decade of Development was well and truly under way. This development spirit would soon spread to Iran.

A New Frontier in US–Iranian Relations

Recent analyses of US–Iranian relations during the Kennedy era have de-emphasized America's role in Iran's "interlude of reform" of the early 1960s.[37] April Summitt contends that although Kennedy "talked about reforming Iran," he made very little effort to achieve results and was more interested in using Iran as a military ally against communism.[38] Victor V. Nemchenok frames Kennedy's policy and any promotion of reform therein as merely a means to secure stability rather than promote democracy.[39] Although both analyses have their merits, they fail to examine either the intellectual rationale for Kennedy's interventionist policy in Iran or the practical effects the policy had on Iran's internal development.[40] Stability was the policy's immediate goal, but democracy was its end point. Based on Rostovian plans for building self-sustaining democracies, Kennedy's ambitious and far-reaching policy sought to position democratic institutions above the shah's power. Its genesis and application were almost entirely external and forced upon a shah who no longer had the ability to resist external intervention.

During the Eisenhower years, American leverage was compromised by the shah's flirtation with the Soviet Union and American reliance on the shah as an ally. But with leverage now restored and a detailed blueprint for reform drawn up, Kennedy had a window of opportunity to push Iran firmly toward democracy and away from disaster. A National Intelligence Estimate report released a month after Kennedy assumed office stated that the shah's position had become so perilous that "a political upheaval could take place in Iran at any time."[41] The shah was immediately made to feel pressured by the new administration. Kennedy had publicly identified Iran during his campaign as a country in need of a new relationship with the United States in order to stamp out corruption and the misappropriation of US aid.[42] The shah, in the hope of averting what he considered undue attention, nervously wrote to Kennedy soon after the latter's inauguration to highlight the progress his country was making.[43] The continued chaos as a result of botched elections, however, told a different story.

As we have seen, the efficacy of American leverage in Iran has depended on the popularity of Iranian leaders, the amount of US financial aid being sent, and whether the Soviet Union or another global power could undermine US influence. With the shah deeply unpopular, Kennedy's plans to increase the levels of financial aid to the developing world, and the Soviet Union's continued propaganda war against the shah, American leverage was high, despite Iran's perilously unstable condition. In an interview with journalist Walter Lippmann in April 1961, Soviet leader Nikita Khrushchev warned that "the misery of the masses and the corruption of the government was [sic] surely producing a revolution" in Iran, making it, in his eyes, the "most immediate example of the inevitable movement of history."[44] Khrushchev personally repeated this prediction to Kennedy a few weeks later when the two met at the Vienna Summit.[45] The United States would have to act quickly while there remained an Iranian leadership over which it had leverage.

Fear of losing out to the Soviets was very real when Kennedy came to power. A possible rapprochement had ended after an American U-2 spy plane was shot down over the Soviet Union in May 1960.

Khrushchev's furious reaction to the plane has led some to argue that this incident delayed détente by fifteen years.[46] Moreover, the Soviets continued to reach out to the developing world and demonstrated their technological advantage by sending the first satellite into space in 1957 and the first man into orbit on April 12, 1961. Fidel Castro was installed as leader of Cuba, and Communist or pro-Communist regimes came to power in Vietnam, Guinea, and Indonesia. As Kennedy took office, Khrushchev joyously declared that one event after another proved Soviet global dominance and that "there is no longer any force in the world capable of barring the road to socialism."[47] Robert McNamara, Kennedy's secretary of defense, later recalled how the incoming administration was immediately made to feel "beset and at risk" by a dominant Soviet Union.[48] In such a climate, it seemed natural, especially to the diplomats of the US State Department, that the safest policy in Iran was simply to back the shah as the best means to ensure Iran's alliance with the West. The New Frontiersmen, however, favored bold action.

An Administration Divided

Walt Rostow and National Security Adviser McGeorge Bundy jointly led Kennedy's foreign-policy apparatus. So as not to step on each other's toes, the two men sportingly delineated distinct global zones of influence. Bundy would deal with countries to the West of the Suez, and Rostow would be responsible for those to the east.[49] Iran therefore fell under Rostow's purview, and the advocates of development formed the new Iran policy. Distinctly Rostovian policies would emerge to tackle Iran's problems as well as those in the wider Middle East, which included the Arab–Israeli conflict and cooperation with Arab nationalists.[50] Behind each policy would be the guiding light of modernization theory. Despite its beam shining brightly on Iran in the early 1960s, many studies of Kennedy's foreign policy have curiously ignored it.[51]

Iran quickly became a focus for the modernization theorists within the administration. In February 1961, Richard Bissell, CIA director of planning and an academic who had studied with Rostow and Millikan in their student days at Yale, argued that the administration must "press upon" and "convince" the shah to make "drastic changes" to avert disaster and preserve future US military and economic aid assistance.[52] In agreement, Kenneth Hansen, assistant director of the Bureau of the Budget, wrote a month later that the United States had to provide the "prompting and prodding" necessary to force the shah to undertake those economic reforms the administration felt were urgently required.[53] Most vocal of all was Robert Komer, a member of the NSC Iran Bureau. According to his assistant at the time, Komer quickly "got under everyone's saddle and made them itch" in his efforts to force interventionist policies to calm the crisis in Iran. Komer and Hansen quickly became the administration's "centers of agitation," pushing the modernization agenda onto other officials in the Kennedy administration.[54]

Opposed to this new thinking were, according to James Goode, the "traditionalists in the State Department and the Defense Department . . . [who] were satisfied with the status quo in Iran."[55] This group included Secretary of State Dean Rusk as well as outgoing ambassador to Iran Edward Wailes and his replacement, Julius Holmes. John Bowling, head of the Office of Greek, Turkish, and Iranian Affairs at the State Department, summed up the traditionalists' view: any "ultimatums or even heavy-handed hints," he warned in a widely circulated memo in February 1961, "would be regarded by the shah as an intolerable interference in his affairs and would probably result in corresponding moves on his part toward the USSR and neutralism."[56] US policy could instead best maintain stability in Iran, the traditionalists argued, by continuing full support and giving assurances to the shah. Dean Rusk in particular was hostile to many of the New Frontiersmen's ideas and did not feel it was the place of the United States to be a "crusader" or to "preach" to Iran the best way to manage its internal politics.[57]

Between the two groups, tension bubbled, but the New Frontiersmen initially reigned supreme. In a governmental memo, Rostow explained that "efforts at reform and development are a legitimate part of the struggle to maintain [Third World countries] against communist pressure . . . [and so there should be no] excuse for deferring thought and effort on development problems."[58] Kennedy's agreement with Rostow's view meant that the traditionalists were forced to fall into line. Owing to Khrushchev's focus on Iran, Iran's strategic position, and the personal interest in Iran taken by Robert Kennedy and Justice William O. Douglas, two close confidantes of the president, Iran was a key area in which to test the applicability of modernization theory.[59]

Pressure Too Strong to Resist: The Appointment of Ali Amini

The shah was aware that Kennedy represented change and immediately sent close confidante General Timur Bakhtiar to meet the new American leadership in February 1961 and to make sure that these officials would continue their predecessors' generous military aid program. Nothing could more greatly emphasize the contrast between the two regimes than the shah's choice of emissary. Bakhtiar was head of Iran's secret police, a symbol of the shah's authoritarian rule and thus in viewpoint far away from the new reform-minded US administration. He was given a distinctly Rostovian message that the fight against communism required not only military strength but also social and economic progress, for which the United States would provide assistance.[60] Although not clear to the shah at the time, this statement was a direct warning that the United States fully intended to promote the modernization and eventual democratization of Iran.

A key part of Rostow's development agenda was to ensure that moderates and reformers be appointed to key government positions in the target country.[61] Continued chaos in Iran immediately gave the United States an opportunity to appoint whoever it wanted to the highest civilian position in the land. In May 1961, Prime Minister Jafar Sharif-Emami resigned, and longtime US ally Ali Amini became the sixty-seventh prime minister of Iran. Most studies of the period assume that Amini was the shah's selection, with some even praising his decision as a means to mollify the United States and the increasingly enraged Iranian opposition.[62] Summitt has written that at the time "no-one [in Washington] knew whether Amini would be a good ally or not," and Ben Offiler has stated more recently that the appointment "forced the Kennedy administration to reassess its policy towards Iran."[63] A close reading of the evidence, however, confirms that the Americans selected Ali Amini and thrust him upon a reluctant shah, who was willing to submit to American pressure in the hope of ensuring high levels of US aid for his regime. American leverage was once again paramount.

Arguments that Amini's appointment was made for any reason other than orders from the Kennedy administration are unconvincing. Despite ongoing public protests on the streets of Iran's cities, the shah still did not see an immediate threat to his rule. Indeed, he had even become convinced that many of the protests were manufactured by the United States as a means to topple Sharif-Emami.[64] The shah's lack of concern for internal protest was illustrated by his lenient response to those caught conspiring against him. The Qarani coup plotters, for instance, were given only three-year prison sentences and upon release were able to roam and organize freely despite continued widespread agitation against the shah's rule.[65] When General Bakhtiar himself was accused of plotting against the shah, he was merely dismissed rather than punished.[66]

Since his clampdown on opposition following the coup in 1953, the shah had been concerned not so much with internal threats but rather with external dangers to his regime.[67] In response to internal opposition, he was confident that this merely temporary unrest would soon dissipate owing to the actions of SAVAK and support from the United States.[68] He therefore felt no compulsion to appoint a prime minister to mollify the internal opposition, as has been suggested. Furthermore, the shah did not favor Ali Amini, and it is unlikely he would have appointed a politician he so distrusted and disliked without some external pressure forcing him to do so. The shah's negative feelings toward Amini were deep rooted. Amini's mother had been a Qajar princess and thus a member of the royal family that the shah's father had ousted in 1925. Moreover, Amini was a close associate and relative by marriage of Ahmad Qavam, a politician the shah detested more than any other, believing him guilty of attempting to remove him from the throne.

Amini had also worked closely with another of the shah's great nemeses, Mohammad Mossadegh. As a member of Mossadegh's cabinet in the early 1950s, Amini had demonstrated his commitment to the anti-shah nationalist movement, and by publicly criticizing the shah's management of elections in 1960 he showed himself a continued advocate for democracy and the rule of law.[69] Once Amini returned to Iran in early 1958 following his stint as ambassador to the United States, he continued to antagonize the shah by openly campaigning for the premiership in flagrance of tradition and custom.[70] Even if one could ignore Amini's history with Qavam and Mossadegh as well as his involvement with opposition movements and the Qarani plot, it is still unlikely that the shah would have chosen Amini. Since his removal of General Fazlollah Zahedi from the premiership in 1955, the shah had selected only prime ministers who were subservient and sycophantic, traits that Amini did not possess. Before accepting the position, Amini wanted confirmation that he would be able to rule independently, and so he demanded he have the right to name his own cabinet ministers (with the exclusion of the minister of war); that the Majles be dissolved; and that a special court be established to handle corruption cases.[71] The shah was not used to a prime minister making such demands, and yet he meekly agreed to each condition. The evidence points decidedly to the major role played by the United States in Amini's appointment.

It was the New Frontiersmen who fretted over Iran's internal situation and the shah's ability to ward off domestic challenges. It was they who saw a window of opportunity in Sharif-Emami's resignation and who put forward Amini's name. As news of the current Iranian prime minister's resignation reached Washington, Kennedy convened an NSC meeting to discuss Iran and formed a task force to organize US policy.[72] The day after the meeting, Amini's appointment was made. The Americans had identified Amini as a committed reformer and skilled politician during the Eisenhower era and trusted him to work closely with Washington to implement Rostow's visions.

According to William G. Miller, a State Department official working in Iran at the time, "there was certainly . . . pressure" from the United States on the shah to appoint Amini.[73] US ambassador Edward Wailes went so far as to personally make clear "by name" that Amini should be appointed prime minister, and a senior CIA official in Iran informed the shah in a face-to-face meeting that the United States desired Amini's appointment.[74] In addition to applying diplomatic pressure, the United States advised the shah that future US aid to Iran was dependent on the appointment being made.[75] Using the same kind of pressure that had been placed on the shah to appoint General Razmara in 1950, the Americans promised a $35 million loan if the appointment were made. The United States therefore made full use of its linkage and leverage and gave the shah little option but to concede to its demands. Later recalling the incident in his memoirs, the shah wrote that the "US wanted . . . its own man in as Prime Minister. This man was Ali Amini, and in time the pressure would become too strong for me to resist."[76]

Phillips Talbot, assistant secretary of state for Near Eastern and South Asian affairs, noted the importance of Amini's appointment to the administration's goals in Iran, declaring it now possible "to see Iran moving toward a government with a somewhat broader base than it has had and to move towards strengthening its public life."[77] The Kennedy administration hoped that Amini's history of opposition to the shah would allow him to "construct a broad political synthesis" of support for his rule among the public, while pressure would be maintained on the shah to prevent him from undermining Amini's position.[78] Previous US attempts to bring to power men not in the shah's favor, such as Razmara and Qavam, had failed because of the shah's intriguing against them. To ensure history did not strike a third time, close attention would be paid to ensure the shah remained committed to and supportive of the US program of reform. The first step in modernizing Iran had been taken, and the experiment had begun.

Building a Development Program

President Kennedy's new Task Force on Iran had the job of turning Rostow's vision into workable policy, but because it was composed equally of New Frontiersmen and traditionalists, its subsequent report contained mixed strategies. Published on May 15, 1961, it stated not only that "vigorous action" was necessary to stop Iran's descent into chaos but also that the shah was essential to maintaining stability.[79] Therefore, although it was agreed that a "major effort" was needed to support Amini, any pressure on the shah had to "be given in such a manner to avoid so far as possible arousing the shah's active opposition."[80] Nevertheless, enough agreement was found to create a plan of action based on the idea of promoting staged development and giving the new Amini government the space necessary to implement reforms. To support him and perhaps to further quiet a disgruntled shah, an additional cash grant of $15 million was made payable to Iran.

It was also the Task Force on Iran that demanded the Iranian Parliament be dissolved and that new elections be put on hold. Although democratization was the end goal of Rostow's theory, the task force feared the emergence of forces that could stymie rather than support Amini in the short term, in particular another Mossadegh. Democratization would instead be achieved gradually as the shah was encouraged "to move toward a more constitutional role," support was given to "the formation and growth of broadly based political parties," and greater emphasis was placed on education and speeding up the process modernization so that Iran would move "towards the growth of responsible government."[81] National Security Adviser McGeorge Bundy summed up the New Frontiersmen's mood and signaled the difference between their policy and that of the traditionalists: "We had better do everything we could to give the Amini 'experiment' a fighting chance even at the cost of irritating the shah . . . [T]he time has come to abandon this policy of [cautious intervention], on the grounds that if Amini fails, the shah will probably go down the drain too."[82]

The Iran Task Force concluded that the United States was in a position to "do much to encourage the Government of Iran to move in promising directions" and detailed specific areas for immediate focus.[83] These areas included a refocus on land reform, a more effective anticorruption campaign, changes to the taxation system, a broadening of the cabinet to bring in more members of the opposition, and efforts to improve the Iranian economy.[84] The New Frontiersmen were determined to dispense aid solely on the condition that reform targets were met, and they took an active and direct role in Iran's internal politics to ensure progress along Rostow's stages of development.[85]

President Kennedy approved the Iran Task Force recommendations on May 24, 1961, and they immediately became policy. A few weeks later the US embassy reported that already the shah had publicly expressed support for Amini and withdrawn from interfering in the government's daily operations.[86] Swift action was also taken to ensure the inclusion of reformers throughout the Iranian government, including those who had in the past criticized the shah.[87] One notable example was the appointment of Mohammad Derakhshesh as minister for education, an opposition figure who had been a leader of the recent teachers' strike that had toppled Sharif-Emami.[88] Close contact between the New Frontier and Amini's government was quickly established through the creation of joint committees of American and Iranian officials.[89] With such close cooperation, the New Frontiersmen were able to inject their influence directly into Iranian governmental policies. In addition, regular meetings were held between Amini and the US ambassador to Iran as well as between the ambassador and the shah to allow US direction from the top.

Amini worked quickly on those areas identified for reform by Kennedy's task force. He targeted what he called the "thieves and embezzlers" in the government and arrested or fired more than one thousand civil servants and government ministry bureaucrats, including former cabinet officials, along with 33 generals and 270 colonels from Iran's graft-ridden army.[90] Amini's purge against bribery proved so successful that one Tehran lawyer was quoted as saying that in Iran "an empty pocket now holds as much power as a fat purse."[91] Amini even went after powerful members of Iran's elite, such as Ehsan Nikkhah Davaloo, Iran's caviar queen and close friend of the shah's influential twin sister, Princess Ashraf. Davaloo was arrested on charges of receiving a $450,000-a-year caviar concession through the bribery of officials and for packaging low-grade caviar as high grade.[92] After his first year, Amini claimed to have cut high-level corruption "by about 60 percent."[93] Meanwhile, hundreds of inefficient bureaucrats in the Ministry of Education were forced out of their offices and sent to the countryside to teach literacy programs to the peasants.

Desmond Harney, a diplomat at the British embassy, recalled how "everything changed with Amini and things opened up" as civil liberties such as freedom of the press and the right to free assembly were reestablished.[94] To tackle inflation, Amini curbed prices and clamped down on tax evasion and government expenditures.[95] Before long, the government brought inflation under control and by the end of 1961 also managed to bring a halt to three years of hectic speculation and the wastage of foreign exchange on luxury and other consumer products. So successful were Amini's reforms that they began a period of bubbling prosperity that allowed Iran to reduce its debt to the International Monetary Fund by $30 million and to pay off $69 million in foreign loans by the end of the year.[96]

The renowned Iran scholar James Bill concludes that the shah's shift from political repression to political reform during this time demonstrated that Iran "undoubtedly had the assistance of an American hand on the gearshift."[97] A more appropriate analogy might be that as well as an American hand on the gearshift, Iran had an American hand on the steering wheel of a car with an American engine, running on gas paid for with American money! Although the reforms were being enacted by the Iranian government, it was a government put in place by America, based on US reform priorities, guided by American officials, and financed by US economic assistance.

American leverage allowed the Kennedy administration to begin an ambitious reform program in Iran and ensured that Iran reaffirmed its allegiance to the West after repeated threats by the shah during the final months of Eisenhower's presidency to move closer to the Soviet Union. Amini confirmed Iran's allegiance to the West and announced Iran's ongoing participation in the anti-Soviet security alliance previously known as the Baghdad Pact but called the Central Treaty Organization since the coup in Iraq. The Iranian prime minister adamantly announced that Iran would not adopt neutralism despite the growing calls for such a policy from Iranians themselves.[98] An article in the *Economist*, released in May 1961, two weeks before Amini's announcement, reported that it was very hard to find an Iranian in support of the Central Treaty Organization and that if Amini continued Iran's involvement in it, many would feel "confirmed in their belief that the new prime minister is the choice of Mr. Dean Rusk [the US secretary of state], rather than the shah."[99] In Washington, however, the auspicious start of the Amini experiment gave hope that Iran would be stabilized and modernized in close alliance with the United States.

Land Reform

Probably the most important area of action highlighted by the Kennedy administration was land reform. Rostow called it essential for a successful movement into the takeoff phase of development and a key element in the democratization of a largely rural state such as Iran.[100] To modernization theorists, the peasant embodied the concept of a premodern personality who required transformation to become a modern, politically active citizen.[101] Rostow also hoped that in addition to pushing countries toward takeoff, modernizing the peasantry would put "television sets in the thatch hutches of the world," shorthand for the defeat of communism through Western concepts of mass consumption.[102] Just as land reform became a key part of Kennedy's policy for Latin America, it also became a top priority for Iran.[103]

Iran's peasantry made up three-quarters of the entire population but owned no land and held very little wealth. The Ford Foundation had argued in the late 1950s that Iran's stark socioeconomic inequalities and political instability meant that the country and much of the region could be lost if the Soviets began to manipulate this weakness.[104] The Kennedy administration therefore pressed the new Iranian government to quickly address the issues and worked closely with it to ensure they were acted upon correctly.[105] Amini and his energetic new minister of agriculture, Hassan Arsanjani, duly obliged. Government-owned land was reassessed, and large portions were given to landless peasants. A long-ignored law restricting individual families to one thousand acres of irrigated lands and two thousand acres of nonirrigated lands was resurrected and used to break up the large holdings of the landed gentry, and any land that exceeded this quota was redistributed among the peasantry.[106] It was further declared that up to two-thirds of all farmland would be moved from private hands to peasant cooperatives. "First we will tackle those who own 150 villages and whose only talent is for drink and drugs and for beating and torturing peasants," declared the ambitious Arsanjani.[107] Such reforms, he said, would "rescue as soon as possible" the peasants from a status that is "little more than that of bonded slaves."[108]

Studies on Amini's land-reform program found clearly that it was "external rather than internal pressure that persuaded Iran's ruling class to do something about its rural population."[109] To further assist and monitor the situation, Kennedy sent US secretary of agriculture Orville Freeman to meet with Amini and Arsanjani in Tehran to discuss the best way to implement the program.[110]

Although such reforms would transform the country, they would be slow and gradual. Aware of the steady pace of change, members of the Iran Task Force continued to advise against the holding of elections in case reactionary forces gained enough power to disrupt the task force's long-term plans.[111] "In the interim," its members concluded, "the goal is gradually increased participation by the literate and politically conscious elements of the country who are now largely in the urban areas."[112] Democracy would therefore be introduced slowly and carefully so as not to derail the Rostovian development plans. Land reform was a "necessary precondition" before any free election could be held in Iran because, in the view of the New Frontiersmen with clear memory of the Mossadegh era, "Iran simply is not ready yet for democratic consensus."[113]

Arsanjani shared the American view of the importance of modernizing the countryside and called it a "key reform" for the eventual establishment of a "healthy democracy" in Iran.[114] The most important step was to break down the power of large absentee landowners and transfer lands to peasant control, thus forming a new class of peasant proprietors. From there, the plan was to establish democratically elected village councils and proceed upward to the election of town and city councils, with each level administered by the people with authority over all local matters.[115] The *Economist* likened the plan to Pakistan's "basic democracy" program, allowing Iranians to gradually experience democracy while assuring that stability was maintained.[116]

The idea of incorporating basic democracy in Iran came directly from American officials, and yet recent studies of Kennedy's policy toward Iran have concluded that the administration wanted political reform as long as it did not coincide with democratization.[117] This conclusion is clearly not correct: Kennedy's "Amini experiment" was intrinsically designed to lead to democracy, albeit in a gradual and controlled manner. In this sense, it was similar to Truman's hopes regarding Razmara and the Seven-Year Plan: first build the foundations upon which democracy would later be able to flourish. Whereas Truman's policy had been an almost entirely top-down approach, Kennedy's was meant to instigate reforms from the top and bottom simultaneously.

Although this plan suited American needs, it did not suit Iran's expectant urban population, who still demanded a return to full constitutionalism, as in the early 1940s. But Washington was not overly concerned about the populace, believing Amini's history with opposition forces would grant him the necessary time to institute his reforms. By October 1961, therefore, members of the task force were in a triumphant mood. They declared that "largely as a result of United

States representations" the shah had assumed a more withdrawn constitutional role, and progress was being made on the reforms Rostow identified as essential to move Iran toward the "takeoff" stage of development.[118] Despite the administration traditionalists' constant warnings of the dangers of such aggressive intervention, the New Frontiersmen remained confident, so much so that when the shah finally signaled opposition to their obtrusive interventions, Ambassador Julius C. Holmes was instructed to firmly impress upon him that Amini ruled with US backing and that the shah should continue to support him rather than consider a return to personal control.[119]

The shah not only jumped back into line but one week later also issued a royal decree giving Amini even greater powers. Ambassador Holmes was praised in Washington for convincing the shah to continue his support for Amini and ensuring that the US Amini experiment received added strength and impetus.[120] The prime minister's new powers enabled him to turn his policies into law without the need for approval by the Majles, which had by this time been shut down for more than a year. American dominance over the shah within his own country was never demonstrated so clearly: an aggrieved shah had made his feelings known to Washington but had been convinced not only to cease complaining but also to cede more powers to Amini. With linkage and leverage, the United States held virtual dominion over Iran's internal system, and yet rumblings of discontent from the disenfranchised urban population continued, threatening the peaceful continuation of the Amini experiment.

The Experiment Falters

The United States used close linkage and strong leverage to force the shah into line but held no such control over the Iranian opposition. The Kennedy administration believed Amini would have the opposition's support owing to his history with Mossadegh, but this support did not materialize. America's linkage to Iran's urban population had deteriorated over the previous decade, and Washington had only a superficial understanding of the people's concerns and aspirations.

Although US officials assumed Amini was a popular and effective politician, they failed to monitor the changing popular mood brought about by their close relationship to Amini. By the summer of 1961, the Iran Task Force lamented that Amini "has not been able to capture the imagination of large sectors of the population"—its hopes for a popularly supported prime minister were fading.[121] Much of this lack of popular support had to do with the American failure to understand the Iranian people's demands. Although linkage to government officials, the military, and economic sources was strong, the United States had not kept up close linkage with the opposition. US officials assumed that Amini's history would bring him popular support, but they ignored that since working with Mossadegh, Amini had chaired the Iranian delegation that had agreed to the deeply unpopular oil consortium arrangement in 1954, which had caused him to be branded a traitor to the cause of oil nationalization.[122] His refusal to allow new elections further ostracized him, as did his backing by the United States.[123] Shortly after his appointment, eighty thousand Nationalist Front members met to protest against any premier imposed upon them by the United States, even if that person were a member of their own organization.[124]

Writing to President Kennedy in August 1961, Robert Komer of the NSC Iran Bureau worried about Amini's lack of popular support as well as the difficulty Amini was having in executing US reform plans "in a gimcrack country like Iran."[125] The shah's granting of extra emergency powers to the prime minister in October merely reignited public anger and reinforced the popular opinion that Amini was not an ally of the Iranian people. As protests swept across Tehran, Washington realized that Amini could not count on public support, and if the US Amini experiment were to have a chance, the shah's support must be unfaltering.

A growing reliance on the shah meant that as the year 1962 began, American leverage was becoming precarious. An Iran Task Force meeting in January reflected the Americans' increasingly nervous position. Although firm "US advice, pressure and financial assistance" had "successfully prevented the shah from dumping the Prime Minister or reducing him to a puppet status," there was doubt whether they could or should apply such pressure again.[126] The shah remained dissatisfied with having to support Amini, and there was fear he could resurrect a positive relationship with the Soviet Union if the United States were to continue to force him into line. Within the Iran Task Force, the traditionalists' arguments therefore became more convincing. The Amini experiment was supposed to stabilize Iran but had instead exacerbated the problem and given rise to increased anti-American ferment on the streets. With Iran's continued allegiance to the West being the ultimate priority, the task force report concluded that the best policy at present was to "support governments acceptable to the shah" rather than dictate to him.[127] This recommendation was a clear deviation from previous task force reports and reflected the diminished support that Washington had for Amini. It was also a clear indication to the shah that he could reassert his authority to provide stability on the streets.

The ensuing crackdown began almost immediately. A few weeks after the release of the task force report, a teacher pay dispute coupled with a large student protest at Tehran University led to a brutal government response. Police and paratroopers stormed the university campus, leaving almost two hundred injured and taking more than one hundred into custody.[128] University grounds were considered safe and honored spaces, so the security forces' actions merely invigorated the opposition.[129] The National Front organized additional protests the next day, and the crowds chanted "Down with Amini" and "Down with the shah."[130]

The New Frontiersmen despaired at the growing chaos in Iran and the renewed emphasis on support for the shah. Bob Komer was particularly vocal, saying that US policy was "going to hell in a hack" by siding with an authoritarian monarch at a time when intelligence reports showed his days would "certainly [be] numbered" unless actions were taken on reform.[131] Komer felt the US officials should instead pursue greater "interference in Iranian internal affairs than they had permitted themselves in the past." In agreement, fellow New Frontiersman T. Cuyler Young of Princeton University argued, "We are damned if we do, and damned if we don't, so let's get blamed for doing something worthwhile."[132]

By early 1962, the Amini experiment had achieved very little. Despite initial gains, many of the government's reform plans were floundering. Attempts at land reform, the centerpiece of US-backed development efforts, proved particularly fruitless. Owing to well-known administrative "flexibilities" favoring the landlords, a law to limit each landlord's holdings to one village affected only a small percentage of Iran's estimated sixty thousand villages.[133] Other problems—such as corruption, slow implementation, and a lack of officials—further impeded progress. Amini's harsh measures had succeeded in curbing inflation, but they had also led to a dramatic drop in business confidence and investment rates as well as a slowdown in new construction—all of which contributed to a sharp increase in unemployment.[134] Amini had similarly been ineffectual in targeting tax dodgers. Despite a flurry of arrests, difficulties in assembling the necessary evidence meant convictions were few and far between.

The calls for greater intervention therefore carried little weight because even after the United States intervened more strongly than at any time since 1953, Iran remained in chaos, and the shah grew increasingly frustrated. Faced with the facts that Iran shared a border with the Soviet Union and was awash with oil, the Kennedy administration now began to focus more on expedience. The destabilization of the country owing to the administration's ambitious reform policies could not be allowed to continue.

Failure Here, Failure There

The declining situation in Iran replicated Rostovian failures in other developing countries by late 1961 and early 1962. The Alliance for Progress in Latin America had all but failed amid poor economic growth, instability, and a series of military coups across the continent.[135] In response, Kennedy began to move away from such policies toward a focus on stability and security, which often meant cozying up to authoritarian leaders.[136] Rostow himself was an early casualty of this change in focus and was moved to a position away from the White House. Kennedy explained at the time that "Walt is full of ideas . . . perhaps one in ten of them is absolutely brilliant. Unfortunately six or seven are not merely unsound, but dangerously so. I admire his creativity, but it will be more comfortable to have him creating at some remove from the White House."[137]

Ralph Dungan, a special assistant to the president, went further and said that Rostow had proved to be a "bloody bore . . . [who] got on everybody's nerve," and even senior officials, Dungan claimed, wanted "him off the premises."[138] Proving that nothing propinks like propinquity, Rostow's new position in the State Department meant he saw little of Kennedy, and his influence as well as the domination of the New Frontiersmen over Iran policy waned.[139] Other New Frontiersmen were also culled, such as Chester Bowles, who was replaced as undersecretary of state by George Ball, a tough and traditional pragmatist.[140]

Amini would soon become another casualty of this shift. He continued to toil without success, and the CIA reported in mid-1962 that he was "ill, exhausted and unable or unwilling to assert his will" on the government.[141] The shah continued to stifle Amini's actions and, sensing the Americans were losing patience, wasted no opportunity to vent his spleen regarding their intervention in Iranian politics. He routinely criticized the Kennedy administration for not removing Amini and backing his own return to personal rule, and on one occasion he threatened abdication if the Americans persisted in their policy.[142] On another, he angrily snapped in a meeting with Kennedy and Dean Rush, "We are not your stooges," and warned of rapprochement with the Soviets if they continued to ignore him.[143]

Without the support of the shah or the people, the Amini experiment was soon declared a failure and wound down. The onset of an economic and budgetary crisis was the final straw, and the Americans finally signaled their permission for the shah to resume personal authority over the government. However, the form and timing of Amini's dismissal illustrated that the Americans were still able to influence events through high degrees of linkage and leverage.

Had they held greater faith in Amini and believed their policy had the potential to succeed, it is possible that the pressure they applied could have kept the shah on the periphery. However, angering the shah over a failing policy was not a trade-off the Americans deemed worthy in mid-1962.

Once the decision had been made in Washington, the US embassy in Tehran informed the shah that the United States now looked to him to personally "enforce discipline and order." Combined with a refusal to assist Amini with the budget crisis, this communication was a clear "invitation to the shah to jettison the Prime Minister," according to Ambassador Holmes.[144] Wishing to leave before being pushed, Amini summarily resigned from office on July 19, 1962.[145]

Summitt argues that the "US watched in apprehension as the shah took more control of the government" in mid-1962, and Nemchenok contends that US policy changed *because* of Amini's departure rather than *before* it.[146] Both are incorrect. The United States played a deciding role in Amini's downfall and gave prior backing to the shah before Amini's departure. An aggrieved Amini was certainly aware of the US role in his downfall and publicly stated on the day of his resignation that he had been forced out by the Americans.[147] In fact, without US support of Amini, it is likely the shah would have removed him from office far sooner. Writing in his memoirs some years later, the shah was moved to admit that by this point "even the Americans had lost faith in [Amini's] abilities . . . [and now looked to me to take] better control of the situation."[148]

The United States had made a concerted effort to lay the groundwork for a future modern democratic Iran. Blocked by popular unrest, an increasingly aggrieved shah, and the need to maintain stability to ensure Iran's westward allegiance, these efforts were abandoned in favor of a return to support for the shah. Iran's interlude of reform can only be understood by examining the role of the United States and its ability to control Iran's internal policies. With leverage and linkage, the United States succeeded in forcing the shah away from personal rule, but the failure to understand or control the Iranian people's demands as well as the lost faith in the policies of modernization ultimately meant that Iran moved from an interlude of reform back to a time of authoritarianism. The shah promised a return to stability through force, but the continued refusal to acknowledge the people's demands meant that their frustration would persist.

The Making of an Uncontrollable Revolution

The Amini experiment would be Washington's final attempt to bring about democratic reform in Iran.[149] Its failure and the absence of an alternative plan returned the United States to a position in which it felt it had to support the shah's authoritarian rule. Despite intelligence reports showing the shah's Iran would soon be lost unless major reforms were made, the United States had no backup plan besides returning to the unsuccessful Eisenhower policy followed some eighteen months earlier: looking to the shah for leadership and stability and applying gentle persuasion to make some progress on reform. The shah, however, was determined not to be dictated to again.

He wasted little time in reasserting his authority. Asadollah Alam, a close and devoted servant of the shah, was immediately—within a week—appointed prime minister to replace Amini in a move that the CIA concluded meant that "for all practical purposes it is the shah himself who will be Prime Minister." However, the CIA remained optimistic, saying that it was "not a setback for the reform program . . . [because] with the right drive from the shah and with the right advice and pressure from the United States, it should be possible to significantly advance" US reforms.[150] The incongruity of following the same policy as Eisenhower in the late 1950s and expecting different results did not temper the feelings of victory among the traditionalists in Washington.

The New Frontiersmen, however, were incensed. Before Amini's resignation, Komer hoped the United States would offer him more support, not less, stating that "in the current Iran flap, I urge as strongly as I know how that we base our policy on saving Amini. . . . [O]ur intervention at this crucial moment, risky though it may be, could spell the difference between success and failure."[151] Amini's resignation did not dampen Komer's insistence. After meetings with other New Frontiersmen, including Kenneth Hansen and William R. Polk, a Harvard professor and member of the State Department's Policy Planning Council, Komer developed what he hoped would be the new blueprint for promoting development in Iran. "We're being blamed by the Iranians for this crisis anyway," he wrote to National Security Adviser Bundy in mid-July, "and I'd rather be hanged for a goat than a sheep."[152] He criticized support for the shah as merely waiting for the inevitable uncontrollable revolution by the people. The shah might keep the peace for a while, but Komer warned that "anyone familiar with this feeble country knows this is just another lull before the storm."[153] He feared that without extensive reform the people would soon rise up, seize power, and install a new government that would have no allegiance to the West.

One alternative would be to remove the shah altogether, but Komer felt that doing so would only lead to the formation of weak and ineffectual governments that would incite chaos in the same way as an uncontrollable revolution. Therefore, Komer attempted to map out a policy that would maintain the shah as a figurehead while achieving a controlled revolution of modernization and democratization. He regarded this controlled revolution as the very rationale for the Amini experiment in the first place and did not feel it should be rejected over one failure or the inability to find a suitable successor to continue the experiment. Convincing the shah to reappoint Amini alongside another reformist cabinet was highly unlikely, so Komer suggested that the Kennedy administration itself "provide what is missing."[154]

This meant the United States would have to take an even more proactive role in Iran by applying more pressure on the shah. Key to this approach would be to convince the shah to install and maintain a reform-minded cabinet consisting of "a series of Aminis" who could work with the United States toward a shared goal. Cognizant of the traditionalist argument that an already disgruntled shah would just reach out to the Soviets in protest against a more interventionist policy, Komer believed that US leverage could be maintained by increasing the amount of financial aid to Iran. Kenneth Hansen supported this approach, stating that the United States should "do a really hard-hitting job of political meddling" in Iran—that it should identify as many future Aminis as possible, engineer "them into a position of some prominence," and then back them with coaching and a staff, like a "damn good CIA operator."[155] Almost a decade after the CIA had helped bring an end to democracy in Iran, Komer and Hansen felt another CIA-style operation was necessary to resurrect it.

Although Komer and Hansen's plan gained some favorable response among officials in the Kennedy administration, little attention was given to Iran in the immediate months after Amini's resignation. The Bay of Pigs fiasco and the Cuban Missile Crisis dominated the Americans' attention for the remainder of the year, and it was not until January 1963 that senior officials in the State Department and National Security Adviser Bundy agreed that a review of Iran policy was necessary.[156] Although likely watered down in meetings with State Department officials, Komer's report seemed set to serve as the first step in developing a new policy to democratize Iran.

However, while the United States was distracted, the shah had already cultivated his own reform program. Since dispensing of Amini, he was determined never again to allow the Americans to control his actions. In doing so, he would make academic the necessity of Komer's plan. Rather than leave himself open to a revolution by the people or by the Americans, the shah determined to become a revolutionary monarch and lead reform personally from above. But this would not be reform in the American sense; rather than democracy, the shah's goal would be to use the language of reform as a means to increase his own authoritarian hold on power. In January 1963, just as the Americans were beginning to return their gaze to Iran, the shah unveiled his White Revolution.

Forced to "Ride This Tiger": Kennedy and the White Revolution

The shah's idea for a revolution came after a long, soul-searching trip to the countryside in late 1962. Angry at external intervention, he wanted a policy that would rid him of its menace while also strengthening his authoritarian rule. After meeting with farmers and peasants, he returned to Tehran with new heart, confidence, and determination to personally lead his country without foreign interference. After months of planning, he unveiled a six-point reform program. Known as the White Revolution, the program was concerned predominantly with land reform but also included changes to the election law, the addition of women's suffrage, the nationalization of the forests, the formation of a literary corps to help educate the peasant population, and an industrial-revenue profit-sharing agreement between management and labor. The Kennedy administration viewed the program as a continuation of the Amini experiment and called it "without precedent," an "irrevocable break" that "changed the context and background of Iranian politics."[157]

However, for the shah the White Revolution was anything but a continuation of the American experiment. Although similar in rhetoric, it differed vastly in goals, most notably in its absence of political reform. Amini's land reform had been pursued to modernize and eventually democratize the countryside; the White Revolution conceived land reform to be a means to increase the Pahlavi dynasty's power and authority.[158] By abolishing the feudal system and gifting land to the peasantry, the shah hoped to create a large and powerful base of support for his rule. The grateful peasants would serve as domestic protection against any popular revolution emanating from Iran's urban centers. Although in the process the shah would make enemies among the landed gentry and clergy who were also large landowners, the sheer size of the peasant population, which made up 75 percent of Iran's total, would inoculate him not only against the landowners' protestations and Iran's urbanites but also against any complaints coming from the United States. Happy to see the shah gain internal support, the United States cheered on his reforms, and Komer's policy suggestion for greater US intervention became moot.

The success of the White Revolution's unveiling reinvigorated the shah, who quickly clamped down on opposition groups and put the nationalists in an awkward position. They were in favor of many of the reforms he had introduced but could not accept a revolutionary monarch and so were forced to come out in opposition to his program. This position allowed the shah to paint them as opponents of reform, which seriously undermined their popular support.[159] Many opposition leaders were arrested as protests against the shah began but were not allowed to escalate to dangerous levels thanks to the shah's new allies. In January 1963, to preempt any unrest, the shah transported three thousand people from the countryside to Tehran for a pro-shah rally. The rally soon escalated into an attack on Tehran University, where students denounced the White Revolution as dictatorial and unconstitutional.[160]

After defeating the students, the shah next sent his peasant army to the holy city of Qom, where the clergy had also begun to protest. Five thousand peasants quickly dispersed the protesters.[161] The shah then staged a national referendum both to demonstrate to the international community the popularity of his program and to show that he was indeed committed to fulfilling the role of a constitutional monarch by aligning his policies with the wishes of the people. According to the highly unlikely results of this referendum, almost 5.6 million people voted in favor of the reform program, giving it a 99.9 percent approval rating.[162] Nevertheless, the Persian and American press called the program a triumph and heaped praise on the shah's action.[163] The White Revolution was a resounding success in forming the idea that the shah was a progressive and dominant force in Iran.

American policy makers were overjoyed by the surprising events in Iran. Emblematic was the response from Robert M. Macy, director of USAID operations in Iran, who saw the shah's program as "self-help at its best" and, with a nod to the failed Alliance for Progress, called it something "we have been clamoring for in Latin America and other areas" for years, before breathlessly exclaiming, "This darn thing is for real!"[164] When Kennedy asked "whether we should be doing anything to guide" the shah's new program, Secretary of State Dean Rusk assured him that it would be better for the United States to withdraw. Rusk saw the events as "an Iranian revolution which will evolve at a Persian tempo and produce Persian results," a much better situation, he cautioned, than forcing unpopular US reforms upon a reluctant shah and an ungrateful populace.[165] Even Robert Komer was moved to remark that although the White Revolution was unexpected, the administration had invested too much money to give up its support for reform in Iran and was "going to have to ride this tiger" by supporting the shah.[166] Kenneth Hansen was one of the few not won over by the revolution, writing that the reversion of the United States to the role of mere adviser to a regime that dealt with "short-term expediency" would inevitably produce chaos.[167] His voice, however, was increasingly isolated.

The shah's success in limiting US intervention in Iran was illustrated by an Iran Task Force meeting in late May 1963. Once dominated by the ideology of the New Frontier, the group now concluded that the "shah had substantially satisfied US pressure for reform by his unilateral program of January 1963."[168] An NSC Standing Group concurred one month later, saying that the shah's revolution "promises to achieve some of our fundamental policy objectives . . . [so] we have been using and will continue to use every opportunity to reiterate our confidence in him."[169]

The shah had successfully co-opted the American reform program and negated the need for the Americans to push for a separate reformist government. After two years of direct external intervention in his affairs, he had reclaimed personal control of Iran. His ability to deflect American pressure under Eisenhower pointed to his self-confidence, but his ability to switch Kennedy administration officials from advocates of change to supporters of his reign was remarkably impressive. As illustrated by Komer's report, the Kennedy administration had been prepared to intervene more extensively in Iranian affairs than ever before, but the shah's actions changed the entire landscape. US intervention was no longer felt necessary, and the United States took a backseat as the shah carried out the White Revolution.[170]

The shah later boasted that the White Revolution had succeeded in "put[ting] a stop to foreign interference" in Iran.[171] The years of American interference, especially under the Kennedy administration, had galvanized him to strike out independently. He had experienced a measure of independence after 1953 but soon lost it as internal unrest and external pressure returned to the country toward the end of the decade. Although in a position of weakness in January 1961, when Kennedy assumed the White House, he had regained confidence and now struck out on his own path. After privately upbraiding the president and the secretary of state for their attempts to treat Iran as a mere stooge in April 1962, the shah skillfully developed a plan to rid his country of their interference.

The Shah's Consolidation of Power

The shah was able to assert himself over the Americans in part because of the steady decay of US linkage and leverage in the months following Amini's departure. Starting in July 1962, the shah ordered his new prime minister, Asadollah Alam, to curtail American influence, and many American-trained economists and planners were dismissed. Among them was Minister of Agriculture Hassan Arsanjani, the driving force behind Amini's land-reform program.[172] The shah also reached out to the Soviet Union in the latter half of 1962 and announced on September 15 that he would unilaterally forbid the placement of any US missiles in Iran that would threaten the Soviet Union. Although a symbolic gesture because the United States currently had no missiles in Iran, this announcement was also, as Bill points out, a "not-so-subtle warning to the United States not to take him for granted or push him too far."[173] In addition, by this point the American focus was moving to Southeast Asia and to the domestic issues growing in the United States, so less attention was given to Iran so long as stability was maintained there.

The White Revolution strengthened the shah's internal position, and he confidently put down all demonstrations against his policy. The largest such protest occurred in early June 1963 and was squashed with such ferocity that some estimates put the death toll in the thousands.[174] Although it was likely substantially less than that, the shah's firm response ensured that no similar such demonstration was held again for almost fifteen years. More arrests followed, including that of the increasingly infamous cleric Ayatollah Ruhollah Khomeini, which effectively decapitated the leading opposition groups and forced others underground.

Rather than chastise the shah, the Americans approved of the steps being taken to restore stability. A Special National Security Estimate from the CIA issued the same month as the uprising concluded that the shah's radical policy shift had strengthened his personal position and weakened the opposition to the extent that he should now be able to surmount all "threats to his position and programs during the next few years."[175] The US press dismissed the uprising as the work of reactionaries incensed that the shah's modernization program would limit their traditional power. Secretary of State Dean Rusk wrote to the shah soon after the uprising in June 1963 and the shah's brutal repression of it, but rather than criticize the dramatic loss of life he merely said that "such manifestations will gradually disappear as your people realize the importance of the measures you are taking to establish social justice and equal opportunity for all Iranians."[176] US diplomat William Miller recalled that after the uprising was brutally crushed and the situation stabilized, the Kennedy administration "forgot about it . . . as though it never happened. They just forgot."[177]

This response illustrates the change of emphasis within the Kennedy administration, which had once been concerned with limiting the shah's power in favor of greater liberalism and democratization. Now faced with increasing authoritarianism committed to brutally suppressing all forms of opposition, the United States chose to sit back and focus on more pressing matters in other parts of the world and at home. Rather than find an alternative to the shah, the Americans were happy so long as he ensured stability and made good on his promises of reform. So satisfied were they that they even began to disengage from Iran. The country had been a focus for American foreign-policy makers for more than a decade, but in the final few months of the Kennedy administration interest or intervention in Iran fell precipitously, weakening US linkage.

Despite general satisfaction over the events in Iran, the US embassy's report on the riots in June 1963 did contain one ominous warning for the future: "Khomeini is now the most important figure with whom the regime has to deal in this situation," it cautioned. "He has become in recent months the best known Mullah, the outstanding opposition leader against the shah, the government and the reform program."[178] Although the shah had overcome the challenge presented by the democracy and nationalist movements, the main opposition now came from the clergy, which had become increasingly politicized owing to the White Revolution. They would ultimately lead their own revolution fifteen years later, but in 1963 the significance of the rise of a religious opposition was lost on the Americans.[179] They similarly ignored the notion of political reform, once felt vital to avoid an uncontrollable uprising in Iran. Although the Americans did not realize it at the time, by supporting the shah's White Revolution and ignoring political reform, they were making inevitable the very eventuality they feared the most.

The Shah's Democratic Facade

In the final few months before the tragic assassination of President Kennedy, the shah continued to assert control while simultaneously convincing the Americans that he really was a constitutional monarch. In a nationally broadcast speech in July 1963, he called Iran "a society of free men and free women" and promised an improved administration with stable economic policies that would transform the country into a modern and prosperous state.[180] The referendum on the White Revolution had for the first time given women the vote, and this right was continued as a new parliamentary election was finally announced for September 1963, the first since the debacle of 1960. The *New York Times* reported that the election would be revolutionary not only because the vote had been extended to women but also because the new electoral laws required voter registration. People would no longer be able to vote more than once, and the traditional routine of ballots "cast on behalf of animals, babies or villagers who

died years ago" would be wiped out.[181] With echoes of his assurances to Eisenhower in 1960, the shah impressed upon Ambassador
Holmes that the election would be free even if it returned a Majles
opposed to his rule. It would, he claimed, be the first step toward the
formation of a new Iranian political party system that would "have a
platform and a purpose" rather than be "fictional as Iranian political
parties have been in the past."[182] Reporting to Washington, Ambassador Holmes said it was the shah's "hope that [in time] political
parties and representative government may be achieved as near the
Western pattern as possible."[183]

Holmes knew that such rhetoric would appeal to Washington
and undermine those who persisted in arguing for the United States
to reassert control in Iran. The election came and went amid American praise that reflected little of the election's actual management.
Rather than a free election, only a single slate of candidates was
put forward, with all candidates screened beforehand to ensure their
allegiance to the shah. All opposition figures were barred from running, and the slate instead included peasants, workers, a national
wrestling champion, and movie and TV actors who specialized in
country-bumpkin parts—anyone so long as he could prove his loyalty to the shah. Not one elected deputy could claim an independent
mandate or would ever likely achieve one; all were loyal to the shah,
the only thing that mattered.[184] His previous crackdown on opposition and the continued strong presence of his security forces made
sure there would be no repeat of the protests of 1960. The lack of
protest convinced the rather obtuse Americans that the election was
a success, and the *New York Times* inexplicably called it the "fairest
and most representative election Iran has ever had."[185]

For the previous five years, first Eisenhower and then Kennedy
had pressed the shah to open Iran up to liberalization. Not wishing to share power with publicly elected democratic institutions, the
shah looked instead to find a balance between repression and reform:
not so much of the former to warrant external intervention but also
not so much of the latter to encourage actual democratization.
Newspapers and journals not directly controlled by the government

were closed down, and SAVAK ensured that political life was strictly regulated.[186]

Although the shah made sure to balance repression with reform to satisfy US demands, the prospects of democracy in Iran were reduced still further. Since the coup in 1953, the shah had involved himself in the day-to-day running of government but still essentially shared power with the prime minister. Now, however, he decided to take more complete control without worrying about maintaining political support.[187] He would not permit challengers to his regime, whether they came from the ranks of the military, such as Zahedi; from the political class, such as Mossadegh or Amini; or from the clergy, such as Khomeini. The success of his return to authoritarianism can be judged by comparing public reaction to similar events at different times. The public reaction to rigged elections in 1960, for instance, so weakened the shah that he was forced to submit to Kennedy's demands, but in 1963 the rigged elections resulted in very little protests from the now cowed population. Similarly, the death of one teacher during a demonstration in May 1961 had brought down the Sharif-Emami government, but during the summer of 1963 the shah's government remained strong and secure despite its killing of numerous protesters.

In essence, a "quantum jump had occurred in the level of oppression" the shah was able to impose and get away with.[188] The United States refused to intervene as it had done previously and instead approved of the shah's rhetoric on reform and his ability to maintain stability. Increasingly distracted by events elsewhere, in particular Vietnam, where Kennedy sent sixteen thousand military advisers in November 1963, stability and peace were all that the United States required from Iran. Interest and control over Iran's reform program was no longer a priority for the now stretched administration. Kennedy instead wanted to believe that the shah's program for reform and democracy was sincere and chose to ignore all glaring evidence to the contrary.[189]

The shah was careful not to dispense of democratic talk completely because he knew the Americans would not condone blatant moves toward authoritarianism. In an interview with the *New York Times*, he therefore claimed his long-term desire was to continue to bring democracy to his people. Although conceding that the election was not completely free, despite the paper's own high praise of it, he hoped that with patience and discipline he "may be able to assume the same role in political affairs as do most European monarchs"— that is, a secondary position behind a representative government.[190] By continually praising the democratic ideal and promising reforms similar to those the United States had called for, he appeased many New Frontiersmen as well as other Western governments.

Dean Rusk later recalled that US officials applauded the shah's actions without realizing that instead of continuing the reforms started by Amini, the shah was actually ending US intervention while increasing his authoritative hold on the country.[191] Instead of responding with skepticism to such events as the reported 99.9 percent vote in favor of the referendum on the White Revolution, Kennedy merely praised the shah. In correspondence, he wrote of his hope that the result would "renew your confidence in the rightness of your course and strengthen your resolve to lead Iran to further achievements in the struggle to better the lot of your people."[192] The shah's statements professing democratic ideals and the wish to modernize Iran convinced the Americans that stability and reform were safe in his hands.

The shah's sudden move to formulate his own revolution was a direct preemption and co-option of the American reform program and of US efforts to impose modernization and democratization in Iran. John Bowling recalled later how State Department officials "shamelessly led JFK to believe that the shah's White Revolution was the greatest thing since cellophane" and overly hyped the shah's reforms so as to maintain the president's support for them.[193] Even Robert Komer, the staunchest of the New Frontiersmen, admitted in June 1963 that "we are all committed to the shah's revolution" and later identified Iran as the only bright spot in the Middle East, "where the shah's White Revolution is rocking along."[194] By successfully co-opting US policy for reform, the shah was able to ensure that US intervention in Iran was scaled back. The only remaining source of tension in the relationship was now military aid—a perennial obsession for the shah.[195]

Conclusion

The Kennedy administration came to power hoping for a controlled revolution toward democracy in Iran. It left office with a shah back in full control and a course set for an inevitable uncontrollable revolution. Kennedy was "the only American president to press seriously . . . for political reform," but the sad irony is that in the last year of Kennedy's presidency the shah was able to sweep "away all opposition to his regime."[196] Nevertheless, the period of reform was real and substantial, despite its absence in much of the literature on this time.[197] Ben Offiler claims that in order to maintain the shah as an ally the Kennedy administration focused almost entirely on "attempts to appeal to [his] ego" rather than actively push him toward policies of reform.[198] Bill's analysis focuses little on the Amini experiment, and Goode argues that Amini's reforms occurred independently of the United States.[199] Summitt has said that Kennedy "ignored those who argued for a fresh approach" toward Iran, and while Amini sought to institute reforms, "Kennedy continued to view Iran in terms of a military ally to contain communism."[200] The military aspect of Iran's relationship with the West was important to the Americans, but the reform program they attempted to impart was a radical change and almost wholly planned and supervised by Washington. The administration was aware that Iran could not be saved through military means alone. It hoped instead to transform the country into a self-sustaining democracy and thereby prevent it from falling to the spread of communism. Nemchenok's study of the period correctly observes that the desire for stability ultimately trumped efforts at reform in Iran. However, Nemchenok, too, ignores the political development goals of the Amini experiment. Any political reform that took place, he argues, occurred only to stabilize Iran and was not part of a policy to push Iran toward democracy.[201] Although it is true that stability within the borders of a Cold War ally neighboring the Soviet Union was of utmost importance, Kennedy's development program was focused on democracy as the best means to achieve lasting stability. Far from being poorly conceptualized or a mere complement to economic development, as Nemchenok charges, political reform was key to ensuring Iran's lasting stability and an integral aspect of Rostovian development plans.

Reform did not occur independently of the White House, but as modernization theory failed to achieve the administration's goals across the developing world, the similar failure of the Amini experiment also caused the administration to abandon the theory. Some scholars have argued that Iran's "interlude of reform" ended with Kennedy's assassination in November 1963,[202] but the beginning of the end in fact began as early as the fall of 1961. In what became known as the Thanksgiving Day Massacre, Kennedy replaced influential New Frontiersmen in his cabinet, including Walt Rostow and Chester Bowles, with more pragmatic personnel. Kennedy likewise began shifting support away from reformist politicians and toward right-wing dictators in Iran, Latin American, and Africa. Modernization theory was failing in practice and, although still the dominant paradigm in the social sciences, had come under increasing pressure from real-world events. Hans Morgenthau, one of the foremost realist thinkers of the twentieth century, launched an attack on the theory in 1962, dismissing the idea that democracy and development could be promoted through "transfers of money and services" and claiming that the United States was engaged in a "policy of make believe."[203]

Kennedy biographer James Giglio believes that over the course of his presidency Kennedy became increasingly conservative, cautious, and aware that Cold War exigencies had to be prioritized over destabilizing policies that promoted modernization.[204] Jeffrey F. Taffet similarly concludes that Rostow's ambitious development projects failed because they were "too idealistic for policymakers to implement."[205] The failure of these policies exacerbated social unrest in the countries where they were applied, which, coupled with an increasing sense of caution, caused Kennedy to shift support from support for reform to support for authoritarianism.

The failure of the Amini experiment was a watershed moment in US–Iranian relations. It drew to a close almost two decades of attempts to seek reform in order to prevent social unrest and to promote development. In its place arose a policy of support for the shah's authoritarianism that would continue until his ousting in 1979. Even Eisenhower, who returned the shah to power in 1953, soon realized the importance of political reform to avoid an uncontrollable revolution. Kennedy's progression was the opposite of his predecessor's, coming to see repressive authoritarianism as the safer solution than reform in Iran. Two decades after his premiership, Amini remained insistent that the Kennedy administration should have done more to press the shah to institute democratic reforms. "They [American officials] are particularly guilty," he said during an interview in 1981, "because they should have put the shah on the right road before it was too late."[206] William Miller, a diplomat in the US embassy in Tehran during this period, agrees and has since argued that the failure to do so was a "missed opportunity of rather sizable proportions." Influencing the shah to give greater respect for constitutional government, he continued, "should have been the foundation of our policy towards Iran."[207] Summitt has argued that this missed opportunity was even greater considering that Kennedy ruled at a unique time when he was not constrained by an Arab–Israeli war and the regional instability that such wars caused throughout the Middle East.[208]

More than this, however, Kennedy entered office with high linkage and leverage. The shah was weakened by internal strife; the prospects of an Iranian–Soviet alliance had temporarily ended; and there existed a determination among American officials to place conditions on aid to alter the shah's behavior. The administration achieved much from this strong position of influence, but when US leverage began to decrease, the administration lost heart. Coupled with the failures of modernization policies and an increasingly resentful shah, the Soviet Union had returned to its efforts to reach out to Iran. As

US leverage weakened, it became more important to maintain Iran as an ally rather than to force the country to reform on American terms. Similarly, Washington's disengagement from Iran as the Cold War began to heat up again in Asia meant that its linkage and understanding of what was happening in Iran also suffered.

This decline in linkage and leverage as well as greater support for the shah's position would accelerate over the next fifteen years until Komer's prediction of an uncontrollable revolution became reality.

7 Shah's in Charge, 1963–1974

Lyndon Baines Johnson came to office unaware that American linkage and leverage with Iran were on the wane or that the shah was seeking to alter the US–Iran relationship. Replacing the American reform program with his own signaled the start of the shah's true dominance over Iran and the beginning of the end for the client–patron relationship that had existed between the two countries since 1941. For the previous two decades, the shah had been at the beck and call of foreign powers, especially the United States. With the Kennedy era now behind him, he was determined to start a new chapter and finally realize his dream of becoming a respected world leader in the dominant style of his father. The United States, however, would be slow to realize this change.

The period 1963–74 was one of steady centralization of Iran's socioeconomic development and restructuring of the US–Iranian relationship dynamic. The two powers would grow ever closer during these years, cooperating both militarily and economically. However, with regard to this book's focus, the period witnesses little but the gradual movement away from constitutionalism in Iran and the steady decline of US leverage. The shah would become both master of his domain and the dominant regional player in the Middle East. He would become so powerful that he would soon be dictating to the United States rather than following orders as he had in years past. When able to act independently of American pressure, the shah showed little thought for US interests, especially if they clashed with his own. Therefore, although Johnson and Richard Nixon would support his rise to dominance, the shah would not show any compulsion to support their policies when they clashed with his own.

External interference had been the defining aspect of Iranian politics in the first half of the twentieth century, but this situation would change as the next fifteen years witnessed the final consolidation of Pahlavi power with American consent and support. Pressure for reform, which had become a staple of US policy toward Iran, would vanish along with the ability to influence the shah's actions.

President Johnson and Declining US Leverage

To the British ambassador to Iran in 1966, the shah remarked how he could "never forget" how the Americans had forced governments of their choosing onto Iran. With the White Revolution helping him to emerge from under the yoke of foreign domination, he hoped the Americans had now "learned their lesson and would treat Iran as a truly independent country."[1] Three years earlier he had been overjoyed at news of Kennedy's assassination, reportedly asking for a drink to celebrate when the news came through to Tehran.[2] He felt confident that Kennedy's successor would not pursue similarly intrusive policies, and he was right. Johnson was already the shah's close friend, having first met him in Washington and then again when as vice president Johnson traveled to Iran in the summer of 1962. There, Johnson had been treated like Persian royalty, and a most favorable and long-lasting impression of the shah was formed. Upon his return to Washington, Johnson lobbied Kennedy to give the shah greater authority and cautioned against dictating policy to Iran. "We must accept [him] with his shortcomings, as a valuable asset," he reported.[3] In return, the shah saw Johnson as a kindred spirit and someone more likely than Kennedy to maintain support for his personal rule.[4]

Although Johnson had initially supported Kennedy's early foreign-policy idealism, he also supported the evolution of that policy toward more immediate security demands. And just as Kennedy had become distracted by issues other than Iran, so too did President

Johnson. The civil rights movement in the United States had created deep fissures in the American psyche as segregationists and integrationists clashed in increasingly violent protests. In addition, protests against and opposition to the Vietnam War added to the incessant unrest on the home front. Although Johnson inherited a recovering economy, unemployment remained high, and poverty levels were a growing source of concern. Bob Dylan captured the popular mood at the time of Johnson's inauguration with the release of his seminal song "The Times They Are A-Changin'." The United States was no longer a paragon for other states to emulate but rather a country in the midst of its own internal transformation. Johnson's signature policy, the Great Society, reflected this shift, focused as it was on tackling poverty, civil rights, and issues of inequality inside America rather than seeking to solve all the world's problems.[5]

Improved relations with the Soviets as well as a relative peace in Europe allowed Johnson to focus on domestic issues but meant that his foreign policy was often developed ad hoc as events occurred.[6] He continued Kennedy's policy of abandoning adventurous modernization programs in favor of focus on issues such as the growing conflagration in Vietnam. The shah's assertion that under his rule Iran would not become another problem for an already overstretched US foreign-policy apparatus was therefore very much welcomed in Washington. Johnson administration officials later recalled how Iran "was not at the top of the agenda nor near the top" when they entered the White House.[7] The White Revolution was seen as the perfect solution to Iran's ills—a robust reform package coupled with the strong leadership by a man they knew and trusted—and US intervention was neither warranted nor called for. Underpinning this trust in the shah's rule was the personal relationship of the two leaders, a relationship that has been called the key "that determined Johnson's foreign policy toward Iran."[8] Confidence in the shah's supremacy and reports that "opposition is disorganized and . . . no longer a threat" meant that the Johnson administration could focus more fully on other problems and leave Iran, a once notorious trouble spot, in the shah's seemingly strong and capable hands.[9]

What Johnson and Kennedy before him failed to appreciate, however, were the history and perseverance of democratic struggle in Iran. Political reform was not a major piece of the shah's reform package, but it was vital to appease internal demands and ensure the country remained peaceful. In early January 1964, Johnson wrote to the shah expressing admiration for his return to personal rule but made no mention of the necessity of political rights for the Iranian people to go alongside the social and economic reforms of the White Revolution. He instead praised the shah's program as "a new birth of freedom and justice" that will "free . . . the energies of Iran's peasantry and laborers, as well as the women." He also praised the shah for his "resistance to alien pressures," and any internal dissatisfaction that remained, Johnson assured him, was merely "the price of progress." The president was sure that in time the White Revolution would lead to the shah's becoming "admired and loved by [his] people."[10]

Robert Komer, who remained on the NSC despite the change in presidency, gleefully stated that "one of JFK's unheralded achievements was to con our nervous shah into stressing reform . . . instead of constantly bleating to us about his need for more arms. . . . Now we've got the shah thinking he's a 20th century reformer."[11] Rather than the Americans having tricked the shah, however, the reality was that the shah's White Revolution tricked the Americans. His reforms did much to strengthen his own authoritarian rule but little to garner the love and admiration of the Iranian people, who were kept repressed by an aggressive use of SAVAK and the military. The reforms were solely socioeconomic, not political ones that would lead to democracy. Johnson was nonetheless smitten with the man, remarking in June that "what is going on in Iran is about the best thing going on anywhere in the world."[12] Two years later this admiration remained strong, with the US ambassador reporting that the "shah is making [a] show-case of modernization in this part of the world."[13] Fears of revolution evaporated as the shah's authoritarian rule delivered reform and effectively suppressed any internal protest.

Shah's in Charge

The shah now dominated Iran but still wished to convince Washington of the need to send more military aid. The military was the shah's obsession, and he dreamed of building the grandest and most modern army that money could buy. This obsession had long been a source of tension between Washington and Tehran, and although Johnson committed to the shah's personal rule more than any other previous president, he continued to restrict the shah's military expenditure. This tension would continue throughout his presidency as the United States preferred a balance of power in the Middle East and rejected the shah's wish to become the region's dominant power.[14] Moreover, Iran's economy was still weak and seen as unable to absorb massive injections of aid, and, aside from these factors, Congress continued to call for reductions in the US foreign-aid program.[15] Johnson therefore informed the shah that contrary to the shah's view that Iran needed greater military aid to better protect itself, "we simply do not yet foresee much likelihood of a substantial Arab threat to Iran" or any amount of military aid being sufficient to guard against Soviet invasion, itself an unlikely eventuality.[16] When Armin H. Meyer arrived to replace Julius Holmes as the new US ambassador to Iran in early 1965, he was given strict instruction to move the shah away from demands for "fancy military hardware."[17] Nevertheless, the shah's persistence did result in the eventual signing of a five-year program of military credit for the period 1965–69, contingent upon annual reviews.[18]

It was on the issue of the military that the United States continued to use leverage to alter the shah's behavior. Despite the fact that the United States was no longer pressing the shah to pursue political reform, leverage remained an effective tool to use on a shah still dependent on US support. Its effectiveness was shown when in 1964 the United States demanded Iran's acceptance to a new Status of Forces Agreement (SOFA). Such arrangements are common between a country hosting foreign military forces, but the one written by the US Defense Department for Iran proved unprecedented in scope. The main source of outrage was that it would grant complete freedom from conviction in Iranian courts for any and all crimes that Americans committed while in the country.[19] This stipulation proved massively unpopular in Iran, yet American pressure on the shah convinced him to force the agreement through the Majles. US assistant secretary of state Strobe Talbott admitted in December 1964 that the SOFA was "rammed through the Iranian Parliament, at our insistence, and with considerable domestic political risk to [the shah's] domestic position."[20] Martin Herz of the US embassy concurred and remarked regarding the Majles's passing of the SOFA that "a very high price had been paid for something that isn't of commensurate value."[21]

So sure were the Americans of the longevity of the shah's new rule, however, that they felt no qualms about forcing him to pass such an unpopular law. Although the opposition was indeed riled by the shah's capitulation, the Americans happily observed his swift crackdown on the ensuing protests. One particular firebrand, Ayatollah Ruhollah Khomeini, who had come to prominence during the protests a year earlier, was exiled to Iraq for his continued agitation and criticism of the government. The Johnson administration merely noted without attaching too much significance to it that Khomeini's sharp denunciation of the shah had "aroused dormant nationalist feelings" and that the SOFA episode had "tarnished our formerly favorable image."[22] Indeed, had the Americans been aware of the level of anti-Americanism in Iran following the Majles's passing of the agreement, they would undoubtedly have been shocked.[23] Even the shah himself cultivated these anti-American feelings, welcoming public anger directed toward the United States rather than toward his own rule.

Despite a good personal relationship with Johnson, the shah still bristled from his experience with Kennedy and resented the Americans' refusal to submit more fully to his demands for more military aid. As the 1960s progressed, the shah moved farther from the United States. The failure of the United States to support Pakistan, a member of the Central Treaty Organization, in the dispute with India over Kashmir in 1965 served only to increase the shah's dissatisfaction. The shah angrily asserted, "We see now what [the treaty] really is. It is a device to protect the West only."[24] To underline his new independent position, he undertook a state visit to Moscow in June and later concluded a deal with the Soviets to build a steel mill, a gas pipeline, and a mechanical engineering plant in Iran. According to Ambassador Meyer, the shah was now a leader who

> is no longer [a] ward of [the] US as in 1941–45 [or the] vacillating youth of [the] late forties. . . . He is becoming more and more like [his] father . . . independent-minded, impulsive and autocratic. . . . [The] shah wants [an] independent stance for his country. . . . [He] is fully aware how [the] US saved his regime in [the] Azerbaijan crisis and in [the] Mosaddeq days. . . . Yet in [his] present state of mind he conjures up all sorts of specters.[25]

Despite the shah's growing independence from American control, the Johnson administration refused to be overly concerned by his actions. Washington's laissez-faire attitude can be explained in part by the shah's ability to dominate those very linkages that had once given the United States control. Instead of American officials suggesting policies to the shah, it was the shah who now used his contact with Americans to control Washington's perceptions of him. Senior officials—such as Averell Harriman, Johnson's roving ambassador-at-large; Walt Rostow, who had returned to the White House as national security adviser; and the new ambassador to Iran, Armin Meyer—were won over by the shah's personality and endeavor.[26] Meyer in particular has been described in the literature as a "silver-haired, friendly man of modest talent . . . [who was] manipulated by the shah, and for four years his actions approached those of a public relations officer for the Persian king."[27] Despite the shah's increasingly independent stance, Johnson was hard-pressed to find a dissenting view of him within the entire senior establishment of his administration.

With allies in the US government and continued threats to move even closer to the Soviet Union, the shah was able to change the status of the relationship between Iran and the United States by altering the balance of linkage and leverage between them. Although he had been forced to submit regarding SOFA in 1964, two years later he in turn successfully forced the US administration to submit to his demands for greater military aid. After the shah's repeated attempts to acquire greater military aid and continued flirtations with the Soviet Union, Rostow decided in May 1966 that "since he is determined to buy arms somewhere, the best we can do is to lean on the brakes. . . . [I]f we cannot dissuade him, no point in losing a good sale."[28] This was a sorry statement on the decline of US leverage over Iran: short-term economic gain was preferable to understanding the dynamics that underpinned the relationship. An extensive report by the *Washington Post* in July described the dangers of this change in the relationship, interpreting the shah's support for US action in Vietnam even as he also leaned toward the Soviets as indicating that the US ability "to set conditions for his military and foreign policy may no longer be a plausible notion."[29]

The Americans had broken in the struggle of wills and extended to the shah additional credit sales, but these concessions were still not enough to satiate his appetite for modern military equipment. Specifically, the new deal included only a fraction of the number of F-4E Phantom jets that he had requested, so he continued to lobby for more both in person and through his American surrogates.[30] Kermit Roosevelt, who had maintained a close friendship with the shah since the coup and was now vice president of the Gulf Oil Company, informed the US government that the shah was "tired of being treated like a schoolboy."[31] Armin Meyer also continued to support the shah, roundly criticizing the US attitude of "Papa knows best" in trying to manipulate and inhibit the shah's military purchases.[32] The shah himself warned that he should not be "taken for granted" or thought of as an American "lackey."[33] To prove that he meant what he said, he followed through with his threats and signed a $100 million arms deal with Moscow to the shock of officials in both Washington and

London. It was the first deal of its kind between the Soviet Union and a country allied with the United States.[34]

This was now a make-or-break moment for US–Iranian relations.[35] The Johnson administration saw additional arms sales to Iran as unnecessary for its security and a needless burden on its economy. The shah also preferred not to deal with the Soviets but would no longer accept Washington's continued refusal of his requests. Constrained by not wishing to disrupt the balance-of-power relationship between Iran and Saudi Arabia but understanding that the United States no longer held leverage in its relationship with Iran, the Johnson administration finally consented to supply additional military credit sales of up to $200 million to Iran. The shah of course welcomed the change of heart, and Walt Rostow consoled the defeated Johnson by informing him that the deal had "gone a long way toward keeping the shah from going overboard . . . [and kept] the worst we had feared from happening." However, the change in the relationship was made clear when Rostow cautioned Johnson that "we will undoubtedly have to adjust to [the shah's] increasingly independent tendencies" because without US leverage he could no longer be so easily controlled.[36]

The shah had backed up his words with actions, and the Johnson administration was forced to accept the new reality of an independent Iran. Although Johnson had successfully used leverage to ensure the passing of SOFA, the shah quickly turned the tables and effectively forced the United States to submit to his demands. The 1960s had been a great struggle for the shah, but he now emerged victorious in his relationship with the United States. Pushed to the periphery of decision making at the start of the decade, he was renewed with vigor and finally free of American control by its end. He not only ended foreign interference in the conduct of governance in Iran but also demonstrated a newfound international independence. A United States weakened both at home by race issues and abroad by the continuation of the Vietnam War and the Cold War struggle, accepted the new relationship in return for the maintenance of an important international ally. It could no longer force the shah to address internal problems, and so it instead chose to ignore them. Rostow and Meyer made sure that the steady stream of letters complaining of internal corruption and repression in Iran were kept far away from the president's desk.[37]

Voices within the administration that were critical of US–Iranian policy therefore became few and far between. One was Harold Saunders, Robert Komer's assistant, who persistently called for greater US action to prevent a long-predicted but now largely ignored revolution in Iran. He hoped the United States would return to the "political battlefield, where the fight will be won or lost . . . [because] we still haven't scratched the surface in figuring out what we can do to encourage political institutions that will, over the long haul, take the steam out of insurgency."[38] William R. Polk, who fluttered between administration positions and academia, had also remained consistent in his opposition to US policy since the fall of Amini. He warned the Johnson administration of the dangers of pursuing socioeconomic reforms while restricting political rights in Iran. "As a historian," he wrote in 1965, "I can tell you that a similar situation existed before each of the major revolutions in the last two centuries. . . . [I]f [the opposition] fail[s] through peaceful means to bring about a sharing of political power . . . [these means] will be thrust aside and others will use more violent means."[39] Equally prescient but similarly unheeded was a report by the State Department's Bureau of Intelligence and Research in 1966:

> On the political side, the shah has alienated the landlords and the clergy without winning the bulk of the reform-minded intellectuals and members of the middle-class. . . . [He] has shown no inclination to accept some of the reform-minded opposition elements and thus has, in effect, lost for his cause some of the elements most capable of making the reform program effective. . . . Eventually, the various opposition factions may be driven together by a common desire to limit the shah's power. Should the shah fail to follow through on the reforms he has begun, the opposition will have an immediate cause and may eventually also acquire the necessary

popular support to unseat him. . . . Long before such an impasse is reached, however, some measure of political compromise would be profitable.[40]

All such warnings were ignored. Senior officials were instead enamored of both the shah and his White Revolution. As instability spread in other regions, the Johnson administration was pleased that on the surface Iran appeared to be stable, modernizing, and, most important of all, allied to the administration's cause.

Iran's Internal Development during the 1960s

Throughout the 1960s, persistent use of the security forces to quiet any protest curtailed the opposition in Iran. Much like Lee Kuan Yew in Singapore, the shah felt that his socioeconomic reforms would produce benefits in time that would negate any popular desire for democratization. To carry out his agenda, he formed the Iran-e Novin (New Iran Party, NIP) in December 1963. Composed of young, Western-educated technocrats, it represented a fundamental change for the shah. Since coming to power in 1941, he had depended on advisers and prime ministers from his father's generation. Homa Katouzian describes the younger shah as someone who "disliked older men of knowledge and wisdom because he felt dwarfed by them."[41] But he did look to elder statesmen such as Ahmad Qavam, Mohammad Sa'ed, Ebrahim Hakimi, and Hossein Ala for patriarchal assistance while he grew into his role. By the end of 1963, he had been on the throne for more than two decades and had successfully overcome challenges to his authority from both Mossadegh and the Kennedy administration. It was a sign of renewed confidence in his ability therefore that he now saw himself as Iran's senior political figure, ready to dispense with the old guard and their patriarchal judgment.

The formation of the NIP therefore marked a break between the past, characterized by American domination, and the future, imagined by the White Revolution and an independent shah. The party's leader, Hasan-Ali Mansur, became the first prime minister younger than the shah when appointed in March 1964. The *Washington Post* described Mansur as a "young intellectual" with a "fresh approach" to achieving progress on the shah's reform programs.[42] Similarly, the *New York Times* heralded the appointment as a sign that Tehran was now "stirring with new life."[43] The NIP was committed to realizing the shah's vision for a modern, developing nation united under his rule, and its formation propelled a new generation of politicians to the forefront of Iranian politics, including Jamshid Amuzegar, who became minister of labor; Dr. Houshang Nahavandi, appointed to the Ministry of Development and Housing; and Mansur's close associate Amir-Abbas Hoveyda, who became the minister of finance.

In 1965, Hoveyda became prime minister and continued the obsequious relationship that had grown between the shah and successive prime ministers since the fall of Ali Amini. Hoveyda would remain in office for an unprecedented twelve years, thanks largely to his willingness "to embrace and affirm the prime ministerial role as defined by the shah."[44] Rather than an independent source of authority, the office of prime minister was now a mere extension of royal prerogative. Whereas previous prime ministers such as Mossadegh and Qavam had first experienced politics during the Constitutional Revolution of 1905–11, the new generation knew only the shah's primacy and demanded that he remain central to the political process.[45]

Hoveyda, like the shah, disdained attempts to assert democracy over the monarchy and devoted himself to realizing the shah's reformist visions. Devoid of political reform, the NIP nevertheless began what has been called "a phase of unprecedented prosperity and economic planning."[46] By mid-1965, the shah was moved to praise his prime minister for bringing "about a great transformation in the economic and social condition of the country. . . . Class privileges have disappeared . . . [and] superiority is now based on qualifications." He also demanded more action: "Poverty must gradually disappear from our midst. The word 'poverty' must be stricken from our dictionary [as the White Revolution becomes] an un-penetrable political school of thought throughout my country."[47] These were not just words; real change had come to Iran. A US State Department report noted that "between 1963 and 1968 Iran's Gross National Product rose at an average rate of 7 per cent per year to a total of $6.9 billion in March 1968. The nation's per capita GNP grew during the same time from $215 to an estimated $263 per annum. Iran's progress was one of the notable success stories of the period."[48]

Urbanization accelerated throughout the decade as development rates reached two to three times that of other developing nations. The Johnson administration noted with approval that one of their "staunchest allies" was now "surging forward."[49] Administration officials praised themselves for having made redundant Khrushchev's prediction of revolution in Iran, but they still made no mention of the need for political reform. The shah's White Revolution completely satisfied the Americans' wishes for economic development, and they praised his strong leadership for effectively protecting US security priorities. Even Walt Rostow seemed to have abandoned his goal of achieving democratization through development, stating in June 1968 that Iran was now at "that point on the development ladder where the 'take off' is just about finished and the nation is beginning to diffuse its resources and technology into broad range of new industries."[50]

Economic growth reduced fears of a social revolution and convinced Washington that the shah was correct to focus on the economy rather than on political reform. Development during the Cold War dictated that political reform was of little importance compared to stability, economic progress, and an alliance with the West. By orchestrating the White Revolution in line with modernist principles, albeit devoid of political reform, the shah had seemingly made US intervention redundant.

Internal Opposition Simmers

Despite growing prosperity, social development, and a more liberal use of SAVAK, opposition to the shah's regime remained active. Protests against SOFA, colloquially known as the Capitulations

Agreement, became one of the first internal challenges since Kennedy's assassination. As mentioned, these protests in 1964 were led by Ayatollah Khomeini, who excoriated the shah for having reduced "the Iranian people to a level lower than that of an American dog. If someone runs over a dog belonging to an American, he will be prosecuted. Even if the shah himself were to run over a dog belonging to an American, he would be prosecuted. But if an American cook runs over the shah, the head of state, no one will have the right to interfere with him."[51]

Although Khomeini was quickly exiled, opposition to the shah simmered for the rest of the decade and would occasionally boil over. In January 1965, for example, Khomeini's supporters assassinated Prime Minister Mansur. The US embassy reported that Khomeini's exile had given him a "new aura of martyrdom," but Mansur became a real martyr for the cause of the shah's White Revolution. He was announced dead on the third anniversary of the shah's referendum, shot by a member of the Feda'iyan-e Islam (Devotees of Islam) with a gun reportedly provided by a young cleric named Ali-Akbar Hashemi Rafsanjani.[52]

A few months after Mansur's assassination, an attempt was made on the shah's life when a disgruntled guard opened fire outside the Marble Palace. Remarkably, the shah emerged from the incident unscathed. However, symbolic of the apathetic and dissatisfied population, the threat to the shah's life did not spur a wave of public support for him, as had the previous assassination attempt in 1949. Furthermore, when festivities began to celebrate the shah's silver jubilee in September 1965, a British diplomat assessing the public mood noted that apart "from the habitual eulogizers of the regime, the reactions of most sophisticated Iranians in Tehran seem to have ranged from unenthusiastic to openly critical."[53]

Other sources of unrest became noticeable even as the shah's economic reforms continued apace. The White Revolution was supposed to create a foundation of regime support among the peasantry, but Iran's rapid industrial development largely negated this element. Emphasis was placed on capital-intensive industries, petrochemicals, pharmaceuticals, and consumer goods—all sectors that encouraged people to move away from the countryside to find work. The shah's reforms largely ignored small-scale production and the agricultural sector.[54] The shah admitted his disdain for the countryside when talking to the US ambassador. "I don't want [rural] villages to survive," he said, "I want them to disappear. We can buy the food cheaper than they can produce it. I need the people from those villages in our industrial labor force. They must come into the cities and work in industry."[55] Come into the city they did: urbanization had increased by 50 percent since 1941.[56]

Those who flocked to the cities, however, were largely unskilled and could find little work in an economy desperate for skilled labor. Economic progress and the benefits therein bypassed the vast majority of Iran's population and created a general feeling of sullen resentment that figures such as Ayatollah Khomeini were quick to take advantage of.[57] Those with the necessary experience and skills thrived and enjoyed relatively high wages, but those without experience or skills were left behind, leading to the creation of a dual society. Uneven development and rapid urbanization promoted income inequality, while continued import substitution put pressure on government finances and the balance of trade.[58]

Progress under the White Revolution was therefore fragile, and recession loomed large if Iran's oil revenues were to fall. Because the shah was unable to count on internal support, a serious economic crash would seriously threaten the longevity of his reign. He had never been able to develop a solid base of internal support, and the White Revolution did not change this situation as his regime was quick to ignore the peasants. Lacking internal support and not wishing to be beholden to the West, the shah was forced to tighten his tools of repression to maintain his grip on power. Bitterness and hatred of the shah bubbled under the surface of daily life. Denied public space to organize, the opposition was forced to congregate at the mosques, the one space left largely untouched by the shah's crackdown. "The banning of political parties, the turning of the Parliament into a club for sycophants, the muzzling of the press, and the continued underdevelopment of trade unions and other associations," wrote one Iranian political commentator in retrospect in 1978, "deprived society of its natural means of self-expression and political activity. This led to a gradual return to the mosque as a multipurpose institution that could counter the inordinate expansion of the state as a super institution."[59] Should the state's tools of repression be weakened or space for free expression somehow be made available, these feelings would quickly sweep the nation and imperil both stability and the shah's reign.

Johnson's Legacy: Sowing the Seeds of Revolution

Johnson's presidency therefore saw a rise in internal dissatisfaction in Iran—the very thing once predicted to lead to an uncontrollable revolution. However, the decline in linkage, illustrated by Ambassador Meyer's almost sycophantic and uncritical support for the shah, meant that the administration had little knowledge of this trend. Even if American officials became aware of such a trend, their lack of leverage meant they no longer had ability to alter it. This lack of both awareness and influence was compounded by the decision in late November 1967 to end direct financial assistance through USAID and declare Iran a developed country.[60] To the Americans, the aid program had served their purpose in helping with what they called the transformation of Iran into a country "enjoying political stability, economic growth, and social change unique in this part of the world."[61] The absence of any major protests, like those in 1960 and 1963, fostered the false impression that the shah was maintaining stability thanks to his reform program. Illustrative of this view was a Bureau of Intelligence and Research report published in the last year of Johnson's presidency. It concluded that the "shah's personal rule of Iran is probably more secure now than at any time since he succeeded to the throne."[62] From the American officials' minimal vantage point, the White Revolution had undercut the nationalist opposition, and his policy of independence in the international sphere seemed to have removed the stigma of subservience to American demands.

President Johnson left office in January 1969 blissfully unaware of the perilous nature of Iranian stability. The administration was instead satisfied that Iran did not present any cause for concern. Democratization had been abandoned, but Iran's economy and alliance with the West remained strong. The high monetary and human price of the conflict in Vietnam was a major reason why the "Decade of Development" concluded without political gains around the world in general.[63] Rapid modernization had caused instability and anomie not only in the developing world but also in the United States itself, the supposed paragon that other countries esteemed. The apparent stability in Iran was therefore a source of rare pleasure that the United States did not feel the need or desire to investigate further.

If Johnson was pleased with the situation in Iran, he should have been uneasy with the price paid to achieve it. Relinquishing leverage meant that should the shah decide to move away from an alliance with the West or should he succumb to internal unrest, the United States would be powerless to control subsequent events. Although an increase in military aid had been seen as necessary to maintain the shah's westward allegiance, the Johnson administration became increasingly ignorant of internal events as the 1960s drew to a close. Iran was therefore a country in the balance: if anything affected the status quo, the prospects of an uncontrollable revolution would become all too real.

The Johnson years therefore witnessed both the gradual decline in US linkage and leverage as well as the rise of the shah as an actor willing and able to stand up to the Americans and even make his own demands in certain situations. The only remaining form of leverage Washington held over the shah was in the form of military aid. As Ambassador Meyer wrote in April 1969, "The military sales relationship remains the most essential aspect of our ties with Iran."[64] The incoming administration of Richard Nixon understood this fact. Shortly after Nixon took office, a briefing summary on Iran designed for the new national security adviser, Henry Kissinger, remarked that unless the United States remains "Iran's principal military supplier . . . our ability to maintain our own strategic interests there and to influence the shah in the direction of constructive foreign and domestic policies will be seriously weakened."[65]

A resurgent shah with a booming economy changed the dynamic of the US–Iran relationship.[66] Military aid was the only form of leverage the United States had left, but its clout even in this area had been badly compromised by the shah's willingness to deal with the Soviets. By surrendering linkage and leverage to the shah, the Johnson presidency had begun to sow the seeds for revolution. Over the next ten years, these seeds would take root and eventually change the Iranian landscape completely.

The Nixon Presidency

The shah greeted Richard M. Nixon's victory in the presidential elections of 1968 with even greater enthusiasm than when he had heard the news that Johnson had replaced Kennedy four years earlier. Nixon and the shah had developed a close bond, and one of Nixon's former speechwriters recalled how "the shah was [just] about the president's favorite confidant in the world."[67] As Eisenhower's vice president, Nixon had visited Iran shortly after the coup in 1953, and his presence at such a difficult time helped forge a symbolic feeling of unity with the newly restored monarch. Their relationship almost grew too close, and three years later Nixon was accused of failing to disclose receipt of an expensive Persian rug sent to him as a gift from the shah.[68] Similarly, in 1960, desperate for his old friend to succeed to the White House, the shah was alleged to have secretly donated "hundreds of thousands of dollars to the Nixon campaign."[69]

In 1967, while preparing for a second presidential run, Nixon traveled to Iran and had "an unusually long meeting with the shah."[70] The two talked about regional security, among other topics, and the shah repeated his hope that the United States would finally abandon the balance-of-power approach and "pick Iran as its 'chosen instrument' in the Middle East."[71] Nixon was taken with the shah both as man and as a leader, praising him for his "profound social conscience" and for running "a virtual dictatorship in a benign way."

Talking about democracy in the Middle East, Nixon exclaimed, "Good God, it wouldn't work. . . . They aren't ready [for democracy]."[72] He praised Iran's "strong monarchy" as the best system of government for Iran and American interests.[73]

Since Kennedy's demise, the shah had gradually become more of a partner than a client of the United States.[74] The United States no longer dictated policies to him, but there still remained some restrictions on how much US military aid Iran could receive. Once the shah's old friend Richard Nixon was in the White House, these final restrictions would be swept away. Arms sales that had averaged around $100 million a year during Johnson's tenure ballooned to $289 million for 1969–70 alone.[75] This increase was not based solely on Nixon's personal admiration for and trust in the shah but also on the new president's view of how best to combat communism. Wishing to prevent another Vietnam War, Nixon began to look at ways to prevent such conflicts from occurring elsewhere. The United States "must avoid the kind of policy that will make countries . . . so dependent upon us that we are dragged into conflicts such as the one we have in Vietnam," he stated to reporters shortly after his inauguration.[76]

The Nixon Doctrine declared that rather than leading the response to international conflicts, the United States would give greater responsibility and military aid to allied countries. In essence, as Odd Arne Westad has concluded, the United States would become "an overseer, not an intervener," in international affairs.[77] The new doctrine largely dispensed with the notion that economic aid was a useful tool in the fight against communism. Massive economic aid projects that over the past decade had become the signature of America's shift toward modernization theory were instead blamed for sinking the country into the quagmire of Vietnam.[78]

The developing world held little interest for the Nixon administration, which also viewed Wilsonian concerns for promoting democracy as naïve; geopolitical realism became dominant in its approach to foreign policy.[79] "What happens in those parts of the world," Nixon told his advisers, "is not, in the final analysis, going to have any significant effect on the success of our foreign policy in the foreseeable future."[80] The focus would instead be on Great Power politics and how the United States could best supply its allies to protect its strategic interests, in particular the oil resources of the Middle East, against Communist aggression.

American attention to Iran's internal development had been moribund for years, and with Nixon's new national security posture, any remaining vestigial interest was terminated as talk of modernization theory left the administration's lexicon.[81] Stability through any means necessary was a position welcomed by the shah, who now felt comfortable dispensing with the notion that he was a democratizing monarch. After decades of praising democracy, the shah was finally able to speak his mind without fear of a negative reaction from the Americans. In an interview in 1973, he rejected democracy for Iran and spat, "It's all yours, you can have it! Your wonderful democracy! You'll see, in a few years, where your wonderful democracy leads."[82]

Now that there was no compulsion to continue reforms, the early 1970s saw little attention paid to Iran's internal situation. The shah tightened his authoritarian control, and a reign of terror enveloped Iran as prisons were filled, people disappeared, and the use of torture and executions rose considerably.[83] By 1974, a time of much competition for the title of worst dictator among the likes of Pol Pot and Idi Amin, Amnesty International concluded that Iran had the worst human rights record in the world.[84] Despite this record, the United States remained privately pleased that the shah at least seemed secure on his throne and maintained an alliance with the West.

Increased Internal Strife

There were, of course, signs that Iran was not as stable as it appeared, but the Americans ignored them, even when those signs threatened the life of the president himself. Coinciding with Nixon's state visit to Iran in 1972, a series of bombs exploded at numerous locations across Tehran, including at the United States Information Service office and under a US Air Force brigadier general's car. An explosion designed to coincide with Nixon's ceremonial visit to the tomb of Reza Shah Pahlavi went off early thanks to a faulty timer, but it forced the president to wait nervously in his car until news came that it was safe to travel. He eventually left the area surrounded by a special motorcycle guard and two dozen Jeeps bursting with soldiers.[85]

The bombings were part of a growing number of attacks that exploded across Iran in the early 1970s. Although most opposition groups had been forced underground or abroad following the shah's crackdown, others remained active despite SAVAK's attentions. With secular organizations such as the Tudeh and the National Front largely constrained since 1953, the main form of opposition came from Islamic groups. Many of these groups drew inspiration from armed struggles elsewhere in the developing world and pursued increasingly violent means to achieve their goals.[86] The Hey'at-ha-ye Mo'talefeh-ye Eslami (Coalition of Islamic Associations), which now included the Feda'iyan-e Islam, the group responsible for the assassination of Prime Minister Ali Razmara in 1951, repeated the Feda'iyan's success by dispatching Prime Minister Hasan-Ali Mansur in 1965.[87] The Mujahadeen-e-Khalq (MEK, People's Mujahideen of Iran), formed in 1965 by leftist Islamic students, also followed the Feda'iyan's violent lead.[88] By 1968, MEK was in contact with other revolutionary movements, such as the Palestinian Liberation Organization, and sent a number of its members to learn insurgency techniques at the al-Fatah (Conquering) training camps. Spurred on by the Feda'iyan's high-profile attacks, MEK endangered the life of the US president in 1972.[89]

Although Nixon was unharmed, General Saeed Taheri, chief of police in Tehran, was assassinated, and additional bombs were detonated at the Imperial Club, the Civil Defense Organization Center, the Municipal Department Store, the Police Armory in Qom, and the exhibition hall of the Department of Military Industries. The MEK's campaign received much publicity, culminating in a major street battle with police in the middle of Tehran later that year. Nixon was interested in who was responsible, but the shah successfully restricted any talk of Iran's internal situation by blaming the

Soviet-backed regime in Iraq for the troubles. Although the MEK made clear the true reasons behind its attacks in a series of publications and communiqués, the Americans felt the attacks to be but a trifling internal matter that the shah would no doubt deal with in his customary manner. Despite having his life threatened, Nixon did not increase monitoring of Iran's internal situation and maintained utmost faith in his friend's permanency on the throne.

"Stronger Than Horseradish": The Final Loss of Leverage

So great was Nixon's faith in the shah that he finally consented to a readjustment of America's Middle East strategy. Relations with the Saudi Kingdom had soured following strong American support for Israel during the Arab–Israeli war of 1967. An NSC policy statement issued in November 1969 cautioned that King Faisal had become increasingly disenchanted with the United States, and it was unclear whether the "political and social order upon which US–Saudi cooperation was built" could be maintained.[90] In addition, the chaos following the Soviet-backed Ba'athist coup in Iraq in July 1968 brought increased instability to the region. These trends, coupled with the vacuum left by Britain's extraction from "east of Suez" and the strong personal relationship between Nixon and the shah, meant that Iran became the prime candidate to protect US interests in an increasingly unstable region.[91] Kissinger praised Iran for being "the most powerful and most stable state in the area" and argued that the shah, "despite the travesties of retroactive myth," was really "a dedicated reformer."[92] In Nixon's analysis, the shah was a true friend: "I'm stronger than horseradish for him," Nixon declared. "I like him, I like him, and I like the country. And some of those other bastards out there I don't like." Of Iran's internal situation, he was content only to note approvingly that the shah "runs a damn tight shop."[93]

Iran was therefore chosen to be the Nixon administration's "chosen instrument" for regional stability in the Middle East.[94] This was news the shah had long waited for, and he was told face to face during Nixon's state visit in 1972. Meeting in Tehran's Saadabad Palace on the morning of May 31, as protests and explosions outside demonstrated the shah's inability to maintain stability in his own country, Nixon looked the shah in the eyes and said, "Protect me."[95] In an instant, the shah was given his greatest wish: freedom to order as much military aid as he wished, the whole Milky Way. An internal US governmental memo stated that it was now to be US policy that all "decisions of the acquisition of military equipment should be left primarily to the government of Iran." Lest any confusion emerge, Kissinger clarified that "we will accede to any of the shah's requests for arms purchases from us."[96]

Congress, which had once served to limit US arms sales during the Johnson years, failed to prevent this change in policy owing to what Senator Frank Church (D–ID) at the time called the legislative body's "impotence" in standing up to Nixon, a president he called an "autocrat supreme."[97] Nixon's centralization of domestic power allowed him to strongly support his chosen instrument in the Middle East. His plea for protection was therefore a revolutionary change in US arms policy and in US–Iranian relations as the last vestiges of the patron–client relationship were washed away and Iran became a full partner of the United States.[98] The United States was now fully dependent on the shah for security in the region, and so US leverage, which had gradually eroded since the downfall of Amini in 1962, finally fell away. The United States now depended on the shah as much as he depended on US aid. Conditionality, which had once been so effective, was lost.

With his dream realized, the shah wasted little time in placing orders that totaled a staggering $9 billion in the first four years after this shift in relations.[99] Between July and November 1972 alone, his orders reached $3.5 billion, more than the combined US military assistance budget for all other countries for the entire year.[100] Much of this equipment was far beyond anything Iran could actually use or even absorb into its economy. An example of acquisition for acquisition's sake was the purchase of F-14 Tomcats, the most sophisticated and state-of-the-art swing-wing fighters on the planet. So advanced were they that even the US Navy had trouble implementing the F-14 program. Iranian air force mechanics meanwhile were still trying to become accustomed to the less-sophisticated F-4 and F-5 fighters previously purchased. So pleased was the shah, however, that Iranian air force commanders restricted use of the F-14s so as not to lose or damage the jets and threaten disfavor from the monarch: despite the hundreds of millions of dollars spent on the program, the F-14s were flown only during good weather in daylight hours and even then only for simple training runs rather than for dogfight training.[101]

"Chosen Instrument": The Final Loss of Linkage

In addition to the surrender of leverage, the Nixon administration also lost any remaining linkage to Iran's internal affairs. The Americans seemed perfectly at ease with the shah's permanency and felt no compulsion to continue monitoring Iran for signs of unrest. Fears of the inevitable uncontrollable revolution were long forgotten, and links with anyone but the shah were regarded as superfluous. Henry Precht, who served as chief political officer in the US embassy in Tehran at this time, remembered how the staff was no longer encouraged to monitor the opposition in Iran: "I think Henry Kissinger and Nixon didn't want to know that the shah had any problems domestically. They didn't encourage the embassy to inquire if the country was stable before making a military commitment. They assumed it was stable and didn't want to look further into such questions." As a result, Precht continued, the US embassy's knowledge of the internal situation was nonexistent: "it was assumed that the country people loved the shah," he recalled in an interview many years later.[102]

The embassy and CIA stations were instead directed to focus their attentions outward and use Iran as a base to monitor the neighboring Soviet Union. Intelligence officials sent to Iran were chosen not for their knowledge of Iran but for their Soviet expertise.[103] Emblematic of this approach was Richard Helms's transfer from his post as director of the CIA to a new position as ambassador to Iran in February 1973. His close relationship with the shah ensured that any critical thinking about the shah's regime was stamped out. Precht recalled the visit of one embassy official to Mashhad, a city some five hundred miles to the east of Tehran. When the official returned to the embassy and commented, "I just wish the shah had bought one fewer of those F-4s and paved the road," he was quickly removed from his position for his insolence.[104] On another occasion, a visiting delegation asked a high-ranking embassy official about human rights in Iran. When a researcher later quizzed the official on whether in his response he had mentioned the ongoing torture in Iran's prisons, the official replied, "Of course not": he had instead given the delegation a ninety-minute presentation extolling the virtues of the shah's White Revolution.[105] It was both the ambassador's and the administration's view that no criticism of the shah by American officials should be allowed either in public or in private. One State Department official at the time explained that it became standard practice not to "report on an ally once he's become 'The Chosen Instrument.' It's bad manners."[106]

The result of this policy was that the United States became totally ignorant of Iran's opposition movement and of the shah's inability to maintain stability. A report drawn up by the US embassy in 1972 falsely concluded that even if "a marked faltering of the economy or an apparent weakening of the government's firm hand [should occur] . . . it is unlikely [the opposition] will ever return to a historic role such as that of 1892, when they [*sic*] led the attacks against the Belgian Tobacco Concession, or of 1907, when they played a big role in the Constitutional Revolution, or in 1952, when they rallied behind the government in the break with the British."[107] The errors in this statement—that it was the British tobacco concession rather than the Belgian and that protests began in 1890, not in 1892—point to the lack of attention given to Iran. Three years later, in 1975, Ambassador Helms exhibited the same low degree of oversight of the Iranian opposition. Just two years before the revolution began, he remarked that it was "difficult to find any grouping which was in opposition to the government . . . [let alone anything that could constitute] a threat to stability."[108]

Divergent Interests: The Oil Crisis

This lack of linkage and leverage went unnoticed in the early 1970s as Iran remained relatively stable and the shah was willing to protect US interests. However, conditions change, especially in a country as capricious as Iran. When the shah eventually diverged from the US position, Washington would be shown how ineffective it was in controlling the now all-powerful Iranian monarch. The first sign of disharmony came as early as 1970, when the shah proved unwilling to follow the US position on oil policy. When Nixon requested the shah's assistance in influencing the Organization of the Petroleum Exporting Countries (OPEC) to reduce the price of oil, he was rebuffed because the shah was quite taken with getting more dollars for his oil. Without fear of punishment from the Americans, the shah acted as he pleased. "These guys think they can for example spend one or two million dollars in Iran and stage a coup," the shah confided to his minister of court; "the time for such things has passed."[109] Events swung more in the shah's favor after October 4, 1973, when the combined armies of Egypt and Syria attacked Israel on Yom Kippur, the holiest day of the Jewish calendar. Nixon supported Israel in the conflict, so the Persian Gulf states quickly imposed an oil embargo on the United States. Iran abstained from the embargo, but the shah pushed strongly for an increase in the price of oil to help fund his ongoing military purchases.[110]

This demand brought him in direct confrontation with the Nixon administration, which quickly felt the effects of the embargo and rise in the price of oil. If administration officials expected loyalty in return for building the shah's power, they were disappointed. Nixon was instead taught the lesson that realism and national self-interest drove other countries besides the United States. From the outset of the fourth Arab–Israeli war, the shah followed a policy that would increase Iranian power and prestige even if it undermined and weakened the United States. The "chosen instrument" was now striking his own key. "He *was* our baby," complained one CIA official, "but now he has grown up."[111] With the United States more dependent than ever on Iranian oil, the shah was keen to reap the advantage. Lacking leverage and experiencing continued political paralysis in Washington from incessant political scandals, the United States was at the shah's mercy.

The impact of the oil crisis hit Americans hard in late 1973.[112] Christmas decorations in major cities were cancelled or dimmed; Governor Ronald Reagan reduced the speed limit on California's highways in hopes of conserving ten million gallons of fuel a year, and other states soon followed suit.[113] Taxis in Manhattan ran out of gas; lights on bridges and monuments were turned off; and predictions were made that unemployment would reach levels not seen since the Great Depression.[114] Citizens attempted to rise to their civic duty and took whatever measures they could to ameliorate the crisis. One conscientious commuter in Kentucky traded his car for a pony to ride the six blocks to work every day; Alfred Pauly of Belle Plaine, Minnesota, decided to wrap his concrete house in transparent plastic, which allowed his impressed wife to reduce the thermostat by ten degrees compared to the previous winter.[115] Joe Conforte, owner of the Mustang Ranch in Nevada, the first legal brothel in the United States, also lowered the thermostat and "ordered all his girls to wear nightgowns rather than bikinis while waiting for customers."[116]

Less responsible were the men and women on Capitol Hill, who, while holding long sessions into the night, were rather unfairly accused of having increased their own energy consumption.[117] Despite ordinary Americans' best efforts, the US economy began to slump. In the third week of November 1973, the Dow-Jones Industrial witnessed the sharpest back-to-back drop since the Great Depression and a few days later saw the fifth-largest one-day decline in US history.[118]

American officials' efforts to convince the shah to lower oil prices were ignored. The shah knew he held the upper hand in negotiations because the United States was starved of oil-producing allies. Iran was therefore vital for both refueling American ships in the region and supplying Israel with fuel. The Nixon administration could not take a firm line with the shah lest the shah take umbrage and join the embargo. Moreover, the shah was well aware that the president's perilous domestic situation following the uncovering of the Watergate scandal meant that any demands would unlikely be backed up by force. Kissinger recalled two years later how they had not been in a position to move against the shah for fear of pushing him to join the embargo against the United States.[119] Free from US leverage, therefore, the shah was able to defiantly inform the United States that oil prices were a nonnegotiable issue.[120] His military and development plans depended on greater oil revenues, and as a firm believer in peak-oil theory he was determined to extract as much money as possible before the oil ran out. He hoped that a soft landing could be reached as modernization and industrialization made up for the decline in revenues when the oil wells slowly petered out.[121] The current crisis gave the shah the chance to make even more money from oil, and no gesturing from an increasingly desperate United States could dissuade him. When questioned by reporters on whether oil prices would continue to rise, the shah answered with excitement: "Certainly! And how!"[122] In an interview with the *New York Times* in December 1973, he stated that "in 20 or 25 years I want [Iran] to be ahead of the greatest nations of the world" and that with higher oil prices "we can be the most advanced country and do better than any other."[123]

Although increased revenue would greatly benefit Iran's development, the reality was that the shah had already spent any additional income he might derive from price increases. Since Nixon's invitation to the shah to take his pick from the US military arsenal, the shah had racked up estimated expenditures for 1974–78 that were $5 billion in excess of projected oil revenues for that period. These expenditures included 177 F-4 Phantoms, 141 F-5E Tigers, 80 F-14 Tomcats, 489 attack and utility helicopters, 460 M-60 tanks, and additions to what was already the world's largest hovercraft fleet.[124] The shah needed an increase in oil prices just to pay off his account with the US Treasury.

When OPEC met in Tehran in December to discuss future price increases, the United States lobbied desperately but unsuccessfully for a reduction. Not only was the shah able to act independently of

US pressure, but he was able to make American oil consumers foot the bill for his arms expenditures by raising prices as much he could. He also refused to give any discounts to the US military and instead made large profits on oil sold to the US fleet in Oman.[125]

In meetings at the time, Nixon was "listless, [he] looked sad; his mind elsewhere; [he] shook his head now and then, but he was clearly not interested."[126] Kissinger was less concerned, feeling that a spike in prices had been inevitable owing to the market conditions of the early 1970s.[127] But the situation continued to deteriorate. Just as the United States was braced for OPEC to increase the price of oil from the current $5.11 a barrel to around $7 a barrel, the shah convinced the organization to set the price at $11.65. The previous price, $5.11, had itself been a 70 percent increase from the price set in October, and with this second substantial raise OPEC producers effectively gave themselves a 400 percent increase in profit per barrel over the space of just a few months.[128] While the developed countries were swept toward economic turmoil, the unsentimental shah declared triumphantly that the West's "era of . . . terrific progress and even more terrific income and wealth based on cheap oil is finished."[129]

The loss of leverage had cost the Americans dearly. Their ineffective response to the shah's actions illustrated how far away they were from being able to successfully mount an objection. Ambassador Helms was instructed to bring diplomatic pressure to bear on the shah, but it was ineffective. In one conversation, the shah replied, "Well, I've tried in the past to get oil price rises and the American and British companies wouldn't give them to me. Now I've got them and you're going to have to live with them."[130] So great had Iranian leverage over the United States become that the shah was even able to exact more concessions from his beaten allies. In return for increasing oil production for the embargoed West, he insisted that the United States provide and deliver additional construction materials to Iran.[131] Again the United States had no option but to oblige.

The shah's bonanza was staggering. It was predicted that Iran's oil revenues would increase from $4 billion in 1973 to an incredible $18 billion the following year.[132] Nixon had given the shah the entire Milky Way when he asked for protection in return for virtually unlimited arms sales, and the spike in oil prices gave the shah part of Andromeda as well. The shah happily received news from his chief economist in mid-1974 that "we have no real limit on money, none."[133] It was reported in the West that among the people the shah's development of Iran had finally made him a worthy successor to the great Persian emperors of old. One Iranian summed up the sense of prosperity the shah had given his country when he remarked that "every teacher and bank clerk [now] has a Volkswagen; they didn't have a bicycle twenty years ago."[134]

In December 1974, *New York* magazine ran a fictional piece on the possible result of the ongoing oil crisis. On its cover, like something out of a GI Joe catalog, an illustration showed hovercrafts speeding toward the reader as the headline warned of "the coming oil war: how the shah will win the world." The article spelled out what it called an "all-too-plausible scenario" of a shah totally free of American control and increasingly aligned with the Soviet Union. The story went that a dominant Iran would use its sophisticated American-made military to launch a blitzkrieg offensive to reclaim the Middle East and successfully capture Iraq, Kuwait, Bahrain, Qatar, Dubai, and Oman, all within two days. The shah would then be in control of all the oil in the region. While American officials in the story frantically discussed ways to react, including the nuclear option, the shah released a statement: to compensate himself for liberating the Middle East, he would have to double the price of Persian Gulf oil. The story concluded as if looking back from a dystopian future:

> That did it. Within two months Italy and Britain were bankrupt. The dollar had collapsed, along with a few thousand banks. Wall Street lay in ruins. . . . [U]ltimately [the price increase led to] the End of the Industrial Era. Today in 1984, most survivors say that it has all been for the good. At least the ones here in California don't have to worry about starving or freezing to death. I'm not sure. Sometimes I like to stop and think back on the world—but, right now, the cows need milking.[135]

This was the level of fear that swept the United States as the oil crisis continued. The United States appeared helpless against the seemingly all-powerful shah. Thankfully for the West, the *New York* story was mere fiction. Reality was to be quite different and altogether less prosperous for the shah.

8 The Predictable Storm, 1974–1979

It was said that "not a sparrow falls in the kingdom without [the shah's] knowledge," but the shah of Iran was slow to take action as the warning signs of unrest grew during the 1970s.[1] On May 26, 1974, the *Washington Post* listed these signs: "The shah has proclaimed nationwide programs of free education for which there are not enough teachers or schools; free health care, for which there are not enough hospitals or doctors; free milk for school children, for which there are not enough cows, and other sweeping changes which most Iranians expect to take effect immediately."[2]

Analysts noted that the shah's failure to manage expectations—indeed, his tendency to balloon them beyond all possible and practical proportions—could hurt him if they were not met. "The shah is aiming for the sky," said one observer in May 1974, "but he might just hit a big tree." He "thinks he knows the oil business inside out but he doesn't, you know," said another, "in fact, his ideas on economics are bloody naïve!"[3] An early warning that the shah's economic policy was backfiring was seen in reports that same month showing that "inflation is running wild . . . anywhere from 15 to 22 percent."[4] In response, stern punitive measures were quickly put in place, with hoarders facing the prospect of either fifteen years in prison or the death penalty if persistent offenders.[5] Prime Minister Amir-Abbas Hoveyda told Iranians to prepare for inevitable food shortages caused by the increase in demand owing to the continued high rate of urbanization and newfound prosperity.[6]

260

As economic problems became more prevalent, so, too, did examples of opposition and repression. It was rumored that political prisoners in Iran numbered between twenty-five thousand and forty-five thousand, and at least seventy-five people were executed for subversive activities between 1972 and 1974.[7] In March 1974, five bombs exploded in one night across the capital city. Tehran University resembled more a police station than a place of learning, with the shah keen to ensure that students did not take to the streets.[8] It was estimated that by the end of the 1970s at least half a million people had at one time in their lives been beaten, whipped, or tortured by SAVAK.[9] A huge public backlash was coming unless the shah could make good on his promise to supply benefits to everyday Iranians—a promise that demanded higher oil prices.

The shah therefore refused to back down in the standoff with his old friend in the White House. Realizing that the shah could not be dissuaded, Nixon looked elsewhere for assistance. In March 1974, the Nixon administration succeeded in convincing Saudi Arabia to break OPEC's embargo of the United States and to hold firm on oil prices. In return, the Saudis were offered military and economic deals that would consolidate King Faisal's regime and make Saudi Arabia, not Iran, America's chosen instrument for maintaining stability in the Middle East. A few months later Nixon was forced to resign, and it was left to his successor to solve both the oil crisis and the problem of Iran.

The five years between Gerald R. Ford's inauguration and the fall of the shah's regime illustrate the failures of US policy toward Iran that date back to 1941. They also further highlight the importance of linkage and leverage because the absence of these two elements for much of this period made impossible the formulation of any coherent strategy to deal with renewed crisis in Iran. Both Ford and Carter have been blamed for the revolution that swept Iran toward the end of the decade, but without these two vital elements of influence there was little that either of these presidents could do to alter what happened.[10] President Ford took action to overcome the oil crisis, not realizing that those very actions would kick-start Iran's revolutionary period. His successor, Jimmy Carter, was handed the task of trying to save the situation but without linkage was unable to understand or respond in a cogent manner. These five years therefore show clearly the dangers of not having linkage or leverage.

President Ford and the Breaking of the Shah

Gerald Ford's ascendance to international politics occurred simultaneously with the oil crisis. On the day Egyptian troops crossed the Sinai, October 6, 1973, starting the Yom Kippur War, Ford was toiling as House Minority leader. A few days later, October 10, Vice President Spiro Agnew resigned, and Ford was suddenly selected as his replacement. Although Ford had served in the House of Representatives for twenty-five years, he had failed to write a single piece of major legislation. He instead had developed a reputation as a highly skilled negotiator and dealmaker.[11] Becoming vice president amid corruption scandals, the energy crisis, and chaos in the Middle East was not ideal for a figure new to the international scene. The situation for Ford would only get worse: he would be vice president for only eight months before Nixon's resignation made him president. All of America's woes were now placed on his shoulders. He had no relationship with the shah, so his appointment of Nelson Rockefeller as vice president ensured that the shah still had a close personal friend in the White House.[12] Defeat in the presidential election of 1976 meant Ford departed the international scene almost as quickly as he arrived, but his fleeting presidency was by no means insignificant for US–Iranian relations. He would pass on to his successor, Jimmy Carter, as many presidents had done before him, an Iran in turmoil.

Upon entering the White House, Ford immediately learned that unless he brought inflation under control in three months, the United States itself would suffer severe social unrest.[13] A member of the offensive line for the Michigan Wolverines while in college, Ford followed his instincts and went on the attack. He demanded that oil prices move with the market rather than be kept high through what he called the "artificial rigging and distortion of world commodity markets."[14] The shah, however, had played this particular game far longer than the White House freshman and knew the rules. His instant reply was that "no one can dictate to us. No one can wave a finger because we will wave one back."[15] To his minister of court, the shah confided, "Ford is an utter booby."[16] Neither side was willing to back down. In a meeting with Secretary of State Henry Kissinger days after his inauguration, Ford was told that "the shah is a tough, mean guy. But he is our friend. . . . We can't tackle him without breaking him."[17] Such advice would prove prescient but did not alter Ford's calculation. If the choice were between breaking the shah and breaking the United States through economic recession, Ford would push for the former.

Economic Chaos and a Return to Liberalization

The oil crisis and union between the United States and Saudi Arabia soon brought discomfort to Iran. The worldwide recession had forced many countries to reduce their petroleum consumption, and in reply many producers began to lower output so as not to flood a saturated market. In alliance with the Americans, however, Saudi Arabia instead called for a reduction in prices rather than output. This decision immediately affected Iran. Its Consumer Price Index increased, and inflationary pressures led to a shortage of goods and rising prices for imports.[18] As unskilled workers continued to sweep into the cities in search of work and opportunity, they created even more shortages of food items, while power blackouts, traffic jams, overcrowding, and eventually riots began to spike.[19] The twelfth anniversary of the demonstrations of 1963 brought the largest antigovernment protests seen since the event they were commemorating. Inflation reached 20 percent by June 1975 and increased to 30 percent just two months later.[20] The shah, while awaiting the next OPEC meeting, at which he hoped to secure a large price increase, was forced to take desperate measures and so declared forced price cuts of up to 57 percent on hundreds of key products. Shopkeepers protested at the decline in revenue, but the shah was unmoved; 7,500 individuals were arrested for profiteering, and more than five hundred stores were closed in Tehran. In early August, the *Wall Street Journal* commented sardonically that "Iran will undoubtedly have stable prices until it runs out of shops and shopkeepers."[21]

As the situation spiraled out of control, protests erupted, and rumors of antigovernment sabotage operations abounded. Desperate to maintain order and, as the shah said, "to squelch such intrigues," he finally returned to political reform in the hope of releasing internal pressure.[22] Political reform and liberalization had been a way of tempering social unrest in the past, and the shah hoped that doing so again could ensure calm until he could achieve an increase in oil price. The move began with the reorganization of the country's political party system in May 1975. The current two-party system had been instituted to mirror the state of modern democratic nations such as the United States, but the shah now decided that just one party would be better. The watchword for the new political system was *participation*, and the shah expected everyone to join the Rastakhiz (National Resurgence) Party. Prime Minister Hoveyda assured Iranians that the party would encourage free discussion of issues and promote domestic reform.[23] James Bill argues that the shah's inspiration for this restructuring came from American-trained Iranian social scientists.[24] The shah had first incorporated social science thinking when promoting the White Revolution and wished to do so again to prove to the world that he was a forward-thinking monarch. Scholars such as Samuel P. Huntington argued that development was best ensured through participation. "In much of Asia, Africa, and Latin America," Huntington wrote in 1968, "political systems face simultaneously the needs to centralize authority, to differentiate structure, and to broaden participation. It is not surprising that the system which seems most relevant to the simultaneous achievement of these goals is a one-party system."[25] Not included in Huntington's prescription, however, was the shah's insistence that all Iranians either join the party or leave the country.[26]

Other policies were announced with the intention of gaining public support, including free health insurance to the increasingly fractious student population and encouragement of private benevolence and official largesse. To support workers in Tehran who had to deal with unremitting traffic jams and poor roads, the shah agreed to the construction of a subway system to ease their travels.[27] The concept of participation was extended to the parliamentary elections of June 1975, with Hoveyda urging high turnouts: "We have been economic animals and now we must be political animals too," he belatedly informed prospective voters long deprived of any political representation.[28] More ominously, he warned that those who failed to vote would have to explain their reasons to the party. Although the system was run solely by the shah, with all candidates personally selected by him, it was hoped that encouragement and forced participation would give his crumbling regime a badly needed fillip in the form of a popular mandate. However, of course, such threats amid rising public anger did not satisfy demand for real change, and only 10 percent of the population consented to vote.[29]

Rather than a new beginning for political participation, the reality of the new party system was just a continuation of the shah's control over the political process. John D. Stempel, a Foreign Service officer in Tehran at the time, saw it as a missed opportunity. He reported that many Iranians initially welcomed the emergence of the Resurgence Party and noted that around six hundred individuals among Tehran's intelligentsia expressed a willingness to give the party a chance in return for a greater say in Iran's political system.[30] With significant official prodding, seven to eight million membership applications were completed in the run-up to the election.[31] However, the party was never allowed to achieve independence from the shah, who maintained close control over its operation. Although he had ostensibly returned to populist policies to protect his regime against a crumbling economy, the reforms were largely window dressing and reminiscent of his policy in the late 1950s. Unable to secure public backing, the shah saw an increase in oil prices as even more essential to avert disaster.

Defeat at Doha

In alliance with the Saudis, the United States had so far been able to stall Iranian demands for higher prices, thus devastating the Iranian economy.[32] By February 1976, Iran's economic growth rate had contracted by 60 percent from the previous spring, and it was estimated that a budget deficit of $2.4 billion should be expected over the next twelve months. Income inequality more than tripled from a decade earlier as a severe recession set in.[33] Nevertheless, military expenditures continued unabated and even rose 8 percent to more than $8 billion in 1975.[34] In exile, Ayatollah Ruhollah Khomeini continued to protest against the shah and used the failure of modernization and industrialization to add further pressure. "Take a look at the south of [Tehran]," he urged people. "Go look at those pits, those holes in the ground where people live, dwellings you reach by going down about a hundred steps into the ground; homes people have built out of rush matting or clay so their poor children can have somewhere to live."[35]

With unrest rising, the shah doubled his efforts to avoid losing Iran before higher oil prices could be attained. He employed an army of twenty thousand official price watchers to clamp down on profiteering and encouraged ordinary citizens to inspect merchandise with greater scrutiny to ensure there were no irregularities. One diligent woman counted the number of sheets in her toilet roll and concluded that the number had been reduced by 10 percent while the price stayed the same. Her case was taken to court, where judges routinely confiscated stock or decreed large fines or passed lengthy prison sentences for violators. One managing director of a building-materials firm was convicted of profiteering and ordered to spend ninety days in the Dasht-e Kavir, the Iranian equivalent of Siberia, where, instead of cold, temperatures could reach an intolerable 130 degrees Fahrenheit. In the latter half of 1975 alone, 85 people were banished there, 11,500 were charged with profiteering, and 180 businesses were closed down.[36] Social unrest was bubbling amid economic difficulties and government repression. The upcoming OPEC meeting in Doha in December 1976 seemed to offer the final opportunity for the shah to secure significant oil-price increases before his country was lost to chaos.

The meeting has been called "the showdown at Doha" and pitted the Saudi–US alliance against the Iranians in a decisive confrontation.[37] A significant increase in the price of oil would seriously hinder the US economy, whereas no increase would cause untold problems in Iran. Ford lobbied hard for the Saudis to support his policy of no further oil-price increases. He also requested leniency from the shah and warned that the future sale of military equipment could be in jeopardy if the shah were to force through a significant increase. Despite the shah's position since the start of the oil crisis, the United States had continued to supply him with military aid and equipment. Indeed, both Kissinger and Ford felt that continued military deals were vital for sustaining the US economy during the tough economic period.[38] Only now did they consider adding conditions to force an end to the standoff. This would be the first use of conditionality since the Americans had successfully pushed through the ratification of SOFA in 1964. However, the shah remained confident in his ability to convince his OPEC allies to push for higher prices. After intense negotiation, he emerged from one round of the talks in a joyous mood, announcing a 15 percent increase. Iran was saved, while much of the Western world prepared for desolation.

But not so fast. Before the shah could bask in his success, the Saudis made their move. In connivance with the Americans, the kingdom rejected the deal and walked out of the meeting along with the delegates of the United Arab Emirates. The summit collapsed, and Iranian oil was undercut, pushing Iran's economy to the edge of the abyss. In the first nine days of 1977 alone, hundreds of millions of dollars in anticipated revenue were erased.[39] The shah was forced to take out an emergency $500 million loan from Western banks to cover immediate expenses. "We're broke," he declared on January 2, 1977. "Everything seems doomed to grind to a standstill, and meanwhile many of the programs we had planned must be postponed. . . . It's going to be very tough."[40] Minister of the Court Asadollah Alam dejectedly confided to his diary that "we have squandered every cent we had only to be checkmated by a single move from Saudi Arabia."[41]

Shortly thereafter, Ford's brief tenure in the White House ended. Under presidents Johnson and Nixon, the United States had lost all leverage over the shah and had been unable to alter his behavior. By consistently failing to control the shah since 1941, especially his profligate spending, the United States had laid the foundation for the crisis. In the first half of the 1970s, "the days when Washington called the tune in relations with Iran, if remembered at all," wrote Gary Sick, a member of the NSC under Presidents Ford, Carter, and Reagan, "were remembered with irony as Washington scrambled to accommodate the latest requests of the shah."[42] Nixon and Kissinger in particular were notable for allowing personal friendship and admiration for the shah to distract them from establishing policies that would maintain US strategic interests. The shah's refusal to remain obsequious to the United States when in a position of leverage was something the United States was unprepared for. It was left to Gerald Ford to save the United States from a crisis caused in large part by the shah, but in doing so he sent a country tasked with protecting the United States in the Middle East spiraling out of control.

However, just as the inheritance of chaos had allowed Kennedy to dictate to the shah, the result of the OPEC meeting in December 1976 placed the incoming Carter administration in a position once again to wield influence over the shah. The outbreak of significant unrest in Iran and a nervous and desperate shah meant that the United States could control his actions. In contrast to the US position in 1961, however, Carter did not inherit linkage and so had little understanding of what impact this control would have internally in Iran. Movement toward revolution had been accelerated by the oil crisis, yet Washington remained blissfully ignorant of that movement.

Carter: The Mirage of Change

Economic crisis had led the shah to return to political liberalization in 1975 in an attempt to quell public unrest. He was also driven by a more personal goal. A year earlier, unbeknownst to the Americans, he was diagnosed with leukemia. His eldest son was only thirteen at the time, and the shah wished for stability to allow him to smoothly pass on his crown and maintain the Pahlavi dynasty. Although these two explanations for the shah's return to liberalization were largely internal, the movement was hastened by external factors. Besides his defeat at Doha, the most influential of these factors was the emergence of Jimmy Carter, a politician seen as the reincarnation of John F. Kennedy. The Kennedy era and the extent of American intervention in Iran at that time were the shah's darkest days. He refused to return to a patron–client relationship and hoped instead to prove to Carter that he was taking the necessary steps to maintain stability and progress.

The shah's fear of returning to a period of intrusive external intervention was great. Reminiscing in 1969, he told an American journalist that his "worst period was 1961 and 1962 . . . [with] your great American 'liberals' wanting to impose their way of 'democracy' on others, thinking their way is wonderful."[43] Since then, he had successfully prevented foreign intervention, but as his economy plunged into chaos, his confidence and independence suddenly evaporated. Carter's ascension was therefore well timed to coincide with a weakened and increasingly desperate shah. Because of the collapse of the Iranian economy and the shah's perception of Carter as the new Kennedy, the United States could once again approach Iran from a position of leverage, albeit one devoid of strong linkage.

To some extent, the shah was right to worry about the new president. During his campaign, Carter had committed himself to the promotion of democracy at home and abroad. He made clear that democracy required more than the occasional holding of elections but was a complex system of rules with ethical standards and open debate on social policies and problems.[44] Of special interest to him was the promotion of human rights, as he made clear in his Inaugural Address:

> Because we are free, we can never be indifferent to the fate of freedom elsewhere. Our moral sense dictates a clear-cut preference for

those societies which share with us an abiding respect for individual human rights. We do not seek to intimidate, but it is clear that a world which others can dominate with impunity would be inhospitable to decency and a threat to the well-being of all people.[45]

Congress had already begun to focus on the promotion of human rights abroad and had held hearings on the abuses carried out under the shah's regime.[46] As part of his campaign for president, Carter had promised to go further, declaring that human rights would become the "soul of US foreign policy."[47] In the second presidential candidates' debate, he had directly criticized Nixon and Ford for making the United States little more than an "arms merchant" for the world, saying specifically that "Iran is going to get 80 F-14's before we even meet our own Air Force orders for F-14's, and the shipment of Spruance Class Destroyers to Iran are much more sophisticated than the Spruance Class Destroyers that are being delivered to our own Navy. This is ridiculous, and it ought to be changed."[48]

Carter's election therefore suggested an end to the Nixon–Ford brand of realism in foreign policy and the reemergence of idealism. It promised a return to the idea that reform rather than authoritarianism was the best way to ensure the protection of US national interests. Striking fear in the shah, Carter singled out his regime in particular as one that should do more to safeguard human rights.[49]

The shah quickly reached out to the new president, as he had done with Kennedy, to try and prevent any undue interference in his rule. Before Carter's inauguration, the shah sent a congratulatory and introductory telex, but he received no reply from the White House. This lack of a response caused great consternation in Tehran and led the shah to remark that he "perceived a new coolness towards" his rule.[50] For twenty-seven days, the telex went unanswered, sparking rumors and gossip that the United States was displeased with the shah. According to an American correspondent in Iran, Iranian officials worried why no reply had been sent from the White House and would often take US contractors and diplomats aside at parties to try and gauge the mood in Washington.[51] Almost a month later, in late

February, a formal and perfunctory reply was sent, with the delay put down to "sloppy staff work"; the shah, however, understood it as a sign that change was coming.[52]

In response, the shah sped up his process of liberalization. He released 357 political dissidents in February 1977 and a few months later set free an additional 343.[53] Censorship laws were relaxed, and commissions were established to give a platform for Iranians wishing to air their grievances. International human rights organizations were invited to conduct studies and surveys of the conditions in Iran, upon whose findings the shah promised to enact additional reforms.[54] Because of these reforms, a US intelligence report issued in November 1977 found that Iran had made a decisive move away from human rights abuses: not a single case of torture had been reported in the previous twelve months.[55] The shah once again began to talk of democracy and even contemplated the holding of free elections in 1979.[56] An example of his eagerness to please exogenous forces was the dismissal of Hoveyda, his long-serving prime minister, whom the shah felt was unpopular in Washington.[57] Many in Tehran saw Hoveyda's demise as the beginning of the end for the shah himself because it was hoped Carter would next pressure the shah himself to vacate the throne.[58]

Therefore, even before the Carter administration had developed an Iran policy, the shah accelerated reforms in the hopes of placating possible future demands.[59] Cognizant of his weakened position and not wishing to return to the servile relationship of the past, he increased his liberalization policies so as to preempt and deflect what he felt would be the inevitable return of external pressure. However, such moves failed to satisfy internal demands and instead merely exacerbated the situation. The deflationary policies put in place by Hoveyda's replacement, Jamshid Amuzegar, "brought a sudden growth in unemployment[,] . . . [which,] coming after rising expectations, helped create a classic prerevolutionary situation."[60]

The late Barry Rubin, commenting in 1980 on this moment in Iran's history, dismissed the notion that pressure from the United States forced the shah "to become too soft, and thus encouraged the upheaval" that followed, stating categorically that "[it has] no basis in fact."[61] Although it is true that Carter did not force the shah's liberalization program, which began before Carter took office, the shah's perception of the new administration and, as we will see, Carter's eventual Iran policy did convince him to speed up the process. This acceleration of reform ironically had drastic consequences for the shah's regime and brought the end undeniably closer. With international attention once more focused on his style of government, the shah was made to feel insecure and fearful of a return to what he remembered as the darkest days of US–Iranian relations.

External and Internal Influences on the Opposition

Since 1963, the shah had moved away from the aegis of the United States to become a largely independent regional power. The opposition, however, continued to view him as a lackey of the West. The coup of 1953 had crystallized the opinion that anything that happened in Iran happened with America's blessing. When translated into Persian, the moniker "Policeman of the Gulf," given to him after the announcement of the Nixon Doctrine, means "gendarme," carrying connotations of servility.[62] The view that the shah was a puppet of the United States remained prevalent even at the height of his independence in the early 1970s. From this perspective, it was natural for Iranians to see his return to liberalization as being ordered by the US government. Mehdi Bazargan, a founding member of the Nahzat-e Azadi-e Iran (Liberation Movement of Iran), recollected that "we did not believe the shah when he started the liberalization policy, but when Carter's human rights drive lifted the hope of the people, all the built-up pressure exploded."[63] It was because of the popular vision of the shah as puppet of the West that Carter's presidency proved so important in the promotion of popular protest against the shah's rule. Hoveyda's resignation was seen as a clear sign of US dominance and displeasure in the shah. In Tehran's notorious Evin prison, for example, future leaders of the Islamic Republic, such as Ali-Akbar Hashemi Rafsanjani and Ayatollah Hussein-Ali

Montazeri, men who generally shunned the prison television as a matter of principle, broke their self-imposed rule to watch in awe and satisfaction at news of Hoveyda's resignation.

A report around this time by Parviz Sabeti, head of SAVAK's internal security branch, warned the shah of the dangers to stability if it were perceived that the Americans had lost faith in the shah. He explained how the forces that had risen up against the shah's rule in 1963 had not been defeated but were merely waiting for the right moment to challenge him again. Continued liberalization, Sabeti warned, would create space for this challenge and lead to turmoil in Iran.[64] Furthermore, if protests took to the streets, as in 1963, the extensive changes in Iranian society that had taken place since then would make any repeat performance far more disruptive and damaging. The White Revolution may have failed in many respects to constitute reform, but it had modernized Iranian society and massively expanded the middle class. The population in urban areas increased from 10 percent to 30 percent, and the number of cities in Iran doubled between 1956 and 1976.[65] In total, Iran's population increased by roughly one-third.[66] Any repeat of the uprising, as Sabeti warned, was therefore guaranteed to be on a much larger scale, much more persistent, and much more of a threat to the shah's continued rule.

SAVAK's analysis was supported by British officials, who concluded that after fifteen years of repressive control of the opposition, any relaxation of discipline would inevitably lead to a violent release of popular emotion.[67] The shah was therefore stuck between clamping down on the opposition and thus risking external pressure or proceeding with liberalization and thus risking the unification of Iran's opposition and the United States. Having faith that his people would not turn against him, he proceeded with the latter. More political prisoners were released, including many members of the MEK and other opposition groups, while controlled policies of liberalization continued.

As happened in other periods of liberalization in Iran's history, Iran's indigenous opposition movement quickly filled the space now made available for it. Believing that the United States was forcing liberalization on the shah, more and more groups began to test the waters. In January 1977, the Iranian author Ali-Asghar Haj Seyed Javadi published an open letter criticizing the government and calling for greater reform. Human rights activists at the time wondered why Javadi was not punished for his letter, one of them commenting that had it been written "five years earlier, they [the security forces] would have seized him and thrown him in prison."[68] The absence of punishment encouraged others to write similar letters. Still in exile in neighboring Iraq, Ayatollah Khomeini welcomed such testing of the shah's return to liberalization. "A new opportunity has appeared in Iran today. . . . This is [one] that should not be lost," he told his followers.[69] Iran's mosques took full advantage, having been one of the few venues of social gathering and, increasingly, political action not to have been broken up by the shah. They were easily able to reach out to the masses thanks to weekly sermons and the interconnection of mullahs across the country. The shah's policies were routinely denounced as un-Islamic as even secular opposition began to cloak its protests with the mantle of religion.[70]

Nevertheless, the shah continued to permit opposition, and other tests of his liberalization program soon followed. Public meetings that had previously been banned were now held without disruption by SAVAK. One meeting in particular consisted of ten consecutive nights of poetry organized by the oppositional group Kanun-e Nevisandagan-e Iran (Writers' Association of Iran), drawing an audience of thousands. The gathering was ostensibly a literary event, but the performers spoke on topics such as censorship, oppression, and freedom of thought, which aroused the crowd "to a peak of emotional communion unprecedented in Iranian cultural history."[71]

As more and more open letters were published and grievances were increasingly aired in public, the professional class—lawyers, writers, and university professors—began to organize.[72] Civil society reemerged with gusto as opposition groups once forced into exile began to return. The Liberation Movement of Iran, an offshoot of the National Front, reformed under the leadership of Mahmud Taleqani and Mehdi Bazargan. It was more overtly religious than the National

Front, but secular groups also emerged, such as the Nehzat'e Radi-kal (Radical Movement), led by Moqaddam Maragheh'i; the Hezb-e Mellat-e Iran (Party of the Iranian Nation), led by Dariush Forou-har; and the Hezb-e Iran (Iran Party), led by Shapur Bakhtiar.[73] By November 1977, secular nationalists had even reformed the National Front, but this was one step too far for the shah, who ordered SAVAK to break up its first public meeting. Favorable references to Khomeini and his politics, however, continued to circulate widely.[74]

A modernized and expectant population therefore combined with a weakened shah and a United States seemingly in favor of greater liberalization and political reform. If revolution were to be avoided, it seemed movement toward democratization was essential. During this time, Iran was relatively peaceful as its urban elite continued to see how far they could go in freely organizing opposition to the shah's splintering authoritarianism. James Bill, in Iran at the time, explains how it seemed as though they were patiently waiting for "the Ameri-can president and the shah to publicly state their joint support for a new, open political system in which 'liberalization' would become a reality."[75] However, they would soon be disappointed; Iranians' perception of the Carter administration did not match reality. The United States was not in a position to facilitate a move to democracy by one of their key strategic allies, so external factors would once again intervene to spoil Iran's democratic aspirations.

The Perception: Carter as Kennedy

The view that Carter was a new Kennedy initially seemed well grounded because the similarities were striking. Both came from naval backgrounds and assumed the presidency after eight years of Republican rule. Both championed democracy and liberalization and campaigned on the need to revive a stagnant US economy while restoring American prestige abroad. A newspaper article at the end of Carter's first one hundred days in office compared the two and remarked how both Carter and Kennedy had "relied heavily on sym-bolic gestures and personal style to capture public affection."[76] It also noted that they had "virtually identical" public and congressional support. Just as during his campaign Kennedy had identified Iran as a country badly in need of development, so Carter, too, focused on Iran as a country in need of human rights reform.

An outgoing official from the Ford administration described Carter's newcomers, like Kennedy's New Frontiersmen, as "think-tank types, academics," and such like.[77] Soon after his inauguration, Carter declared that the United States would not continue to support dictatorships out of an "inordinate fear of communism" and would reassess its support for authoritarianism.[78] Proving that his declaration was not mere words, his administration duly cut assistance for regimes that violated human rights in places such as Argentina, Ethiopia, Uruguay, El Salvador, Chile, and Nicaragua. This trend was worrying for the shah but good news for an expectant Iranian opposition.

And the administration initially did pay greater attention to Iran's internal situation. Since 1963, successive presidents had been satisfied that top-down development would solve all of Iran's problems and that the United States need have relations only with the shah. The Carter administration, however, took a less-sanguine approach. "In the last fifteen years," read a State Department report in early 1977, "a very traditional society has been going through as massive a social and economic change as any country in the world. . . . [This has created] rising expectations in all sectors of national life . . . [and has led to increased opposition from those who] do not accept the present monarchy or its reform policies."[79] To ease the internal dissatisfaction in Iran, Carter began to reapply pressure that the shah had not felt since the Kennedy years.[80] For example, he appointed William H. Sullivan to replace Richard Helms as ambassador. Sullivan had previously served in Laos and the Philippines, where he had gained a reputation as a "tamer of dictators."[81]

In response to the shah's new liberalization program, Sullivan reported back that "it would do no harm and some positive good to express our approval of the opening up process."[82] In discussion with Prime Minister Amuzegar, Sullivan urged the continuation of liberalization and the allowance of peaceful protests to ensure that opposition did not resort to violence or terrorism.[83] This comment furthered the shah's belief that the United States would increase intervention if he did not continue to expand liberalization. As if to encourage further action, after five years of virtually open-check military sales to the shah, the United States cancelled an arms shipment of 250 F-16 fighter jets to Iran. Carter then blocked the shah's efforts to purchase Pershing missiles, and a bitter and public debate ensued over whether to supply him with an Airborne Warning and Control System.[84] Deputy National Security Adviser David Aaron remarked that the shah "has got to learn that Jimmy Carter's presidency is going to be very different from Nixon's. We've got to exhibit a new attitude, and Iran is a glaring case of excessive arms sales, and if our policy is going to have meaning, it's got to be in this case. We have to draw the line here."[85] As well as wanting to draw a line, the new administration also looked to protest the human rights situation in Iran through official diplomatic channels and high-level meetings in which Carter personally directly asked the shah questions on torture and sham trials.[86]

The Iranian leader therefore received a stark warning, which, coupled with fears brought on by the return of idealism to US foreign policy, pushed him to accelerate his liberalization policy. Leaders of the Resurgence Party, members of the royal family, and senior government officials began to give speeches extolling the shah's desire for democracy, human rights, and justice.[87] Although the shah was reported to have been "irritated by the criticism," he was no longer in a position to protest the renewed American attention.[88] He proved almost as amenable to foreign control as he had been in the early 1960s.

The Reality: Carter as Nixon

However, Carter was no Kennedy. Although some similarities existed between them, Carter's actual Iran policy most replicated that of Richard Nixon. Despite calling for political reforms abroad,

Carter also emphasized that he would not intervene in other nations to enforce the promotion of such reforms. He also made clear that if his human rights policy came into conflict with US self-interest, the latter would always be prioritized. This was the case in the Philippines, where Carter supported the subjugation of human rights, and to a lesser extent in South Korea and El Salvador.[89] Of his administration's priority in foreign affairs, Carter made clear that "[we cannot] conduct our foreign policy by rigid moral maxims. We live in a world that is imperfect and which will always be imperfect; a world that is complex and confused, and which will always be complex and confused. I understand fully the limits of moral suasion."[90]

As the historian Scott Kaufman notes, "Carter repeatedly demonstrated a preparedness to push aside morality in the name of protecting geopolitical or strategic interests."[91] Despite the change in administration, US strategic interests in Iran remained the same from Nixon to Carter.[92] The shah's international and regional support, his oil, and the need to use his country as a base to acquire intelligence on the Soviet Union were held in higher esteem than the desire to push Iran toward democracy. In reality, Sullivan had been sent to Iran not to tame a dictator but to continue the strategic relationship established by his predecessor.[93] The administration did not consider Iran, according to Gary Sick, Carter's chief adviser on Persian Gulf affairs, to be a problem worthy of undue attention or interference. "On the contrary," Sick later wrote, "the concept of relying on regional powers . . . in the pursuit of policy objectives and interests was embraced as a cardinal tenet of Carter's foreign policy."[94]

Although some effort was made to limit the shah's military spending, little actual progress was made in this regard. Far from being a portent for an overall reduction in US arms sales to Iran, the cancellation of the F-16 sale was a one-off. Increased opposition to unlimited sales by Congress and the American public forced the cancellation of one deal, but it was largely a gesture to appease Capitol Hill.[95] Many other deals were concluded, and the delayed sale of the Airborne Warning and Control System, worth $1.23 billion, was eventually confirmed in September after the president personally

lobbied the House Foreign Affairs Committee to remove its obstruc-
tion to the sale (although actual delivery of the warning system was
eventually cancelled because of the Iranian Revolution).[96] Furthermore, Carter approved $1.1 billion of additional military sales to
Iran in what was a clear and unmistakable message that he intended
no dramatic shift away from the tight security relationship with Iran
established during the Nixon era.[97] The shah had made the armed
forces central to his grip on power since 1941, and by continuing to
support the shah's desire for ever more military hardware, Carter
signaled his support for the shah's regime. As Gary Sick recalled in
2012, the new president "had no desire to damage the relations with
Iran or to see anything go wrong."[98] His preference for good relations with the shah was made explicit when Secretary of State Cyrus
Vance visited Iran in May 1977. A US embassy official confirmed
that Vance's meeting with the shah focused on finalizing arms deals
and mentioned human rights only in passing. "There were many
more important issues to be discussed," concluded the official when
questioned.[99]

Even as Carter was at pains to convince the shah that he supported him, the opposition groups in Iran continued to believe the
United States supported them. It was widely felt that Vance had come
to Iran with instructions that the shah must liberalize or be removed
from power.[100] Conflicting messages convinced the opposition groups
that the United States was on their side and confused the shah as to
Carter's true intentions.[101] A chance to end the confusion face to face
came when the shah visited the United States in November 1977.
Again, however, he received mixed messages. The meeting began on
the White House lawn, where the two leaders faced the press and
were forced to cough and choke their way through prepared statements as tear gas wafted over the ceremony. For a week before the
meeting, Iranian students in the United States had converged on the
capital to protest against the shah. On the day of the two leaders'
meeting, the students' skirmishes with royalist supporters on the
Ellipse resulted in the firing of tear gas, which, aided by an unhelpful
wind, gradually drifted over the assembled dignitaries with perfect

timing. Humiliating footage of the shah wiping tears away from his face were beamed worldwide, much to the glee of the Iranian opposition groups. They saw it as a deliberate sign that the United States was displeased with the shah and desirous of greater concessions to democracy.[102] Gary Sick relates a conversation he had four years after the event with an anonymous leader of demonstrations in Iran: "He informed me that the timing of [demonstrations in Iran] . . . was no coincidence. When the dissidents learned of the tear gas incident on the White House lawn, they reasoned that such an event could have occurred only at the president's behest. Thus they quickly concluded that Carter had abandoned the shah and launched a series of protest demonstrations and meetings."[103]

Their perception was incorrect. Carter had no wish to embarrass the shah and intended to use the visit to stress the importance of their alliance and convince him that the United States was not disengaging from the relationship. In subsequent meetings, he mentioned human rights but, as with Vance before him, only in passing and clearly as secondary to more important issues. That Carter was no Kennedy was demonstrated by the discomfort Carter felt in telling the shah how best to promote liberal reforms. "How do I say these things to another head of state?" he complained to an aide before meeting with the shah.[104] The answer, according to Gary Sick, was to place the emphasis on "gentle persuasion" rather than "heavy pressure or fundamental shifts of alliance."[105] The shah had spent decades deflecting "gentle pressure," and even Carter understood that his "expression of concern would not change the policies of the shah."[106] However, the mere mention of liberalization and human rights, no matter how soft, left the shah with nagging doubts as to Washington's true intention.[107]

Overall, the meeting in Washington largely convinced the shah that Carter supported his continued personal rule. He returned to Tehran more confident and more determined to crack down on the protests. Opposition meetings that had previously been permitted were now interrupted, and police and the security forces once again attacked protestors. Mehdi Bazargan was moved to note that "following the shah's visit to Washington, repression again seemed the order of the day," and another group noted that the shah "threw himself into a new course intended to seek revenge against the insurgent people of Iran and freedom seekers."[108] The belief that Jimmy Carter was a friend of the Iranian people began to waver. Once feted as the harbinger of democracy, he was increasingly seen for what he in fact was: a determined supporter of the shah's regime. All semblance of doubt were washed away when the president visited Iran to celebrate the New Year. As 1978 began amid continued protests in Tehran, Carter raised his glass and delivered the following statement to his host: "Iran, because of the great leadership of the shah, is an island of stability in one of the more troubled areas of the world. This is a great tribute to you, Your Majesty, and to your leadership, and to the respect, admiration and love which your people give to you."[109]

As Sick explains, the statement, once the hyperbole common at such occasions is peeled away, was an accurate summation of the American position at the time. To expectant Iranians anticipating support, however, it was a sea change.[110] Now it was clear whose side the Americans were on. Ayatollah Khomeini quickly moved to cement his position as the true leader of the opposition movement and responded to Carter's eulogy by stating, "[The president] says human rights are inalienable, and then he says, 'I don't want to hear about human rights.' . . . He fooled people for a time . . . [but now he says,] 'we have military bases in Iran; we can't talk about human rights there. Respect for human rights is feasible only in countries where we have no military bases.'"[111]

Khomeini's identification of the stark hypocrisy at the center of Carter's message was deeply influential and brought Khomeini the support of many people who had once hoped the United States would lead them to freedom. Conversely, Carter's strong public message of support for the regime further convinced the shah that the United States favored stability over democracy, and so he quickly clamped down even harder on sources of opposition. Khomeini's growing reputation made him a regime target, and attacks were launched in the press defaming his character. This tactic led to more protests, which in turn drew a fierce response from the police, who in one instance opened fire in the religious city of Qom, killing two dozen and injuring many more. This event, Sick concludes, marked the start of the revolution in earnest—a revolution that had been building for almost a century.[112]

The deaths in Qom began a series of cyclical demonstrations throughout Iran as, in accordance with Shi'ite tradition, memorial services were held forty days after each death. These memorial services would include fiery sermons and demonstrations against the regime, which continued from the mosques to the streets. As the regime continued to crack down, demonstrations intensified: more deaths meant more memorial services, which resulted in more deaths and more memorial protests, and so on. Events culminated with a huge sit-in at Jaleh Square in September 1978, which the military forcibly dispersed, leaving hundreds dead.

By this time, the revolution was in full swing, yet the United States still failed to grasp the situation as critical. Other countries were not so oblivious. Shortly after Carter's "island of stability" speech, Israeli intelligence likened Iran to Ethiopia just before the fall of Haile Selassie and predicted radical regime change as highly likely.[113] But National Security Adviser Zbigniew Brzezinski urged the president to immediately signal continued US support for the shah.[114] A phone call Carter placed to the shah shortly after the massacre in Jaleh Square contained only expressions of friendship and "concern" rather than condemnation of the massacre.[115] When news of Carter's phone call was leaked to the public, it convinced the opposition that the United States approved of the massacre and had therefore orchestrated the crackdown.[116] As Bill concludes, the shah's "bullets ultimately only stitched together the fragmented protesting organizations until the bloodstained patchwork quilt of opposition forces covered the entire nation. . . . [T]he country was [soon] literally afire."[117]

US Influence during the Iranian Revolution

Amazingly, given that a revolution was under way, the United States still refused to take a close interest in Iran's internal travails. During the summer of 1978, the State Department felt it a good time for the US ambassador there to take a two-month vacation, despite having been on the job for less than a year.[118] Stopping by Washington on his way to Mexico, Sullivan blithely assured the administration that the shah had triumphed when in similar situations before and would likely do so again.[119] The CIA concurred, arguing that Iran was not in a "prerevolutionary situation."[120] This ignorance was made possible only by the lack of linkage to Iran's internal situation. Gary Sick, the man most responsible for Iran in the Carter administration, recalled that during this time preparation and organization of the Camp David Peace process commanded around 80 percent of the administration's time, leaving little left to focus on Iran.[121] By the end of October 1978, not one high-level policy meeting had been convened to formulate a coherent response to the situation in Iran.[122]

The shah was instead informed of continued US support for his rule and the Carter administration's belief that he should assert strong leadership to surmount the troubles, as he had in 1963. So strong was the American officials' opinion that the shah would muddle through that when outside experts were asked for their assessment, these officials were shocked and bemused by the experts' fears. A discussion at the Department of State that included professors James Bill and Marvin Zonis centered not on talk of how the shah would prevail but on whether the situation could best be described as a raging forest fire (Bill) or an avalanche of catastrophe (Zonis).[123] Neither apocalyptic vision interested the administration.

It was not until the last few weeks of 1978 that officials began to truly appreciate the disaster looming in Iran. But even then the United States could not take decisive action as deep splits formed between officials such as Brzezinski who argued for the formation of a military government to clamp down heavily on the protesters and officials such as Secretary of State Cyrus Vance and Ambassador

Sullivan who called for the co-optation of Iran's opposition through the formation of a civilian government made up of members of the secular and moderate opposition. The result was a mix of contradictory messages. Henry Precht, then in charge of the State Department's Iran desk, recalled how

> the shah, poor fellow, was confused by the conflicting advice. He was getting one line from Brzezinski and another from Sullivan and was desperate to know what to do. Then there were the divisions within the Department of State. There were the human rights folks pulling in one direction, there were other people pulling in another direction and the Defense Department pulling in their direction, as was the CIA. Everyone was pursuing his own ends, leaking to the press to obtain those ends. It was a textbook case of how not to conduct diplomacy in the modern era.[124]

The shah himself remarked on the incongruity of the messages coming from the United States during the crisis. Shortly after the revolution, he wrote, "The messages I received from the United States . . . continued to be confusing and contradictory. Secretary of State Vance issued a statement endorsing my efforts to restore calm and encouraging the liberalization program. Such Herculean fantasies left me stunned. . . . Zbigniew Brzezinski at least had his priorities straight. He called me in early November to urge that I establish law and order first."[125]

The result of the mixed signals from the Americans was a mixed response from the shah to the protests.[126] The brutal clampdown on the peaceful protest in Jaleh Square had shocked the revolutionaries and, according to Steven Ward, a former Iran analyst at the CIA, led to "one of [the regime's] best opportunities to reassert control."[127] Unsure whether the Americans would support continued bloodshed, however, the shah followed up the clampdown with concessions and continued liberalization, which only reenergized the opposition.

Finally, in late 1978 the State Department began in earnest to formulate a plan to allow for a transition from royal authoritarianism to a more representative government based on the long-forgotten Constitution. George Ball, a former undersecretary of state under Kennedy and Johnson, was brought in to prepare a report on the matter. With him returned the specters of the New Frontiersmen, who had demanded greater US intervention in Iran's internal affairs. His report, completed in December, accurately explained that "all parties are looking to the United States for signals. . . . We made the shah what he has become. We nurtured his love for grandiose geopolitical schemes and supplied him the hardware to indulge his fantasies." It concluded that now "that [the shah's] regime is coming apart under the pressures of imported modernization," the United States should intervene to ensure the formation of a "responsible government that not only meets the needs of the Iranian people but the requirements of our own policy."[128]

However, the decline in linkage over the previous fifteen years meant that the Americans were no longer able to ensure movement toward such a government. In particular, the religious aspect of the revolution was largely unknown to them. Although the US embassy in Iran was the fifth-largest embassy in the world at the time, its knowledge of Iran's internal situation was pitiful. "I doubt if anyone in the embassy ever knew a mullah," recalled one official stationed there in the early 1970s.[129] Information received by the embassy was instead strictly controlled by the shah, who allowed embassy officials access only to a small number of establishment figures.[130] Ambassador Sullivan was particularly out of his depth. No expert on Iran or Islam, he was unable to provide leadership on the ground and routinely misunderstood the country and the forces at play.[131]

In his article on US government missteps in the buildup to the revolution, Luca Trenta details numerous opportunities the United States had to gain greater insight into the looming opposition to the shah. In May 1978, Mehdi Bazargan, an opposition leader and soon to be the first prime minister in the Islamic Republic of Iran, approached US embassy officials to suggest a compromise of reform in return for the opposition's acceptance of the monarchy. As Trenta notes, the embassy officials were confused about who he was and whether he really spoke for the real opposition. In October, an envoy for the moderate Grand Ayatollah Kazem Shariatmadari put forward an offer of cooperation between religious leaders headed by Shariatmadari and the Iranian government but was similarly rebuffed.[132]

It was not until very late in 1978 that the embassy sent out official feelers to build bridges with Ayatollah Khomeini's followers and discuss the formation of a government with his support.[133] These attempts, however, were both too little and too late, and Brzezinski eventually overruled them, maintaining that strong support for the shah must be sustained. It has been said that Brzezinski's opposition to all proposals to limit the shah's power were based on "a profound ignorance" and a dependence on "distorted information" of events in Iran given to him by the embassy and by the shah's loyal ambassador to the United States, Ardeshir Zahedi.[134] US officials' mistaken belief that the shah would win out remained such orthodoxy even in the final few weeks of his imperiled reign that when one State Department official submitted an alternative, dissenting strategy, he included with it a note remarking, "I doubt I have much of a future [here]."[135] Intelligence predictions continued to conclude that the shah would retain power despite the protests. The Defense Intelligence Agency put forward its expectation in late September that the shah would "remain actively in power over the next ten years."[136] Even by December 12, one month before the shah was forced to flee Iran, Carter publicly declared, "I fully expect the shah to maintain power in Iran, and for the present problems in Iran to be resolved. . . . I think the predictions of doom and disaster that come from some sources have certainly not been realized at all."[137]

Such obstinate views that the shah would prevail went unchanged until a meeting of leaders from the United States, Great Britain, France, and Germany was held in Guadeloupe on January 5 and 6, 1979. It would be the first time since World War II that the leaders of these countries had met to discuss a range of global problems. Although reports indicate that issues such as nuclear disarmament, the price of oil, China, European security, the future of Rhodesia, and the economy of Turkey were among those discussed, Iran dominated the schedule. The *Washington Post* reported with some skepticism that Carter intended to inform his European allies that the United States continued to support the shah.[138] At the resort of Saint-François, the leaders—pictured in short sleeves and meeting in an open-air cabana—enjoyed eighty-degree weather, tennis, swimming, sailing, and sunshine. The press quickly dubbed the meeting the "sunshine summit" or "swimsuit summit."[139] A nervous shah, by contrast, enjoyed a far less relaxing time, anxiously waited for news on whether the West still supported his rule. There were no minutes made of the meeting, but it became clear that support for the shah among the UK, French, and German leaders was nonexistent. Carter was instead met by international unity in the belief that the shah had to go.[140] Officials at the US embassy in Iran concluded that this international unity at that meeting "convinced President Carter that the shah was doomed."[141] The president later revealed in his memoirs, "I found little support for the shah among the other three leaders. . . . [They] were unanimous in saying that the shah ought to leave as soon as possible."[142]

Realization that the shah was doomed finally dawned on the American president. By January 7, one day after the swimsuit summit, the *Boston Globe* reported a shift in US policy. "There is a realization within the administration," led the *Globe*, "that the shah is incapable of restoring order in his country." It concluded that, according to its sources, "order in Iran enjoys a higher priority in the Carter administration than does the shah."[143] Although no public change in policy was announced, it was understood that the United States would now notify the shah that it was time to go. A few days later the *New York Times* similarly reported a shift in US policy away from the shah that would "remain unarticulated by an administration that does not want to be seen at home or abroad to be undercutting a long and valued ally."[144] However, both White House and State Department officials acknowledged the shift to be true. The United States would try to assist in the formation of a civilian government supported by the military. US officials in Iran were instructed not to suggest to the shah that he must leave Iran, but if the shah mentioned the possibility to them, they should appear supportive.

The shah did not need to be told. The new Bakhtiar government's failure to quell the protests and the lack of international support following the Guadeloupe summit finally convinced him that the jig was up. Although he still maintained control over much of the armed forces, he refused to sanction a forceful military crackdown without US support because he was afraid that such action against the people would threaten the continuity of the Pahlavi dynasty once he died. According to Precht, the Americans informed the shah that they "had this place for him and he packed his bags and around the 15th of January flew out to Egypt."[145] His long reign was finally over.

A Predictable End

> Those who make peaceful revolution impossible will make violent revolution inevitable.
> —John F. Kennedy, speech at the White House, 1962

The Iranian Revolution was the culmination of more than fifteen years of failed US policy. Despite being in possession of high levels of linkage and leverage for much of the shah's reign and thus able to direct Iran toward peace, democracy, and prosperity, the United States failed to achieve a consistent and sustained policy to promote the necessary reforms to avert the long-predicted disaster. Since the failure of the Amini experiment in 1962, the United States gradually surrendered control and, together with the shah, ignored the political reform once seen as vital. With American support and a liberal use of SAVAK, the shah remained in power far beyond his regime's natural life, but he could not escape the inevitable forever. Without political reform, an uncontrollable revolution was always coming, and when it did, the Iranian–American alliance was ripped asunder.

The loss of linkage and leverage between 1963 and 1978 made the United States dependent on the shah. The United States looked to Iran to provide regional stability and therefore became beholden to his wishes. This was not an issue so long as Washington and Tehran worked toward the same goals, but when the two powers came into disagreement over weapons sales and the oil crisis in the 1970s, the weakness of the US position became abundantly clear. When the United States was pushed to economic collapse, Nixon and Ford, unable to alter the shah's course, instead undercut him by reaching a deal with the Saudis. The United States was saved from the economic pit of despair but only by sacrificing Iran. The fallout from the failure to achieve higher oil prices was the catalyst to the events that brought about the shah's inevitable end.

Lack of linkage also prevented Jimmy Carter from understanding events as Iran entered a prerevolutionary state. Whereas American officials had a good understanding with the shah, they did not understand Iranian society. During the height of US engagement with Iran in the early 1960s, the US embassy had as many as seventeen staffers devoted to political reportage; by 1977, however, this number had dropped to just two, neither of whom was encouraged to develop sources outside the royal court.[146] This change is emblematic of a complete failure to understand Iran's internal situation at a time when such understanding was essential.[147] The failure to comprehend revolutionary Iran resulted in a muddled and unclear US response to the volatile situation, which gave hope and despair to both the shah and the opposition in equal measure. More extreme Islamic forces were able to take advantage of this confusion. By supporting the shah's restriction of secular opposition following the 1953 coup, the United States ensured that when the next moment of liberalization arrived, Islamic forces were best prepared to prevail. The shah's weakness had given the Carter administration a measure of leverage over his actions; had the administration also inherited linkage, it might have encouraged a more controlled and managed transition centered on the democracy activists who had begun the protests in the mid-1970s.

Although much has been written on the internal causes of the revolution, little has been said about the significant role played by international factors.[148] And even when the latter factors are mentioned, they are largely misunderstood. At one point in his largely exculpatory book on events of the late 1970s, Gary Sick expresses surprise at how otherwise "sophisticated, well-educated Iranians . . . [could ask,] 'Why did the United States want to bring Khomeini to power?'" Sick feels such questions were "patently absurd" yet "accepted by virtually every Iranian from the shah down."[149] The fact that such questions so baffled Carter administration officials such as Sick illustrates how little appreciation or understanding they had of the historic role the United States had played in Iranian affairs since 1941.

The revolution did not begin in the 1970s. It was instead the conclusion of a struggle that had begun in the nineteenth century—a struggle between the shahs' desire for total control and the people's desire for freedom. Throughout this struggle, external forces influenced both sides' fortunes. It should not have been surprising to the Americans that some Iranians believed the United States brought Khomeini to power because the United States had been behind many of the key decisions taken in Iran over the previous three decades. In fact, American decisions in Iran over this time—in bolstering the shah and ignoring the need for political reform—made the revolution inevitable.

Numerous scholars and officials have missed this point. They have called the shah's fall "unthinkable," "unpredictable," and "a sudden surprise."[150] Yet it was actually predicted as early as January 1962. As the United States discussed shifting support from Prime Minister Ali Amini to the shah, NSC official Robert Komer remarked that US policy toward Iran was "going to hell in a hack."[151] Intelligence showed that unless the shah coupled political change with extensive socioeconomic reforms, he would inevitably face uncontrollable public protests and the eventual overthrow of his regime. Even earlier, Eisenhower understood that unless he pressed the shah to concentrate on liberalization and political reform, his reign would be finished. US aid and support as well as the shah's White Revolution and intelligence services extended his reign but did little to address the Iranian people's demands for political reform.

It was not prescient guesswork by Komer or other officials who predicted the shah's demise but a keen understanding of the political currents that characterized Iranian life.[152] Komer likened US policy that supported the shah but ignored political reform to "running a holding action that will sooner or later fail."[153] For the Americans, the early success of this holding action blinded them to its temporary nature and instead made it permanent US policy.

The history of US–Iran relations since the assassination of President Kennedy shows the growth of the shah and his transformation of the relationship with Washington to one of near equality. Once a pawn of the United States in the 1940s, by the early 1970s he was an important global leader who refused to accept orders from the United States.[154] Even before the coup in 1953, he demonstrated his ability and willingness to act independently when US leverage weakened. For example, following the outpouring of support after the assassination attempt on his life in 1949, he took swift and decisive action that went against American wishes. Washington could no longer call the shots and was instead forced to follow his lead. Unfortunately for the shah, his moment of independence ended almost as quickly as it began when he lost public support and was again made dependent on the West.

The shah was indignant at his reliance on the United States, especially during the Amini years. After that, he was determined to break free from American control and so worked toward this goal with skill and persistence.[155] He understood that repression alone would not quiet internal unrest and that continued unrest would precipitate additional US interference. He therefore coupled repression with socioeconomic reform through the White Revolution, believing that rising prosperity would dampen internal agitation. With Iran seemingly peaceful, the shah next worked on convincing American officials that he represented both stability and reform. During the late 1960s and early 1970s, through persistent diplomacy and an understanding of the forces of linkage and leverage, the shah achieved his goals of massive military assistance and independence from US control.

Convinced that the shah was the best option for Iran, the United States disengaged from the country during the Johnson and Nixon presidencies. The shah was given more authority both internally and externally, and calls for political reform became but a distant memory. Through clever manipulation of senior American officials, repressive control of the people by means of his security services, and his own brand of socioeconomic reforms, the shah was able to extend his run another seventeen years. By not combining these socioeconomic reforms with political reform, however, he was only prolonging the inevitable fall of his regime.

Had US officials maintained close linkage and leverage, they could have foreseen this inevitable end and pressed the shah for political reform earlier and potentially have avoided the disaster at Doha. Alternatively, had they not stuck to the rigid position that US interests would be best assured through the shah's personal rule rather than through democratic institutions, it is possible the shah could far sooner and in a peaceful, controlled manner have been removed or placed in a position of reigning but not ruling. When revolution came, however, the United States was powerless and ignorant, groping to understand events that US officials had once predicted so clearly.

Even a late realization that change had to occur may have ensured a transition to a government more agreeable than the Islamic regime that eventually took over. A better-informed administration could have promoted a move toward constitutional monarchy before it was too late. By this point, the shah was more concerned with maintaining his dynasty than with furthering his personal rule and was amenable to conceding to democratic forces as well as to American direction. If the Carter administration had acted quickly and returned the shah to the periphery of politics as the Kennedy administration had in 1961, much of the secular opposition could have been co-opted before it became truly revolutionary. By the time Bakhtiar, a longtime member of Iran's nationalist opposition, was appointed prime minister in early January 1979, it was too late for compromise; the opposition had already united in the belief that the shah must go. The ultimate result of the loss of linkage and leverage after 1963 therefore meant the Americans were unable to effect a transition to democracy when the time to do so finally seemed ripe. Repressed by the shah and ignored by the Americans, the opposition instead became radicalized, and the ability for secular moderates to fill the void left by the shah was lost as people looked increasingly to Khomeini and Islamic rule for guidance.

Conclusion

Thrown to the Wind

The Importance of Linkage and Leverage

In 2002, Ibrahim Karawan complained about the "excessive preoccupation with the United States and its policies" in studies of the Middle East. Although the United States is clearly "an important actor," he argued, many scholars tend to attribute to it "more power, more coherent strategic purpose, and more ability to produce its desired outcomes than it can possibly possess."[1] This study examines this claim and finds that in the case of the shah's Iran, the ability of the United States to influence events varied in relation to the amount of linkage and leverage it possessed: sometimes US pressure was highly influential and effective; other times it was not. Vital to understanding the US ability to control events, therefore, is understanding what makes linkage and leverage wax and wane. This greater understanding today can help formulate policies that better achieve US goals in the future while avoiding the nefarious and unintended outcomes described in these pages.

The times when the United States held both linkage and leverage with respect to Iran—roughly 1941 to 1950, 1953 to 1958, and 1961 to 1964—US policy largely achieved its aims. During the 1940s, for example, the United States forced the shah to withdraw from personal rule, succeeded in getting numerous ministers and prime ministers of its choosing appointed to office, and controlled Iran's reform agenda. When the return to constitutionalism threatened to provoke instability and threaten wider US interests during the late 1940s, Truman was able to return the shah to a more active role. But to prevent him from returning Iran to a dictatorship, the United States pushed him back from personal control and convinced him to instead appoint General Ali Razmara.

This study shows that international pressure is effective only when both elements are present.[2] With only linkage in the late 1950s, Eisenhower was unable to push the shah toward meaningful reform because the shah knew there would be no punishment if he refused to comply. Similarly, with only leverage in the late 1970s, Carter was unable to understand the revolutionary situation in Iran and thereby failed to develop a coherent strategy to deal with the growing crisis. During these times, American pressure was still important but was not determinative in whether US goals were achieved. When both linkage *and* leverage were absent—for instance, during the oil crisis between 1972 and 1976—the United States was both ignorant of events inside Iran and too feeble to affect the shah's policies one way or the other.

How Leverage Is Won and Lost

The story of US relations with the shah demonstrates how the United States both gained and lost these vital instruments of influence. Financial aid was an important factor in convincing Iran to submit to American demands. After the Iran Declaration in 1943, which promised financial assistance to help the country rebuild, the shah and Iranian politicians followed American direction to speed up the transmittal of funds. This acquiescence gave the United States control in the relationship, but that control was soon lost as Washington failed to furnish the expected aid and the Iranian elite no longer felt an obligation to pursue US-favored policies. When financial aid resumed—for example, after the coup and during the Kennedy era—Iranian elites were again beholden to the United States, and conditional pressure was again effective. The pressure placed on the shah to agree to the appointment of Ali Amini was in part the threat that failure to do so would jeopardize a proposed $35 million loan. The levels and expectations of economic assistance therefore contribute to a country's susceptibility to external control.

A second factor that affected the US ability to control events in Iran was the power of the people. This factor was illustrated most strongly in the early 1950s when the popular nationalist movement identified Western interference as the root of Iran's ills. The movement eventually coalesced around Mohammad Mossadegh, who remained stubbornly determined not to bend to foreign pressure. With internal support of Mossadegh holding firm, the Americans and British were unable to force his submission despite leveraging economic weapons such as sanctions and the closure of the AIOC oil refinery. Prime ministers and even the shah had previously depended on foreign support to both attain and maintain power, which allowed exogenous forces considerable influence. Mossadegh's popular support protected him from such dependency and gave him space to chart an independent course. Similarly, during the short period when the shah gained popular support after the attempt on his life, he was able to act without first receiving foreign powers' approval. When this internal support evaporated, he was once again beholden to American demands, such as the appointment of Razmara, a man whom the shah disliked and distrusted.

A third factor shown to determine the efficacy of US leverage is the status of global polarity. As the country least affected by the ravages of World War II, the United States emerged from it as the supreme global power. US dominance of the international system allowed its officials to pursue policies without having to balance against competing power centers. This period, however, did not last long. Germany and Japan had been vanquished, and the British Empire was in decline, but the Soviet Union soon grew to greatly affect American decision making during the 1950s and beyond. The rise of the Soviet Union and its determination to use aid to draw countries into its alignment allowed the shah to play one superpower off against the other in the late 1950s. Although the shah depended on the United States for diplomatic and financial support, the specter of a resurgent Soviet Union made the Americans less likely to force him to take action against his wishes. Similarly, in the early 1960s Kennedy withdrew from forcibly pushing the shah toward reform in part owing to the fear that Iran would move away from the West and toward an alliance with the Soviets.

These factors, clearly illustrated in this history of US–Iranian relations, are the predominant inhibitors of leverage and greatly affected the ability of the United States to dictate policy to the shah.

Understanding Linkage

While American leverage ebbed and flowed in the first two decades of US engagement with Iran, the 1940s and 1950s, linkage remained strong. Diplomatic, economic, and personal relations were maintained not only with the shah but also with other prominent Iranian politicians, various opposition groups, and Iran's civil society leaders. The United States monitored and kept in close contact with these groups through its embassy, economic and military aid missions, CIA stations, and influential American officials and businessmen who made regular trips to Iran. The extent of linkage was demonstrated by American officials' ability to work secretly with numerous Iranian groups to successfully oust Mossadegh as well as to maintain knowledge of various opposition movements, such as those involved in the Qarani conspiracy. That such high-ranking officials within the Eisenhower administration had direct knowledge of the plot before the shah did demonstrates how in tune the Americans were with feelings of opposition and unrest in Iran. It was such strong linkage that allowed the United States to achieve its aims so effectively in the early 1960s.

Linkage remained strong until around 1963, when it began a steady decline. With the onset of the White Revolution, Washington no longer felt it necessary to take such an invasive and proactive interest in Iran's internal situation. It was felt the shah had finally seen the light in regards to the necessity of dramatic reforms, and the United States was desperate to turn away from Iran and focus on other areas of the world, such as Israel and Vietnam, and on the wider Cold War. This view was encapsulated in Richard Helms's stint as ambassador from 1973 to 1977, who ended all criticism or surveillance of the shah. Embassy officials once devoted to internal monitoring were replaced by others trained to spy on the Soviet Union. The result was that embassy officials got their information on Iran's internal situation from the shah himself, and the CIA relied on intelligence supplied directly by the shah's intelligence and security apparatus, SAVAK.[3]

The shah masterfully ensured that the United States did not rekindle an interest in Iran's internal affairs. He convinced the Americans to allow him to rule independently through the cultivation of personal relations with senior American officials, who would argue his case in Washington. The result was that by 1976, when the United States was again in a position of leverage and able to influence events in Iran, the Carter administration had little linkage and therefore little knowledge of the internal situation, its opposition, or the Islamic revolutionary forces therein. This information was available, but the administration overlooked it owing to blind faith in the shah's longevity. A study in 1976, for instance, found that Tehran was now home to forty-eight publishers of purely religious books, more than half of which had been established in the previous decade.[4] Also noteworthy were the uptick in the number of pilgrims to Mecca and other holy sites, the greater amounts of money being donated to religious causes, and the revival of books promoting more traditional interpretations of Shi'ism, such as *Keys to the Garden of Heaven* by Abbas Qumi. This work reached number two in the best-seller list of the time, second only to the Qur'an.[5] Other evidence of a coming revolution that any respectable embassy should have noted included increased media reports on instability in Iran, the movement of capital out of the country, and a surge in embassy contacts seeking visas to leave Iran.[6]

All these signs were missed, and, as a result, the understanding prevalent in the late 1950s and early 1960s that without reform the shah would soon be toppled was forgotten. By the late 1970s, the view that the shah was safe on his throne had become so institutionalized that even evidence to the contrary brought directly to the Americans was dismissed out of hand. In early 1978, Sadegh Ghotbzadeh, a close confidante of Ayatollah Khomeini, met with a State Department official to enlighten him on the precarious nature of the shah's position. According to the journalist David Harris, "The State Department man considered the meeting so insignificant that he didn't even bother to write up an account of it until more than a year later."[7] By that time, Ghotbzadeh had joined Khomeini's circle in France and days after the shah's departure would return to Iran with Khomeini as a leading figure in the revolution. Likewise, US officials generally saw Khomeini as an apolitical man with no interest in holding power, despite the fact that he had published his template for Islamic governance in 1970. The CIA instead reported as late as November 1978 that "Khomeini promises social equality and political democracy in his new Iran."[8]

The Strangling of Democracy

> There is nothing stable in the world; uproar's your only music.
> —John Keats to George and Thomas Keats,
> January 13–19, 1818

James Bill's authoritative book on US–Iranian relations labels as tragedy the history of the United States and Iran.[9] The most tragic aspect of this history is perhaps the failure of Iran's internal democratic opposition to consolidate the various transitions that began during the shah's reign. A major contributing factor to this failure was American interference. Even when in possession of linkage and leverage, the United States refused to ally with Iran's indigenous democratic movement. Roosevelt's early attempts to restructure Iran through the work of advisers such as Arthur Millspaugh ran contrary to Iran's own attempts to formalize independent democratic institutions such as the Majles and office of prime minister. Similarly, Truman chose Razmara over Mossadegh, and as the oil nationalization crisis took off, he saw Mossadegh more as an enemy than as an ally. Kennedy's policy also failed to work with Iran's own democrats and instead saw them as a hindrance to US reform plans.

The failure to work with the indigenous democratic movement had a massive impact on Iran's internal development. By restricting the opposition's goals, Truman succeeded in turning a largely healthy democratic movement into one organized around nationalism and anger at foreign interference. Rather than finding common ground, American intervention was based on dictating to Iran how best to reform and on restricting any efforts that it was felt might lead to instability. By encouraging the shah's crackdown on secular opposition following the coup in 1953, the United States contributed to the rise of Islamic movements as the main source of opposition to the shah. This trend continued throughout the 1960s and 1970s, so that by the time of the revolution militant Islamic groups were better prepared than democrats to take advantage of the chaos and confusion that ensued. Although secular democrats attempted to apply leadership to the revolution, Islamic forces led by Ayatollah Khomeini were in a stronger position and eventually won out.

In 1912, W. Morgan Shuster published a book entitled *The Strangling of Persia.* It documented Iran's struggle to establish an effective government following the Constitutional Revolution, which began in 1905.[10] From his vantage point as the country's treasurer-general, Shuster explained how Iranian aspirations were negated and destroyed by Great Britain's and the Soviet Union's combined predatory intentions. In 1906, a US official reported hearing chants of "vive la liberté des peuples" on the streets of Iran, but the discovery of huge reserves of oil in Iran's southern region two years later led the Great Powers to undermine democracy and supplant Iran's sovereign independence for their own interests. Shuster would later write:

> Time with whose passage certain pains abate
> But sharpens those of Persia's unjust fate.[11]

Just as Britain and Russia strangled Iran's nascent democratic movement in the early twentieth century, so, too, the United States and the shah squeezed the life from it between 1941 and 1979. The return of revolution seventy years after the first demand for constitutionalism should have heralded the return of constitutionalism. After decades of restriction by SAVAK and democratic states' refusal to support the opposition, however, public demand turned instead to the more extreme Westoxification and Islamism. Whereas Western-style democracy had once been something to aspire to, Western support for repression and autocracy turned the people away from emulating such models. Anti-Western sentiments grew, influenced by such writers as Jalal Al-e Ahmad and Ali Shariati, who argued for development based on Iranian cultural and religious values rather than on the replication of Western institutions.[12] The history of US foreign policy during this period is a story of the consistent negation of Iran's democrats by the United States and the shah as well as of the tremendous influence American actions had in ensuring the Islamic Revolution.

History could have been so different. If in February 1953, for example, the United States had not intervened to prevent Mossadegh from placing the shah in a permanent position of reigning but not ruling, there would have been no coup and all that came after it. But US policy instead led directly to the coup, the Islamic Revolution, and the persistence of a regime in opposition to the West that remains to this day.

Epilogue

After the Shah

US linkage to and leverage over Iran were lost not because of the shah's departure from Iran but because of the fear and distrust that had built up among Iranians over decades of US intervention. In late October 1979, the ousted shah entered the United States for medical reasons, but many Iranians felt the real reason was so the Americans could plan his return to power in a repeat of the events that occurred in 1953. On November 4, 1979, demonstrators entered the US embassy in protest at what they saw as continued foreign intervention, an action that resulted in the holding of fifty-two American embassy workers hostage for 444 days.[1] Ayatollah Ruhollah Khomeini called the capture of the Americans "a second revolution, more glorious than the first," as Iranians took over what many called the "Den of Spies," the main source of linkage with which the Americans had influenced the shah and numerous prime ministers for more than thirty-five years.[2]

In protest, the Americans ended diplomatic relations, and the web of linkages that once joined the two countries lay in tatters. In the agreement to free the hostages in 1981, the Iranians demanded that the United States promise not to "intervene, directly or indirectly, politically or militarily, in Iran's internal affairs."[3] Today, with diplomatic relations still not restored, the embassy building is used to train members of Iran's Revolutionary Guard Corps and other secret activities.[4] Mutual resentment and suspicion characterize what is left of the relationship between the United States and Iran as each

302

frequently accuses the other of atrocities or nefarious acts. Iran has been charged with complicity in the attacks on September 11, 2001, as well as in a suicide bombing in Lebanon in 1983 that killed 241 US military personnel, prompting the State Department to place Iran on a list of governments supporting terrorism. In turn, Iran accuses the United States of such things as purposefully shooting down an Iranian passenger plane in 1988, killing 290 passengers and crew on board, and more recently playing a role in the assassination of Iranian scientists who worked on its nuclear program.

But over the past three decades, the two countries have also cooperated. Efforts were being made to renew relations when the secret dealings of the Iran–Contra Affair were made public in late 1986, and both sides retreated from negotiation.[5] Again, after the surprise election of Mohammad Khatami in 1997 on a platform of liberalization and reform, Iran renewed attempts to reach out to the US government and its people.[6] However, progress on making a connection was slow, and mutual distrust precluded action. The more conservative elements in Iran gradually restricted Khatami's outreach, and after a sluggish response from Washington, the attempt came to nothing. Yet another opportunity arose soon after, however, when Iran offered to assist the United States in the war against the Taliban and al-Qaeda after September 11, 2001. According to Flynt Leverett, then senior director for Middle Eastern affairs in the NSC, and his wife, Hillary Mann Leverett, who was part of the team negotiating with the Iranians, Tehran offered to put the "Northern Alliance at the United States' disposal as the primary ground force component in the campaign to topple the Taliban" in Afghanistan.[7] Iran also offered to support Afghanistan's first post-Taliban government. But these attempts at cooperation were weakened when President George W. Bush included Iran in his "Axis of Evil" speech, which "dismayed Iranians of all political stripes."[8]

Nevertheless, Iran persevered and in 2003 presented the Americans with a comprehensive plan to address all points of contention, including its nuclear program, its support for terrorist groups such as Hamas, US sanctions, and recognition of legitimate Iranian security interests.[9] But the grand bargain came at a time of American trium-phalism a few weeks after US armed forces had easily dispatched Saddam Hussein's regime. The view in Washington was "Why talk to Iran when you could simply dictate from a position of strength?"[10] The administration therefore responded flatly, "We don't speak to evil," and instead discussed continuing the war into Iran and Syria.[11]

Barbara Slavin has summarized this period of missed opportu-nities as a case of the two countries being continually out of sync.[12] When one side was prepared to talk, the other was unresponsive. This was most apparent during the first term of Barack Obama's presidency. After a US overture to Iran in 2009 was spurned, the Ira-nians attempted to revive negotiations a year later, but by that time the Americans were no longer in a position to compromise.[13]

It was not until 2013 that the two sides finally began to synchro-nize. President Obama began his second term in January 2013. and a few months later Hassan Rouhani was elected president of Iran. Much more of a pragmatist than his predecessor, Mahmud Ahma-dinejad, Rouhani gained the nickname the "Diplomat Sheikh" for his former role as chief nuclear negotiator.[14] He immediately pledged to recalibrate Iran's relations with the world, and a door was opened to return to the negotiation table. Later that year the two leaders broke a thirty-five-year absence of high-level communication by dis-cussing Iran's nuclear program via telephone.[15]

Synchronization of goals between Washington and Tehran, the reestablishment of high-level linkage, as well as an element of lever-age brought on by the continued economic sanctions placed on Iran finally brought the two sides together.[16] After twenty months of high-level meetings and negotiation, the historic Joint Comprehen-sive Plan of Action was signed on July 14, 2015, in which Iran prom-ised to eliminate its medium-enriched uranium stockpile, reduce its centrifuges by two-thirds, and limit the extent of future uranium enrichment.[17] Since the nuclear deal was signed, implementation day has come and gone successfully, meaning that Iran has taken the steps required of it for the deal to begin, and in return the United

States has relaxed a number of nuclear-related sanctions and unfrozen much of Iran's assets held abroad.

The success of the nuclear deal raises questions of what comes next and what this deal means for Iran's struggle for democracy. A major outcome of the nuclear deal was the triumph of cooperation over decades of distrust. Both sides agreed to a set of compromises, and both sides have fulfilled their commitments so far. The increase in trust between them was highlighted when Iran seized ten US Navy sailors who mistakenly trespassed in Iranian waters in January 2016. Previous Americans taken hostage in Iran, such as the embassy staff in 1979 and three hikers picked up in the Zagros Mountains and accused of spying in 2011, were held for years before being released. The errant sailors, however, were returned in less than twenty-four hours after direct discussion between Secretary of State John Kerry and his Iranian counterpart, Mohammad Javad Zarif. According to one analyst, "It helped that Kerry could call 1-800-Zarif and get an answer right away."[18] Also in January 2016, another diplomatic channel successfully concluded a prisoner swap that freed four additional Americans imprisoned in Iran. A senior administration official declared that "this [swap] proves that we are able to resolve issues when we have diplomatic channels."[19]

This rebuilding of trust should include further attempts to recreate the web of linkages at all levels that once existed between the two countries. This has been happening but at a slow pace. Nevertheless, the continued reestablishment of economic links and the promise of increased trade routes to Europe and the United States could be used as rewards for the continuation of good relations, thus drawing Iran out of its international isolation. The danger lies in waiting too long and falling again out of sync. We are already hearing grumblings in Tehran about the slow progress of economic normalization.[20] If Rouhani's outreach fails to achieve progress, he could be undermined by Iran's hard-liners, as Khatami was in 1999. Similarly, the more aggressive posture adopted by the Trump administration could dismantle the gradual rebuilding of trust between the two sides.

To prevent backsliding, the reestablishment and expansion of cultural and business links are vital and should be used as stepping stones toward the reopening of the US embassy and the institutionalization of trust and cooperation. A permanent and direct point of contact is essential for any linkage regime and will mark a huge leap in the levels of mutual trust and cooperation between the two countries. The eventual reopening of the US embassy will demonstrate that the United States trusts Iran with the safety of its diplomats, and Iran's acceptance will show that it in turn trusts that the embassy will not become another "Den of Spies" intent on controlling Iranian affairs. And there is precedence for this step. In November 1978, the British embassy was also stormed by protesters angry at the United Kingdom's support for the shah. History repeated itself in 2011 after relations became strained over Iran's nuclear program. After both occasions, once tempers cooled, the British embassy was reopened. Speaking in Tehran at its most recent reopening in August 2015, British foreign secretary Philip Hammond remarked, "We will not always agree but as confidence and trust grows [sic], there should be no limit to what over time we can achieve together."[21] The British experience may not have been as traumatic as the US embassy takeover, but rekindling diplomatic relations is essential for sound and peaceful long-term relations between the United States and Iran.

The danger of the revival of linkage with Iran and the use of economic levers to gain leverage is the temptation for the United States to use them to promote its idea of democracy and to try to effect regime change. Such a mindset is no longer possible for lasting US–Iranian relations, if it ever was. The days in which the United States can control the development of other countries should be consigned to the trashcan of history, most of all with respect to a country that has a tragic history of US intervention. When questioned about the United States using the threat of sanctions to deter Iranian missile tests, for example, Foreign Minister Zarif replied tersely, "That's the problem with the United States, it believes it can control everybody's behavior."[22] Mutual respect rather than forced intervention would be more conducive to the healthy and peaceful growth of democracy in Iran.

Meaningful and beneficial relations can be used to create space for Iran's own democrats to complete their more than century-long struggle. The global move toward democracy from autocracy in the 1980s and 1990s was aided by the international environment, which heightened the cost of suppression for authoritarian regimes.[23] If a regime allows space for democracy, it can be rewarded through greater aid, trade concessions, or membership in international organizations; if a regime suppresses its people, it can be punished through diplomatic condemnation, economic punishment, and international isolation. This system of rewards and punishments is not a return to the application of leverage as used by the United States during the reign of the shah because the choice of action remains in Iranian hands. If it sees benefit from closer relations to the West, it will be less likely to pursue policies that might threaten those relations. This form of soft leverage will be more conducive to achieving lasting change in Iran—change that, as Dean Rusk said in 1963, will "evolve at a Persian tempo and produce Persian results."[24] Both the shah's regime and the current Islamic system sprung from Iran's history of foreign intervention, which repeatedly undermined the country's democracy movement. Given freedom to organize without interference, those who favor democracy will undoubtedly succeed in making a free and democratic Iran.

The Arab Spring demonstrated the intransigent nature of Middle Eastern authoritarianism, but Iran does not share many of the problems faced in countries such as Egypt, Libya, Syria, and Bahrain. These countries had little experience with democracy prior to the uprisings, and for many opposition protestors the establishment of an accountable and effective government rather than a democratic government was the true goal. Iran's long history of experimentation with civil society, party formation, deliberative politics, peaceful protest, and electioneering has created a sound democratic legacy upon which lasting democracy can be built.

It is only through linkage and leverage that the United States can support Iran's evolution. The response to the disputed election of 2009 showed the weakness of the US position when the two countries are estranged. Obama was able only to condemn the human rights violations because he held no leverage and could not risk jeopardizing progress on the nuclear issue.[25] If a similar uprising were to occur after economic and political linkages have been established, the Iranian regime would have to take into consideration a host of new factors before deciding on how to respond to civil protest. It is possible that rather than threaten lucrative international trade deals and international integration, the regime would seek greater internal dialogue and compromise rather than clamp down on free expression.

Using influence to protect space for freedom of expression in Iran is important. Iran maintains a strong democratic movement, both on the streets and among its intellectuals. Its current system is a hybrid of democracy and theocracy, with elections far more free than they were during the shah's reign. The Islamic Republic is centered on the concept of *vilayat-e faqih*, "guardianship of the jurist," which places the supreme leader at the top of Iran's power structure. He has power over the entire system, including the ability to set the tone for all foreign and domestic policies; he serves as commander in chief; and he decides appointments to key positions within the judiciary, military, and Guardian Council. The twelve-member Guardian Council interprets Iran's Constitution to ensure that all legislation passed by the Majles conforms to Islamic principles. The democratic institutions, such as the office of president and the Majles, still depend on a mandate from the people but are checked by the supreme leader and the Guardian Council. Nevertheless, functioning democratic institutions continue Iran's democratic legacy and lead to active democratic discussion about both everyday politics and the future of the Iranian system.

This debate generally falls into three camps. The hard-line camp argues that democracy is incompatible with the concept of *vilayat-e faqih* and is therefore neither desirable nor beneficial.[26] The second argues the opposite: Islam does not provide a specific system of government, so democracy is also legitimate and less of a religious dictatorship than *vilayat-e faqih*. Encapsulated by the writings of Abdolkarim Soroush, this view argues that Islamic democracy is both possible and preferential to the current system.[27] The third camp lies in the middle and argues that *vilayat-e faqih* is an acceptable system but can be made even more so through adjustments to enhance its democratic component. One suggested reform proposes that the position of supreme leader become an elected office, with candidates selected by the clergy.[28] Preference for either of the first two options will likely be achieved only through a violent clash between advocates of *vilayat-e faqih* and democrats. The third option, however, could be an organic and evolutionary process, adapting democracy to fit Iran's cultural and religious criteria, thereby making it a legitimate system in ways that forced Western-style democracy is not.[29] Political discourse in Iran is vibrant, and, according to Laura Secor, a journalist who has reported from Iran since 2004, Iran "does not have a culture of passive citizenship but a restless determination to challenge injustice and to seize control of its destiny."[30]

For more than a century, foreign powers have repeatedly prevented the Iranian people from seizing control of their own destiny. The United States needs to rebuild relations with Iran based on the notion of fair dealing regardless of which of the three camps gains the upper hand in Iran's internal political discussion. The United States should not seek to control or intervene in this discussion but rather patiently pursue a policy that does no harm. Linkage and leverage can raise the costs of suppression, but true democracy, whether through reform of the current system or through its overhaul, must be carried out by the Iranian people. Talking about Iran's revolutions in 1905 and 1979, Simin Behbahani, Iran's national poet, who passed away in 2014, stated in 2011 her belief that although both movements eventually saw "the people's dream of freedom turned into a national tyranny. . . . I believe that these kinds of experiences and setbacks are necessary to attaining freedom and real rule by the people."[31]

The United States can support the Iranian people's dream by continuing to rebuild political, economic, and social linkages. The severance of these linkages after the hostage crisis badly affected Iran's democracy movement and allowed the Islamic regime to stifle opposition with little punishment from the West. Without political or economic links, the only form of leverage is military force. The gradual rebuilding of links is therefore essential. Shortly before his final departure from Iran, the shah was surprised to hear from Ambassador William Sullivan that Washington had canceled the ambassador's meeting with Ayatollah Khomeini. In response, the shah asked, "How can you expect to have any influence with these people if you won't meet with them?"[32]

The United States should refrain from a policy of "not speaking with evil" because it is only through dialogue that trust and understanding can grow. Through linkage and leverage, the United States can support Iran's attainment of freedom so long as it learns the lessons of the past. The Iranian democracy movement is persistent, and with a favorable internal and external climate the quest for democracy in Iran will eventually succeed.

My country, I will build you again,
If need be, with bricks made from my life.
I will build columns to support your roof,
if need be, with my bones.
I will inhale again the perfume of flowers
favored by your youth.
I will wash again the blood off your body
with torrents of my tears.
Once more, the darkness will leave this house.
I will paint my poems blue with the color of our sky.
The resurrector of "old bones" will grant me in his bounty
a mountains splendor in his testing grounds.
Old I may be, but given the chance, I will learn.
I will begin a second youth alongside my progeny.
I will recite the Hadith of "love and country"
with such fervor as to make each word bear life.
There still burns a fire in my breast

to keep undiminished the warmth of kinship
I feel for my people.
Once more you will grant me strength,
though my poems have settled in blood.
Once more I will build you with my life,
though it be beyond my means.

  Simin Behbahani, "My Country, I Will Build You Again"[33]

Notes

Bibliography

Index

Notes

Abbreviations Used in Notes

CF	Confidential File
DDE	Dwight D. Eisenhower
DDEL	Dwight D. Eisenhower Presidential Library
FDRL	Franklin D. Roosevelt Presidential Library
FRUS	*Papers Relating to the Foreign Relations of the United States*
HSTL	Harry S. Truman Presidential Library
JFKL	John F. Kennedy Presidential Library
LoC	Library of Congress
NARA	National Archives and Records Administration
NSC	National Security Council
NSF	National Security Files
OCB	Operations Coordinating Board
PSF	President's Secretary's File
RG	Record Group
WHO	White House Office

Introduction: The United States, Iran, and the Legacy of Democracy

1. For more on this protest and the legal situation regarding disputed elections in Iran, see Tanya Otsuka, "'Where Is My Vote?': Democratizing Iranian Election Law through International Legal Recourse," *Boston College International and Comparative Law Review* 33, no. 2 (2010): 339–56.

2. "Khamenei: 'No Proof' of Chaos Plot," *Al Jazeera News*, Aug. 27, 2009, at http://www.aljazeera.com/news/middleeast/2009/08/200982784942708215.html; Golnaz Esfandiari, "Iran State TV Suggests Neda's Iconic Death Was Faked," Radio Free Europe/Radio Liberty, July 1, 2010, at http://www.rferl.org/content/Iran _State_TV_Suggests_Iconic_Protest_Death_Faked/1923414.html; "Iran Accuses US and Britain of Role in Killing of Nuclear Scientist," *Guardian*, Jan. 12, 2012, at

http://www.theguardian.com/world/2012/jan/14/iran-accuses-us-britain-scientist; Almed Vahdat and Harriet Alexander, "Iran Accuses 'Foreign Agents' of Being behind Acid Attacks on Women," *Daily Telegraph*, Oct. 28, 2014, at http://www .telegraph.co.uk/news/worldnews/middleeast/iran/11193259/Iran-accuses-foreign -agents-of-being-behind-acid-attacks-on-women.html; Aryn Baker, "Why Iran Believes the Militant Group ISIS Is an American Plot," *Time*, July 19, 2014, at http:// time.com/2992269/isis-is-an-american-plot-says-iran/.

3. See Daniel Brumberg, *Reinventing Khomeini: The Struggle for Reform in Iran* (Chicago: Univ. of Chicago Press, 2001), 92.

4. Anthony Parsons, *The Pride and the Fall: Iran, 1974–1979* (London: J. Cape, 1984), x.

5. Ahmad Ashraf, "Conspiracy Theories," *Encyclopædia Iranica* 6 (1992): 138–47, at http://www.iranicaonline.org/articles/conspiracy-theories.

6. Ibid.

7. Steven Levitsky and Lucan A. Way, *Competitive Authoritarianism: Hybrid Regimes after the Cold War* (Cambridge: Cambridge Univ. Press, 2010), 23–24.

8. Steven Levitsky and Lucan A. Way, "International Linkage and Democratization," *Journal of Democracy* 16, no. 3 (2005): 21.

9. Levitsky and Way, *Competitive Authoritarianism*, 43–44.

10. Ibid., 43.

11. Ibid., 44.

12. Iran never became a democracy, so in this study "movement toward democracy" refers to Iranian governance moving away from the shah's personal rule and toward the institutions of the prime minister's office and/or parliament. It also includes reforms that open up the political and electoral process.

13. Fakhreddin Azimi, *The Quest for Democracy in Iran: A Century of Struggle against Authoritarian Rule* (Cambridge, MA: Harvard Univ. Press, 2008); Ali Gheissari and Vali Nasr, *Democracy in Iran: History and the Quest for Liberty* (Oxford: Oxford Univ. Press, 2006).

14. H. E. Chehabi, "The Shah's Two Liberalizations: Re-equilibration and Breakdown," in *Iran and the Challenges of the Twenty-First Century: Essays in Honour of Mohammad-Reza Djalili* ed. H. E. Chehabi, Khosrokhavar Farhad, and Clement Therme (Costa Mesa, CA: Mazda, 2013), 25.

15. See, for example, Ervand Abrahamian, *The Coup: 1953, the CIA, and the Roots of Modern US–Iranian Relations* (New York: New Press, 2013); Luca Trenta, "The Champion of Human Rights Meets the King of Kings: Jimmy Carter, the Shah, and Iranian Illusions and Rage," *Diplomacy and Statecraft* 24, no. 3 (2013): 476–98; Christian Emery, *US Foreign Policy and the Iranian Revolution:*

The Cold War Dynamics of Engagement and Strategic Alliance (Basingstoke, UK: Palgrave Macmillan, 2013); Roham Alvandi, *Nixon, Kissinger, and the Shah: The United States and Iran in the Cold War* (New York: Oxford Univ. Press, 2014), 29; Ben Offiler, *US Foreign Policy and the Modernization of Iran: Kennedy, Johnson, Nixon, and the Shah* (Basingstoke, UK: Palgrave Macmillan, 2015); Claudia Castiglioni, "No Longer a Client, Not Yet a Partner: The US–Iranian Alliance in the Johnson Years," *Cold War History* 15, no. 4 (2015): 491–509; Javier Gil Guerrero, *The Carter Administration and the Fall of Iran's Pahlavi Dynasty: US–Iran Relations on the Brink of the 1979 Revolution* (New York: Palgrave Macmillan, 2016); Andrew Scott Cooper, *The Fall of Heaven: The Pahlavis and the Final Days of Imperial Iran* (New York: Holt, 2016).

16. Jimmy Carter, "The President's News Conference," Feb. 13, 1980, at http://www.presidency.ucsb.edu/ws/index.php?pid=32928.

17. For more on the Constitutional Revolution, see Janet Afary, *The Iranian Constitutional Revolution, 1906–1911: Grassroots Democracy, Social Democracy, the Origins of Feminism* (New York: Columbia Univ. Press, 1996).

18. Juan J. Linz and Alfred C. Stepan, *Problems of Democratic Transition and Consolidation: Southern Europe, South America, and Post-Communist Europe* (Baltimore: Johns Hopkins Univ. Press, 1996), 452.

19. Samuel P. Huntington, *The Third Wave: Democratization in the Late Twentieth Century* (Norman: Univ. of Oklahoma Press, 1991), 270. For more on democratic stock, see John Gerring, Philip Bond, William T. Barndt, and Carola Moreno, "Democracy and Economic Growth: A Historical Perspective," *World Politics* 57 (2005): 323–64.

20. Geoffrey Pridham, *The Dynamics of Democratization: A Comparative Approach* (New York: Continuum, 2000).

21. For more on Baskerville, see Hooshang Guilak, *Fire beneath the Ashes: The United States and Iran, a Historic Perspective* (Bloomington, IN: Xlibris, 2011), 7.

22. Thomas M. Ricks, quoted in Nasrin Alavi, *We Are Iran: The Persian Blogs* (Brooklyn, NY: Soft Skull Press, 2005), 40–41.

23. W. Morgan Shuster, *The Strangling of Persia: Story of the European Diplomacy and Oriental Intrigue That Resulted in the Denationalization of Twelve Million Mohammedans, a Personal Narrative* (Washington, DC: Mage, 2006), 5; Guilak, *Fire beneath the Ashes*, 13.

24. Ali M. Ansari, *Modern Iran since 1921: The Pahlavis and After* (New York: Pearson Education, 2003), 22.

25. James Bill, *The Eagle and the Lion: The Tragedy of American–Iranian Relations* (New Haven, CT: Yale Univ. Press, 1988), 9.

1. Roosevelt and the Return of Constitutionalism, 1941–1945

1. Dean Acheson, *Present at the Creation: My Years in the State Department* (New York: Norton, 1969), 133.

2. Quoted in "National Affairs: Out, Swin[g]ing," *Time*, Dec. 10, 1945, 5.

3. Quoted in Drew Pearson, "Washington Merry Go-Round: Hurley's Near East Plan Stirs Row in High Places," *Washington Post*, May 19, 1944, 4.

4. Quoted in ibid.

5. Philip Zelikow, "Practical Idealism: Present Policy in Historical Perspective," US Department of State, May 6, 2005, at http://2001-2009.state.gov/s/c/rls/rm/45851.htm.

6. Frank Friedel, *Franklin D. Roosevelt: A Rendezvous with Destiny*, vol. 1 of the *Franklin D. Roosevelt* series, paperback reprint (Boston: Little, Brown, 1990), 107.

7. Tony Smith, *America's Mission: The United States and the Worldwide Struggle for Democracy in the Twentieth Century* (Princeton, NJ: Princeton Univ. Press, 1994), 114–15.

8. Franklin D. Roosevelt, "Annual Message to Congress on the State of the Union," Jan. 6, 1941, at http://www.fdrlibrary.marist.edu/pdfs/ffttext.pdf.

9. Quoted in Friedel, *Franklin D. Roosevelt: A Rendezvous with Destiny*, 360.

10. Franklin D. Roosevelt, "Address of the President Delivered by Radio from the White House," Dec. 9, 1941, at http://www.mhric.org/fdr/chat19.html.

11. *The Atlantic Charter*, Aug. 14, 1941, at http://avalon.law.yale.edu/wwii/atlantic.asp.

12. Woodrow Wilson, "Making the World Safe for Democracy," Apr. 2, 1917, at http://historymatters.gmu.edu/d/4943/.

13. Conrad Black, *Franklin Delano Roosevelt: Champion of Freedom* (New York: Public Affairs, 2003), 655; William Manchester and Paul Reid, *The Last Lion: Winston Spencer Churchill, Defender of the Realm, 1940–1965* (New York: Little, Brown, 2012), 659.

14. Sattareh Farman-Farmaian and Dona Munker, *Daughter of Persia: A Woman's Journey from Her Father's Harem through the Islamic Revolution* (New York: Crown, 1992), 73.

15. Reza Shah to Franklin D. Roosevelt, radiogram, Aug. 25, 1941, Official File Box 134, Franklin D. Roosevelt Presidential Library (FDRL), Hyde Park, NY.

16. Homa Katouzian, "Riza Shah's Political Legitimacy and Social Base, 1921–1941," in *The Making of Modern Iran: State and Society under Riza Shah, 1921–1941*, ed. Stephanie Cronin (New York: Routledge Curzon, 2003), 33; Shaul Bakhash "Britain and the Abdication of Reza Shah," *Middle Eastern Studies* 52, no. 2 (2016): 318–34.

17. Mohammad Reza Pahlavi, *Mission for My Country* (New York: Hutchinson, 1961), 12, 36. The shah's relationship with his father was a complex one with equal parts admiration, jealousy, and resentment. For more on this relationship, see Abbas Milani, *The Shah* (Basingstoke, UK: Palgrave Macmillan, 2011).

18. Cooper, *The Fall of Heaven*, 45–46.

19. Ibid., 45; Ashraf Pahlavi, *Faces in a Mirror: Memoirs from Exile* (Englewood Cliffs, NJ: Prentice-Hall, 1980), 9.

20. A. Milani, *The Shah*, 10.

21. Alidad Mafinezam and Aria Mehrabi, *Iran and Its Place among Nations* (Westport, CT: Praeger, 2008), 28–29.

22. "Pro-Allied Policy Announced in Iran," *New York Times*, Sept. 21, 1941, 24.

23. Louis G. Dreyfus to Secretary of State, telegram, Sept. 18, 1941, 891.00, Box 5818, National Archives and Records Administration (NARA), Washington, DC; Dreyfus to Secretary of State, dispatch, Sept. 24, 1941, 891.001, Mohammad Reza Pahlavi/4, Box 5820, NARA.

24. Shah to Roosevelt, telegram, Jan. 31, 1942, Official File 134, NARA.

25. Azimi, *Quest for Democracy in Iran*, 135.

26. Dreyfus to Secretary of State, telegram, Sept. 18, 1941; "Iran Gets Wealth of Abdicated Shah," *New York Times*, Sept. 19, 1941, 4; "Pro-Allied Policy Announced in Iran," *New York Times*, Sept. 21, 1941, 24; Azimi, *Quest for Democracy in Iran*, 126; Ervand Abrahamian, *Iran between Two Revolutions* (Princeton, NJ: Princeton Univ. Press, 1982), 176–77; Gholam Reza Afkhami, *The Life and Times of the Shah* (Berkeley: Univ. of California Press, 2009), 81.

27. "Autocracy Opposed by Iran's Young Shah," *New York Times*, Oct. 20, 1941, 9.

28. Dreyfus to Secretary of State, dispatch, Oct. 6, 1941, 891.00/1843, Box 5820, NARA.

29. Afkhami, *Life and Times of the Shah*, 82.

30. See, for example, Mark J. Gasiorowski, *US Foreign Policy and the Shah: Building a Client State in Iran* (Ithaca, NY: Cornell Univ. Press, 1991), 43, and Abrahamian, *Iran between Two Revolutions*.

31. A. Milani, *The Shah*, 104.

32. Abrahamian, *Iran between Two Revolutions*, 178.

33. The shah's true ambition and lack of belief in democracy were revealed in the early 1940s by his repeated attempts to receive Allied approval for a return to authoritarianism. See A. Milani, *The Shah*, 104.

34. Stephen McGlinchey, *US Arms Policies towards the Shah's Iran* (New York: Routledge, 2014), 7.

35. Ibid., 178.

36. Roosevelt to Edward R. Stettinius, memo, Mar. 10, 1942, Official File 134, NARA.

37. Nikki R. Keddie, *Modern Iran: Roots and Results of Revolution* (New Haven, CT: Yale Univ. Press, 2003), 106.

38. Abrahamian, *Iran between Two Revolutions*, 184, 107.

39. "Schwarzkopf Is in Iran," *New York Times*, Aug. 6, 1944, 12.

40. Bill, *The Eagle and the Lion*, 19.

41. Quoted in Fakhreddin Azimi, *Iran: The Crisis of Democracy* (New York: St. Martin's Press, 1989), 58.

42. US Legation to Secretary of State, telegram, July 7, 1942, 891.00/1894, Box 5818, NARA.

43. Azimi, *Iran*, 64.

44. Azimi, *Quest for Democracy in Iran*, 53–54.

45. Abrahamian, *Iran between Two Revolutions*, 183.

46. David Halberstam, *The Best and the Brightest* (New York: Random House, 1972), 250.

47. Mark H. Lytle, *The Origins of the Iranian–American Alliance, 1941–1953* (New York: Holmes and Meier, 1987), 19.

48. Wallace Murray, memo, Aug. 3, 1942, in *Papers Relating to the Foreign Relations of the United States* [FRUS], *1942*, vol. 4: *The Near East and Africa* (Washington, DC: US Government Printing Office, 1975), 242; Richard A. Stewart, *Sunrise at Abadan: The British and Soviet Invasion of Iran, 1941* (New York: Praeger, 1988), 230.

49. Wallace Murray to Sumner Welles, letter, Nov. 21, 1942, 891.00/2951, Box 5818, NARA.

50. Vaughan Russell (British consulate in Kirmanshah), May 19, 1942, quoted in Azimi, *Iran*, 58.

51. Lytle, *Origins of the Iranian–American Alliance*, 21.

52. Department of State to US Legation, telegram, June 3, 1942, 891.00/1882, Box 5818, NARA.

53. Murray to Welles, letter, Nov. 21, 1942.

54. State Department to US Legation, telegram, Nov. 20, 1942, 891.00/1950, Box 5818, NARA.

55. Ibid.

56. Wallace Murray and John Jernegan, "American Policy in Iran," report, US Department of State, Jan. 23, 1943, 711.91/91, Box 2236, NARA.

57. Welles to Murray, memo, Nov. 21, 1942, and Sumner Welles to Secretary of State, telegram, Dec. 7, 1942, Sumner Welles Papers, Folder 02, Box 165, NARA.

58. Welles to Secretary of State, telegram, Dec. 7, 1942.

59. Dreyfus to Secretary of State, telegram, Mar. 20, 1943, 891.00/2007, Box 5819, NARA.

60. Welles to Dreyfus, memo, Mar. 13, 1943, 711.91/91, Box 2236, NARA.

61. "British and American Policy in Iran," Memorandum of Conversation, Jan. 8, 1943, 891.00/2004, Box 5819, NARA.

62. US Legation to Secretary of State, telegram, Feb. 10, 1943, 891.00/1984, Box 5819, NARA.

63. Secretary of State to US Legation, telegram, Feb. 12, 1943, 891.00/1988, Box 5819, NARA.

64. "Iran Parliament Backs Premier," *Washington Post*, Feb. 23, 1943, 3.

65. Dreyfus to Secretary of State, memo, Mar. 9, 1943, 711.91/92, Box 2236, NARA.

66. A. Milani, *The Shah*, 104.

67. Quoted in ibid.

68. Habib Ladjevardi, "The Origins of US Support for an Autocratic Iran," *International Journal of Middle Eastern Studies* 15, no. 2 (1983): 225.

69. Murray to Adolf A. Berle and Sumner Welles, letter, Apr. 6, 1943, 891.00/2003, Box 5819, NARA.

70. "Iranian Political Parties and the Forthcoming Election for the XIVth Parliament," July 22, 1943, 891.00/2037, Box 5819, NARA.

71. R. Mustawfi, quoted in Abrahamian, *Iran between Two Revolutions*, 187.

72. Abrahamian, *Iran between Two Revolutions*, 187.

73. Ibid., 184.

74. Ibid.

75. British Military Attaché to Foreign Office, memo, Jan. 24, 1944, quoted in Abrahamian, *Iran between Two Revolutions*, 199; Sir Reader Bullard to Foreign Office, memo, Jan. 20, 1944, quoted in Azimi, *Quest for Democracy in Iran*, 137–38.

76. Manucher Farmanfarmaian and Roxanne Farmanfarmaian, *Blood and Oil: Memoirs of a Persian Prince, from the Shah to the Ayatollah* (New York: Random House, 2005), 166.

77. Abrahamian, *The Coup*, 38.

78. Abrahamian, *Iran between Two Revolutions*, 189.

79. Homa Katouzian, *Musaddiq and the Struggle for Power in Iran* (New York: St. Martin's Press, 1999), 51.

80. Azimi, *Iran*, 94.

81. Abrahamian, *Iran between Two Revolutions*, 203.

82. See ibid., 204–5.

83. Azimi, *Iran*, 129.

84. Ibid., 132.

85. Abdol Hossein Hamzavi, "Iran and the Tehran Conference," *International Affairs* 20, no. 2 (1944): 201.

86. Robert L. Beisner, *Dean Acheson: A Life in the Cold War* (New York: Oxford Univ. Press, 2006), 15.

87. Acheson, *Present at the Creation*, 9.

88. Dean Acheson, *Fragments of My Fleece* (New York: Norton, 1971), 129.

89. Ibid.

90. Quoted in Ted Morgan, *FDR: A Biography* (New York: Simon and Schuster, 1985), 371.

91. Acheson, *Present at the Creation*, 11; Cordell Hull quoted in Friedel, *Franklin D. Roosevelt: A Rendevous with Destiny*, 108.

92. Quoted in Lynne Olson, *Citizens of London: The Americans Who Stood with Britain in Its Darkest, Finest Hour* (New York: Random House, 2010), 56.

93. Robert L. Beisner, *Dean Acheson: A Life in the Cold War* (New York: Oxford Univ. Press, 2006), 19; see also Friedel, *Franklin D. Roosevelt: A Rendevous with Destiny*, 569–70.

94. Quoted in Susan Butler, *Roosevelt and Stalin: Portrait of a Partnership* (New York: Knopf, 2015), 114.

95. Declaration of the Three Powers, Dec. 6, 1943, in *FRUS: Diplomatic Papers, the Conferences at Cairo and Tehran, 1943* (Washington, DC: US Government Printing Office, 1961), 640–41.

96. Declaration signed at Tehran, Dec. 1, 1943, in *FRUS: Diplomatic Papers, the Conferences at Cairo and Tehran, 1943*, 861–62.

97. Dreyfus to Secretary of State, dispatch, Dec. 10, 1943, 891.00/2079, Box 5820, NARA.

98. Hamzavi, "Iran and the Tehran Conference," 200.

99. Andre Visson, "Successful Test: On United Nations' Inside Front," *Washington Post*, Dec. 12, 1943, B6.

100. All quoted in Hamzavi, "Iran and the Tehran Conference," 200.

101. Arthur Millspaugh to the President, letter, Dec. 1, 1943, in *FRUS: Diplomatic Papers, the Conferences at Cairo and Tehran, 1943*, 630.

102. Friedel, *Franklin D. Roosevelt: A Rendevous with Destiny*, 486.

103. Warren F. Kimball, *The Juggler: Franklin Roosevelt as Wartime Statesman* (Princeton, NJ: Princeton Univ. Press, 1991), 64.

104. Patrick Hurley to the President, memo, Dec. 21, 1943, President's Secretary's File (PSF)/Confidential File (CF), Box 40, FDRL.

105. Ibid.

106. The President to Secretary of State, memo, Jan. 12, 1944, PSF/CF, Box 40, FDRL.

107. Stettinius to the President, memo, Feb. 18, 1944, PSF/CF, Box 40, FDRL.

108. Ibid.; see also Russell D. Buhite, *Patrick J. Hurley and American Foreign Policy* (Ithaca, NY: Cornell Univ. Press, 1973), 130.

109. Memorandum of Conversation between Wallace Murray, George V. Allen and John J. McCloy, Jan. 29, 1944, in *FRUS, 1944*, vol. 5: *The Near East, South Asia, and Africa, the Far East* (Washington, DC: US Government Printing Office, 1965), 309.

110. Memorandum of Conversation, Apr. 13, 1944, in *FRUS, 1944*, 5:324.

111. The President to Patrick Hurley, Mar. 25, 1944, PSF/CF, Box 40, FDRL.

112. Office of Strategic Services, Research and Analysis Branch, "The Three-Power Problem in Iran," report, July 13, 1944, 711.91/7-2844, Box 2236, NARA.

113. W. Averell Harriman and Elie Abel, *Special Envoy to Churchill and Stalin, 1941–1946* (New York: Random House, 1975), 191; Wilson D. Miscamble, "Roosevelt, Truman, and the Development of Postwar Grand Strategy," *Orbis* 53, no. 4 (2009): 559.

114. Office of Strategic Services, Research and Analysis Branch, "The Three-Power Problem in Iran."

115. Quoted in Farmanfarmaian and Farmanfarmaian, *Blood and Oil*, 167.

116. Azimi, *Iran*, 106.

117. Ibid., 107.

118. Abrahamian, *Iran between Two Revolutions*, 200.

119. Ibid., 206.

120. Ladjevardi, "Origins of US Support for an Autocratic Iran," 226.

121. Ibid., 208

122. "The Revolt in Isfahan," *Ra'ad-e Emruz*, May 15–25, 1944, quoted in Abrahamian, *Iran between Two Revolutions*, 207.

123. Quoted in Katouzian, *Musaddiq*, 53–54.

124. Acheson, *Present at the Creation*, 133.

125. Dean Acheson to Secretary of State, memo, Jan. 28, 1944, 891.00/1-2844, Box 5820, NARA.

126. Murray to Secretary of State, Jan. 31, 1944, 891.00/1-2844, Box 5820, NARA.

127. Acheson to Mr. Taft, memo, Apr. 12, 1944, 891.00/3037, Box 5820, NARA.

128. Quoted in Abbas Milani, "Hurley's Dream—How FDR Almost Brought Democracy to Iran," *Hoover Digest*, July 30, 2003, at http://www.hoover.org /publications/hoover-digest/article/6280.

129. Quoted in A. Milani, *The Shah*, 107.

130. Abdol Hossein Hamzavi, *Persia and the Powers: An Account of Diplomatic Relations, 1941–1946* (New York: Hutchinson, 1946), 41.

131. As transmitted in Leland B. Morris to Secretary of State, Dec. 6, 1944, 891.00/12-644, Box 5820, NARA.

132. See Irene L. Gendzier, *Notes from the Minefield: United States Intervention in Lebanon and the Middle East, 1945–1958* (New York: Columbia Univ. Press, 2006), 21–34.

133. Dreyfus to Secretary of State, telegram, Nov. 15, 1943, in *FRUS, 1943*, vol. 4: The Near East and Africa (Washington, DC: US Government Printing Office, 1964), 625.

134. Secretary of State to Dreyfus, telegram, Nov. 23, 1943, in *FRUS, 1943*, 4:625–26.

135. Abrahamian, *Iran between Two Revolutions*, 210; "Iranian Oil Deal Sighted," *New York Times*, Mar. 30, 1944, 6.

136. US Ambassador to Secretary of State, telegram, Oct. 27, 1944, in *FRUS, 1944*, 5:461.

137. Quoted in Abrahamian, *Iran between Two Revolutions*, 210.

138. Ibid., 211.

139. Miscamble, "Roosevelt, Truman, and the Development of Postwar Grand Strategy," 553.

140. Ibid., 555; John Lewis Gaddis, *We Now Know: Rethinking Cold War History* (New York: Oxford Univ. Press, 1997), 198.

141. "Text of Ambassador Hurley's Statement," *New York Times*, Nov. 28, 1945, 3.

142. W. H. Lawrence, "Hurley Contends Acheson Defeated Our Policy in Iran," *New York Times*, Dec. 7, 1945, 1.

143. Azimi, *Iran*, 115.

144. Robert Dallek, *Franklin D. Roosevelt and American Foreign Policy, 1932–1945* (New York: Oxford Univ. Press, 1979), 537.

145. Abrahamian, *Iran between Two Revolutions*, 212–15.

146. US Legation to Secretary of State, telegram, Dec. 9, 1942, 891.00/1963, Box 5818, NARA; US Legation to Secretary of State, telegram, Dec. 10, 1942, 891.00/1960, Box 5818, NARA.

147. See Memo of Conversation between Shah and Richard Ford, George V. Allen, and John Jernegan, Nov. 6, 1943, 891.00/2066, Box 5820, NARA; US Legation to Secretary of State, telegram, Aug. 12, 1944, 711.91/8-1244, Box 2236, NARA; US Embassy in Iran to Secretary of State, telegram, June 26, 1945, in *FRUS, 1945*, vol. 8: The Near East and Africa (Washington, DC: US Government Printing Office, 1969), 384; British Ambassador to Foreign Office, May 2, 1944, quoted in Abrahamian, *Iran between Two Revolutions*, 205.

2. A More Selfish Iran Policy, 1945–1951

1. Truman's middle name was simply the letter S, but he often added a period to make it look like an initial. When asked in the early 1960s whether he had a preference, he replied, "It makes no difference to me." Since then, the *Associated Press Stylebook* and the Truman Presidential Library have included the period.

2. To this belief his mother-in-law stuck, even after Truman had been inaugurated as the thirty-third president of the United States.

3. It was his persistence that enabled Truman to rebound from the rejection of his first proposal to his childhood sweetheart, Bess Wallace, in 1911 to eventually wed her eight years later, despite ongoing protestations from Bess's mother. Similarly, after denied entrance to West Point, a determined Truman memorized the eye chart to gain entrance into the Missouri Army National Guard in 1905 ("Harry Truman Joins Battery B of the Missouri National Guard," June 14, 1905, Harry S. Truman Presidential Library [HSTL], Independence, MO, at http://www.truman library.org/anniversaries/nationalguard.htm).

4. Truman was mockingly referred to as "the senator from Pendergast" after he first arrived in Washington. For more on Truman's relationship with Pendergast, see Robert H. Ferrell, *Truman and Pendergast* (Columbia: Univ. of Missouri Press, 1999).

5. Robert Dallek, *Harry S. Truman* (New York: Times Books, 2008), 16. A classic example of "what might have been" in regard to US–Iran policy is that Roosevelt's own preference for running mate was Supreme Court justice William O. Douglas. See Robert H. Ferrell, *Choosing Truman: The Democratic Convention of 1944* (Columbia: Univ. of Missouri Press, 2000), 10–13.

6. The quote appeared on the dust jacket to Bert Cochran, *Harry Truman and the Crisis Presidency* (New York: Funk and Wagnalls, 1973).

7. Quoted in David McCullough, *Truman* (New York: Simon and Schuster, 1992), 436.

8. For more on the "compulsion for continuity," see Nicole L. Anslover, "An Executive Echo Chamber: The Evolution of America's Vietnam Policy from Truman to Johnson," PhD diss., Univ. of Kansas, 2007; for more on Truman's desire to promote freedom and liberty, see his first major foreign-policy speech: Harry S. Truman, "Address on Foreign Policy at the Navy Day Celebration in New York City," Oct. 27, 1945, at http://www.presidency.ucsb.edu/ws/index.php?pid=12304#axzz1abPSJ8K6.

9. J. V. Stalin, speech delivered at the Meeting of Voters of the Stalin Electoral District, Moscow, Feb. 9, 1946, in *Stalin: Speeches Delivered at Meetings of Voters of the Stalin Electoral District, Moscow, December 11, 1937 and February 9, 1946* (Moscow: Foreign Language Publishing House, 1950), 19–43.

10. George Kennan to Secretary of State, Feb. 22, 1949, National Security Archive, George Washington Univ., at http://www.gwu.edu/~nsarchiv/coldwar /documents/episode-1/kennan.htm.

11. See Jamil Hasanli, *At the Dawn of the Cold War: The Soviet–American Crisis over Iranian Azerbaijan, 1941–1946* (Lanham, MD: Rowman and Littlefield, 2006).

12. See James A. Thorpe, "Truman's Ultimatum to Stalin on the 1946 Azerbaijan Crisis: The Making of a Myth," *Journal of Politics* 40, no. 1 (1978): 188–95. For more on the crisis in general, see William J. Daugherty, "Truman's Iranian Policy, 1945–1953: The Soviet Calculus," *International Journal of Intelligence and Counterintelligence* 15 (2002): 583.

13. Thorpe, "Truman's Ultimatum," 190.

14. George V. Allen, "Mission to Iran," unpublished memoirs, Correspondence File/Manuscript File/Family File, George V. Allen Papers, Box 1, HSTL.

15. General Hassan Arfa, quoted in Bill, *The Eagle and the Lion*, 36.

16. Beisner, *Dean Acheson*, 45.

17. Lloyd C. Gardner, *Three Kings: The Rise of an American Empire in the Middle East after World War II* (New York: New Press, 2009), 3. For more on the imperial presidency, see Arthur M. Schlesinger Jr., *The Imperial Presidency* (Boston: Houghton Mifflin, 1973).

18. See Harry S. Truman, "Recommendation for Assistance to Greece and Turkey, Address of the President of the United States," in *Our Documents: 100 Milestone Documents from the National Archives*, foreword by Michael Beschloss (New York: Oxford Univ. Press, 2003), 194–99.

19. McGlinchey, *US Arms Policies*, 8.

20. Quoted in Michael A. Palmer, *Guardians of the Gulf: A History of America's Expanding Role in the Persian Gulf, 1883–1992* (New York: Free Press, 1992), 29.

21. Secretary of State to Ambassador in Iran, telegram, Mar. 24, 1946, in *FRUS, 1946*, vol. 7: *The Near East and Africa* (Washington, DC: US Government Printing Office, 1969), 378.

22. Daniel Yergin, *Shattered Peace: The Origins of the Cold War and the National Security State* (Boston: Houghton Mifflin, 1977), 180.

23. Quoted in ibid.

24. See Overseas Consultants Inc., *Interim Report to the Plan Organization of the Government of Iran, May 16, 1949* (New York: Overseas Consultants Inc., 1949).

25. "Hull Names Oil Man to Post," *New York Times*, Aug. 7, 1941, 12.

26. Max Weston Thornburg to Henry Luce, Jan. 6, 1946, quoted in Linda Wills Qaimmaqami, "The Catalyst of Nationalism: Max Thornburg and the

Failure of Private Sector Development in Iran, 1947–1951," *Diplomatic History* 19, no. 1 (1995): 4.

27. Ibid., 3–4; Bill, *The Eagle and the Lion*, 40.

28. A. Milani, *The Shah*, 128.

29. George Allen to Secretary of State, telegram, Mar. 27, 1947, in *FRUS, 1947*, vol. 5: *The Near East and Africa* (Washington, DC: US Government Printing Office, 1971), 900.

30. Ladjevardi, "Origins of US Support for an Autocratic Iran," 230.

31. Quoted in ibid.

32. Abrahamian, *Iran between Two Revolutions*, 121.

33. "Notes from Qavam's Diaries," *Kvandaniha*, Sept. 28–Nov. 2, 1955, quoted in Abrahamian, *Iran between Two Revolutions*, 225.

34. See Democrat Party, "Party Program," *Demokrat-e Iran*, Oct. 24, 1946, quoted in Abrahamian, *Iran between Two Revolutions*, 233.

35. Quoted in Abrahamian, *Iran between Two Revolutions*, 233.

36. Allen to Secretary of State, telegram, Sept. 25, 1947, in *FRUS, 1947*, 5:957–58. For more on Qavam's reforms, see Abrahamian, *Iran between Two Revolution*, 233–34.

37. Abrahamian, *Iran between Two Revolutions*, 242–43.

38. Katouzian, *Musaddiq*, 60; Abrahamian, *Iran between Two Revolutions*, 241.

39. Azimi, *Iran*, 166.

40. Gasiorowski, *US Foreign Policy and the Shah*, 47.

41. Azimi, *Iran*, 166.

42. Acting Secretary of State to US Embassy, telegram, Sept. 26, 1947, in *FRUS, 1947*, 5:960–61.

43. Lytle, *Origins of the Iranian–American Alliance*, 179.

44. John Jernegan to Loy Henderson, telegram, Dec. 4, 1947, in *FRUS, 1947*, 5:990–91.

45. Ibid., 5:991.

46. Quoted in Ladjevardi, "Origins of US Support for an Autocratic Iran," 232; see also A. Milani, *The Shah*, 128–29.

47. Ladjevardi, "Origins of US Support for an Autocratic Iran," 233–34.

48. Azimi, *Iran*, 176–77.

49. Ibid., 177 n. 90.

50. A. Milani, *The Shah*, 130.

51. Allen to Jernegan, telegram, Dec. 26, 1947, in *FRUS, 1947*, 5:998.

52. Ibid.

53. Ladjevardi, "Origins of US Support for an Autocratic Iran," 233.

54. Azimi, *Iran*, 178.

55. Allen to Secretary of State, telegram, Jan. 5, 1948, in *FRUS, 1948*, vol. 5, part 1: *The Near East, South Asia, and Africa* (Washington, DC: US Government Printing Office, 1976), 91.

56. In fact, Allen called the Majles an "almost entirely negative body with no apparent ability to take positive action" (Allen to Secretary of State, telegram, Jan. 16, 1948, in *FRUS, 1948*, 5:96).

57. Abrahamian, *Iran between Two Revolutions*, 246.

58. Ibid., 185.

59. Azimi, *Iran*, 201.

60. See *FRUS, 1947*, 5:952.

61. For more on sequencing, see Thomas Carothers, "The 'Sequencing' Fallacy," *Journal of Democracy* 18, no. 1 (2007): 12–27.

62. Dean Acheson, Princeton Univ. Seminar, May 15, 1954, Princeton Seminars File, Dean G. Acheson Papers, Box 81, HSTL.

63. Quoted in Bill, *The Eagle and the Lion*, 52.

64. James F. Goode, *The United States and Iran, 1946–1951: The Diplomacy of Neglect* (New York: St. Martin's Press, 1989), 17.

65. US Department of State, "Policy Statement on Iran," Feb. 1, 1949, in *FRUS, 1949*, vol. 6: *The Near East, South Asia, and Africa* (Washington, DC: US Government Printing Office, 1977), 474.

66. Ibid.

67. A. Milani, *The Shah*, 131.

68. Pahlavi, *Mission for My Country*, 57.

69. "Ruler of Iran Wounded Slightly by Two Bullets Fired by Assassin," *New York Times*, Feb. 5, 1949, 1.

70. Abrahamian, *Iran between Two Revolutions*, 249.

71. "Ruler of Iran Wounded," 1.

72. "Iran Suppresses 60 Newspapers Because of Shooting of Shah," *Chicago Daily Tribune*, Feb. 7, 1949, 14.

73. Abrahamian, *Iran between Two Revolutions*, 250.

74. "A Red Coup in Iran Reported Thwarted," *New York Times*, Feb. 24, 1949, 8.

75. "Iran Election Decreed," *New York Times*, Mar. 2, 1949, 19; Abrahamian, *Iran between Two Revolutions*, 250.

76. Abrahamian, *Iran between Two Revolutions*, 250.

77. David S. McLellan, *Dean Acheson: The State Department Years* (New York: Dodd, Mead, 1976), 137.

78. James Somerville to Secretary of State, telegram, Feb. 17, 1949, in *FRUS, 1949*, 6:482; Abrahamian, *Iran between Two Revolutions*, 203.

79. Hamzavi, "Iran and the Tehran Conference," 202.

80. See *FRUS, 1947,* 5:918.

81. "Developments of the Quarter: Comment and Chronology," *Middle East Journal* 3, no. 4 (1949): 448.

82. George McGhee to Secretary of State, Nov. 17, 1949, in *FRUS, 1949,* 6:569.

83. John C. Wiley to State Department, memo, Jan. 30, 1950, 788.00/1/2350, Box 4106, NARA.

84. Wiley to Secretary of State, memo, Feb. 15, 1950, 611.88/2-1550, Box 2853, NARA.

85. Ibid.

86. Wiley to McGhee, letter, Jan. 30, 1950, 788.00/1-3050, Box 4106, NARA.

87. McGhee to Jernegan, letter, Mar. 23, 1950, 788.00/3-2350, Box 4106, NARA.

88. McGhee to Secretary of State, memo, Apr. 19, 1950, 788.00/4-1950, Box 4106, NARA.

89. Wiley to Secretary of State, memo, Feb. 15, 1950, 611.88/2-1550, Box 2853, NARA.

90. Secretary of State to US Embassy, telegram, Feb. 22, 1949, in *FRUS, 1949,* 6:484.

91. Quoted in Azimi, *Iran,* 216.

92. Bill, *The Eagle and the Lion,* 51–52.

93. Wiley to McGhee, letter, Jan. 30, 1950, 788.00/1-3050, Box 4106, NARA.

94. Dean Acheson to US Embassy, telegram, Mar. 25, 1950, 788.00/3-2550, Box 4106, NARA.

95. US Department of State, "The Present Crisis in Iran," report, in *FRUS, 1950,* vol. 5: *The Near East, South Asia, and Africa* (Washington, DC: US Government Printing Office, 1978), 512.

96. Azimi, *Iran,* 219; Abrahamian, *Iran between Two Revolutions,* 261.

97. Acheson to US Embassy, telegram, Mar. 25, 1950, 788.00/3-2550, Box 4106, NARA.

98. US Department of State, "The Present Crisis in Iran," 5:509–10.

99. Wiley to Secretary of State, telegram, June 5, 1950, 788.00/5-2950, Box 4106, NARA.

100. Ibid.

101. General Razmara also literally had a fine head of hair, but of Mossadegh Dean Acheson remarked that he was "completely bald with no hair on his head at all" (Princeton Univ. Seminar, May 15, 1954).

102. M. Reza Ghods, "The Rise and Fall of General Razmara," *Middle Eastern Studies* 29, no. 1 (1993): 22.

103. Quoted in ibid., 23.

104. Katouzian, *Musaddiq*, 79.

105. Quoted in ibid., 24.

106. Ibid.

107. Ibid., 78.

108. James F. Goode, *The United States and Iran: In the Shadow of Musaddiq* (New York: St. Martin's Press, 1997), 6–7.

109. Quoted in Katouzian, *Musaddiq*, 1.

110. Quoted in ibid., 25.

111. Stephen Kinzer, *All the Shah's Men: An American Coup and the Roots of Middle East Terror* (Hoboken, NJ: Wiley, 2003), 60.

112. Mossadegh received more votes than any of the other eleven Tehrani deputies elected that day (Katouzian, *Musaddiq*, 51).

113. Ibid., 51–54.

114. Abrahamian, *The Coup*, 52–53.

115. Bill, *The Eagle and the Lion*, 55.

116. US Department of State, "The Present Crisis in Iran," 5:509–10.

117. McGhee to Phillip Jessop, Apr. 17, 1950, 788.00/4-1750, Box 4106, NARA; Working Group Paper—Iran, June 1950, Bureau of Near Eastern and South Asian Affairs/Office of Greek, Turkish, and Iranian Affairs, US Department of State, Lot 54, D363, Box 9460, NARA.

118. Quoted in Hussein Fardust and Ali Akbar Dareini, *The Rise and Fall of the Pahlavi Dynasty: Memoirs of Former General Hussein Fardust* (Delhi: Motilal Banarsidass, 1999), 74.

119. Qaimmaqami, "Catalyst of Nationalism," 2.

120. Ibid., 3–6.

121. William Rountree to McGhee, memo, July 13, 1950, 3.41 Greek, Turkish, and Iranian Office Iranian File, Box 36, NARA; Qaimmaqami, "Catalyst of Nationalization," 17.

122. Ghods, "Rise and Fall of General Razmara," 23–24.

123. Bill, *The Eagle and the Lion*, 52.

124. Wiley to Secretary of State, telegram, June 5, 1950, 788.00/5-2950, Box 4106, NARA.

125. A. Milani, *The Shah*, 147.

126. Qaimmaqami, "Catalyst of Nationalization," 17.

127. Wiley to Secretary of State, telegram, June 8, 1950, 788.00/6-850, Box 4106, NARA; US Embassy to Secretary of State, telegram, June 19, 1950, 788.00/6-1950, Box 4106, NARA.

128. Azimi, *Iran*, 223.

129. Quoted in ibid., 224. Shepherd's tour in Iran ironically came after a torrid spell as ambassador to Indonesia, where he almost lost his life during the conflict

against the Dutch. Foreign Secretary Ernest Bevin appointed him to Tehran, promising him an easier time in a "place where we never have any trouble with the natives," clearly not anticipating the looming crisis in Iran (Christopher de Bellaigue, *Patriot of Persia: Muhammad Mossadegh and a Tragic Anglo-American Coup* [New York: Harper, 2012], 160).

130. A. Milani, *The Shah*, 147–48.

131. Barry M. Rubin, *Paved with Good Intentions: The American Experience in Iran* (New York: Oxford Univ. Press, 1980), 47.

132. McGhee to Secretary of State, memo, Jan. 30, 1951, 788.00/1-3051, Box 4107, NARA.

133. Goode, *The United States and Iran, 1946–51*, 69.

134. Summary of conversation with President Harry S. Truman regarding intentions of the Chinese Communists vis-à-vis Korea, June 26, 1950, George M. Elsey Papers, HSTL.

135. Bill, *The Eagle and the Lion*, 53.

136. Gasiorowski devotes a paragraph and a half to Razmara in *US Foreign Policy and the Shah*, 49.

137. Rubin, *Paved with Good Intentions*, 47. See also Ansari, *Modern Iran since 1921*; Gheissari and Nasr, *Democracy in Iran*; Azimi, *Quest for Democracy in Iran*.

138. US Embassy to Secretary of State, telegram, June 21, 1950, 788.00/6-2150, Box 4106, NARA; Ghods, "Rise and Fall of General Razmara," 25; Azimi, *Iran*, 228–29.

139. Azimi, *Iran*, 228.

140. McGhee to Secretary of State, memo, July 7, 1950, 788.00/7-750, Box 4106, NARA.

141. Secretary of State to Henry Grady, July 22, 1950, 788.00/7-2050, Box 4106, NARA.

142. Grady to Secretary of State, telegram, Sept. 18, 1950, 788.00/9-1850, Box 4106, NARA.

143. US Embassy to Secretary of State, memo, Nov. 30, 1950, 611.88/11-3050, NARA.

144. "Background Memoranda on Visit to the United States of His Imperial Majesty Mohammad Reza Pahlavi Shahinshah of Iran, Nov. 1949—Prepared by the Department of State," Nov. 1, 1949, White House Central Files, CF, Correspondence Box 40, HSTL; State Department to the Iranian Embassy, telegram, Jan. 26, 1950, 788.5 MAP/1-2650, in *FRUS, 1950*, 5:452.

145. Quoted in Rubin, *Paved with Good Intentions*, 49.

146. US embassy report, quoted in Rubin, *Paved with Good Intentions*, 50.

147. Wiley to William O. Douglas, letter, Sept. 1, 1949, William O. Douglas Papers, Box 639, Library of Congress (LoC), Washington, DC.

148. Douglas to the President, letter, Oct. 6, 1950, William O. Douglas Papers, Box 1718, LoC.

149. Grady to Rountree, letter, Oct. 27, 1950, Henry F. Grady Papers, Box 1, HSTL.

150. US Embassy report, quoted in Rubin, *Paved with Good Intentions*, 50.

151. Quoted in Ghods, "Rise and Fall of General Razmara," 26.

152. Muzaffar Baghai, quoted in ibid.

153. Abrahamian, *Iran between Two Revolutions*, 265; Ghods, "Rise and Fall of General Razmara," 26.

154. Baghai quoted in Abrahamian, *Iran between Two Revolutions*, 265.

155. Ghods, "Rise and Fall of General Razmara," 30.

156. See ibid., 30; Abbas Milani, *Eminent Persians: The Men and Women Who Made Modern Iran, 1941–1979* (Syracuse, NY: Syracuse Univ. Press, 2008), 1010; Azimi, *Iran*, 233.

157. McGhee to Secretary of State, memo, Jan. 30, 1951, 788.00/1-3051, Box 4107, NARA.

158. Bill, *The Eagle and the Lion*, 52.

159. Azimi, *Iran*, 236; Secretary of State to US Embassy, memo, Jan. 19, 1951, 788.00/1-3051, Box 4107, NARA.

160. Henry F. Grady, "What Went Wrong in Iran?" *Saturday Evening Post*, Jan. 5, 1952, 57.

3. Mossadegh and the Anglo-Iranian Oil Crisis, 1951–1953

1. George McGhee, Princeton Univ. Seminar, May 15, 1954, Princeton Seminars File, Dean G. Acheson Papers, Box 81, HSTL.

2. Bill, *The Eagle and the Lion*, 64.

3. Ervand Abrahamian, "The 1953 Coup in Iran," *Science and Society* 65, no. 2 (2001): 185.

4. Sam Falle, an Iran expert in the British Foreign Office at the time, later remarked (with a bit of ethnocentricity) that the AIOC's stubbornness to renegotiate equity so that the Iranians would receive a greater share was owing in part to the company's "Scottish management" (Abrahamian, *The Coup*, 48).

5. Bill, *The Eagle and the Lion*, 64.

6. Kinzer, *All the Shah's Men*, 67.

7. Bill, *The Eagle and the Lion*, 63.

8. Kinzer, *All the Shah's Men*, 67–68.

9. Farmanfarmaian and Farmanfarmaian, *Blood and Oil*, 184–85.

10. Quoted in de Bellaigue, *Patriot of Persia*, 118.

11. Bill, *The Eagle and the Lion*, 61.

12. Quoted in Mostafa Elm, *Oil, Power, and Principle: Iran's Oil Nationalization and Its Aftermath* (Syracuse, NY: Syracuse Univ. Press, 1992), 75.

13. See ibid., 76.

14. Ronald W. Ferrier, "The Development of the Iranian Oil Industry," in *Twentieth Century Iran*, ed. Hossein Amirsadeghi (New York: Holmes and Meier, 1977), 106.

15. Quoted in Bill, *The Eagle and the Lion*, 62–63.

16. Kinzer, *All the Shah's Men*, 76.

17. Quoted in ibid.

18. Quoted in de Bellaigue, *Patriot of Persia*, 147.

19. Kashani quoted in Abrahamian, *Iran between Two Revolutions*, 266–67.

20. Azimi, *Iran*, 238.

21. "Maus" to William O. Douglas, Mar. 10, 1951, William O. Douglas Papers, Box 1718, LoC.

22. Ironically, the leader of the group responsible for the assassination, Navvab Safavi, had once been an employee of the AIOC. See Farhad Kazemi, "Fedā'īān-e Eslām," *Encyclopædia Iranica* 9 (1999): 470.

23. Quoted in Azimi, *Iran*, 236.

24. Ibid.

25. Secretary of State to US Embassy, telegram, Nov. 18, 1950, in *FRUS, 1950*, 5:613–16.

26. George McGhee, quoted in Beisner, *Dean Acheson*, 540.

27. Quoted in ibid., 538.

28. Director of the Office of Greek, Turkish, and Iranian Affairs (US Department of State) to the Assistant Secretary of State of Near Eastern, South Asian, and African Affairs, memo, Dec. 20, 1950, in *FRUS, 1950*, 5:634.

29. Edmund Stevens, "Huge Oil Refinery in Iran Closed by Striking Pickets," *Christian Science Monitor*, Apr. 16, 1951, quoted in Bill, *The Eagle and the Lion 65*.

30. *Bakhtar-e Emrooz*, n.d., quoted in de Bellaigue, *Patriot of Persia*, 154.

31. US Embassy to Secretary of State, telegram, Mar. 9, 1951, 788.00/3-951, Box 4107, NARA.

32. For full text of the nine-point bill, see Goode, *The United States and Iran: In the Shadow of Musaddiq*, app. B, 191. For British attempts to bring Sayyid Zia Tabataba'i to power, see Azimi, *Iran*, 251.

33. Mossadegh's appointment reportedly came as the shah was meeting with Tabataba'i about forming a new government. See Katouzian, *Musaddiq*, 93, and Azimi, *Iran*, 257.

34. Mossadegh, speech before the Majles, Apr. 11, 1951, quoted in Azimi, *Iran*, 257.

35. Acheson, *Present at the Creation*, 506, 503.

36. Rubin, *Paved with Good Intentions*, 58.

37. Dean Acheson, Princeton Univ. Seminar, May 15, 1954, Princeton Seminars File, Dean G. Acheson Papers, Box 81, HSTL.

38. Katouzian, *Musaddiq*, 7.

39. Schymen Nussbaum to the President, letter, June 6, 1951, White House Central File, Official File, 1945–1953, Box 691, HSTL.

40. M. J. Williams, Director of the Executive Secretariat, to William Hopkins, White House, memo, Oct. 25, 1951, White House Central File, Official File, 1945–1953, Box 691, HSTL.

41. Acheson, Princeton Seminar, May 15, 1954.

42. William E. Warne, US Director of Technical Cooperation for Iran, to Joseph Short, Secretary to the President, letter, Feb. 5, 1952, Harry S. Truman Papers, White House Central File, Official File, Box 169, HSTL.

43. W. Averell Harriman, Princeton Univ. Seminar, May 15, 1954, Princeton Seminars File, Dean G. Acheson Papers, Box 81, HSTL.

44. Acheson, Princeton Seminar, May 15, 1954.

45. Loy Henderson, oral history interview, Dec. 14, 1970, OH-191, Oral History Project, Columbia Univ., New York.

46. Katouzian, *Musaddiq*, 262.

47. "Challenge of the East," *Time*, Jan. 7, 1952, 20.

48. Azimi, *Iran*, 261.

49. Kinzer, *All the Shah's Men*, 112.

50. Lord Fraser's title has often been mistaken as "First Lord of the Admiralty"; for example, see Elm, *Oil, Power, and Principle*, 162. The Office of First Lord of the Admiralty is an honorary position reserved for members of the royal family. Now called "Lord High Admiral," this position is currently bestowed upon His Royal Highness the Duke of Edinburgh. Lord Fraser was Admiral of the Fleet, a rank equivalent to five-star general and the Royal Navy's highest honor for a member of the service. He also held the position of First Sea Lord, the professional head of the Royal Navy.

51. Quoted in Kinzer, *All the Shah's Men*, 112, and Elm, *Oil, Power, and Principle*, 162–63.

52. Quoted in A. Milani, *The Shah*, 152.

53. Quoted in de Bellaigue, *Patriot of Persia*, 158.

54. National Security Council (NSC), "A Report to the President by the NSC on the Position of the US with Respect to Iran," NSC 107/2, June 27, 1951, White House Office (WHO), NSC Staff: Papers, 1948–61, Disaster File, Box 65, HSTL.

55. See Abrahamian, *The Coup*, 83–85; US Department of State, "US Position on Iranian Oil Situation," May 18, 1951, Oil Crisis in Iran, 1951–1953, Box 1, Student Research File, HSTL.

56. See Abrahamian, *The Coup*, 85.

57. Memo of Conversation between George McGhee and Sir Oliver Franks, British Ambassador to Iran, July 11, 1951, Dean G. Acheson Papers, Memoranda of Conversation File, 1949–1953, Box 69, HSTL; Abrahamian, *Iran between Two Revolutions*, 268.

58. Quoted in Elm, *Oil, Power, and Principle*, 134.

59. Henry Grady to State Department, telegram, Aug. 19, 1951, Harry S. Truman Papers, PSF: Subject File, 1940–53, Box 180, HSTL; Grady to State Department, telegram, Aug. 19, 1951, 888.2553/8-1951, NARA.

60. Harriman, Princeton Seminar, May 15, 1954.

61. UK Ministry of Fuel and Power, Sept. 5–6, 1951, quoted in Abrahamian, *The Coup*, 122–23.

62. Quoted in Mary Ann Heiss, *Empire and Nationhood: The United States, Great Britain, and Oil, 1950–1954* (New York: Columbia Univ. Press, 1997), 89.

63. W. Averell Harriman to Secretary of State, telegram, Aug. 22, 1951, Harry S. Truman Papers, PSF: Subject File, 1940–53, Foreign Affairs File, Box 158, HSTL.

64. Harriman to Secretary of State, telegram, Aug. 24, 1951, Harry S. Truman Papers, PSF: Subject File, 1940–53, Foreign Affairs File, Box 158, HSTL; Harriman, Princeton Seminar, May 15, 1954.

65. Tim Weiner, *Legacy of Ashes: The History of the CIA* (New York: Doubleday, 2007), 83–84.

66. Kinzer, *All the Shah's Men*, 164; Darioush Bayandor, *Iran and the CIA: The Fall of Mosaddeq Revisited* (New York: Palgrave Macmillan, 2010), 126.

67. Kinzer, *All the Shah's Men*, 170.

68. Mark J. Gasiorowski, "The 1953 Coup d'État in Iran," *International Journal of Middle East Studies* 19, no. 3 (1987): 268.

69. Ibid., 268–69.

70. Ibid., 269.

71. Ibid.

72. Quoted in Elm, *Oil, Power, and Principle*, 157.

73. "History of the 16th Independent Parachute Group Signal Squadron, 1948–1959," n.d., at http://www.216parasigs.org.uk/history/16ipbgss.htm; Elm, *Oil, Power, and Principle*, 166.

74. Elm, *Oil, Power, and Principle*, 160; Goode, *The United States and Iran: In the Shadow of Musaddiq*, 33.

75. Hugh Gaitskell, *The Diary of Hugh Gaitskell, 1945–1956*, ed. Philip Maynard Williams (London: Cape, 1983), 260.

76. Goode, *The United States and Iran: In the Shadow of Musaddiq*, 34.

77. William Roger Louis, *The British Empire in the Middle East* (Oxford: Clarendon Press, 1985), 739.

78. Quoted in ibid., 122. Sir Alfred's great-great-grandson, David Cameron, was the prime minister of the United Kingdom from 2010 to 2016.

79. Quoted in Elm, *Oil, Power, and Principle*, 165.

80. Morrison's grandson is Peter Mandelson (now Lord Mandelson), one-time member of the Young Communist League and later key architect in rebranding Labour away from the political left and into "New Labour."

81. Quoted in Elm, *Oil, Power, and Principle*, 162.

82. Heiss, *Empire and Nationhood*, 96.

83. Elm, *Oil, Power, and Principle*, 154.

84. See Steve Marsh, "Anglo-American Relations and the Labour Government's 'Scuttle' from Abadan: A 'Declaration of Dependence'?" *International History Review* 35, no. 4 (2013): 817–43.

85. Quoted in Bill, *The Eagle and the Lion*, 76.

86. Acheson, Princeton Seminar, May 15, 1954.

87. Memo of Conversation between Winston Churchill and the US Secretary of State, Jan. 6, 1952, Dean G. Acheson Papers, Memoranda of Conversation File, 1949–53, Box 69, HSTL.

88. Quoted in Steve Neal, *HST: Memories of the Truman Years* (Carbondale: Southern Illinois Univ., 2003), 10.

89. Harriman to Secretary of State, telegram, Aug. 24, 1951, Harry S. Truman Papers, PSF: Subject File, 1940–53, Foreign Affairs File, Box 158, HSTL.

90. Quoted in Beisner, *Dean Acheson*, 546.

91. State Department to Grady, telegram, Sept. 7, 1951, Henry F. Grady Papers, Box 1, HSTL.

92. State Department to Grady, telegram, Aug. 17, 1951, Henry F. Grady Papers, Box 1, HSTL.

93. "CIA Analysis of Iranian Political Situation," report, Oct. 12, 1951, Harry S. Truman Papers, PSF: Subject File, 1940–53, Foreign Affairs File, Box 158, HSTL.

94. Acheson, *Present at the Creation*, 504.

95. Mohammad Mossadegh to Harry S. Truman, letter, Nov. 9, 1951, Harry S. Truman Papers, White House Central File, Official File, 1945–53, Box 691, HSTL.

96. Memo for the Director of Central Intelligence from Assistant Director for National Estimates, Jan. 17, 1952, Harry S. Truman Papers, PSF: Subject File, 1940–53, Foreign Affairs File, Box 158, HSTL.

97. Paul Nitze, Princeton Univ. Seminar, May 15, 1954, Princeton Seminars File, Dean G. Acheson Papers, Box 81, HSTL; "Telegram to US Embassy Containing Message from President to Mossadegh," Feb. 1952, Harry S. Truman Papers, White House Central Files, Confidential File, Correspondence, Box 40, HSTL.

98. Memorandum of Dinner Meeting on SS *Williamsburg* between Truman and Churchill, Jan. 5, 1952, Dean G. Acheson Papers, Memoranda of Conversation File, 1949–53, Box 69, HSTL.

99. Quoted in US Ambassador to State Department, telegram, Sept. 30, 1951, in *FRUS, 1952–1954*, vol. 10: *United States Department of State / Iran, 1952–1954* (Washington, DC: US Government Printing Office, 1989), 187. See also Steering Group on Preparations for the Talks between the President and Churchill, Jan. 5, 1952, George M. Elsey Papers, Truman Presidency Subject File, Box 115, HSTL, and Azimi, *Iran*, 268.

100. Azimi, *Iran*, 269.

101. Ibid.

102. UK Ministry of Fuel and Power, report, Sept. 5–6, 1951, quoted in Abrahamian, *The Coup*, 122–23.

103. Loy Henderson to Harriman, memo, Nov. 6, 1951, W. Averell Harriman Papers, Special Files: Public Service, 1918–86, LoC.

104. Azimi, *Iran*, 277.

105. Goode, *The United States and Iran: In the Shadow of Musaddiq*, 75; Abrahamian, *Iran between Two Revolutions*, 269; Azimi, *Iran*, 278; Katouzian, *Musaddiq*, 120.

106. Kenneth M. Pollack, *The Persian Puzzle: The Conflict between Iran and America* (New York: Random House, 2004), 61. See also Abrahamian, *Iran between Two Revolutions*, 269.

107. Abrahamian, *Iran between Two Revolutions*, 269.

108. National Front deputy, quoted in ibid., 270.

109. Fakhreddin Azimi, "Unseating Mossadegh: The Configuration and Role of Domestic Forces," in *Mohammad Mossaddeq and the 1953 Coup in Iran*, ed. Mark J. Gasiorowski and Malcolm Byrne (Syracuse, NY: Syracuse Univ. Press, 2004), 52.

110. A. Milani, *The Shah*, 153.

111. For possible reasons why Mossadegh made this request, see Katouzian, *Musaddiq*, 121–23; Abrahamian, *Iran between Two Revolutions*, 271; A. Milani, *The Shah*, 153.

112. Katouzian, *Musaddiq*, 123; Kinzer, *All the Shah's Men*, 135.

113. Pollack, *Persian Puzzle*, 62.

114. Quoted in Azimi, *Iran*, 284.

115. A. Milani, *The Shah*, 153.

116. Quoted in Goode, *The United States and Iran: In the Shadow of Musaddiq*, 79.

117. Quoted in Kinzer, *All the Shah's Men*, 139.

118. William Roger Louis, "Britain and the Overthrow of the Mosaddeq Government," in Gasiorowski and Byrne, *Mohammad Mosaddeq*, 143.

119. Acheson, Princeton Seminar, May 15, 1954.

120. Meeting between the President [and Dean Acheson] on the Iranian Situation, July 21, 1952, Dean G. Acheson Papers, Memoranda of Conversation File, 1949–53, Box 70, HSTL.

121. Memo for File, July 24, 1952, W. Averell Harriman Papers, Special File, Public Service, 1918–86, LoC; "Memorandum of Telephone Conversation between Acheson and President," July 31, 1952, Dean G. Acheson Papers, Memoranda of Conversation File, 1949–53, Box 70, HSTL.

122. Loy Henderson, quoted in Goode, *The United States and Iran: In the Shadow of Musaddiq*, 80.

123. Quoted in Elm, *Oil, Power, and Principle*, 242.

124. Heiss, *Empire and Nationhood*, 133.

125. Katouzian, *Musaddiq*, 125; Azimi, *Iran*, 290; Abrahamian, *Iran between Two Revolutions*, 272.

126. Goode, *The United States and Iran: In the Shadow of Musaddiq*, 80.

127. For little to no mention of American policy during Qavam's brief premiership at this time, see Heiss, *Empire and Nationhood*; Ivan L. G. Pearson, *In the Name of Oil: Anglo-American Relations in the Middle East, 1950–1958* (Eastbourne, UK: Sussex Academic Press, 2010). It received only two sentences in Bill's otherwise excellent book *The Eagle and the Lion* (66) and similar scant consideration in Rubin's book *Paved with Good Intentions* (73).

128. Sir Oliver Franks, quoted in Steve Marsh, "Continuity and Change: Reinterpreting the Policies of the Truman and Eisenhower Administrations toward Iran, 1950–1954," *Journal of Cold War Studies* 7, no. 3 (2005): 108.

129. Acheson, Princeton Seminar, May 15, 1954.

130. Pollack, *Persian Puzzle*, 62.

131. Sepehr Zabih, *The Mossadegh Era: Roots of the Iranian Revolution* (Chicago: Lake View Press, 1982), 66; Katouzian, *Musaddiq*, 125; Kinzer, *All the Shah's Men*, 141.

132. For more on Mossadegh's views on the role of the monarchy, see Mohammad Mossadegh, *Khaterat va ta'allomat-e Mossadegh* (Memoirs and Musings of Mossadegh), ed. Iraj Afshar (Tehran: Elmi, 1986), 209–37.

133. Quoted in Zabih, *Mossadegh Era*, 66, and Kinzer, *All the Shah's Men*, 141.

134. Albion Ross, "Iranian Deputies Rebuff Mossadegh over Martial Law," *New York Times*, Aug. 11, 1952, 1.

135. Abrahamian, *Iran between Two Revolutions*, 273.

136. Azimi, *Iran*, 293.

137. Ibid., 295; Abrahamian, *The Coup*, 145.

138. Homa Katouzian, "Mosaddeq's Government in Iranian History: Arbitrary Rule, Democracy, and the 1953 Coup," in Gasiorowski and Byrne, *Mohammad Mosaddeq*, 5.

139. Heiss, *Empire and Nationhood*, 3; Bill, *The Eagle and the Lion*, 84; Pearson, *In the Name of Oil*, 38; Abrahamian, *The Coup*, 150. See also Alan S. Milward, *The Reconstruction of Western Europe, 1945–1951* (Berkeley: Univ. of California Press, 1984), and Fraser J. Harbutt, *The Iron Curtain: Churchill, America, and the Origins of the Cold War* (New York: Oxford Univ. Press, 1986).

140. Acheson to State Department, telegram, Nov. 10, 1951, in *FRUS, 1952–1954*, 10:279.

141. Harriman, quoted in Acheson, Princeton Seminar, May 15, 1954.

142. Secretary of State to US Embassy in London, telegram, July 26, 1952, in *FRUS, 1952–1954*, 10:415.

143. See Abrahamian, *The Coup*, 140–41.

144. Ibid., 142–47.

145. Acheson, *Present at the Creation*, 680.

146. Memorandum of Telephone Conversation between Secretary of State and Truman, July 31, 1952, Dean G. Acheson Papers, Memoranda of Conversation File, 1949–53, Box 70, HSTL.

147. Memorandum of Conversation between Secretary of State and Franks, Aug. 11, 1952, Dean G. Acheson Papers, Memoranda of Conversation File, 1949–53, Box 70, HSTL.

148. Acting Secretary of State to US Embassy in London, telegram, Aug. 18, 1952, in *FRUS, 1952–1954*, 10:447.

149. Quoted in Louis, "Britain and the Overthrow of the Mosaddeq Government," 158.

150. Personal and Secret Message from Churchill to Truman, Aug. 22, 1952, Harry S. Truman Papers, PSF, General File, 1940, 1953, Box 99, HSTL.

151. Minutes of Meeting, White House, Aug. 21, 1952, Dean G. Acheson Papers, Memoranda of Conversation File, 1949–53, Box 70, HSTL; Text of the Report Submitted by Mossadegh to the Seventeenth Majles, Sept. 16, 1952, Henry F. Grady Papers, General File, General Correspondence, 1954-H, Box 3, HSTL; Acheson, *Present at the Creation*, 681.

152. Quoted in Elm, *Oil, Power, and Principle*, 252.

153. Katouzian, *Musaddiq*, 143.

154. Memorandum of Meeting at White House between Truman and Eisenhower, Nov. 18, 1952, Dean G. Acheson Papers, Memoranda of Conversation File, 1949–53, Box 70, HSTL.

155. Memorandum of Meeting at White House between Truman and Eisenhower, Nov. 18, 1952, Dean G. Acheson Papers, Memoranda of Conversation File, 1949–53, Box 70, HSTL; Memorandum of Meeting between Acheson and Oil Company Representatives, Dec. 4, 1952, Dean G. Acheson Papers, Memoranda of Conversation File, 1949–53, Box 70, HSTL; Acheson, *Present at the Creation*, 681.

156. Acheson, *Present at the Creation*, 683.

157. Ibid, 684.

158. Henry Byroade, oral history interview, HSTL, at https://www.trumanlibrary.org/oralhist/byroade.htm#note.

159. Dean Acheson, Princeton Seminar, May 15, 1954.

160. Acheson, *Present at the Creation*, 681; Anthony Eden, *Full Circle: The Memoirs of Anthony Eden* (Boston: Houghton Mifflin, 1960), 232, 236.

161. Katouzian, "Mosaddeq's Government in Iranian History," 5.

162. George Allen to Secretary of State, telegram, Mar. 27, 1947, in *FRUS, 1947*, 5:900; Ladjevardi, "Origins of Support for an Autocratic Iran," 230.

4. The Overthrow of Democracy, 1953

1. Jean Edward Smith, *Eisenhower in War and Peace* (New York: Random House, 2012), 394.

2. Ibid.

3. McCullough, *Truman*, 887.

4. John Foster Dulles, "Thoughts on Soviet Foreign Policy and What to Do about It," *Life*, June 3, 1946, 112–26, and June 10, 1946, 119–30.

5. Ronald W. Pruessen, *John Foster Dulles: The Road to Power* (New York: Free Press, 1982), 291.

6. Quoted in ibid., 292.

7. John Foster Dulles, *War or Peace* (New York: Macmillan, 1950), 17.

8. Ibid., 154, 157.

9. Dulles became the fifty-second secretary of state, following a tradition established by his grandfather, the thirty-second secretary of state, and his uncle, the forty-second.

10. Smith, *Eisenhower in War and Peace*, 553.

11. Quoted in ibid., 553.

12. Ibid., 569.

13. Quoted in David A. Nichols, *Eisenhower 1956: The President's Year of Crisis—Suez and the Brink of War* (New York: Simon and Schuster, 2011), 7.

14. Andrew Goodpaster, quoted in ibid., 7–8.

15. Quoted in ibid., 7.

16. Smith, *Eisenhower in War and Peace*, 617.

17. Dwight D. Eisenhower to Edward E. "Swede" Hazlett, June 21, 1951, quoted in ibid., 621.

18. Cooper, *Fall of Heaven*, 72; Kinzer, *All the Shah's Men*, 3; Lytle, *Origins of the Iranian–American Alliance*, 204; Gasiorowski, *US Foreign Policy and the Shah*, 83; Mostafa T. Zahrani, "The Coup That Changed the Middle East: Mossadegh v. the CIA in Perspective," *World Policy Journal* 19, no. 2 (2002): 93–99; Pollack, *Persian Puzzle*, 64.

19. Dwight D. Eisenhower, *The Eisenhower Diaries*, ed. Robert H. Ferrell (New York: Norton, 1981), 223, 224.

20. Heiss, *Empire and Nationhood*, 229.

21. Executive Secretary to the Members of the National Security Council, memo, NSC 4-A, Dec. 9, 1947, Minutes of the Fourth NSC Meeting, NSC Records, Record Group (RG) 273, NARA.

22. Otis Pike, *CIA: The Pike Report* (Nottingham, UK: Spokesman Books, 1977), 204–5; F. Mark Wyatt, "Episode 3: Marshall Plan—Interview," *The Cold War*, CNN, at http://www.cnn.com/SPECIALS/cold.war/episodes/03/interviews/wyatt; Beisner, *Dean Acheson*, 566.

23. See Douglas Little, "Cold War and Covert Action: The United States and Syria, 1945–1958," *Middle East Journal* 44, no. 1 (1990): 51–76; Miles Copeland, *The Game of Nations: The Amorality of Power Politics* (New York: Simon and Schuster, 1970), 50–56.

24. Sarah-Jane Corke, *US Covert Operations and Cold War Strategy: Truman, Secret Warfare, and the CIA, 1945–1953* (New York: Routledge, 2008), 2. For more on BGFIEND, see Nicholas Bethell, *Betrayed* (New York: Times Books, 1985).

25. William Stueck, "Reassessing US Strategy in the Aftermath of the Korean War," *Orbis* 53, no. 4 (2009): 574.

26. John Prados, *Safe for Democracy: The Secret Wars of the CIA* (Chicago: Ivan R. Dee, 2006), 99.

27. "Kermit Roosevelt; Arranged Iran Coup," *Los Angeles Times*, June 11, 2000, at http://articles.latimes.com/2000/jun/11/local/me-39909.

28. Quoted in "Kermit Roosevelt," *Daily Telegraph*, June 22, 2000, at http://www.telegraph.co.uk/news/obituaries/1344246/Kermit-Roosevelt.html.

29. Kermit Roosevelt, *Countercoup: The Struggle for the Control of Iran* (New York: McGraw-Hill, 1979), 110.

30. Ibid., 107.

31. See, for example, Douglas Little, "Gideon's Band: America and the Middle East since 1945," *Diplomatic History* 18, no. 4 (1994): 513–40; Beisner, *Dean Acheson*, 566; Heiss, *Empire and Nationhood*, 229; Kinzer, *All the Shah's Men*, 149. Although the British were of the opinion that Eisenhower would be more amenable to their coup plans, there is no evidence they discussed the matter with Truman.

32. Roosevelt, *Countercoup*, 115.

33. Quoted in ibid., 115.

34. Gasiorowski, *US Foreign Policy and the Shah*, 73–74.

35. Discussion at the 132nd NSC Meeting, Feb. 18, 1953, memo, Dwight D. Eisenhower (DDE) Papers as President, 1953–1961, Ann Whitman File, NSC Series, Box 4, Dwight D. Eisenhower Presidential Library (DDEL), Abilene, KA.

36. Quoted in *Department of State Bulletin* 29, July 20, 1953, 76–77, Harry N. Howard Papers, Middle East Chronological File, 1950–54, HSTL.

37. "Probable Developments in Iran through 1953," National Intelligence Estimate 75, Nov. 13, 1952, Harry N. Howard Papers, Middle East Chronological File, 1950–54, Box 14, HSTL.

38. See Mark J. Gasiorowski, "The 1953 Coup d'État against Mosaddeq," in Gasiorowski and Byrne, *Mohammad Mossaddeq*, 231.

39. Abrahamian, *The Coup*, 161–62.

40. Loy Henderson to State Department, telegram, Mar. 9, 1953, in *FRUS, 1952–1954*, 10:705–6.

41. Quoted in Heiss, *Empire and Nationhood*, 171.

42. "The Reminiscences of Loy Henderson," Dec. 14, 1970, OH-191, Center for Oral History Archives, Rare Book and Manuscript Library, Columbia Univ., New York.

43. Henderson to State Department, telegram, Feb. 22, 1953, in *FRUS, 1952–1954*, 10:674.

44. Henderson to State Department, telegram, Feb. 23, 1953, in *FRUS, 1952–1954*, 10:677.

45. A. Milani, *The Shah*, 161.

46. Henderson to State Department, telegram, Feb. 22, 1953, in *FRUS, 1952–1954*, 10:677.

47. Ibid., 676. See also Mansoureh Ebrahimi, *The British Role in Iranian Domestic Politics (1951–1953)* (Geneva: Springer Science and Business Media, 2016), 77.

48. Henderson to State Department, telegram, Feb. 22, 1953, 675–76; Henderson to State Department, telegram, Feb. 24, 1953, in *FRUS, 1952–1954*, 10:680.

49. Henderson to State Department, telegram, Feb. 25, 1953, in *FRUS, 1952–1954*, 10:681.

50. Ibid., 10:682.

51. Ibid.

52. For more on this linkage, see Ebrahimi, *British Role*.

53. See Abrahamian, *The Coup*, 160–61.

54. Stephen Dorril, *MI6: Inside the Covert World of Her Majesty's Secret Intelligence Service* (New York: Free Press, 2000), 583.

55. Robert Dreyfuss, *Devil's Game: How the United States Helped Unleash Fundamentalist Islam* (New York: Metropolitan Books, 2005), 115.

56. Abrahamian, *The Coup*, 169.

57. Ebrahimi, *British Role*, 78.

58. Henderson to State Department, telegram, Feb. 28, 1953, in *FRUS, 1952–1954*, 10:688–89.

59. Ibid., 10:688.

60. Ibid.

61. Ebrahimi, *British Role*, 79.

62. A. Milani, *The Shah*, 167.

63. Mossadegh, *Khaterat va ta'allomat*, 262–66, quoted in Azimi, "Unseating Mosaddeq," 81.

64. US Embassy to Secretary of State, memo, Mar. 4, 1953, 611.88/3-453, Box 2853, NARA.

65. State Department to Henderson, telegram, Mar. 2, 1953, 788.00/3-253, RG 59, NARA.

66. Ibid.

67. Secretary of State to US Embassy, telegram, Mar. 2, 1953, in *FRUS, 1952–1954*, 10:691.

68. Elm, *Oil, Power, and Principle*, 295; Kinzer, *All the Shah's Men*, 157.

69. Henderson to Secretary of State, telegram, Mar. 4, 1953, in *FRUS, 1952–1954*, 10:692.

70. CIA to the President, memo, Mar. 1, 1953, WHO, NSC Staff: Papers, 1948–61, Disaster File, Box 65, DDEL.

71. Discussion at the 135th NSC Meeting, Mar. 4, 1953, memo, in *FRUS, 1952–1954*, 10:693.

72. Although Mossadegh was accused of being a Communist in the run-up to the coup, there is no evidence of this being the case. Recent research at the Russian State Archives found that the Soviets already considered Iran lost to the Western sphere. See Artemy M. Kalinovsky, "The Soviet Union and Mosaddeq: A Research Note," *Iranian Studies* 47, no. 3 (2014): 403.

73. Kinzer, *All the Shah's Men*, 206.

74. Kalinovsky, "Soviet Union and Mosaddeq," 405. The Soviet impression of Mossadegh did change following his return to power after Qavam's brief premiership in 1952, but instead of seeing him as a fellow traveler, the Soviets viewed him as a weakling who would not last long. Their efforts were directed more at recruiting Kashani to their side (see Kalinovsky, "Soviet Union and Mosaddeq").

75. Discussion at the 135th NSC Meeting, Mar. 4, 1953, memo, in *FRUS, 1952–1954*, 10:693.

76. Ibid., 10:698.

77. Ibid., 10:697.

78. Ibid., 10:699.

79. Ibid.

80. Elm, *Oil, Power, and Principle*, 282.

81. Quoted in Smith, *Eisenhower in War and Peace*, 573.

82. Quoted in ibid., 575.

83. Memorandum of Discussion at the 136th NSC Meeting, Mar. 11, 1953, DDE Papers as President, 1953–1961, Ann Whitman File, NSC Series, Box 4, DDEL.

84. Roosevelt, *Countercoup*, 117.

85. Memorandum of Discussion at the 136th NSC Meeting, Mar. 11, 1953, DDE Papers as President, 1953–1961, Ann Whitman File, NSC Series, Box 4, DDEL.

86. Ibid.

87. Smith, *Eisenhower in War and Peace*, 624–25.

88. Stephen E. Ambrose, *Eisenhower, the President* (New York: Simon and Schuster, 1983), 111–12.

89. Quoted in Stephen Kinzer, *Overthrow: America's Century of Regime Change from Hawaii to Iraq* (New York: Holt, 2006), 111.

90. The veracity of Ambrose's work on Eisenhower in particular has been called into question. For more information on this criticism, see Richard Rayner, "Channeling Ike," *New Yorker*, Apr. 26, 2010, at http://www.newyorker.com/talk/2010/04/26/100426ta_talk_rayner.

91. Dorril, *MI6*, 583.

92. Central Intelligence Agency, "Overthrow of Premier Mossadeq of Iran, November 1952–August 1953," Mar. 1954, 3, at https://archive.org/details/CIA-Mossadeq-Iran-1953.

93. Quoted in Roosevelt, *Countercoup*, 8.

94. Ibid.

95. Geoffrey Wawro, *Quicksand: America's Pursuit of Power in the Middle East* (New York: Penguin, 2010), 136.

96. Ibid., 17; Kinzer, *All the Shah's Men*, 164.

97. Quoted in Goode, *The United States and Iran: In the Shadow of Musaddiq*, 82.

98. Quoted in Roosevelt, *Countercoup*, 18.

99. Ibid., 14.

100. Gasiorowski, "1953 Coup d'État against Mosaddeq," 245.

101. See ibid.; Wilbur, "Overthrow of Premier Mossadeq of Iran, November 1952–August 1953."

102. John Foster Dulles and Allen W. Dulles, telephone conversation, July 24, 1953, transcript, John Foster Dulles Papers, 1951–59, John Foster Dulles Chronological Series, Box 4, DDEL.

103. Roosevelt, *Countercoup*, 135.

104. "Appendix B: 'London' Draft of the TPAJAX Operational Plan," 3, at http://www.gwu.edu/~nsarchiv/NSAEBB/NSAEBB28/appendix%20B.pdf.

105. Cooper, *Fall of Heaven*, 37, 114–16, 328–30.

106. Quoted in A. Milani, *The Shah*, 179.

107. Roosevelt, *Countercoup*, 156–57, emphasis in original.

108. Abrahamian, *The Coup*, 180.

109. Henderson to Roy M. Melbourne, letter, Apr. 19, 1980, Loy Henderson Papers, Subject File, LoC.

110. Kinzer, *All the Shah's Men*, 14.

111. US Ambassador Burton Y. Berry to State Department, telegram, Aug. 17, 1953, in *FRUS, 1952–1954*, 10:747.

112. Kinzer, *All the Shah's Men*, 15.

113. Walter Bedell Smith to the President, memo, Aug. 18, 1953, DDE Papers as President, 1953–1961, Ann Whitman File, International Series, Box 32, DDEL.

114. Henderson to State Department, telegram, Aug. 18, 1953, 788.00/8-1853, Box 4111, NARA.

115. William M. Rountree, interview by Arthur L. Lowrie, Dec. 22, 1989, Foreign Affairs Oral History Project, Association for Diplomatic Studies and Training, LoC.

116. "The People Take Over," *Time*, Aug. 31, 1953, 16–18.

117. Ibid.

118. William A. Dorman and Mansour Farhang, *The US Press and Iran: Foreign Policy and the Journalism of Deference* (Berkeley: Univ. of California Press, 1987), 52.

119. Bill, *The Eagle and the Lion*, 91–92.

120. "Ex-*Times* Reporter Accused of Role in '53 Coup in Iran," *New York Times*, Sept. 26, 1980, A11.

121. Dorman and Farhang, *US Press and Iran*, 53; Gasiorowski, "1953 Coup d'État against Mosaddeq," 251.

122. Quoted in James Risen, "CIA Tried, with Little Success, to Use US Press in Coup," *New York Times*, Apr. 16, 2000, A14.

123. See Katouzian, *Musaddiq*, 185–88.

124. Fakhreddin Azimi, "The Overthrow of the Government of Mosaddeq Reconsidered," *Iranian Studies* 45, no. 5 (2012): 694.

125. A. Milani, *The Shah*, 174.

126. De Bellaigue, *Patriot of Persia*, 186–87.

127. Ibid., 187.

128. Ahmad Razavi, quoted in ibid., 209.

129. Nosratollah Amini, "Where Have All the Good Men Gone?" *Guardian*, May 24, 2007, at http://www.guardian.co.uk/commentisfree/2007/may/24/where haveallthegoodmengo.

130. Foreign Office, quoted in Ali Rahnema, "Overthrowing Mosaddeq in Iran: 28 Mordad/19 Aug. 1953," *Iranian Studies* 45, no. 5 (2012): 661.

131. NRM General Committee to Selden Chapin, letter, 1955 (no specific date given), William O. Douglas Papers, Box 640, LoC.

132. Quoted in Elm, *Oil, Power, and Principle*, 336.

133. Quoted in Bill, *The Eagle and the Lion*, 94.

134. Quoted in Edgar Snow, *The Other Side of the River: Red China Today* (New York: Random House, 1962).

135. For more on the Tudeh turning away from Mossadegh, see Bayandor, *Iran and the CIA*; Ali Mirfetros, *Doktor Mohammad Mossadegh: Asib shenasi yek shekast* (Dr. Mohammad Mossadegh: Pathology of a Failure) (Los Angeles: Ketab, 2008); and Jalal Matini, *Nigahi beh Karnamah-i siyasi-i Doktor Moham-mad Mossadegh* (A Glance at the Political Career of Dr. Mohammad Mossadegh) (Los Angeles: Ketab, 2005).

136. CIA, *The Battle for Iran*, report, 62, approved for public release Feb. 26, 2014, at https://archive.org/details/CIA-Battle-For-Iran.

137. According to research by Ebrahim Mohseni of the University of Maryland, 85 percent of Iranians say it is very important for Iran to have a civilian nuclear program (cited in Geneviève Abdo, "Abdo: Iranians Support Their Nuclear Program," *Newsday*, Oct. 26, 2012, at http://www.newsday.com/opinion/oped /abdo-iranians-support-their-nuclear-program-1.4156752).

5. US Policy after Mossadegh, 1954–1960

1. Memorandum of Discussion at the 160th NSC Meeting, Aug. 27, 1953, DDE Papers as President, 1953–61, Ann Whitman File, NSC Series, Box 4, DDEL.

2. US Embassy to State Department, dispatch, Mar. 10, 1954, 788.00/3-1054, Interagency Security Committee Staff Papers, Operations Coordinating Board (OCB) Central File Series, OCB 091, DDEL.

3. US Ambassador to Secretary of State, memo, Sept. 16, 1953, 611.88/9-1653, Box 2853, NARA. See also US Embassy to State Department, dispatch, Feb. 8, 1954, Interagency Security Committee Staff Papers, OCB Central File Series, Box 42, DDEL.

4. "Progress Report on NSC 5402," Sept. 28, 1954, WHO, NSC Staff Papers, 1948–61, OCB Central File Series, Box 42, DDEL.

5. Katouzian, *Musaddiq*, 208.

6. Mahmud Farjami, "Political Satire as an Index of Press Freedom: A Review of Political Satire in the Iranian Press during the 2000s," *Iranian Studies* 47, no. 2, (2014): 217. For more on the history of the Iranian press during the early Pahlavi period, see Mohammad Sadr Hashemi, *Tarikh-e jarayed va majallat-e Iran* (The History of the Press and Magazines in Iran) (Esfahan, Iran: Kamal, 1949), 143–47.

7. Azimi, *Quest for Democracy in Iran*, 158; Gasiorowski, *US Foreign Policy and the Shah*, 86.

8. H. E. Chehabi, *Iranian Politics and Religious Modernism: The Liberation Movement of Iran under the Shah and Khomeini* (Ithaca, NY: Cornell Univ. Press, 1990), 134.

9. Abrahamian, *Iran between Two Revolutions*, 419.

10. Ibid., 451.

11. Bill, *The Eagle and the Lion*, 100.

12. Abbas William Samii, "The Role of SAVAK in the 1978–1979 Iranian Revolution," PhD diss., Univ. of Cambridge, 1994.

13. Ibid., 65.

14. Azimi, *Quest for Democracy*, 339.

15. The shah's determination to maintain the alliance with the more accommodating Islamic clerics was best illustrated after Queen Soroya was pictured in a bathing suit while on a trip to the United States in 1955. To quell their displeasure with the photo, the shah struck a deal to permit attacks on the rival religious sect, Baha'ism. When mobs converged on the National Baha'i Center in Tehran, the shah's forces looked up but took no action as hundreds were either killed or forced to recant their religion. For more on this incident, see A. Milani, *The Shah*, 199; Bill, *The Eagle and the Lion*, 101–2; Iran Human Rights Documentation Center, *A Faith Denied: The Persecution of the Baha'is of Iran* (New Haven, CT: Iran Human Rights Documentation Center, 2011), at http://www.iranhrdc.org/english /publications/reports/3149-a-faith-denied-the-persecution-of-the-baha-is-of-iran .html?p=1.

16. A. Milani, *The Shah*, 202.

17. Gasiorowski, *US Foreign Policy and the Shah*, 86.

18. Ibid., 91.

19. Abrahamian, *Iran between Two Revolutions*, 451–52.

20. Gasiorowski, *US Foreign Policy and the Shah*, 91 n. 13.

21. Secretary of State to US Embassy, telegram, Dec. 13, 1954, in *FRUS, 1952–1954*, 10:1073.

22. "Progress Report on NSC 5402," Oct. 13, 1954, Freedom of Information Act Electronic Reading Room, at http://www.foia.cia.gov/sites/default/files /document_conversions/5829/CIA-RDP80R01731R003000020001-0.pdf.

23. Ibid.

24. Abrahamian, *Iran between Two Revolutions*, 420.

25. "Progress Report on NSC 5504," May 18, 1955, WHO, NSC Staff Papers, 1948–61, OCB Central File Series, Box 43, DDEL.

26. Memorandum of Discussion at the 162nd NSC Meeting, Sept. 17, 1953, DDE Papers as President, 1953–61, Ann Whitman File, NSC Series, Box 4, DDEL.

27. Loy Henderson to State Department, telegram, Sept. 18, 1953, in *FRUS, 1952–1954*, vol. 10: 799.

28. Leonard Ware to Iran Working Group, OCB, Feb. 15, 1954, WHO, NSC Staff Papers, 1948–61, OCB Central File Series, Box 41, DDEL.

29. Rubin, *Paved with Good Intentions*, 94.

30. Bill, *The Eagle and the Lion*, 109.

31. Quoted in ibid., 109.

32. Ibid., 106.

33. Anthony Sampson, *The Seven Sisters: The Great Oil Companies and the World They Shaped* (New York: Viking Press, 1975), 135.

34. Bill, *The Eagle and the Lion*, 112; Rubin, *Paved with Good Intentions*, 94–95.

35. John Jernegan to Secretary of State, memo, Jan. 11, 1955, in *FRUS, 1955–1957*, vol. 12: *Near East, Iran, Iraq* (Washington, DC: US Government Printing Office, 1991), 684.

36. Raymond Hare, quoted in William J. Burns, *Economic Aid and American Policy toward Egypt, 1955–1981* (Albany: State Univ. of New York Press, 1985), 11.

37. Roby C. Barrett, *The Greater Middle East and the Cold War: US Foreign Policy under Eisenhower and Kennedy* (New York: Palgrave Macmillan, 2007), 15.

38. McGlinchey, *US Arms Policies towards the Shah's Iran*, 10.

39. Joint Chiefs of Staff Joint Intelligence Committee Memorandum for the Joint Strategic Plans Committee and the Joint Logistic Plans Committee, Apr. 13, 1955, in *The United States and Iran: A Documentary History*, ed. Yonah Alexander and Allan S. Nanes (Frederick, MD: Aletheia Books, 1980), 273–74; Bill, *The Eagle and the Lion*, 117.

40. US Embassy to State Department, telegram, Sept. 27, 1956, 688.00/9-2756, Box 2707, DDEL.

41. Quoted in Harry N. Howard, "Regional Pacts and the Eisenhower Doctrine," *Annals of the American Academy of Political and Social Science* 401 (1972): 87. For more on the Baghdad Pact and Eisenhower's policy regarding the wider Middle East, see Salim Yaqub, *Containing Arab Nationalism: The Eisenhower Doctrine and the Middle East* (Chapel Hill: Univ. of North Carolina Press, 2004).

42. Quoted in Bill, *The Eagle and the Lion*, 117.

43. Samii, "The Role of SAVAK," 68.

44. Mark J. Gasiorowski, "Central Intelligence Agency," *Encyclopædia Iranica* 5 (1991): 253–58.

45. Kennett Love, "Tehran Quiet as Voting Ends after Three Days of Disorder," *New York Times*, Mar. 12, 1954, 2; Bill, *The Eagle and the Lion*, 99; Chehabi, *Iranian Politics*, 134–36.

46. Love, "Tehran Quiet," 2.

47. Ibid.; quote also given in Chehabi, *Iranian Politics*, 136.

48. Thomas L. Hughes to Secretary of State, memo, July 31, 1967, quoted in Azimi, *Quest for Democracy*, 160.

49. US Embassy to State Department, telegram, July 3, 1956, quoted in Azimi, *Quest for Democracy*, 161.

50. "Progress Report on NSC 5504," May 18, 1955, WHO, NSC Staff Papers, 1948–61, OCB Central File Series, Box 43, DDEL.

51. Quoted in Azimi, *Quest for Democracy*, 160.

52. Ibid.; Secretary of State to US Embassy, telegram, May 29, 1954, in *FRUS, 1952–1954*, 10:1017.

53. Princess Soraya Esfandiary Bakhtiary, *Palace of Solitude*, trans. Hubert Gibbs (London: Quartet Books, 1992), quoted in Cooper, *Fall of Heaven*, 81–82.

54. Azimi, *Quest for Democracy*, 160.

55. Quoted in A. Milani, *The Shah*, 201.

56. Ibid.

57. Rubin, *Paved with Good Intentions*, 93.

58. "Progress Report on NSC 5504," May 18, 1955.

59. Ervand Abrahamian, *A History of Modern Iran* (New York: Cambridge Univ. Press, 2008), 128.

60. US Embassy to State Department, dispatch, Mar. 26, 1956, 788.00/4-2156, Box 3809, NARA.

61. Foreign Office, quoted in A. Milani, *The Shah*, 204.

62. "Country Team Analysis of the Internal Security Position in Iran," Apr. 1955, in *FRUS, 1955–1957*, 12:735–36.

63. "Progress Report on NSC 5504," July 6, 1955, WHO, NSC Staff Papers, 1948–61, OCB Central File Series, Box 43, DDEL; Rowland Hughes to the President, memo, Feb. 9, 1956, WHO, Office of the Special Assistant for National Security Affairs Records, NSC Series, Policy Papers Subseries, Box 14, DDEL.

64. See NSC 5703, Jan. 28, 1957, WHO, Office of the Special Assistant for National Security Affairs, NSC Series, Policy Papers Subseries, Box 20, DDEL.

65. Sam Pope Brewer, "Iran Is Reported Subversion-Free," *New York Times*, Dec. 2, 1956, 31.

66. Discussion at the 237th NSC Meeting, Feb. 17, 1955, memo, in *FRUS, 1955–1957*, vol. 6: *American Republics: Multilateral, Mexico, Caribbean* (Washington, DC: US Government Printing Office, 1987), 2.

67. "Report of the Interdepartmental Committee on Certain US Aid Programs," July 3, 1956, in *FRUS, 1955–1957*, 12:832.

68. Foreign Office, "Iran Annual Review, 1956," quoted in A. Milani, *The Shah*, 202.

69. "OCB Working Group Report on Current Political Conditions in Iran," Aug. 22, 1956, WHO, NSC Staff Papers, 1948–61, OCB Central File Series, Box 44, DDEL.

70. A. Milani, *The Shah*, 205.

71. US Embassy to State Department, dispatch, Mar. 26, 1956, 788.00/4-2156, Box 3809, NARA.

72. US Embassy to State Department, June 20, 1956, WHO, NSC Staff Papers, 1948–61, OCB Central Files Series, Box 44, DDEL.

73. "OCB Working Group Report on Current Political Conditions in Iran," Aug. 22, 1956.

74. Eric J. Hooglund, *Land and Revolution in Iran, 1960–1980* (Austin: Univ. of Texas Press, 1982), 45.

75. Paul Maris, quoted in Afsaneh Najmabadi, *Land Reform and Social Change in Iran* (Salt Lake City: Univ. of Utah Press, 1987), 68.

76. "Progress Report on NSC 5504," July 12, 1956, WHO, NSC Staff Papers, 1948–61, OCB Central File Series, Box 44, DDEL.

77. See Mark J. Gasiorowski, "The Qarani Affair and Iranian Politics," *International Journal of Middle East Studies* 25, no. 4 (1993): 628.

78. Sam Pope Brewer, "Unrest Is Viewed as Threat in Iran," *New York Times*, Jan. 2, 1958, and "Iran Arrests Reported," *New York Times*, Feb. 25, 1958.

79. Gasiorowski, "Qarani Affair," 628.

80. Quoted in US Embassy to State Department, dispatch, Apr. 27, 1957, 788.00/4-2757, Box 3881, NARA.

81. Ibid.

82. US Embassy to State Department, dispatch, Apr. 27, 1957.

83. US Embassy to State Department, dispatch, June 5, 1957, 788.00/6-557, Box 3881, NARA.

84. John W. Bowling, First Secretary of the Embassy, to State Department, dispatch, Aug. 29, 1957, 788.00/8-2957, Box 3881, NARA.

85. US Embassy to State Department, dispatch, Sept. 3, 1957, 788.00/9-337, Box 3881, NARA.

86. Gasiorowski "Qarani Affair," 628, citing an interview with Kazem Jafrudi, one of the deputies recruited by the shah to go undercover in the Freedom Society.

87. See Memo of Conversation between William O. Douglas, Mohammad Hosein Qashqai, and John Bowling, Feb. 8, 1955, 788.00/2-855, RG 59, Central Decimal File, Box 3808, NARA.

88. See Memo of Conversation between John D. Jernegan and Rahim Atai, May 4, 1957, Box 3810, NARA.

89. Memo for the Record, Feb. 6, 1958, in *FRUS, 1958–1960*, vol. 12: *Near East Region, Iraq, Iran, Arabian Peninsula* (Washington, DC: US Government Printing Office, 1993), 539; Gasiorowski, "Qarani Affair," 625–44.

90. William Rountree to State Department, telegram, Feb. 3, 1958, in *FRUS, 1958–1960*, 12:537.

91. Gasiorowski, "Qarani Affair," 634.

92. Ibid., 632.

93. US Ambassador to State Department, telegram, Feb. 27, 1958, in *FRUS, 1958–1960*, 12:541.

94. State Department to US Embassy, Feb. 28, 1958, telegram, in *FRUS, 1958–1960*, 12:541.

95. Gasiorowski "Qarani Affair," 625.

96. "Supplementary Courses of Action for the Outline Plan of Operations for Iran," OCB, Aug. 22, 1956, WHO, NSC Staff Papers, 1948–61, OCB Central File Series, Box 44, DDEL.

97. Azimi, *Quest for Democracy*, 250.

98. The Baghdad Pact was quickly renamed the Central Treaty Organization following the Iraq coup.

99. Quoted in Wawro, *Quicksand*, 230.

100. Quoted in ibid.

101. Edward T. Wailes to State Department, Aug. 14, 1958, in *FRUS, 1958–1960*, 12:583–84.

102. For the quote from King Farouk of Egypt, see Susan Ratcliffe, *Concise Oxford Dictionary of Quotations* (New York: Oxford Univ. Press, 2011), 144.

103. Allen Dulles, 376th NSC Meeting, Aug. 15, 1958, editorial note, in *FRUS, 1958–1960*, 12:585.

104. Quoted in Elizabeth Kridl Valkenier, *The Soviet Union and the Third World: An Economic Bind* (New York: Praeger, 1983), 4.

105. Quoted in ibid., 13.

106. Smith, *America's Mission*, 198.

107. Rountree to Secretary of State, memo, Sept. 9, 1958, in *FRUS, 1958–1960*, 12:589; Discussion from the 379th NSC Meeting, Sept. 18, 1958, memo, DDE Papers as President, 1953–61, Ann Whitman File, NSC Series, Box 10, DDEL; State Department to Gordon Gray, memo, Sept. 5, 1958, 788.00/8-2958, Box 3881, NARA.

108. Allen Dulles, Discussion at the 376th NSC Meeting, Aug. 15, 1958, in *FRUS, 1958–1960*, 12:585.

109. Karl G. Herr Jr., Special Assistant to the President, memo, Oct. 13, 1958, in *FRUS, 1958–1960*, 12:596.

110. "Operations Coordinating Board Report," NSC 5703/1, Oct. 8, 1958, WHO, Office of the Special Assistant for National Security Affairs Records, 1952–61, NSC Policy Papers, Subseries Box 20, DDEL.

111. Ibid.

112. "National Security Council Report," NSC 5821/1, Nov. 15, 1958, WHO, NSC Staff Papers, 1948–61, Disaster File, Box 66, DDEL.

113. Ibid.

114. Briefing Note for NSC, Nov. 13, 1958, WHO, NSC Staff Papers, 1948–61, Special Staff File, Box 4, DDEL.

115. Memorandum of Discussion of the 186th NSC Meeting, Nov. 13, 1958, DDE Papers as President, 1953–61, Ann Whitman File, NSC Series, Box 10, DDEL.

116. Quoted in Gasiorowski, *US Foreign Policy and the Shah*, 96.

117. Draft Briefing Note for NSC, "US Policy toward Iran," Nov. 12, 1958, WHO, NSC Staff Papers, 1953–61, Special Staff File, Box 4, NARA.

118. John Foster Dulles to US Ambassador, telegram, Sept. 12, 1958, 788.00/9-858, Box 3881, NARA.

119. Quoted in A. Milani, *The Shah*, 238.

120. Board of National Estimates to the Director of the CIA, memo, Nov. 10, 1958, in *FRUS, 1958–1960*, 12:598–99. This order was most likely meant figuratively rather than literally.

121. A. Milani, *The Shah*, 238.

122. Secretary of State to US Embassy, telegram, Jan. 16, 1959, in *FRUS, 1958–1960*, 12:document 260, at https://history.state.gov/historicaldocuments/frus1958-60v12/d260 (document numbers instead of page numbers given for volumes of *FRUS* located online).

123. Quoted in Roham Alvandi, "Flirting with Neutrality: The Shah, Khrushchev, and the Failed 1959 Soviet–Iranian Negotiations," *Iranian Studies* 47, no. 3 (2014): 429.

124. US Consulate, Esfahan, to State Department, dispatch, Apr. 23, 1959, 788.00/4-2359, Box 3812, NARA.

125. A. Milani, *The Shah*, 238.

126. Hooglund, *Land and Revolution in Iran*, 46.

127. Sir Roger Stevens, quoted in Fakhreddin Azimi, "On Shaky Ground: Concerning the Absence or Weakness of Political Parties in Iran," *Iranian Studies* 30, nos. 1–2 (1997): 65.

128. Secretary of State to US Embassy, telegram, Jan. 16, 1959, in *FRUS, 1958–1960*, 12:document 260. John Foster Dulles's view of the shah was also held by George Allen, ambassador to Iran from 1946 to 1948 and director of the US Information Agency starting in 1959. At an NSC meeting, he stated that the shah "was the best blackmailer he knew of" (in *FRUS, 1958–1960*, 12:document 261, editorial note, at https://history.state.gov/historicaldocuments/frus1958-60v12/d261).

129. Memo of Conversation between the President and Secretary of State, Jan. 30, 1959, John Foster Dulles Papers, Telephone Call Series, Box 9, DDEL.

130. Quoted in Steven R. Ward, *Immortal: A Military History of Iran and Its Armed Forces* (Washington, DC: Georgetown Univ. Press, 2009), 192.

131. "Iran 'Two Faced'—Reds," *Montreal Gazette*, Feb. 13, 1959, 1.

132. For details of the Soviets' propaganda campaign, see Alvandi, "Flirting with Neutrality," 435–37.

133. Quoted in ibid., 437.

134. Quoted in ibid., 435.

135. National Intelligence Estimate 34-59, Mar. 3, 1959, in *FRUS, 1958–1960*, 12:document 70, at https://history.state.gov/historicaldocuments/frus1958-60v12/d70.

136. US Ambassador to Secretary of State, telegram, May 5, 1953, 788.00/5-553, Box 4110, NARA.

137. Iraj Amini, *Bar bal-e bohran: Zendegi-ye siyasi-ye Ali Amini* (Flying on the Wings of Crisis: The Political Life of Ali Amini) (Tehran: Nashr-e Mahi, 2009), 101.

138. John Bowling to State Department, dispatch, Feb. 28, 1959, 788.00/2-2859, Box 2859, NARA.

139. US Embassy to State Department, dispatch, July 27, 1959, 788.00/7-2759, Box 3812, NARA.

140. Ibid.

141. Allen Dulles, briefing before the 426th NSC meeting, Mar. 10, 1960, in *FRUS, 1958–1960*, 12:document 287, at https://history.state.gov/historical documents/frus1958-60v12/d287.

142. See Discussion at the 440th NSC Meeting, Apr. 7, 1960, memo, in *FRUS, 1958–1960*, 12:document 288, https://history.state.gov/historicaldocuments/frus 1958-60v12/d288.

143. President Eisenhower before the 426th NSC meeting, Mar. 10, 1960, memo, in *FRUS, 1958–1960*, 12:document 287.

144. Discussion at the 449th NSC Meeting, June 30, 1960, memo, in *FRUS, 1958–1960*, 12:document 291, at https://history.state.gov/historicaldocuments/frus 1958-60v12/d291.

145. Ibid.

146. "National Security Council Report," NSC 6010, July 6, 1960, in *FRUS, 1958–1960*, 12:document 293, at https://history.state.gov/historicaldocuments/frus 1958-60v12/d293.

147. Memorandum of Discussion at the 449th NSC Meeting, June 30, 1960, in *FRUS, 1958–1960*, 12:document 291.

148. Ibid. See also the US Embassy in Iran to State Department, telegram, Aug. 4, 1960, in *FRUS, 1958–1960*, 12:692; Abrahamian, *Iran between Two Revolutions*, 422.

149. Richard P. Hunt, "Iranians Test 2-Party Election," *New York Times*, Aug. 14, 1960, 8.

150. See Andrew F. Westwood, "Elections and Politics in Iran," *Middle East Journal* 15, no. 2 (1961): 154; Richard W. Cottam, *Iran and the United States: A Cold War Case Study* (Pittsburgh: Univ. of Pittsburgh Press, 1988), 123.

151. See Chehabi, *Iranian Politics*, 142.

152. The shah is reported to have told American officials in May 1960 that it was "premature to think in terms of free elections . . . in Iran" (quoted in Azimi, *Quest for Democracy*, 166).

153. Chehabi, *Iranian Politics*, 144.

154. Westwood, "Elections and Politics in Iran," 154.

155. Ibid., 161; Chehabi, *Iranian Politics*, 145.

156. Richard P. Hunt, "Election Frauds Charged in Iran," *New York Times*, Aug. 21, 1960, 20.

157. "Reformer in Shako," *Time*, Sept. 12, 1960, 33.

158. Westwood, "Elections and Politics in Iran," 161–62.

159. Gasiorowski, *US Foreign Policy and the Shah*, 178.

160. National Front, Seventh Annual Conference, "Nashriyeh-e Hezbi," cited in Sepehr Zabih, *The Communist Movement in Iran* (Berkeley: Univ. of California Press, 1966), 221–22.

161. Quoted in "Reformer in Shako," 33.

162. A. Milani, *The Shah*, 246.

163. CIA Position Paper, attached to Sam Belk to McGeorge Bundy, memo, Feb. 24, 1961, National Security Files (NSF), Box 115a, John F. Kennedy Presidential Library (JFKL), Boston; Chehabi, *Iranian Politics*, 148–52.

164. Smith, *America's Mission*, 187.

6. Kennedy's Experiment, 1961–1963

1. Eisenhower was seventy by the time he left the White House. His age record stood until Reagan, who left office when he was almost seventy-eight. On January

20, 2017, Donald J. Trump became the oldest elected president, taking office at the same age as Eisenhower when the latter *left* the White House.

2. See Deborah H. Strober and Gerald S. Strober, *The Kennedy Presidency: An Oral History of the Era* (Washington, DC: Brassey's, 2003).

3. Quoted in Arthur M. Schlesinger Jr., *A Thousand Days: John F. Kennedy in the White House* (Boston: Houghton Mifflin, 2003), 590.

4. Bill, *The Eagle and the Lion*, 131.

5. David Milne, *America's Rasputin: Walt Rostow and the Vietnam War* (New York: Hill and Wang, 2008), 17–30.

6. Quoted in David Wise, "Scholars of the Nuclear Age," in *The Kennedy Circle*, ed. Lester Tanzer (Washington, DC: Luce, 1961), 41.

7. The CIS was formed to assist on Project TROY, an attempt to counter the Soviet's successful jamming of the US propaganda radio station Voice of America (Nick Cullather, "Development Doctrine and Modernization Theory," in *Encyclopedia of American Foreign Policy*, 3 vols., ed. Alexander DeConde, Richard Dean Burns, and Fredrik Logevall [New York: Scribner's, 2002], 1:482).

8. See Walt W. Rostow and Max F. Millikan, *A Proposal: Key to an Effective Foreign Policy* (New York: Harper and Bros., 1957).

9. Ibid., 1.

10. David Ekbladh, *The Great American Mission: Modernization and the Construction of an American World Order* (Princeton, NJ: Princeton Univ. Press, 2010); Smith, *America's Mission*; Nick Cullather, *The Hungry World: America's Cold War Battle against Poverty in Asia* (Cambridge, MA: Harvard Univ. Press, 2010).

11. Howard J. Wiarda, *New Directions in Comparative Politics* (Boulder, CO: Westview Press, 2002), 8.

12. Ibid., 3.

13. Quoted in Nils Gilman, *Mandarins of the Future: Modernization Theory in Cold War America* (Baltimore: Johns Hopkins Univ. Press, 2003), 1.

14. Rostow and Millikan, *A Proposal*, 25.

15. Gilman, *Mandarins of the Future*, 5.

16. Walt W. Rostow, *Eisenhower, Kennedy, and Foreign Aid* (Austin: Univ. of Texas Press, 1985), 136.

17. John F. Kennedy to Eugene Rostow, Oct. 16, 1956, Pre-presidential Papers, Box 550, JFKL.

18. Gilman, *Mandarins of the Future*, 191; Milne, *America's Rasputin*, 66.

19. Rostow and Millikan, *A Proposal*, 56.

20. CIS, "The Objectives of United States Economic Assistance Programs," report prepared for the Special Committee to Study the Foreign Aid Program, US Senate, quoted in Gilman, *Mandarins of the Future*, 193.

21. Rostow and Millikan, *A Proposal*, 63.

22. David Milne has identified these speeches as being "The Choice in Asia—Democratic Development in India," March 25, 1958, and "The Economic Gap," February 19, 1959 (*America's Rasputin*, 264).

23. Milne, *America's Rasputin*, 58. See also Denis Kux, *India and the United States: Estranged Democracies, 1941–1991* (Washington, DC: National Defense Univ. Press, 1992), 148.

24. Rostow and Millikan, *A Proposal*, 1.

25. Ibid., 4.

26. Walt W. Rostow, *The Stages of Economic Growth: A Non-Communist Manifesto* (Cambridge: Cambridge Univ. Press, 1960), 134–42.

27. Walt W. Rostow, *Diffusion of Power: An Essay in Recent History* (New York: Macmillan, 1972), 125; Milne, *America's Rasputin*. Rostow would declare that the title "deputy special assistant for national security affairs" meant he was deputy to the president, not to National Security Adviser McGeorge Bundy (Strober and Strober, *The Kennedy Presidency*, 186).

28. George W. Ball, *The Past Has Another Pattern* (New York: Norton, 1982), 183.

29. Rostow, *Diffusion of Power*, 125.

30. "We stand today on the edge of a New Frontier—the frontier of the 1960's, the frontier of unknown opportunities and perils, the frontier of unfilled hopes and unfilled threats. . . . [This is] not a set of promises. It is a set of challenges. . . . I believe that the times require imagination and courage and perseverance. I'm asking each of you to be pioneers towards that New Frontier" (John F. Kennedy, nomination acceptance address, Democratic National Convention, July 15, 1960, JFKL, at http://www.jfklibrary.org/Historical+Resources/Archives/Reference+Desk /Speeches/JFK/JFK+Pre-Pres/1960/Address+of+Senator+John+F.+Kennedy+Accept ing+the+Democratic+Party+Nomination+for+the+Presidency+of+t.htm).

31. M. B. Schnapper, quoted in H. R. McMaster, *Dereliction of Duty: Lyndon Johnson, Robert McNamara, the Joint Chiefs of Staff, and the Lies That Led to Vietnam* (New York: Harper Collins, 1997), 1.

32. Michael E. Latham, *Modernization as Ideology: American Social Science and "Nation Building" in the Kennedy Era* (Chapel Hill: Univ. of North Carolina Press, 2000), 59.

33. Walt Rostow to JFK, Mar. 2, 1961, President's Office Files, Box 64a, JFKL.

34. John F. Kennedy, "Alliance for Progress Speech, March 13, 1961," in *Let the Word Go Forth: The Speeches, Statements, and Writings of John F. Kennedy 1947 to 1963*, ed. Ted Sorensen (New York: Dell, 1988), 351.

35. Kennedy often invoked the call of Puritan John Winthrop, who while sailing on the ship *Arbella* in 1830 stated that the future Massachusetts Bay colony

would "be as a city upon a hill. The eyes of all people are upon us." Kennedy quoted this passage, for instance, in his speech before the General Court of Massachusetts on January 9, 1961 (in Kennedy, *Let the Word Go Forth*, 56).

36. Lincoln Gordon, "The Alliance at Birth: Hopes and Fears," in *The Alliance for Progress: A Retrospective*, ed. L. Ronald Scheman (New York: Praeger, 1988), 74.

37. Bill, *The Eagle and the Lion*, 131.

38. April Summitt, "For a White Revolution: John F. Kennedy and the Shah of Iran," *Middle East Journal* 58, no. 4 (2004): 567–68.

39. Victor V. Nemchenok, "In Search of Stability amid Chaos: US Policy toward Iran, 1961–1963," *Cold War History* 10, no. 3 (2010): 341–69.

40. David R. Collier, "To Prevent a Revolution: John F. Kennedy and the Promotion of Democracy in Iran," *Diplomacy and Statecraft* 24, no. 3 (2013): 456–75.

41. National Intelligence Estimate, NIE 34-61, Feb. 28, 1961, in *FRUS, 1961–1963*, vol. 17: *Near East* (Washington, DC: US Government Printing Office, 1994), document 16, at https://history.state.gov/historicaldocuments/frus1961-63v17/d16.

42. Assistant Secretary for Near Eastern and South Asian Affairs to the Secretary of State, memo, Feb. 15, 1961, in *FRUS, 1961–1963*, 17:document 11, at https://history.state.gov/historicaldocuments/frus1961-63v17/d11.

43. Mohammad Reza Pahlavi to Kennedy, letter, Jan. 26, 1961, NSF, Box 119, JFKL.

44. Walter Lippmann, "Lippmann Believes Khrushchev Feels Red Triumph Is Inevitable," *Washington Post*, Apr. 18, 1961.

45. Robert Komer to McGeorge Bundy, Mar. 26, 1962, NSF, Box 116, JFKL.

46. Quoted in William Taubman, *Khrushchev: The Man and His Era* (New York: Norton, 2003), 468.

47. Quoted in Schlesinger, *A Thousand Days*, 303.

48. Robert S. McNamara, *In Retrospect: The Tragedy and Lessons of Vietnam* (New York: Vintage Books, 1995), 30; Milne, *America's Rasputin*, 75.

49. Milne, *America's Rasputin*, 81.

50. See Stephen G. Rabe, *John F. Kennedy: World Leader* (Washington, DC: Potomac Books, 2010), 153.

51. See, for example, Philip A. Goduti, *Kennedy's Kitchen Cabinet and the Pursuit of Peace: The Shaping of American Foreign Policy, 1961–1963* (Jefferson, NC: McFarland, 2009), and Rabe, *John F. Kennedy*.

52. Richard M. Bissell Jr., "Position Paper on Iran," attached to Sam Belk to Bundy, memo, Feb. 24, 1961, NSF, Box 115a, JFKL.

53. Kenneth R. Hansen, "Some Notes on the Situation in Iran," Mar. 20, 1961, report attached to "JB" to Bundy, memo, Apr. 1, 1961, NSF, Box 115a, JFKL.

54. Harold Saunders, recorded interviews by William Burr, Feb. 12, 27, Apr. 8, May 1, 1987, Oral History of Iran Collection, Foundation of Iranian Studies, Bethesda, MD, at http://fis-iran.org/en/content/saunders-harold.

55. James F. Goode, "Reforming Iran during the Kennedy Years," *Diplomatic History* 15, no. 1 (2007): 17.

56. John W. Bowling, "The Current Political Situation in Iran," report attached to George A. Morgan to Bundy, memo, Mar. 27, 1961, NSF, Box 115, JFKL.

57. "The Reminiscences of Dean Rusk," interview by William Burr, May 23, 1986, Oral History of Iran Collection, Foundation of Iranian Studies, at http://www.fis-iran.org/en/oralhistory/Rusk-Dean.

58. W. Rostow to Theodore Sorensen, Mar. 16, 1961, NSF, Box 324, JFKL.

59. Ansari, *Modern Iran since 1921*, 152.

60. Memo of Conversation between General Timur Bakhtiar and Dean Rusk, Feb. 21, 1961, in *FRUS, 1961–1963*, 17:document 14, at https://history.state.gov/historicaldocuments/frus1961-63v17/d14.

61. See W. Rostow to George McGhee, memo, Mar. 28, 1961, and Notes on Discussion of Iran between Professor T. Cuyler Young and Messrs. Rostow and Johnson, Apr. 3, 1961, NSF, Box 115a, JFKL.

62. Bill, *The Eagle and the Lion*, 142; Richard W. Cottam, *Nationalism in Iran* (Pittsburgh: Univ. of Pittsburgh Press, 1964), 302; Goode, "Reforming Iran," 19; Summitt, "For a White Revolution," 565; Nemchenok, "In Search of Stability," 350; Michael E. Latham, *The Right Kind of Revolution: Modernization, Development, and US Foreign Policy from the Cold War to the Present* (Ithaca, NY: Cornell Univ. Press, 2011), 147.

63. Summitt, "For a White Revolution," 565; Offiler, *US Foreign Policy and the Modernization of Iran*, 37.

64. A. Milani, *The Shah*, 251. Milani goes on to explain that Sharif-Emami himself claimed that a large amount of money was suddenly deposited in a bank account set aside to support the strikers and that a "foreign officer" was seen riding a motorcycle and dictating the demonstrators' actions and movements. This claim is most likely untrue because opposition to the shah was both real and widespread, but it hints at the belief inherent within the royal court.

65. See Gasiorowski, "Qarani Affair."

66. Constantine P. Danopoulos and Cynthia Ann Watson, *The Political Role of the Military: An International Handbook* (Westport, CT: Greenwood Press, 1996), 215.

67. For more on the shah's fear of external rather than internal threats, see Dr. Khodad Farmanfarmaian, recorded interview by Habib Ladjevardi, Nov. 10, 1982, Iranian Oral History Project, Harvard Univ., at http://www.fas.harvard.edu/~iohp/farmanfarmaian.html.

68. See "Operations Coordinating Board Report," NSC 5703/1, Oct. 8, 1958, WHO, Office of the Special Assistant for National Security Affairs Records, 1952–61, NSC Policy Papers, Subseries Box 20, DDEL. See also Habib Ladjevardi, *Khaterat-e Ali Amini: Nukhust vazir-e Iran, 1340–1341* (Memoirs of Ali Amini: Prime Minister of Iran, 1961–1962) (Cambridge, MA: Iranian Oral History Project, Harvard Univ., 1995), 161.

69. Westwood, "Elections and Politics in Iran," 161.

70. Amini, *Bar bal-e bohran*, 149; A. Milani, *Eminent Persians*, 4–65.

71. US Embassy to Secretary of State, telegram, May 6, 1961, Central Files, 788.13/5-661, RG 59, NARA.

72. Amini, *Bar bal-e bohran*, 260.

73. William G. Miller, recorded interview by Shahla Haeri, Mar. 7–25, 1985, Iranian Oral History Project, Harvard Univ., at http://www.fas.harvard.edu/~iohp /miller.html. See also Abrahamian, *Iran between Two Revolutions*, 423; Pollack, *Persian Puzzle*, 82; Amin Saikal, *The Rise and Fall of the Shah* (Princeton, NJ: Princeton Univ. Press, 1980), 76; Abbas Amirie and Hamilton A. Twitchell, *Iran in the 1980s* (Tehran: Institute for International Political and Economic Studies, 1978), 382.

74. "The Reminiscences of Colonel Gratian Yatsevitch," interviews by William Burr, Nov. 5, 1988, and Jan. 12, 1989, Oral History of Iran Collection, Foundation of Iranian Studies, at http://fis-iran.org/en/content/yatsevitch-colonel-gratian; Amini, *Bar bal-e bohran*, 283; Hooglund, *Land and Revolution in Iran*, 47–48.

75. Amini, *Bar bal-e bohran*, 101, 317.

76. Mohammad Reza Pahlavi, *Answer to History* (New York: Stein and Day, 1980), 22–23. The shah goes on to describe one peculiar form of pressure came from First Lady Jacqueline Kennedy, who "spoke of Amini's wonderfully flashing eyes and how much she hoped I would name him Prime Minister" (*Answer to History*, 146; see also "Back of the Boom in Iran: The Shah's Own Story," *US World & News Report*, Jan. 27, 1969, 49). In his diaries, Asadollah Alam also mentions the shah's belief that Amini was imposed on him by the Americans (Azimi, *Quest for Democracy*, 167; Stuart Rockwell, Deputy Chief of Mission in Iran, 1960–65, recorded interview by Habib Ladjevardi, May 20, 1987, Iranian Oral History Project, Harvard Univ., at http://www.fas.harvard.edu/~iohp/rockwell.html).

77. Quoted in Saikal, *Rise and Fall of the Shah*, 76.

78. Record of Action No. 2427—Taken at the 484th NSC Meeting, May 19, 1961, in *FRUS, 1961–1963*, 17:document 51, at https://history.state.gov/historical documents/frus1961-63v17/d51.

79. "A Review of Problems in Iran and Recommendations for the National Security Council: A Report of the Task Force on Iran," May 15, 1961, NSF, Box 115a, JFKL.

80. Record of Action No. 2427—Taken at the 484th NSC Meeting, May 19, 1961.

81. "A Review of Problems in Iran and Recommendations for the National Security Council."

82. McGeorge Bundy, "Preliminary Comments on Iran Task Force Report," May 15, 1961, NSF, Box 115a, JFKL.

83. "A Review of Problems in Iran and Recommendations for the National Security Council."

84. "Follow-up Measures to Support the Amini Regime—Task Force on Iran," Aug. 11, 1961, NSF, Box 116, JFKL.

85. "A Report on the Task Force on Iran," Oct. 9, 1961, NSF, Box 426, JFKL. See also Komer to JFK, memo, May 18, 1961, NSF, Box 115a, JFKL.

86. US Embassy to Secretary of State, memo, June 15, 1961, NSF, Box 115a, JFKL.

87. W. Rostow to McGhee, memo, Mar. 28, 1961, and Notes on Discussion of Iran between Professor T. Cuyler Young and Messrs. Rostow and Johnson, Apr. 3, 1961.

88. See Abrahamian, *Iran between Two Revolutions*, 423; Mohsen M. Milani, *The Making of Iran's Islamic Revolution: From Monarchy to Islamic Republic* (Boulder, CO: Westview Press, 1988), 44–45; Keddie, *Modern Iran*, 142.

89. Rockwell interview, May 20, 1987, Iranian Oral History Project.

90. "Time, Gentlemen, Please," *Time*, June 9, 1961, 25; "Iran's Shrewd Premier," *New York Times*, May 30, 1962, 2.

91. "Time, Gentlemen, Please," 25.

92. "Reform with Tears," *Time*, June 16, 1961, 25; "Caviar Fraud Alleged," *New York Times*, June 4, 1961, 21.

93. "Iranian Says He Cut Corruption by 60%," *New York Times*, May 6, 1962, 32.

94. Desmond Harney, recorded interview by Habib Ladjevardi, Oct. 15, 1985, tape 1, Iranian Oral History Project, Harvard Univ., at http://ted.lib.harvard.edu/ted/deliver/~iohp/Harney,+Desmond.01.

95. "Last Call in Iran," *New York Times*, June 2, 1961, 30.

96. "Diffident Dr. Amini," *Economist*, July 14, 1962, 49; "Shah Orders Amini to Press Reform," *New York Times*, Nov. 15, 1961, 4.

97. Bill, *The Eagle and the Lion*, 143.

98. "Premier Reaffirms Iran's Ties to West," *New York Times*, June 8, 1961, 6.

99. "Persia at the Edge," *Economist*, May 20, 1961, 50.

100. Rostow, *Stages of Economic Growth*, 22.

101. Cullather, *Hungry World*, 4.

102. Quoted in ibid., 161.

103. L. D. Battle to Bundy, memo, Aug. 11, 1961, NSF, Box 116, JFKL.

104. Victor V. Nemchenok, "That so Fair a Thing Should Be so Frail: The Ford Foundation and the Failure of Rural Development in Iran, 1953–1964," *Middle East Journal* 63, no. 2 (2009): 263.

105. See William Gaud, recorded interview by Joseph E. O'Connor, Feb. 21, 1966, John F. Kennedy Oral History Collection, JFKL. Curiously, in her thorough examination of land reform in Iran, Afsaneh Najmabadi uses this interview with William Gaud, the assistant administrator of USAID for the Near East and South Asia, to prove that the United States had little say in Amini's program of land reform. The confusion lies in Gaud's expression that the shah's land-reform program came "all of a sudden, more or less out of the blue as far as we were concerned." Najmabadi reads this statement as referring to the land-reform legislation of Amini's government in January 1962 (*Land Reform and Social Change in Iran*, 78). In actuality, Gaud explicitly stated that he was referring to the shah's White Revolution, announced a year later.

106. "Time, Gentlemen, Please," 25.

107. Quoted in ibid.

108. Quoted in "Iran Gets Action in Land Reform," *New York Times*, July 29, 1961, 13.

109. Gholam Hossein Kazemian, quoted in Najmabadi, *Land Reform and Social Change in Iran*, 80; George B. Baldwin, *Planning and Development in Iran* (Baltimore: Johns Hopkins Univ. Press, 1967), 93.

110. "Sec. Freeman in Iran," *Boston Globe*, Oct. 13, 1961, 11; "Freeman Visits Iran," *Washington Post*, Oct. 13, 1961, B5.

111. Komer to JFK, memo, Aug. 4, 1961, NSF, Box 116, JFKL; "Embassy Concerns on NEA Study of Possible US Actions re: The Long Term Political Situation in Iran," Aug. 27, 1961, NSF, Box 116, JFKL; US Embassy to Rusk, air gram, Oct. 18, 1961, NSF, Box 116, JFKL.

112. "A Review of Problems in Iran and Recommendations for the National Security Council."

113. "Status of Specific Recommendation as Approved by the President—the Situation in Iran, for Meeting of the Iran Task Force," Aug. 2, 1961, NSF, Box 426, JFKL; Robert Komer, "Our Policy in Iran," Oct. 20, 1962, NSF, Box 119, JFKL.

114. Quoted in "Iran Gets Action in Land Reform," 13.

115. Bissell, "Position Paper on Iran."

116. "Gift for Dr. Amini," *Economist*, Dec. 2, 1961, 57. For more on "basic democracy," see K. B. Sayeed, "Pakistan's Basic Democracy," *Middle East Journal* 15, no. 3 (1961): 249–63.

117. Bissell, "Position Paper on Iran"; Nemchenok, "In Search of Stability," 350–51, 360.

118. "Task Force Report—Iran," Oct. 9, 1961, NSF, Box 426, JFKL.

119. US Embassy to Rusk, telegram, Oct. 19, 1961, NSF, Box 116, JFKL; Rusk to US Ambassador, telegram, Oct. 31, 1961, NSF, Box 116, JFKL; US Ambassador to Rusk, memo, Nov. 6, 1961, NSF, Box 116, JFKL.

120. Battle to Bundy, memo, "Report by Chairman, Iran Task Force," Jan. 18, 1962, NSF, Box 116, JFKL.

121. "Status Report—the Situation in Iran: For Meeting of the Iran Task Force of August, 2, 1961," n.d., in *FRUS 1961–1963*, 17:document 90, at https://history.state.gov/historicaldocuments/frus1961-63v17/d90.

122. Bill, *The Eagle and the Lion*, 109.

123. Amini, *Bar Bal-e Bohran*, 401.

124. Chehabi, *Iranian Politics*, 164.

125. Komer to JFK, memo, Aug. 4, 1961.

126. Battle to Bundy, "Report by Chairman, Iran Task Force."

127. Komer to Carl Kaysen, memo, Jan. 19, 1962, NSF, Box 116, JFKL.

128. "6,000 Students Stone Police, 180 Injured in Iran," *Boston Globe*, Jan. 22, 1962, 6; "6,000 Students Riot on Land Reform,' *Los Angeles Times*, Jan. 22, 1962, 2.

129. "Report from Iran," Jan. 21, 1962, NSF, Box 116, JFKL; Ansari, *Modern Iran since 1921*, 157.

130. Ansari, *Modern Iran since 1921*, 157.

131. Battle to Bundy, "Report by Chairman, Iran Task Force."

132. Komer to Kaysen, memo, Jan. 19, 1962; Komer to JFK, memo, Oct. 3, 1961, NSF, Box 426, JFKL; Harold H. Saunders to W. Rostow (quoting Young), Nov. 24, 1961, NSF, Box 116, JFKL.

133. By 1971, only 3,967 whole villages had been divided under the provisions of the land-reform act (Najmabadi, *Land Reform and Social Change in Iran*, 94).

134. "Diffident Dr. Amini," 49.

135. See Jeffrey F. Taffet, *Foreign Aid as Foreign Policy: The Alliance for Progress in Latin America* (New York: Routledge, 2007), 45–48; Rabe, *John F. Kennedy*, 82–97; Jerome I. Levinson and Juan de Onis, *The Alliance That Lost Its Way: A Critical Report on the Alliance for Progress* (Chicago: Quadrangle Books, 1970).

136. Robert B. Rakove, *Kennedy, Johnson, and the Nonaligned World* (Cambridge: Cambridge Univ. Press, 2013).

137. Quoted in Townsend Hoopes, *The Limits of Intervention: An Inside Account of How the Johnson Policy of Escalation in Vietnam Was Reversed* (New York: McKay, 1969), 21.

138. Quoted in Strober and Strober, *Kennedy Presidency*, 187.

139. Milne, *America's Rasputin*, 9–10.

140. Goode, "Reforming Iran," 21; Strober and Strober, *Kennedy Presidency*, 185.

141. CIA Information Report, May 14, 1962, NSF, Box 116, JFKL; State Department to US Embassy, June 16, 1962, NSF, Box 116, JFKL.

142. Scope Paper for Visit of Shah of Iran, Mar. 27, 1962, NSF, Box 117, JFKL.

143. Memorandum of Conversation, Apr. 13, 1962, NSF, Boxes 116 and 117, JFKL.

144. State Department to US Embassy, memo, June 16, 1962, and State Department to US Embassy, memo, June 20, 1962, NSF, Box 116, JFKL.

145. See Komer to JFK, memo, Aug. 4, 1961; Iran Task Force, "Follow-Up Measures to Support the Amini Regime," Aug. 10, 1961, NSF, Box 116, JFKL; "Iran Aid Planned by US and Bonn," *New York Times*, Aug. 4, 1961, 3; "Dr. Amini's Defeat," *Economist*, July 21, 1962, 20–21.

146. Summitt, "For a White Revolution," 568; Nemchenok, "In Search of Stability," 357.

147. CIA Office of Current Intelligence, Current Intelligence Memorandum, OCI no. 2412/62, July 18, 1962, NSF, Box 116, JFKL; "Worldgram," *US News & World Report*, July 30, 1962, 65–66; "Iran Premier Quits, Holds US to Blame," *Boston Globe*, July 19, 1962, 3. Amini immediately withdrew this statement, possibly to remain in favor with the Americans in the hope of being brought back into government at a later date.

148. Pahlavi, *Answer to History*, 146.

149. US Embassy to Secretary of State, telegram, July 18, 1962, NSF, Box 116, JFKL; David E. Lilienthal, *The Journals of David E. Lilienthal*, vol. 5: *The Harvest Years, 1959–1963*, ed. Helen M. Lilienthal (New York: Harper and Row, 1983), 258–59.

150. CIA to unknown recipient, telegram, July 23, 1962, NSF, Box 116, JFKL.

151. Komer to the President, memo, July 18, 1962, NSF, Box 424, JFKL.

152. Komer to Bundy, memo, July 19, 1962, in *FRUS, 1961–1963*, vol. 18: *Near East, 1962–1963* (Washington, DC: US Government Printing Office, 1995), document 8, at https://history.state.gov/historicaldocuments/frus1961-63v18/d8.

153. Komer, "Our Policy in Iran," Oct. 20, 1962.

154. Ibid.

155. Kenneth Hansen to Komer, memo, Nov. 7, 1962, NSF, Box 424, JFKL.

156. Komer to Bundy, memo, Jan. 15, 1963, NSF, Box 116a, JFKL.

157. William Brubeck to Bundy, memo, Jan. 21, 1963, NSF, Box 116a, JFKL; Komer to Bundy, memo, Jan. 15, 1963.

158. US officials had encouraged the Ford Foundation's efforts to enact land reform in Iran, and its program ran from 1952 to 1964. The Kennedy administration

had also encouraged Amini to continue land reform as a means of moving toward modernization, encouragement that led to rumors inside Iran that development theorists in the US government had imposed the land-reform movement on the shah. See Nemchenok, "That so Fair a Thing Should Be so Frail"; Ansari, *Modern Iran since 1921*, 156; Ali M. Ansari, "The Myth of the White Revolution: Mohammad Reza Shah, 'Modernization,' and the Consolidation of Power," *Middle Eastern Studies* 37, no. 3 (2001): 1–24.

159. Cottam, *Nationalism in Iran*, 307; Azimi, *Quest for Democracy*, 309–10.

160. "Iran Peasants Riot, Beat Election Foes," *Los Angeles Times*, Jan. 25, 1963, 11.

161. CIA to unknown recipient, telegram, Jan. 23, 1963, NSF, Box 116a, JFKL.

162. Roger Hilsman, Bureau of Intelligence and Research, to Secretary of State, memo, Feb. 11, 1963, NSF, Box 116a, JFKL; "Legal Revolution," *US News & World Report*, Mar. 25, 1963. Ironically, when Communist and fascist leaders held elections and announced that 99.9 percent of the vote were cast for the ruling party, the shah wrote in response in 1961, "I wonder how many intelligent people are fooled by that sort of thing" (Pahlavi, *Mission for my Country*, 162).

163. Ansari, "Myth of the White Revolution," 19.

164. Quoted in Warren Unna, "Iran's Shah Conducts Own Social Revolution," *Washington Post*, Jan. 16, 1963, A19.

165. Rusk to the President, memo, Apr. 20, 1963, NSF, Box 116a, JFKL.

166. Komer to Bundy, Jan. 29, 1963, NSF, Box 116a, JFKL.

167. Hansen to Komer, May 7, 1953, NSF, Box 340, JFKL.

168. Iran Task Force, "US Strategy for Iran," report, May 21, 1963, NSF, Box 340, JFKL.

169. NSC Standing Committee Action Program, June 28, 1963, NSF, Box 424, JFKL.

170. White House to US Embassy, memo, June 20, 1963, NSF, Box 116a, JFKL; Secretary of State to US Embassy, memo, July 16, 1963, NSF, Box 424, JFKL.

171. Quoted in "Back of the Boom in Iran," *US News & World Report*, Jan. 27, 1963.

172. Goode, "Reforming Iran," 24.

173. Bill, *The Eagle and the Lion*, 150.

174. For estimates of the number of deaths during the protest in June 1963, see, for example, Abrahamian, *Iran between Two Revolutions*, 461; Keddie, *Modern Iran*, 147; Marvin Zonis, *The Political Elite of Iran* (Princeton, NJ: Princeton Univ. Press, 1971), 63; Cottam, *Nationalism in Iran*, 306–9; Ansari, *Modern Iran since 1921*, 160; Cooper, *Fall of Heaven*, 116.

175. US Embassy to Secretary of State, telegram, June 11, 1963, NSF, Box 116a, JFKL; Special National Security Estimate, 34-63, submitted by the CIA, concurred to by the United States Intelligence Board, Apr. 10, 1963, NSF, Box 116a, JFKL.

176. Rusk to the shah, telegram, July 16, 1963, NSF, Box 119, JFKL.

177. Miller interview, Mar. 7–25, 1985, Iranian Oral History Project.

178. US Embassy to Secretary of State, telegram, June 11, 1963, NSF, Box 116a, JFKL.

179. Chehabi, *Iranian Politics*, 179; Goode, "Reforming Iran," 27.

180. Mohammad Reza Pahlavi, speech, July 16, 1963, noted in Katherine Bracken to Komer, July 29, 1963, NSF, Box 424, JFKL.

181. "Iranian Women to Vote on Tuesday," *New York Times*, Sept. 15, 1963, 8.

182. US Embassy to Secretary of State, Sept. 13, 1963, NSF, Box 116a, JFKL.

183. Ibid.

184. Goode, "Reforming Iran," 28.

185. "Victory for the Shah," *New York Times*, Sept. 20, 1963, 31.

186. Chehabi, *Iranian Politics*, 184–85.

187. Cooper, *Fall of Heaven*, 119.

188. Chehabi, *Iranian Politics*, 184.

189. Summitt, "For a White Revolution," 573.

190. Jay Walz, "Shah Says Reform Program Will Bring Democracy to Iran," *New York Times*, Sept. 25, 1963.

191. "The Reminiscences of Dean Rusk," May 23, 1986, Oral History of Iran Collection.

192. JFK to the shah, Jan. 29, 1963, NSF, Box 119, JFKL.

193. John Bowling, quoted in Goode, "Reforming Iran," 24.

194. Komer to Averell Harriman, David Bell, and Carl Kaysen, memo, June 20, 1963, NSF, Box 424, JFKL; Komer to Bundy, memo, Dec. 3, 1963, in *FRUS, 1961–1963*, 18:document 376, at https://history.state.gov/historicaldocuments/frus 1961-63v18/d376.

195. For instance, after pressure from White House officials to put a stop to the shah's sending of repeated requests for military aid, Ambassador Holmes convinced the shah to recall a letter asking for torpedo boats, patrol boats, and a radar station, much to the monarch's chagrin. This reminder caused the shah to enter "one of his dark and brooding moods" and to complain that he could not use his own country's money to buy material he felt necessary (Holmes to Phillips Talbot, memo, Sept. 4, 1963, NSF, Box 424, JFKL).

196. Goode, "Reforming Iran," 28.

197. For instance, accounts of this reform period are absent in Ansari, *Modern Iran since 1921*; Keddie, *Modern Iran*; Gheissari and Nasr, *Democracy in Iran*;

and Abrahamian, *Iran between Two Revolutions*. Similarly, the standard accounts of Kennedy's foreign policy make little to no mention of Iran. See, for instance, Rabe, *John F. Kennedy*; Robert Dallek, *An Unfinished Life: John F. Kennedy, 1917–1963* (Boston: Little, Brown, 2003); Lawrence Freedman, *Kennedy's Wars: Berlin, Cuba, Laos, and Vietnam* (New York: Oxford Univ. Press, 2000); James N. Giglio, *The Presidency of John F. Kennedy* (Lawrence: Univ. Press of Kansas, 1991); and Latham, *Right Kind of Revolution*, 143–53.

198. Offiler, *US Foreign Policy and the Modernization of Iran*, 51. Offiler writes that the Kennedy administration faithfully pursued a policy of massaging the shah's ego, which undermined the administration's ability to influence his actions. Although niceties characterize all diplomatic communication, this does not explain how the United States was able to push the shah to take action he did not wish to take or why he felt so abused by the Kennedy administration during Amini's premiership. Focus on a "massage policy" does not adequately encapsulate the changes in the relationship between Washington and the royal court between 1961 and 1963, differences that can be better explained by looking at the changing levels of leverage.

199. Bill, *The Eagle and the Lion*, 143–47; Goode, "Reforming Iran."

200. Summitt, "For a White Revolution," 568.

201. Nemchenok, "In Search of Stability," 351.

202. See Bill, *The Eagle and the Lion*, 149; Nemchenok, "In Search of Stability," 363; Goode, "Reforming Iran," 28.

203. Hans Morgenthau, "A Political Theory of Foreign Aid," *American Political Science Review* 56, no. 2 (1962): 302; Latham, *Modernization as Ideology*, 101–2.

204. Giglio, *Presidency of John F. Kennedy*, 238.

205. Taffet, *Foreign Aid as Foreign Policy*, 7.

206. Quoted in Summitt, "For a White Revolution," 572.

207. Miller interview, Mar. 7–25, 1985, Iranian Oral History Project.

208. Summitt, "For a White Revolution," 574.

7. Shah's in Charge, 1963–1974

1. Quoted in Azimi, *Quest for Democracy*, 186–87.

2. Mansur Rafizadeh, *Witness: From the Shah to the Secret Arms Deal—An Insider's Account of U.S. Involvement in Iran* (New York: Morrow, 1987), 124.

3. Quoted in Andrew L. Johns, "The Johnson Administration, the Shah of Iran, and the Changing Pattern of US–Iranian Relations, 1965–1967: 'Tired of Being Treated Like a Schoolboy,'" *Journal of Cold War Studies* 9, no. 2 (2007): 69.

4. See Douglas Little, "Nasser Delenda Est: Lyndon Johnson, the Arabs, and the 1967 Six Day War," in *The Foreign Policies of Lyndon Johnson: Beyond*

Vietnam, ed. H. W. Brands (College Station: Texas A&M Univ. Press, 1999), 149; Bill, *The Eagle and the Lion,* 155.

5. For more details on these domestic struggles, see Mary L. Dudziak, *Cold War Civil Rights: Race and the Image of American Democracy* (Princeton, NJ: Princeton Univ. Press, 2000), 203–48.

6. McGlinchey, *US Arms Policies towards the Shah's Iran,* 38.

7. Phillips Talbot, interview by William Burr, Nov. 21, 1985, Oral History of Iran Collection, Foundation of Iranian Studies, Bethesda, MD, at http://fis-iran .org/en/oralhistory/Talbot-Phillips.

8. Bill, *The Eagle and the Lion,* 154.

9. "Memo on the Substance of Discussion at the Department of State–Joint Chiefs of Staff Meeting," Dec. 6, 1963, in *FRUS, 1961–1963,* 18:document 382, at https://history.state.gov/historicaldocuments/frus1961-63v18/d382.

10. Lyndon B. Johnson to the shah, Jan. 2, 1964, in *FRUS, 1964–1968,* vol. 22: *Iran* (Washington, DC: US Government Printing Office, 1999), document 1, at https://history.state.gov/historicaldocuments/frus1964-68v22/d1.

11. Komer's comment is given in *FRUS, 1964–1968,* 22:document 1, n. 2.

12. Quoted in Bill, *The Eagle and the Lion,* 178.

13. Quoted in Douglas Little, *American Orientalism: The United States and the Middle East since 1945* (Chapel Hill: Univ. of North Carolina Press, 2002), 221.

14. For more on Johnson's aid policy and his restriction of the shah's demands, see McGlinchey, *US Arms Policies towards the Shah's Iran,* 38–60.

15. Walt Rostow to Johnson, memo, May 12, 1966, in *FRUS, 1964–1968,* 22:document 136, at https://history.state.gov/historicaldocuments/frus1964-68v22 /d136; Rostow to Johnson, memo, May 21, 1966, in *FRUS, 1964–1968,* 22:document 141, at https://history.state.gov/historicaldocuments/frus1964-68v22/d141; W. Howard Wriggins to Rostow, memo, May 21, 1966, *FRUS 1964–1968,* 22:document 140, at https://history.state.gov/historicaldocuments/frus1964-68v22/d140.

16. Johnson to the shah, letter, Mar. 19, 1964, in *FRUS, 1964–1968,* 22:document 8, at https://history.state.gov/historicaldocuments/frus1964-68v22/d8.

17. Robert Komer to Johnson, memo, Apr. 15, 1965, in *FRUS, 1964–1968,* 22:document 77, at https://history.state.gov/historicaldocuments/frus1964-68v22 /d77; Johns, "The Johnson Administration," 70.

18. McGlinchey, *US Arms Policies towards the Shah's Iran,* 40–41.

19. Richard Pfau, "The Legal Status of American Forces in Iran," *Middle East Journal* 28, no. 2 (1974): 141.

20. Strobe Talbott to Dean Rusk, Action Memorandum, Dec. 19, 1954, in *FRUS, 1964–1968,* 22:118.

21. Martin Herz to Gordon Tiger, memo, Dec. 16, 1964, RG 59, Box 5, NARA.

22. US Department of State, "The Significance of Khomeini's Opposition to the Iranian Government," paper, Jan. 7, 1965, in *FRUS, 1964–1968*, 22:123–24.

23. See Bill, *The Eagle and the Lion*, 178–79.

24. Quoted in Johns, "The Johnson Administration," 72.

25. Quoted in Abbas Milani, *The Persian Sphinx: Amir Abbas Hoveyda and the Riddle of the Iranian Revolution. A Biography* (Washington, DC: Mage, 2000), 168.

26. Rudy Abramson, *Spanning the Century: The Life of W. Averell Harriman, 1891–1986* (New York: Morrow, 1992), 635–36.

27. Bill, *The Eagle and the Lion*, 173.

28. Rostow to Johnson, May 21, 1966, in *FRUS, 1964–1968*, 22:document 141.

29. Alfred Friendly, "Shah Steers an Independent Course," *Washington Post*, July 9, 1966, A11.

30. McGlinchey, *US Arms Policies towards the Shah's Iran*, 45.

31. Quoted in Johns, "The Johnson Administration," 83.

32. Armin H. Meyer to Johnson, May 23, 1966, in *FRUS, 1964–1968*, 22:document 143, attachment, at https://history.state.gov/historicaldocuments/frus 1964-68v22/d143.

33. Quoted in Bill, *The Eagle and the Lion*, 172.

34. Johns, "The Johnson Administration," 85; Ward, *Immortal*, 193.

35. McGlinchey, *US Arms Policies towards the Shah's Iran*, 47.

36. Rostow to Johnson, memo, Aug. 10, 1966, in *FRUS, 1964–1968*, 22:document 170, at https://history.state.gov/historicaldocuments/frus1964-68v22/d170.

37. Bill, *The Eagle and the Lion*, 174–75.

38. Quoted in Johns, "The Johnson Administration," 91.

39. Quoted in ibid., 93–94.

40. Quoted in A. Milani, *Persian Sphinx*, 169.

41. Katouzian, *Musaddiq*, 48.

42. Joseph Mazandi, "Iran's Regime Shuffled; New Premier Is Pro-US," *Washington Post*, Mar. 8, 1964, A15.

43. Jay Walz, "New Premier Gives Iranians Fresh Confidence," *New York Times*, Apr. 7, 1964, 7.

44. Azimi, *Quest for Democracy*, 186.

45. Ibid., 189. A survey conducted among politicians and officials in Iran in 1960 found a correlation between having spent one's early twenties during the Constitutional Revolution and preference for democracy. Those who spent these formative years during Reza Shah's dictatorship held a greater preference for authoritarianism. See G. Hossein Razi, "Democratic–Authoritarian Attitudes

and Social Background in a Non-Western Society," *Comparative Politics* 14, no. 1 (1981): 64; Chehabi, "The Shah's Two Liberalizations," 38.

46. Castiglioni, "No Longer a Client, Not Yet a Partner," 499. For details on this economic growth, see Vali Nasr, "Politics within the Late-Pahlavi State: The Ministry of Economy and Industrial Policy, 1963–69," *International Journal of Middle East Studies* 32, no. 1 (2000): 97–122.

47. Quoted in Ansari, *Modern Iran since 1921*, 163.

48. "United States Support for Nation-Building," Administrative History of the Department of State, quoted in Roland Popp, "An Application of Modernization Theory during the Cold War? The Case of Pahlavi Iran," *International History Review* 30, no. 1 (2008): 86.

49. Ibid.

50. Quoted in "Memorandum of Conversation," between Mehdi Samii, Governor of the Central Bank of Iran, Walt Rostow, and Harold H. Saunders, June 13, 1968, in *FRUS, 1964–1968*, 22:document 298, at https://history.state.gov /historicaldocuments/frus1964-68v22/d298.

51. Ruhollah Khomeini, *Islam and Revolution: Writings and Declarations of Imam Khomeini*, trans. Hamid Algar (Berkeley, CA: Mizan Press, 1981), 182.

52. A. Milani, *Persian Sphinx*, 172.

53. Quoted in Ansari, *Modern Iran since 1921*, 164.

54. See Gheissari and Nasr, *Democracy in Iran*, 60–61.

55. Quoted in Charles Kurzman, *The Unthinkable Revolution in Iran* (Cambridge, MA: Harvard Univ. Press, 2004), 82.

56. Kurzman, *The Unthinkable Revolution*, 82.

57. Ervand Abrahamian, *Khomeinism: Essays on the Islamic Republic* (Berkeley: Univ. of California Press, 1993), 13–38.

58. Ibid. See also Jahangir Amuzegar, *The Dynamics of the Iranian Revolution: The Pahlavis' Triumph and Tragedy* (Albany: State Univ. of New York Press, 1991); John Foran, *Fragile Resistance: Social Transformation in Iran from 1500 to the Revolution* (Boulder, CO: Westview Press, 1993); Homa Katouzian, *The Political Economy of Modern Iran, 1926–1979* (New York: New York Univ. Press, 1981); Robert Looney, *Economic Origins of the Iranian Revolution* (New York: Pergamon Press, 1982).

59. Amir Taheri, "Return of the Mosque," *Kayhan International*, Oct. 21, 1978, quoted in Cooper, *Fall of Heaven*, 157.

60. Lyndon B. Johnson, "Statement by the President on the Completion of the Agency for International Development Program in Iran," Nov. 29, 1967, in Lyndon Johnson, *Public Papers of the Presidents of the United States: Lyndon B. Johnson, Containing the Public Messages, Speeches, and Statements of the President,*

November 22, 1963, to January 20, 1969 (Washington, DC: US Government Printing Office, 1965–70), 1075–76.

61. US Aid Mission to Iran, *The US Aid Program in Iran* (Washington, DC: US Government Printing Office, Sept. 1966), 15.

62. Thomas L. Hughes to Rusk, Mar. 27, 1968, in *FRUS, 1964–1968*, 22:document 274, at https://history.state.gov/historicaldocuments/frus1964-68v22/d274.

63. Ekbladh, *Great American Mission*, 233.

64. US Embassy to State Department, airgram, Apr. 15, 1969, RG 59, Box 2219, NARA.

65. Benjamin H. Read to Henry A. Kissinger, memo, Jan. 30, 1969, RG 59, Box 2220, NARA.

66. See Castiglioni, "No Longer a Client, Not Yet a Partner."

67. William Safire, *Before the Fall: An Inside View of the Pre-Watergate White House* (New Brunswick, NJ: Transaction, 2005), 458.

68. A. Milani, *The Shah*, 248

69. Jack Anderson, "Did Shah Donate to Nixon?" *Palm Beach Post*, June 10, 1974, 11.

70. A. Milani, *The Shah*, 327.

71. State Department to US Embassy, Nov. 23, 1968, in *FRUS, 1964–1968*, 22:563.

72. Quoted in Andrew Scott Cooper, *The Oil Kings: How the US, Iran, and Saudi Arabia Changed the Balance of Power in the Middle East* (New York: Simon and Schuster, 2011), 50.

73. Richard M. Nixon, address to the Bohemian Club, July 29, 1967, in *FRUS, 1969–1976*, vol. 1: *Foundations of Foreign Policy, 1969–1972* (Washington, DC: US Government Printing Office, 2003), 2.

74. See Castiglioni, "No Longer a Client, Not Yet a Partner."

75. Bill, *The Eagle and the Lion*, 173.

76. Quoted in *FRUS, 1969–1976*, 1:29, editorial note.

77. Odd Arne Westad, *The Global Cold War: Third World Interventions and the Making of Our Time* (Cambridge: Cambridge Univ. Press, 2005), 197.

78. Ekbladh, *Great American Mission*, 223–24.

79. Smith, *America's Mission*, 239.

80. Nixon to Kissinger, H. R. Haldeman, and John Ehrlichmann, memo, Mar. 2, 1970, in *FRUS, 1969–1976*, 1:61.

81. Ekbladh, *Great American Mission*, 255.

82. Oriana Fallaci, "The Shah of Iran: An Interview with Mohammad Reza Pahlavi," *New Republic*, Dec. 1, 1973, 18.

83. There is much confusion and debate surrounding the true nature of the shah's human rights record. Official documents from after the revolution assert

that "60,000 men, women and children were martyred by the Shah's regime," but others estimate as many as 70,000 dead and 100,000 wounded. Later analysis found that between 1963 and 1979 a total of 3,164 Iranian lives were taken by the shah's regime and that 2,781 were killed during the revolution. For more on these numbers, see Cyrus Kadivar, "A Question of Numbers," *Rouzegar-Now*, Aug. 8, 2003, at http://www.emadbaghi.com/en/archives/000592.php.

84. Bill, *The Eagle and the Lion*, 186–87.

85. Cooper, *Oil Kings*, 64.

86. Samii, "The Role of SAVAK," 200.

87. Kazemi, "Fedā'īān-e Eslām," 472.

88. For background on the formation of the MEK, see Naqi Hamidian, *Safar ba balha-ye arezou: Sheklgiri-ye jonbesh-e cheriki-ye Feda'iyan-e Khalq* (Flying on the Wings of Hope: The Formation of the People's Devotees) (Stockholm: Arash, 2004).

89. Despite the MEK's attack on the US president and subsequent bombings that killed US citizens and Iranians alike, the US State Department surrendered to pressure and delisted the MEK as a terrorist organization in 2012. It is alleged that the MEK continues its terror attacks, and it has been implicated in a spate of assassinations of Iranian scientists. For more information on the MEK, see Dan Raviv and Yossi Melman, *Spies against Armageddon: Inside Israel's Secret Wars* (New York: Levant Books, 2014).

90. Joseph J. Sisco to Kissinger, Nov. 21, 1969, in *FRUS, 1969–1976*, vol. 24: *Middle East Region and Arabian Peninsula, 1969–1972* (Washington, DC: US Government Printing Office, 2008), 426–27.

91. Roham Alvandi, "Nixon, Kissinger, and the Shah: The Origins of Iranian Primacy in the Persian Gulf," *Diplomatic History* 36, no. 2 (2012): 362.

92. Quoted in ibid., 356; see also Little, *American Orientalism*, 221.

93. Memo of Conversation among Nixon, Douglas MacArthur III, and Alexander Haig, Apr. 8, 1971, in *FRUS, 1969–1976*, vol. E-4: *Documents on Iran and Iraq, 1969–1972* (Washington, DC: US Government Printing Office, 2006), document 122, at https://history.state.gov/historicaldocuments/frus1969-72ve04/d122.

94. For more detail on the change in policy toward the Middle East from Johnson to Nixon, see McGlinchey, *US Arms Policies towards the Shah's Iran*, 62–79.

95. Ibid., 65; Wawro, *Quicksand*, 297.

96. Quoted in Walter Isaacson, *Kissinger: A Biography* (New York: Simon and Schuster, 1992), 563.

97. Quoted in McGlinchey, *US Arms Policies towards the Shah's Iran*, 78.

98. Alvandi, "Nixon, Kissinger, and the Shah," 338; McGlinchey, *US Arms Policies towards the Shah's Iran*, 61.

99. Gary Sick, *All Fall Down: America's Tragic Encounter with Iran* (New York: Penguin, 1988), 17.

100. McGlinchey, *US Arms Policies towards the Shah's Iran*, 78.

101. See Ward, *Immortal*, 198, 208. Interestingly, the legacy of this purchase by the shah is still being felt today. In 2007, the Pentagon announced plans to shred all its retired F-14 fleet so as to ensure spare parts could not find their way to Iran. "Within a day," wrote Sharon Theimer of the Associated Press, "a $38 million fighter jet . . . can be reduced to shreds of twisted metal at the Davis-Monthan Air Force Base in Tucson, Ariz." ("US to Shred F-14s, Deny Iran Any Parts," *Seattle Times*, July 2, 2007, at http://seattletimes.nwsource.com/html/nationworld/2003771077_webshredding02.html).

102. Henry Precht, interview by Charles Stuart Kennedy, Mar. 8, 2000, Foreign Affairs Oral History Project, Association for Diplomatic Studies and Training, at http://www.adst.org/OH%20TOCs/Precht,%20Henry.toc.pdf.

103. Gary Sick, "Iran: A View from the White House," *World Affairs* 149, no. 4 (1987): 210.

104. Precht interview, Mar. 8, 2000.

105. Bill, *The Eagle and the Lion*, 221.

106. Quoted in Richard Sale, "Carter and Iran: From Idealism to Disaster," *Washington Quarterly* 3, no. 4 (1980): 86.

107. Quoted in M. Milani, *The Making of Iran's Islamic Revolution*, 24.

108. Quoted in Richard Helms, "Iran," in *Contacts with the Opposition: A Symposium*, ed. Martin F. Herz (Washington, DC: Univ. Press of America, 1980), 21–22.

109. Quoted in Rahnema, "Overthrowing Mosaddeq in Iran," 665.

110. Joe Alex Morris Jr., "Oil Talks Deadlocked as Mideast War, Arab Politics Get in the Way," *Los Angeles Times*, Oct. 10, 1973, E15.

111. Quoted in Cooper, *Oil Kings*, 212, emphasis in original.

112. Although the oil crisis hit Americans hard, there is evidence for its being more a result of mismanagement by Western states. Timothy Mitchell argues that it was not an issue of supply and demand but resulted from measures such as emergency policies put in place by Western governments that impeded the distribution of oil. He also explains how big oil corporations profited highly and exacerbated the problem in order to increase profits (*Carbon Democracy: Political Power in the Age of Oil* [New York: Verso, 2011]).

113. "70mph Speed Limit Will Be Cut to 65 in Effort to Save Fuel," *Los Angeles Times*, Nov. 6, 1973, A1.

114. "Yule Lights Won't Shine so Brightly," *Boston Globe*, Nov. 4, 1973, 50; Robert E. Dallos and Ronald L. Soble, "Petroleum Crisis Puts 1.6 Million Jobs on the Line," *Los Angeles Times*, Nov. 7, 1973, A1.

115. Sam Dobbins, "The Lighter Side of the Energy Crunch," *Lewiston Morning Tribune*, Nov. 18, 1973, 14; "Today's Queer Story," *The Bee*, Nov. 20, 1973, 1.

116. Dobbins, "The Lighter Side of the Energy Crunch," 14.

117. "Congress' Use of Energy Rises," *Washington Post*, Nov. 6, 1973, A4.

118. "Market Rebounds in Heavy Trading," *New York Times*, Nov. 22, 1973, 1; "Stocks Plunge 29 Points on Energy Fears," *Chicago Tribune*, Nov. 27, 1973, 1.

119. Cooper, Oil Kings, 143.

120. Ibid., 139.

121. Ibid.

122. Quoted in ibid., 64.

123. Bernard Weinraub, "Shah of Iran Urges Arabs to End Their Oil Embargo," *New York Times*, Dec. 22, 1973, 1; see also Cooper, *Oil Kings*, 139.

124. Cooper, *Oil Kings*, 141.

125. Ibid., 140.

126. Arthur Burns, Federal Reserve Bank chairman, quoted in ibid., 144.

127. McGlinchey, *US Arms Policies towards the Shah's Iran*, 81.

128. Jim Hoagland, "Persian Gulf Oil to Double in Price," *Boston Globe*, Dec. 24, 1973, 1, 16.

129. Quoted in ibid.

130. Quoted in "The Reminiscences of Richard Helms," interview by William Burr, July 10 and 24, 1985, 137–38, Oral History of Iran Collection, Foundation of Iranian Studies, at http://fis-iran.org/en/content/helms-richard.

131. Cooper, *Oil Kings*, 150.

132. Lewis M. Simons, "Shah's Dreams Are Outpacing Iran's Economic Boom," *Washington Post*, May 26, 1974, A6.

133. Quoted in ibid.

134. Quoted in David Holden, "Napoleonic Vision of Iran as a New Japan: Shah of Shahs, Shah of Dreams," *New York Times*, May 26, 1974, 39.

135. Paul E. Erdman, "The Coming Oil War: How the Shah Will Win the World," *New York*, Dec. 2, 1974, at https://iranian.com/History/2002/October/Crash/index.html.

8. The Predictable Storm, 1974–1979

1. David Holden "Napoleonic Vision of Iran as a New Japan: Shah of Shahs, Shah of Dreams," *New York Times*, May 26, 1974, 39.

2. Lewis M. Simons, "Shah's Dreams Are Outpacing Iran's Economic Boom," *Washington Post*, May 26, 1974, A6.

3. Quoted in ibid.

4. Simons, "Shah's Dreams," A6.

5. James F. Clarity, "Hoarders in Iran Facing Execution," *New York Times*, May 15, 1974, 7.

6. Ibid.

7. Clarity, "Hoarders in Iran," 7. See also Reza Baraheni, "The SAVAK Documents," *The Nation*, Feb. 23, 1980, 198–202, and Cyrus Kadivar, "A Question of Numbers," *Rouzegar-Now*, Aug. 8, 2003, at http://www.emadbaghi.com/en/archives/000592.php.

8. Clarity, "Hoarders in Iran," 7.

9. Baraheni, "The SAVAK Documents," 202.

10. Cooper, *Oil Kings*; Bill, *The Eagle and the Lion*; Cottam, *Iran and the United States*; Sick, *All Fall Down*.

11. See James M. Cannon, "Gerald R. Ford, Minority Leader of the House of Representatives, 1965–1973," in *Masters of the House: Congressional Leadership over Two Centuries*, ed. Roger H. Davidson, Susan Webb Hammond, and Raymond Smock (Boulder, CO: Westview Press, 1998), 267–75.

12. Rockefeller was reported to have respected the shah so much that he once asked Asadollah Alam whether the United States could borrow him for a while. "He'd soon teach us how to govern America," he quipped (Asadollah Alam, *The Shah and I: The Confidential Diary of Iran's Royal Court, 1969–1977* [New York: St. Martin's Press, 1991], 477).

13. Cooper, *Oil Kings*, 199.

14. Gerald R. Ford, remarks to the Ninth World Energy Conference, Detroit, Sept. 23, 1974, at http://www.presidency.ucsb.edu/ws/index.php?pid=4732#axzz1x8G5VSCP.

15. Quoted in Cooper, *Oil Kings*, 208.

16. Quoted in Alam, *The Shah and I*, 389.

17. Memorandum of Conversation between President Ford and Secretary Kissinger, Aug. 17, 1974, National Security Advisor's Memoranda of Conversation Collection, Gerald R. Ford Presidential Library, at https://www.fordlibrarymuseum.gov/library/document/0314/1552754.pdf.

18. Andrew Scott Cooper, "Showdown at Doha: The Secret Oil Deal That Helped Sink the Shah of Iran," *Middle East Journal* 62, no. 4 (2008): 589; Harry B. Ellis, "Iran's Race to Modernize Before the Oil Runs Out," *Christian Science Monitor*, Jan. 2, 1976, 14.

19. Keddie, *Modern Iran*, 163.

20. Cooper, "Showdown at Doha," 589.

21. "Iran's Quick Cure for Inflation," *Wall Street Journal*, Aug. 6, 1975, 8.

22. Quoted in Eric Pace, "Shah Courting Popular Support," *New York Times*, May 13, 1975, 4.

23. Ibid.

24. Bill, *The Eagle and the Lion*, 222.

25. Samuel P. Huntington, *Political Order in Changing Societies* (New Haven, CT: Yale Univ. Press, 1968), 137.

26. Azimi, *Quest for Democracy*, 197.

27. Ibid.

28. Quoted in Eric Pace, "Iran's Sole Party Girds for Elections This Week," *New York Times*, June 16, 1975, 10.

29. Azimi, *Quest for Democracy*, 198.

30. John D. Stempel, *Inside the Iranian Revolution* (Bloomington: Indiana Univ. Press, 1981), 34–35.

31. Pace, "Iran's Sole Party Girds for Elections," 10.

32. Thomas O'Toole, "$4-a-Barrel Oil Price Rise Hinted," *Washington Post*, June 6, 1975, A15; Jim Hoagland, "Exporters Raise Price of Oil by 10%," *Boston Globe*, Sept. 28, 1975, 21.

33. Bill, *The Eagle and the Lion*, 216–17.

34. Eric Pace, "Cut in Iran Oil Revenues Forces a Budget Deficit," *New York Times*, Feb. 4, 1976, 1.

35. Khomeini, *Islam and Revolution*, 223–24; see also Kurzman, *Unthinkable Revolution*, 79–80.

36. Ray Vicker, "Caveat Vendor," *Wall Street Journal*, Oct. 5, 1976, 1.

37. Cooper, "Showdown at Doha."

38. McGlinchey, *US Arms Policies towards the Shah's Iran*, 100.

39. Cooper, "Showdown at Doha," 567.

40. Quoted in Alam, *The Shah and I*, 535, and Cooper, "Showdown at Doha," 568.

41. Alam, *The Shah and I*, 537.

42. Sick, *All Fall Down*, 23.

43. Quoted in *US News & World Report*, Jan. 27, 1969, 49.

44. See Itai Nartzizenfield Sneh, *The Future Almost Arrived: How Jimmy Carter Failed to Change US Foreign Policy* (New York: Peter Lang, 2008), 53.

45. Jimmy Carter, "Inaugural Address," Jan. 20, 1977, at http://www.presidency.ucsb.edu/ws/index.php?pid=6575#ixzz1vis44xHj.

46. For a discussion on congressional efforts to address human rights in the 1970s, see Javier Gil Guerrero, "Human Rights and Tear Gas: The Question of Carter Administration Officials Opposed to the Shah," *British Journal of Middle Eastern Studies* 43, no. 3 (2016): 285–301; Emery, *US Foreign Policy and the Iranian Revolution*, 31–33.

47. Quoted in Sneh, *The Future Almost Arrived*, 54.

48. "Presidential Campaign Debate of October 6, 1976," document 854, in Gerald R. Ford, *Public Papers of the Presidents of the United States: Gerald R. Ford, Containing the Public Messages, Speeches, and Statements of the President 1976–1977* (Washington, DC: US Government Printing Office, 1979), 2419, quoted in Trenta, "The Champion of Human Rights Meets the King of Kings," 478.

49. Ervand Abrahamian, *The Iranian Mojahedin* (New Haven, CT: Yale Univ. Press, 1989), 29.

50. Quoted in Sale, "Carter and Iran," 76.

51. Ibid.

52. Ibid.

53. Abrahamian, *Iranian Mojahedin*, 170.

54. Bill, *The Eagle and the Lion*, 222–23.

55. US Department of State, Bureau of Intelligence and Research, "Progress of Human Rights in Iran," quoted in Cooper, *Fall of Heaven*, 238.

56. Cooper, *Fall of Heaven* 234.

57. A. Milani, *The Shah*, 384.

58. Ibid., 384–85.

59. Guerrero, *Carter Administration*, xxii.

60. Keddie, *Modern Iran*, 164.

61. Rubin, *Paved with Good Intentions*, 192.

62. Ansari, *Modern Iran*, 178.

63. Quoted in Henry Munson Jr., *Islam and Revolution in the Middle East* (New Haven, CT: Yale Univ. Press, 1988), 58.

64. The report is discussed in A. Milani, *The Shah*, 375–76.

65. Shahla Kazemipour and Mohammad Mirzaie, "Uneven Growth of Urbanization in Iran," poster presented at the International Union for the Scientific Study of Population Twenty-Fifth International Population Conference, July 2005, Tours, France, at http://iussp2005.princeton.edu/papers/51663.

66. World Bank, graph of the population of Iran from 1960 to 2014, at http://www.google.com/publicdata/explore?ds=d5bncppjof8f9_&met_y=sp_pop_totl&idim=country:IRN&dl=en&hl=en&q=population+iran.

67. A. Milani, *The Shah*, 376–77.

68. Abdol-Karim Lahiji, quoted in Kurzman, *Unthinkable Revolution*, 18.

69. Quoted in Chehabi, "The Shah's Two Liberalizations," 45.

70. "The Shah's Divided Land: Turmoil in Iran Brings Martial Law and a Threat to the Dream," *Time*, Sept. 18, 1989, at http://content.time.com/time/magazine/article/0,9171,916373,00.html.

71. Ahmad Karimi-Hakkak, quoted in H. E. Chehabi "Goethe Institute," *Encyclopædia Iranica* 11 (2001): 43–44.

72. Chehabi, *Iranian Politics*, 227.

73. Ibid., 228.

74. Roy Mottahedeh, *The Mantle of the Prophet: Religion and Politics in Iran* (Oxford: Oneworld, 2004), 372.

75. Bill, *The Eagle and the Lion*, 234.

76. Martha Angle and Robert Walters, "Kennedy, Carter: Similarities Striking," *Prescott Courier*, Apr. 29, 1977, 3.

77. Quoted in Sale, "Carter and Iran," 76.

78. Quoted in Smith, *America's Mission*, 245.

79. Quoted in Little, *American Orientalism*, 223 n. 147

80. Ibid., 224.

81. A. Milani, *The Shah*, 383.

82. Quoted in Azimi, *Quest for Democracy*, 201.

83. Cooper, *Fall of Heaven*, 267.

84. Trita Parsi, *Treacherous Alliance: The Secret Dealings of Israel, Iran, and the United States* (New Haven, CT: Yale Univ. Press, 2007), 74–75; Sick, *All Fall Down*, 30–31.

85. Quoted in Sale, "Carter and Iran," 80.

86. Curtis Wilkie, "Order in Iran a Key US Priority," *Boston Globe*, Jan. 7, 1979, 23.

87. Chehabi, *Iranian Politics*, 225.

88. Wilkie, "Order in Iran," 23.

89. Smith, *America's Mission*, 242–43.

90. Quoted in ibid., 243.

91. Scott Kaufman, *Plans Unraveled: The Foreign Policy of the Carter Administration* (DeKalb: Northern Illinois Univ. Press, 2008), 4.

92. See Emery, *US Foreign Policy and the Iranian Revolution*, 33–34.

93. William H. Sullivan, *Mission to Iran* (New York: Norton, 1981), 19–22.

94. Sick, *All Fall Down*, 28.

95. For more detail on the cancellation of this one arms deal, see McGlinchey, *US Arms Policies towards the Shah's Iran*, 124–43.

96. See Trenta, "Champion of Human Rights," 481.

97. Sick, *All Fall Down*, 31.

98. Quoted in Trenta, "Champion of Human Rights," 481.

99. Quoted in Bill, *The Eagle and the Lion*, 227.

100. Ibid., 228.

101. "The Reminiscences of Charles W. Naas," interview by William Burr, May 31, 1988, Oral History of Iran Collection, Foundation of Iranian Studies, Bethesda, MD, at http://fis-iran.org/en/content/naas-charles.

102. Ansari, *Modern Iran since 1921*, 196; Sick, *All Fall Down*, 36.

103. Sick, *All Fall Down*, 36.

104. Quoted in Sale, "Carter and Iran," 82.

105. Sick, *All Fall Down*, 32.

106. Jimmy Carter, *Keeping Faith: Memoirs of a President* (New York: Bantam Books, 1982), 437; Bill, *The Eagle and the Lion*, 233.

107. Cyrus R. Vance, *Hard Choice: Critical Years in America's Foreign Policy* (New York: Simon and Schuster, 1983), 321.

108. Both quoted in Kurzman, *Unthinkable Revolution*, 20.

109. "Tehran, Iran, Toasts of the President and the Shah at a State Dinner," Dec. 31, 1977, American Presidency Project, Univ. of California at Santa Barbara, at http://www.presidency.ucsb.edu/ws/?pid=7080.

110. Sick, *All Fall Down*, 35.

111. Khomeini, *Islam and Revolution*, 224; see also Bill, *The Eagle and the Lion*, 234.

112. Sick, *All Fall Down*, 40.

113. Cooper, *Fall of Heaven*, 313.

114. Zbigniew Brzezinski, *Power and Principle: Memoirs of the National Security Advisor, 1977–1981* (New York: Farrar, Straus, Giroux, 1985), 361.

115. Ibid., 60.

116. Bill, *The Eagle and the Lion*, 258.

117. Ibid., 235–36.

118. Sepehr Zabir, *Iran since the Revolution* (London: Routledge, 2011), 4; Lloyd C. Gardner, *The Long Road to Baghdad: A History of U.S. Foreign Policy from the 1970s to the Present* (New York: New Press, 2008), 52.

119. Sick, *All Fall Down*, 54.

120. Quoted in Smith, *America's Mission*, 259.

121. Sick, "Iran," 211.

122. Sick, *All Fall Down*, 70.

123. Bill, *The Eagle and the Lion*, 246.

124. Henry Precht, interview by Charles Stuart Kennedy, Mar. 8, 2000, Foreign Affairs Oral History Project, Association for Diplomatic Studies and Training, at http://www.adst.org/OH%20TOCs/Precht,%20Henry.toc.pdf.

125. Pahlavi, *Answer to History*, 164–65.

126. For more on the disagreements on Iran among officials in the Carter administration, see Guerrero, *Carter Administration*, 113–32.

127. Ward, *Immortal*, 214.

128. George Ball, "Issues and Implications of the Iranian Crisis," late 1978, quoted in A. Milani, *The Shah*, 395.

129. Charles W. McCaskill, interview, July 7, 1993, Foreign Affairs Oral History Project, Association for Diplomatic Studies and Training, at http://www.adst.org/OH%20TOCs/McCaskill,%20Charles%20W.toc.pdf.

130. Ibid.; David Crist, *The Twilight War: The Secret History of America's Thirty-Year Conflict with Iran* (New York: Penguin, 2012), 15.

131. Cooper, *Fall of Heaven*, 452–53.

132. Trenta, "Champion of Human Rights," 486–87, 488.

133. Bill, *The Eagle and the Lion*, 244–60; Sick, *All Fall Down*, 124–61; Chehabi, *Iranian Politics*, 248–50.

134. James A. Bill, *George Ball: Behind the Scenes in US Foreign Policy* (New Haven, CT: Yale Univ. Press, 1997), 91.

135. Henry Precht, quoted in Sick, *All Fall Down*, 141.

136. Quoted in Kurzman, *Unthinkable Revolution*, 2.

137. "President's News Conference," Dec. 12, 1978, cited in Alexander and Nanes, *The United States and Iran*, 463–64.

138. Jim Hoagland, "Carter Set to Tell European Allies He Fully Backs Shah," *Washington Post*, Jan. 5, 1979, A5; see also "Carter Flying to Guadeloupe to Meet 3 European Leaders," *Pittsburgh Post-Gazette*, Jan. 4, 1979, 4.

139. Ellen Hume, "Carter, 3 European Leaders Open Talks," *Los Angeles Times*, Jan. 5, 1979, B20; Timothy D. Schellhardt, "Repercussions of Guadeloupe Summit Are Likely to Be Felt throughout 1979," *Wall Street Journal*, Jan. 8, 1979, 5.

140. R. W. Apple Jr., "Enemies Immobilize Iran's Government," *New York Times*, Jan. 10, 1979, A5.

141. Sullivan, *Mission to Iran*, 224.

142. Carter, *Keeping Faith*, 454.

143. Wilkie, "Order in Iran," 23.

144. Jim Hoagland, "US Switches Effort to Post-Shah Regime," *New York Times*, Jan. 10, 1979, A1.

145. Precht interview, Mar. 8, 2000.

146. Sale, "Carter and Iran," 86.

147. See Robert Jervis, *Why Intelligence Fails: Lessons from the Iranian Revolution and the Iraq War* (Ithaca, NY: Cornell Univ. Press, 2010).

148. For a scholarly focus on the revolution's domestic causes, see, for example, Rubin, *Paved with Good Intentions*; Theda Skocpol, "Rentier State and Shi'a Islam in the Iranian Revolution," *Theory and Society* 11, no. 3 (1982): 265–83; Kurzman, *Unthinkable Revolution*; M. Milani, *Making of Iran's Islamic Revolution*; Hossein Bashiriyeh, *The State and Revolution in Iran, 1962–1982* (New York: St. Martin's Press, 1984).

149. Sick, *All Fall Down*, 39.

150. William H. Sullivan to State Department, memo, Nov. 9, 1978, in "The Carter Administration and the 'Arc of Crisis,' 1977–1981, Cold War International History Project," declassified documents prepared for Woodrow Wilson Center conference, July 25–26, 2005, Washington, DC; Kurzman, *Unthinkable Revolution*, viii, 5–6; Skocpol, "Rentier State and Shi'a Islam," 265.

151. Robert Komer to Carl Kaysen, Jan. 19, 1962, NSF, Box 116, JFKL.

152. See Johns, "Johnson Administration," 91–94.

153. Ibid.

154. Louise Fawcett, "Revisiting the Iranian Crisis of 1946: How Much Do We Know?" *Iranian Studies* 47, no. 3 (2014): 379.

155. Saikal, *Rise and Fall of the Shah*, 202–3.

Conclusion: Thrown to the Wind

1. Ibrahim Karawan, "Middle East Studies after 9/11: Time for an Audit," *Journal of Democracy* 13, no. 3 (2002): 100–101.

2. This view runs contrary to Steven Levitsky and Lucan Way's argument that both linkage and leverage do not need to be present for external pressure to be successful (*Competitive Authoritarianism*, 70).

3. Trenta, "Champion of Human Rights," 484.

4. Saïd Amir Arjomand, *The Turban for the Crown: The Islamic Revolution in Iran* (New York: Oxford Univ. Press, 1988), 92.

5. Ibid.; Trenta, "Champion of Human Rights," 485.

6. Trenta, "Champion of Human Rights," 485.

7. David Harris, *The Crisis: The President, the Prophet, and the Shah—1979 and the Coming of Militant Islam* (New York: Little, Brown, 2004), 88, quoted in Trenta, "Champion of Human Rights," 486.

8. Central Intelligence Agency, "Intelligence Memorandum: The Politics of Ayatollah Ruhollah Khomeini," Nov. 20, 1978, quoted in Cooper, *Fall of Heaven*, 467.

9. Bill, *The Eagle and the Lion*.

10. Shuster, *Strangling of Persia*; see also Charles Kurzman, *Democracy Denied, 1905–1915: Intellectuals and the Fate of Democracy* (Cambridge, MA: Harvard Univ. Press, 2008).

11. Shuster, *Strangling of Persia*, lxv.

12. See Chehabi, "The Shah's Two Liberalizations," 30–32.

Epilogue: After the Shah

1. For details on the hostage crisis, see Mark Bowden, *Guests of the Ayatollah: The First Battle of America's War with Militant Islam* (New York: Atlantic Monthly Press, 2006).

2. Ibid., 142, 69.

3. Their demand comes from *Declaration of the Government of the Democratic and Popular Republic of Algeria*, Jan. 19, 1981.

4. "The Great Satan's Old Den: Visiting Tehran's US Embassy," *Time*, July 14, 2009, at http://content.time.com/time/world/article/0,8599,1910361,00.html.

5. See Parsi, *Treacherous Alliance*, 110–26.

6. See ibid., 184–91.

7. Flynt Leverett and Hillary Mann Leverett, *Going to Tehran: Why the United States Must Come to Terms with the Islamic Republic of Iran* (New York: Metropolitan Books, 2013), 118.

8. Haleh Anvari, "Iranians to Bush: Take This Axis of Evil and Shove It," *Salon*, Feb. 7, 2002, at http://www.salon.com/2002/02/07/tehran/.

9. For the full text of this proposal, see Parsi, *Treacherous Alliance*, 241.

10. Gordon Corera, "Iran's Gulf of Misunderstanding with US," *BBC News*, Sept. 25, 2006, at http://news.bbc.co.uk/2/hi/middle_east/5377914.stm.

11. For this response from the Bush administration and an overview of the grand bargain, see Parsi, *Treacherous Alliance*, 243–50.

12. Barbara Slavin, *Bitter Friends, Bosom Enemies: Iran, the US, and the Twisted Path to Confrontation* (New York: St. Martin's Press, 2007).

13. For more on this failed attempt at negotiation, see Trita Parsi, *Single Roll of the Dice: Obama's Diplomacy with Iran* (New Haven, CT: Yale Univ. Press, 2012), 172–209.

14. "New Iranian President Known as the 'Diplomat Sheikh,'" *All Things Considered*, NPR, June 17, 2013, at http://www.npr.org/templates/story/story.php?storyId=192790975.

15. Jasmin Ramsey, "Watching US–Iran History in the Making," *Lobelog: Foreign Policy*, Sept. 27, 2013, at https://lobelog.com/watching-us-iran-history-in-the-making/.

16. Suzanne Maloney, "Why 'Iran Style' Sanctions Worked against Tehran (and Why They Might Not Succeed with Moscow)," Brookings Institution blog, Mar. 21, 2014, at http://www.brookings.edu/blogs/markaz/posts/2014/03/21-iran-sanctions-russia-crimea-nuclear; Trita Parsi, "No, Sanctions Didn't Force Iran to Make a Deal," *Foreign Policy*, May 14, 2014, at http://foreignpolicy.com/2014/05/14/no-sanctions-didnt-force-iran-to-make-a-deal/.

17. US Department of State, "Joint Comprehensive Plan of Action," July 14, 2015, at http://www.state.gov/e/eb/tfs/spi/iran/jcpoa/.

18. Cliff Kupchan, quoted in Rick Gladstone, "With Iran Nuclear Deal Implemented, What Happens Next?" *New York Times*, Jan. 16, 2016, at http://www.nytimes.com/2016/01/17/world/middleeast/why-iran-sanctions-were-lifted-and-what-happens-next.html.

19. Robin Wright, "Prisoner Swap: Obama's Secret Second Channel to Iran," *New Yorker*, Jan. 16, 2016, at http://www.newyorker.com/news/news-desk/prisoner-swap-obamas-secret-second-channel-to-iran.

20. Thomas Erdbrink, "Europe Says US Regulations Keeping It from Trade with Iran," *New York Times*, Apr. 21, 2016, at http://www.nytimes.com/2016/04/22

/world/middleeast/europe-says-us-regulations-keeping-it-from-trade-with-iran. html?_r=0; Robin Wright, "Iran's Javad Zarif on the Fraying Nuclear Deal, US Relations, and Holocaust Cartoons," *New Yorker*, Apr. 25, 2016, at http://www .newyorker.com/news/news-desk/irans-javad-zarif-on-the-fraying-nuclear-deal-u -s-relations-and-holocaust-cartoons.

21. Quoted in Julian Borger, "British Embassy in Iran Reopens," *Guardian*, Aug. 23, 2015, at http://www.theguardian.com/politics/2015/aug/23/british -embassy-iran-tehran-reopens.

22. Quoted in Wright, "Iran's Javad Zarif."

23. Levitsky and Way, *Competitive Authoritarianism*, 24.

24. Dean Rusk to the President, Apr. 20, 1963, NSF, Box 116a, JFKL.

25. Parsi, *Single Roll of the Dice*, 101.

26. Mohsen Kadivar, "God and His Guardians," *Index on Censorship* 33, no. 4 (2004): 64.

27. See Abdolkarim Soroush, *Reason, Freedom, and Democracy in Islam: Essential Writings of Abdolkarim Soroush*, trans. Mahmoud Sadri and Ahmad Sadri (New York: Oxford Univ. Press, 2000).

28. Kadivar, "God and His Guardians," 64.

29. For examples of works that examine the combination of *vilayat-e faqih* and democracy, see Ibrahim Moussawi, *Shi'ism and the Democratization Process in Iran: With a Focus on Wilayat al-Faqih*, (London: Saqi, 2011); Mohsen Kadivar, "*Wilayat al-Faqih* and Democracy," in *Islam, the State, and Political Authority: Medieval Issues and Modern Concerns*, ed. Asma Afsaruddin (New York: Palgrave Macmillan, 2011), 207–24; Abbas Milani, "Iran's Paradoxical Regime," *Journal of Democracy* 26, no. 2 (2015): 52–60; Abbas William Samii, "Iran's Guardian Council as an Obstacle to Democracy," *Middle East Journal* 55, no. 4 (2001): 643–62.

30. Laura Secor, *Children of Paradise: The Struggle for the Soul of Iran* (New York: Riverhead Books, 2016), 466.

31. Simin Behbahani, "The Lioness of Iran," interview by Shiva Rahbaran, *Guernica*, Oct. 11, 2011, at http://www.guernicamag.com/interviews/behbahani _10_1_11/.

32. Sullivan's description of this meeting with shah is quoted in Stephen S. Rosenfeld, "Knowing the Outs as Well as the Ins," *Washington Post*, Dec. 7, 1979, A17.

33. Simin Behbahani, "My Country I Will Build You Again," in *A Cup of Sin: Selected Poems*, trans. Farzaneh Milani and Kaveh Safa (Syracuse, NY: Syracuse Univ. Press, 1999), 68, reprinted by permission of the publisher.

Bibliography

Abrahamian, Ervand. "The 1953 Coup in Iran." *Science and Society* 65, no. 2 (2001): 182–215.

———. "The Causes of the Constitutional Revolution in Iran." *International Journal of Middle East Studies* 10, no. 3 (1979): 381–414.

———. *The Coup: 1953, the CIA, and the Roots of Modern US–Iranian Relations.* New York: New Press, 2013.

———. *A History of Modern Iran.* New York: Cambridge Univ. Press, 2008.

———. *Iran between Two Revolutions.* Princeton, NJ: Princeton Univ. Press, 1982.

———. *The Iranian Mojahedin.* New Haven, CT: Yale Univ. Press, 1989.

———. *Khomeinism: Essays on the Islamic Republic.* Berkeley: Univ. of California Press, 1993.

Abramson, Rudy. *Spanning the Century: The Life of W. Averell Harriman, 1891–1986.* New York: Morrow, 1992.

Acheson, Dean. *Fragments of My Fleece.* New York: Norton, 1971.

———. *Present at the Creation: My Years in the State Department.* New York: Norton, 1969.

Afary, Janet. *The Iranian Constitutional Revolution, 1906–1911: Grassroots Democracy, Social Democracy, and the Origins of Feminism.* New York: Columbia Univ. Press, 1996.

Afkhami, Gholam Reza. *The Life and Times of the Shah.* Berkeley: Univ. of California Press, 2009.

Afsaruddin, Asma, ed. *Islam, the State, and Political Authority: Medieval Issues and Modern Concerns.* New York: Palgrave Macmillan, 2011.

Alam, Asadollah. *The Shah and I: The Confidential Diary of Iran's Royal Court, 1969–1977.* New York: St. Martin's Press, 1991.

Alavi, Nasrin. *We Are Iran: The Persian Blogs*. Brooklyn, NY: Soft Skull Press, 2005.

Alexander, Yonah, and Allan S. Nanes, eds. *The United States and Iran: A Documentary History*. Frederick, MD: Alethia Books, 1980.

Alvandi, Roham. "Flirting with Neutrality: The Shah, Khrushchev, and the Failed 1959 Soviet–Iranian Neogtiations." *Iranian Studies* 47, no. 3 (2014): 419–40.

———. "Nixon, Kissinger, and the Shah: The Origins of Iranian Primacy in the Persian Gulf." *Diplomatic History* 36, no. 2 (2012): 337–72.

———. *Nixon, Kissinger, and the Shah: The United States and Iran in the Cold War*. New York: Oxford Univ. Press, 2014.

Ambrose, Stephen E. *Eisenhower, the President*. New York: Simon and Schuster, 1983.

Amini, Iraj. *Bar bal-e bohran: Zendegi-ye siyasi-ye Ali Amini* (Flying on the Wings of Crisis: The Political Life of Ali Amini). Tehran: Nashr-e Mahi, 2009.

Amirie, Abbas, and Hamilton A. Twitchell. *Iran in the 1980s*. Tehran: Institute for International Political and Economic Studies, 1978.

Amirsadeghi, Hossein, ed. *Twentieth Century Iran*. New York: Holmes and Meier, 1977.

Amuzegar, Jahangir. *The Dynamics of the Iranian Revolution: The Pahlavi's Triumph and Tragedy*. Albany: State Univ. of New York Press, 1991.

Ansari, Ali M. *Modern Iran since 1921: The Pahlavis and After*. New York: Pearson Education, 2003.

———. "The Myth of the White Revolution: Mohammad Reza Shah, 'Modernization,' and the Consolidation of Power." *Middle Eastern Studies* 37, no. 3 (2001): 1–24.

Anslover, Nicole L. "An Executive Echo Chamber: The Evolution of America's Vietnam Policy from Truman to Johnson." PhD diss., Univ. of Kansas, 2007.

Arjomand, Saïd Amir. *The Turban for the Crown: The Islamic Revolution in Iran*. New York: Oxford Univ. Press, 1988.

Ashraf, Ahmad. "Conspiracy Theories." *Encyclopædica Iranica* 6 (1992): 138–47.

Ayoob, Mohammad. "The Muslim World's Poor Record of Modernization and Democratization: The Interplay of External and Internal Factors."

In *Modernization, Democracy, and Islam*, edited by Shireen T. Hunter and Huma Malik, 186–202. Westport, CT: Praeger, 2005.

Azimi, Fakhreddin. *Iran: The Crisis of Democracy*. New York: St. Martin's Press, 1989.

———. "On Shaky Ground: Concerning the Absence or Weakness of Political Parties in Iran." *Iranian Studies* 30, nos. 1–2 (1997): 53–75.

———. "The Overthrow of the Government of Mosaddeq Reconsidered." *Iranian Studies* 45, no. 5 (2012): 693–712.

———. *The Quest for Democracy in Iran: A Century of Struggle against Authoritarian Rule*. Cambridge, MA: Harvard Univ. Press, 2008.

———. "Unseating Mossadegh: The Configuration and Role of Domestic Forces." In *Mohammad Mossaddeq and the 1953 Coup in Iran*, edited by Mark J. Gasiorowski and Malcolm Byrne, 27–101. Syracuse, NY: Syracuse Univ. Press, 2004.

Bakhash, Shaul. "Britain and the Abdication of Reza Shah." *Middle Eastern Studies* 52, no. 2 (2016): 318–34.

Bakhtiary, Princess Soraya Esfandiary. *Palace of Solitude*. Translated by Hubert Gibbs. London: Quartet Books, 1992.

Baldwin, George B. *Planning and Development in Iran*. Baltimore: Johns Hopkins Univ. Press, 1967.

Ball, George W. *The Past Has Another Pattern*. New York: Norton, 1982.

Baraheni, Reza. "The SAVAK Documents." *The Nation*, Feb. 23, 1980, 198–202.

Barrett, Roby C. *The Greater Middle East and the Cold War: US Foreign Policy under Eisenhower and Kennedy*. New York: Palgrave Macmillan, 2007.

Bashiriyeh, Hossein. *The State and Revolution in Iran, 1962–1982*. New York: St. Martin's Press, 1984.

Bayandor, Darioush. *Iran and the CIA: The Fall of Mosaddeq Revisited*. New York: Palgrave Macmillan, 2010.

Baylies, Carolyn. "'Political Conditionality' and Democratization." *Review of African Political Economy* 22, no. 65 (1995): 321–37.

Behbahani, Simin. *A Cup of Sin: Selected Poems*. Translated by Farzaneh Milani and Kaveh Safa. Syracuse, NY: Syracuse Univ. Press, 1999.

———. "Stop Throwing My Country to the Wind." Translated by Farzaneh Milani and Kaveh Safa. On "Iran's National Poet Speaks Out on

Recent Events in Her Country," National Public Radio, June 26, 2009. At http://www.youtube.com/watch?v=wSdF5KCuxy8

Beisner, Robert L. *Dean Acheson: A Life in the Cold War.* New York: Oxford Univ. Press, 2006.

Bellin, Eva. "The Robustness of Authoritarianism in the Middle East: Exceptionalism in Comparative Perspective." *Comparative Politics* 36, no. 2 (2004): 139–57.

Bernhard, Michael, Christopher Reenock, and Timothy Nordstrom. "The Legacy of Western Oveseas Colonialism on Democratic Survival." *International Studies Quarterly* 48 (2004): 225–50.

Bethell, Nicholas. *Betrayed.* New York: Times Books, 1985.

Bill, James A. *The Eagle and the Lion: The Tragedy of American–Iranian Relations.* New Haven, CT: Yale Univ. Press, 1988.

———. *George Ball: Behind the Scenes in US Foreign Policy.* New Haven, CT: Yale Univ. Press, 1997.

Black, Conrad. *Franklin Delano Roosevelt: Champion of Freedom.* New York: Public Affairs, 2003.

Bollen, Kenneth A. "World System Position, Dependency, and Democracy: The Cross-National Evidence." *American Sociological Review* 48 (1983): 468–79.

Bowden, Mark. *Guests of the Ayatollah: The First Battle of America's War with Militant Islam.* New York: Atlantic Monthly Press, 2006.

Brands, H. W. *The Devil We Knew: Americans and the Cold War.* New York: Oxford Univ. Press, 1993.

———, ed. *The Foreign Policies of Lyndon Johnson: Beyond Vietnam.* College Station: Texas A&M Univ. Press, 1999.

Brinks, Daniel, and Michael Coppedge. "Diffusion Is No Illusion: Neighbor Emulation in the Third Wave of Democracy." *Comparative Political Studies* 39, no. 4 (2006): 463–89.

Brumberg, Daniel. *Reinventing Khomeini: The Struggle for Reform in Iran.* Chicago: Univ. of Chicago Press, 2001.

Brzezinski, Zbigniew. *Power and Principle: Memoirs of the National Security Advisor, 1977–1981.* New York: Farrar, Straus, Giroux, 1985.

Buhite, Russell D. *Patrick J. Hurley and American Foreign Policy.* Ithaca, NY: Cornell Univ. Press, 1973.

Burns, William J. *Economic Aid and American Policy toward Egypt, 1955–1981.* Albany: State Univ. of New York Press, 1985.

Butler, Susan. *Roosevelt and Stalin: Portrait of a Partnership*. New York: Knopf, 2015.

Cardoso, Fernando, and Enzo Faletto. *Dependency and Development in Latin America*. Berkeley: Univ. of California Press, 1979.

Carothers, Thomas. "The 'Sequencing' Fallacy." *Journal of Democracy* 18, no. 1 (2007): 12–27.

Carter, Jimmy. *Keeping Faith: Memoirs of a President*. New York: Bantam Books, 1982.

Case, William. "Can the 'Halfway House' Stand? Semidemocracy and Elite Theory in Three Southeast Asian Countries." *Comparative Politics* 28, no. 4 (1996): 437–64.

Castiglioni, Claudia. "No Longer a Client, Not Yet a Partner: The US–Iranian Alliance in the Johnson Years." *Cold War History* 15, no. 4 (2015): 491–509.

Cavatorta, Francesco. "The International Context of Morocco's Stalled Democratization." *Democratization* 12 (2005): 548–66.

———. *The International Dimension of the Failed Algerian Transition—Democracy Betrayed?* Manchester, UK: Manchester Univ. Press, 2009.

Central Intelligence Agency. "Overthrow of Premier Mossadeq of Iran, November 1952–August 1953." Mar. 1954. At https://archive.org/details/CIA-Mossadeq-Iran-1953.

Chehabi, H. E. "Goethe Institute." *Encyclopædia Iranica* 11 (2001): 43–44.

———. *Iranian Politics and Religious Modernism: The Liberation Movement of Iran under the Shah and Khomeini*. Ithaca, NY: Cornell Univ. Press, 1990.

———. "The Shah's Two Liberalizations: Re-equilibration and Breakdown." In *Iran and the Challenges of the Twenty-First Century: Essays in Honour of Mohammad-Reza Djalili*, edited by H. E. Chehabi, Khosrokhavar Farhad, and Clement Therme, 24–49. Costa Mesa, CA: Mazda, 2013.

———. "Sport and Politics in Iran: The Legend of Gholamreza Takhti." *International Journal of the History of Sport* 12, no. 3 (1995): 48–60.

Chehabi, H. E., Khosrokhavar Farhad, and Clement Therme, eds. *Iran and the Challenges of the Twenty-First Century: Essays in Honour of Mohammad-Reza Djalili*. Costa Mesa, CA: Mazda, 2013.

Chehabi, H. E., and Juan J. Linz. *Sultanistic Regimes*. Baltimore: Johns Hopkins Univ. Press, 1998.

Chomsky, Noam. *Deterring Democracy.* New York: Verso, 1991.

Churchill, Winston. *The Gathering Storm.* Vol. 1 of *The Second World War.* Boston: Houghton Mifflin, 1948.

———. *Triumph and Tragedy.* Vol. 6 of Vol. 1 of *The Second World War.* Boston: Houghton Mifflin, 1953.

Cochran, Bert. *Harry Truman and the Crisis Presidency.* New York: Funk and Wagnalls, 1973.

Collier, David R. "To Prevent a Revolution: John F. Kennedy and the Promotion of Democracy in Iran." *Diplomacy and Statecraft* 24, no. 3 (2013): 456–75.

Collier, David, and Steven Levitsky. "Democracy 'with Adjectives': Conceptual Innovation in Comparative Research." *World Politics* 49 (1997): 430–51.

Collier, Ruth Berins, and David Collier. *Shaping the Political Arena: Critical Junctures, the Labor Movement, and Regime Dynamics in Latin America.* Princeton, NJ: Princeton Univ. Press, 1991.

"Concept Misinformation in Comparative Politics." *American Political Science Review* 64, no. 4 (1970): 1033–53.

Cooper, Andrew Scott. *The Fall of Heaven: The Pahlavis and the Final Days of Imperial Iran.* New York: Holt, 2016.

———. *The Oil Kings: How the US, Iran, and Saudi Arabia Changed the Balance of Power in the Middle East.* New York: Simon and Schuster, 2011.

———. "Showdown at Doha: The Secret Oil Deal That Helped Sink the Shah of Iran." *Middle East Journal* 62, no. 4 (2008): 567–91.

Copeland, Miles. *The Game of Nations: The Amorality of Power Politics.* New York: Simon and Schuster, 1970.

Coppedge, Michael. *Democratization and Research Methods.* Cambridge: Cambridge Univ. Press, 2012.

Corke, Sarah-Jane. *US Covert Operations and Cold War Strategy: Truman, Secret Warfare, and the CIA, 1945–1953.* New York: Routledge, 2008.

Cottam, Richard W. *Iran and the United States: A Cold War Case Study.* Pittsburgh: Univ. of Pittsburgh Press, 1988.

———. *Nationalism in Iran.* Pittsburgh: Univ. of Pittsburgh Press, 1964.

Cox, Michael, G. John Ikenberry, and Takashi Inoguchi. *American Democracy Promotion: Impulses, Strategies, and Impacts.* Oxford: Oxford Univ. Press, 2000.

Crist, David. *The Twilight War: The Secret History of America's Thirty-Year Conflict with Iran*. New York: Penguin, 2012.

Cronin, Stephanie, ed. *The Making of Modern Iran: State and Society under Riza Shah, 1921–1941*. New York: Routledge Curzon, 2003.

Cullather, Nick. *The Hungry World: America's Cold War Battle against Poverty in Asia*. Cambridge, MA: Harvard Univ. Press, 2010.

Curtiss, Richard H. "Bush's 'Forward Strategy' for Freedom in the Middle East." *Washington Report on Middle East Affairs*, Jan.–Feb. 2004, 20.

Dafoe, Allan. "Statistical Critiques of the Democratic Peace: Caveat Emptor." *American Journal of Political Science* 55, no. 2 (2011): 247–62.

Dahl, Robert A. *Dilemmas of Pluralist Democracy: Autonomy vs. Control*. New Haven, CT: Yale Univ. Press, 1982.

―――. *Polyarchy: Participation and Opposition*. New Haven, CT: Yale Univ. Press, 1971.

Dallek, Robert. *Franklin D. Roosevelt and American Foreign Policy, 1932–1945*. New York: Oxford Univ. Press, 1979.

―――. *Harry S. Truman*. New York: Times Books, 2008.

―――. *An Unfinished Life: John F. Kennedy, 1917–1963*. Boston: Little, Brown, 2003.

Danopoulos, Constantine P., and Cynthia Ann Watson. *The Political Role of the Military: An International Handbook*. Westport, CT: Greenwood Press, 1996.

Daugherty, William J. "Truman's Iranian Policy, 1945–1953: The Soviet Calculus." *International Journal of Intelligence and Counterintelligence* 15 (2002): 580–93.

Davidson, Roger H., Susan Webb Hammond, and Raymond Smock. *Masters of the House: Congressional Leadership over Two Centuries*. Boulder, CO: Westview Press, 1998.

De Bellaigue, Christopher. *Patriot of Persia: Muhammad Mossadegh and a Tragic Anglo-American Coup*. New York: Harper, 2012.

DeConde, Alexander, Richard Dean Burns, and Fredrik Logevall, eds. *Encyclopedia of American Foreign Policy*. 3 vols. New York: Scribner's, 2002.

"Developments of the Quarter: Comment and Chronology." *Middle East Journal* 3, no. 4 (1949): 441–54.

Diamond, Larry. *Developing Democracy: Towards Consolidation*. Baltimore: Johns Hopkins Univ. Press, 1999.

———. "A Fourth Wave of False Start? Democracy after the Arab Spring." *Foreign Affairs*, Snapshot, May 22, 2011. At http://www.foreign affairs.com/articles/67862/larry-diamond/a-fourth-wave-or-false-start.

———. *Is the Third Wave of Democratization Over? An Empirical Assessment*. Working Paper no. 236. Notre Dame, IN: Kellogg Institute, 1997.

———. "Is the Third Wave Over?" *Journal of Democracy* 7, no. 3 (1996): 20–37.

———. *The Spirit of Democracy: The Struggle to Build Free Societies throughout the World*. New York: Times Books and Holt, 2008.

———. "Why Are There No Arab Democracies?" *Journal of Democracy* 21, no. 1 (2010): 93–112.

Djerejian, Edward P. "The US and the Middle East in a Changing World." Defense Institute of Security Assistance Management, June 2, 1992. At http://www.disam.dsca.mil/pubs/Vol%2014_4/Djerejian.pdf.

Dobriansky, Paula J., and Thomas Carothers. "Democracy Promotion: Explaining the Bush Administration's Position." *Foreign Affairs* 82, no. 3 (2003): 141–45.

Dorman, William A., and Mansour Farhang. *The US Press and Iran: Foreign Policy and the Journalism of Deference*. Berkeley: Univ. of California Press, 1987.

Dorril, Stephen. *MI6: Inside the Covert World of Her Majesty's Secret Intelligence Service*. New York: Free Press, 2000.

Douglas, William O. *The Court Years, 1939–1975*. New York: Random House, 1980.

Dreyfuss, Robert. *Devil's Game: How the United States Helped Unleash Fundamentalist Islam*. New York: Metropolitan Books, 2005.

Drezner, Daniel W. *The Sanctions Paradox: Economic Statecraft and International Relations*. New York: Cambridge Univ. Press, 1999.

Dudziak, Mary L. *Cold War Civil Rights: Race and the Image of American Democracy*. Princeton, NJ: Princeton Univ. Press, 2000.

Dulles, John Foster. *War or Peace*. New York: Macmillan, 1950.

Easterley, William, Shanker Satyanath, and Daniel Berger. *Superpower Interventions and Their Consequences for Democracy: An Empirical Inquiry*. Working Paper no. 13992. Cambridge, MA: National Bureau of Economic Research, 2008.

Ebrahimi, Mansoureh. *The British Role in Iranian Domestic Politics (1951–1953)*. Geneva: Springer Science and Business Media, 2016.

Eden, Anthony. *Full Circle: The Memoirs of Anthony Eden*. Boston: Houghton Mifflin, 1960.

Eisenhower, Dwight D. *The Eisenhower Diaries*. Edited by Robert H. Ferrell. New York: Norton, 1981.

Ekbladh, David. *The Great American Mission: Modernization and the Construction of an American World Order*. Princeton, NJ: Princeton Univ. Press, 2010.

Elm, Mostafa. *Oil, Power, and Principle: Iran's Oil Nationalization and Its Aftermath*. Syracuse, NY: Syracuse Univ. Press, 1992.

Emery, Christian. *US Foreign Policy and the Iranian Revolution: The Cold War Dynamics of Engagement and Strategic Alliance*. Basingstoke, UK: Palgrave Macmillan, 2013.

Emmanuel, Nikolas. "Undermining Cooperation: Donor-Patrons and the Failure of Political Conditionality." *Democratization* 17, no. 5 (2010): 856–77.

Fallaci, Oriana. "The Shah of Iran: An Interview with Mohammad Reza Pahlavi." *New Republic*, Dec. 1, 1973, 15–21.

Fardust, Hussein, and Ali Akbar Dareini. *The Rise and Fall of the Pahlavi Dynasty: Memoirs of Former General Hussein Fardust*. Delhi: Motilal Banarsidass, 1999.

Farjami, Mahmud. "Political Satire as an Index of Press Freedom: A Review of Political Satire in the Iranian Press during the 2000s." *Iranian Studies* 47, no. 2 (2014): 217–39.

Farmanfarmaian, Manucher, and Roxane Farmanfarmaian. *Blood and Oil: Memoirs of a Persian Prince, from the Shah to the Ayatollah*. New York: Random House, 2005.

Farman-Farmaian, Sattareh, and Dona Munker. *Daughter of Persia: A Woman's Journey from Her Father's Harem through the Islamic Revolution*. New York: Crown, 1992.

Fawcett, Louise. "Revisiting the Iranian Crisis of 1946: How Much Do We Know?" *Iranian Studies* 47, no. 3 (2014): 379–99.

Ferrell, Robert H. *Choosing Truman: The Democratic Convention of 1944*. Columbia: Univ. of Missouri Press, 2000.

———. *Truman and Pendergast*. Columbia: Univ. of Missouri Press, 1999.

Ferrier, Ronald W. "The Development of the Iranian Oil Industry." In *Twentieth Century Iran*, edited by Hossein Amirsadeghi, 93–110. New York: Holmes and Meier, 1977.

Flyvberg, Bent. *Making Social Science Matter: Why Social Science Fails and How It Can Succeed Again*. New York: Oxford Univ. Press, 2001.

Foran, John. *Fragile Resistance: Social Transformation in Iran from 1500 to the Revolution*. Boulder, CO: Westview Press, 1993.

Ford, Gerald R. *Public Papers of the Presidents of the United States: Gerald R. Ford, Containing the Public Messages, Speeches, and Statements of the President 1976–1977*. Washington, DC: US Government Printing Office, 1979.

Forrestal, James V. *The Forrestal Diaries*. New York: Viking Press, 1951.

Freedman, Lawrence. *Kennedy's Wars: Berlin, Cuba, Laos, and Vietnam*. New York: Oxford Univ. Press, 2000.

Friedel, Frank. *Franklin D. Roosevelt*. 4 vols. Boston: Little, Brown, 1952–56.

———. *Franklin D. Roosevelt: A Rendevous with Destiny*. Vol. 1 of the *Franklin D. Roosevelt* series. Paperback reprint. Boston: Little, Brown, 1990.

Gaddis, John Lewis. *We Now Know: Rethinking Cold War History*. New York: Oxford Univ. Press, 1997.

Gaitskell, Hugh. *The Diary of Hugh Gaitskell*. Edited by Philip Maynard Williams. London: Cape, 1983.

Gardner, Lloyd, C. *The Long Road to Baghdad: A History of U.S. Foreign Policy from the 1970s to the Present*. New York: New Press, 2008.

———. *Three Kings: The Rise of an American Empire in the Middle East after World War II*. New York: New Press, 2009.

Gasiorowski, Mark J. "The 1953 Coup d'État against Mosaddeq." In *Mohammad Mossaddeq and the 1953 Coup in Iran*, edited by Mark J. Gasiorowski and Malcolm Byrne, 227–60. Syracuse, NY: Syracuse Univ. Press, 2004.

———. "The 1953 Coup d'État in Iran." *International Journal of Middle East Studies* 19, no. 3 (1987): 261–86.

———. "Central Intelligence Agency." *Encyclopædia Iranica* 5 (1991): 253–58.

———. "The Qarani Affair and Iranian Politics." *International Journal of Middle East Studies* 25, no. 4 (1993): 625–44.

———. *US Foreign Policy and the Shah: Building a Client State in Iran.* Ithaca, NY: Cornell Univ. Press, 1991.

Gasiorowski, Mark J., and Malcolm Byrne, eds. *Mohammad Mossaddeq and the 1953 Coup in Iran.* Syracuse, NY: Syracuse Univ. Press, 2004.

Gavin, Francis J. "Politics, Power, and US Policy in Iran, 1950–1953." *Journal of Cold War Studes* 1, no. 1 (1999): 56–89.

Gendzier, Irene L. *Managing Political Change: Social Scientists and the Third World.* Boulder, CO: Westview Press, 1985.

———. *Notes from the Minefield: United States Intervention in Lebanon and the Middle East, 1945–1958.* New York: Columbia Univ. Press, 2006.

Gerring, John, Philip Bond, William T. Barndt, and Carola Moreno. "Democracy and Economic Growth: A Historical Perspective." *World Politics* 57 (2005): 323–64.

Gheissari, Ali, and Vali Nasr. *Democracy in Iran: History and the Quest for Liberty.* Oxford: Oxford Univ. Press, 2006.

Ghods, M. Reza. "The Rise and Fall of General Razmara." *Middle Eastern Studies* 29, no. 1 (1993): 22–35.

Giglio, James N. *The Presidency of John F. Kennedy.* Lawrence: Univ. Press of Kansas, 1991.

Gilman, Nils. *Mandarins of the Future: Modernization Theory in Cold War America.* Baltimore: Johns Hopkins Univ. Press, 2003.

Goduti, Philip A. *Kennedy's Kitchen Cabinet and the Pursuit of Peace: The Shaping of American Foreign Policy, 1961–1963.* Jefferson, NC: McFarland, 2009.

Goode, James F. "Reforming Iran during the Kennedy Years." *Diplomatic History* 15, no. 1 (2007): 13–29.

———. *The United States and Iran, 1946–51: The Diplomacy of Neglect.* New York: St. Martin's Press, 1989.

———. *The United States and Iran: In the Shadow of Musaddiq.* New York: St. Martin's Press, 1996.

Gordon, Lincoln. "The Alliance at Birth: Hopes and Fears." In *The Alliance for Progress: A Retrospective*, edited by L. Ronald Scheman, 73–80. New York: Praeger, 1988.

Guerrero, Javier Gil. *The Carter Administration and the Fall of Iran's Pahlavi Dynasty: US–Iran Relations on the Brink of the 1979 Revolution.* New York: Palgrave Macmillan, 2016.

———. "Human Rights and Tear Gas: The Question of Carter Administration Officials Opposed to the Shah." *British Journal of Middle Eastern Studies* 43, no. 3 (2016): 285–301.

Guilak, Hooshang. *Fire beneath the Ashes: The United States and Iran, a Historic Perspective*. Bloomington, IN: Xlibris, 2011.

Hagen, James M., and Vernon W. Ruttan. "Development Policy under Eisenhower and Kennedy." *Economic Development Center* 87-10 (1987): 1–54.

Halberstam, David. *The Best and the Brightest*. New York: Random House, 1972.

Halliday, Fred. *Iran, Dictatorship, and Development*. New York: Penguin, 1979.

Hamidian, Naqi. *Safar ba balha-ye arezou: Sheklgiri-ye jonbesh-e cheriki-ye Feda'iyan-e Khalq* (Flying on the Wings of Hope: The Formation of the People's Devotees). Stockholm: Arash, 2004.

Hamzavi, Abdol Hossein. "Iran and the Tehran Conference." *International Affairs* 20, no. 2 (1944): 192–203.

———. *Persia and the Powers: An Account of Diplomatic Relations, 1941–1946*. New York: Hutchinson, 1946.

Harbutt, Fraser J. *The Iron Curtain: Churchill, America, and the Origins of the Cold War*. New York: Oxford Univ. Press, 1986.

Harriman, W. Averell, and Elie Abel. *Special Envoy to Churchill and Stalin, 1941–1946*. New York: Random House, 1975.

Harris, David. *The Crisis: The President, the Prophet, and the Shah—1979 and the Coming of Militant Islam*. New York: Little, Brown, 2004.

Hasanli, Jamil. *At the Dawn of the Cold War: The Soviet–American Crisis over Iranian Azerbaijan, 1941–1946*. Lanham, MD: Rowman and Littlefield, 2006.

Hasemi, Nader, and Danny Postel, eds. *The People Reloaded: The Green Movement and the Struggle for Iran's Future*. New York: Melville House, 2010.

Hashemi, Mohammad Sadr. *Tarikh-e jarayed va majallat-e Iran* (The History of the Press and Magazines in Iran). Esfahan, Iran: Kamal, 1949.

Heiss, Mary Ann. *Empire and Nationhood: The United States, Great Britain, and Oil, 1950–1954*. New York: Columbia Univ. Press, 1997.

Herz, Martin F., ed. *Contacts with the Opposition: A Symposium*. Washington, DC: Univ. Press of America, 1980.

Hillman, Richard. *Democracy for the Privileged: Crisis and Transition in Venezuela.* Boulder, CO: Lynne Rienner, 1992.

Hite, Katherine, and Paola Cesarini. *Authoritarian Legacies and Democracy in Latin America and Southern Europe.* Notre Dame: Univ. of Notre Dame Press, 2004.

Hobson, Christopher. "Rethinking Democracy: The End of Democratic Transitions?" *Melbourne Journal of Politics* 29 (2003): 56–67.

Holliday, Shabnam J. *Defining Iran: Politics of Resistance.* Burlington, VT: Ashgate, 2011.

Hooglund, Eric J. *Land and Revolution in Iran, 1960–1980.* Austin: Univ. of Texas Press, 1982.

Hoopes, Townsend. *The Limits of Intervention: An Inside Account of How the Johnson Administration Policy of Escalation Was Reversed.* New York: McKay, 1969.

Howard, Harry N. "The Regional Pacts and the Eisenhower Doctrine." *Annals of the American Academy of Political and Social Science* 401 (1972): 85–94.

Huntington, Samuel P. *The Clash of Civilizations and the Remaking of World Order.* New York: Simon and Schuster, 1998.

———. "Democracy's Third Wave." *Journal of Democracy* 2, no. 2 (1991): 12–34.

———. *Political Order in Changing Societies.* New Haven, CT: Yale Univ. Press, 1968.

———. *The Third Wave: Democratization in the Late Twentieth Century.* Norman: Univ. of Oklahoma Press, 1991.

Immerman, Richard H. *John Foster Dulles: Piety, Pragmatism, and Power in US Foreign Policy.* Wilmington, DE: Scholarly Resources, 1999.

Iran Human Rights Documentation Center. *A Faith Denied: The Persecution of the Baha'is of Iran.* New Haven, CT: Iran Human Rights Documentation Center, 2011. At http://www.iranhrdc.org/english/publications/reports/3149-a-faith-denied-the-persecution-of-the-baha-is-of-iran.html?p=1.

Isaacson, Walter. *Kissinger: A Biography.* New York: Simon and Schuster, 1992.

Jervis, Robert. *Why Intelligence Fails: Lessons from the Iranian Revolution and the Iraq War.* Ithaca, NY: Cornell Univ. Press, 2010.

Johns, Andrew L. "The Johnson Administration, the Shah of Iran, and the Changing Pattern of US–Iranian Relations, 1965–1967: 'Tired of Being Treated Like a Schoolboy.'" *Journal of Cold War Studies* 9, no. 2 (2007): 64–94.

Johnson, Lyndon B. *Public Papers of the Presidents of the United States: Lyndon B. Johnson, Containing the Public Messages, Speeches, and Statements of the President, November 22, 1963, to January 20, 1969.* Washington, DC: US Government Printing Office, 1965–70.

Kadivar, Mohsen. "God and His Guardians." *Index on Censorship* 33, no. 4 (2004): 64–71.

———. "*Wilayat al-Faqih* and Democracy." In *Islam, the State, and Political Authority: Medieval Issues and Modern Concerns*, edited by Asma Afsaruddin, 207–24. New York: Palgrave Macmillan, 2011.

Kalinovsky, Artemy M. "The Soviet Union and Mosaddeq: A Research Note." *Iranian Studies* 47, no. 3 (2014): 401–18.

Karawan, Ibrahim. "Middle East Studies after 9/11: Time for an Audit." *Journal of Democracy* 13, no. 2 (2002): 96–101.

Katouzian, Homa. "Mosaddeq's Government in Iranian History: Arbitrary Rule, Democracy, and the 1953 Coup." In *Mohammad Mossaddeq and the 1953 Coup in Iran*, edited by Mark J. Gasiorowski and Malcolm Byrne, 1–26. Syracuse, NY: Syracuse Univ. Press, 2004.

———. *Musaddiq and the Struggle for Power in Iran.* New York: St. Martin's Press, 1999.

———. *The Political Economy of Modern Iran, 1926–1979.* New York: New York Univ. Press, 1981.

———. "Riza Shah's Political Legitimacy and Social Base, 1921–1941." In *The Making of Modern Iran: State and Society under Riza Shah, 1921–1941*, edited by Stephanie Cronin, 15–37. New York: Routledge Curzon, 2003.

Kaufman, Scott. *Plans Unraveled: The Foreign Policy of the Carter Administration.* DeKalb: Northern Illinois Univ. Press, 2008.

Kazemi, Farhad. "Fedā'īān-e Eslām." *Encyclopædia Iranica* 9 (1999): 470–74.

Keddie, Nikki R. "Comments on Skocpol." *Theory and Society* 11, no. 3 (1982): 285–92.

———. *Modern Iran: Roots and Results of Revolution.* New Haven, CT: Yale Univ. Press, 2003.

————. *Religion and Rebellion in Iran: The Iranian Tobacco Protest of 1891–1892*. Abingdon, VA: Frank Cass, 1966.

Kedourie, Elie. *Democracy and Arab Political Culture*. London: Frank Cass, 1994.

Kennedy, John F. *Let the Word Go Forth: The Speeches, Statements, and Writings of John F. Kennedy 1947 to 1963*. Edited by Ted Sorensen. New York: Dell, 1988.

Khalidi, Rashid. "The Arab Spring." *The Nation*, Mar. 21, 2011. At http://www.thenation.com/article/158991/arab-spring.

Khomeini, Ruhollah. *Islam and Revolution: Writings and Declarations of Imam Khomeini*. Translated by Hamid Algar. Berkeley, CA: Mizan Press, 1981.

————. *Islamic Government: Government of the Jurist*. Translated by Hamid Algar. Tehran: Institute for Compilation and Publication of Imam Khomeini's Work, 2002.

Kimball, Warren F. *The Juggler: Franklin Roosevelt as Wartime Statesman*. Princeton, NJ: Princeton Univ. Press, 1991.

Kinzer, Stephen. *All the Shah's Men: An American Coup and the Roots of Middle East Terror*. Hoboken, NJ: Wiley, 2003.

————. *Overthrow: America's Century of Regime Change from Hawaii to Iraq*. New York: Holt, 2006.

Kisatsky, Deborah. "Voice of America and Iran, 1949–1953: US Liberal Developmentalism, Propaganda, and the Cold War." *Intelligence and National Security* 14, no. 3 (1999): 160–85.

Kramer, Martin. "Islam vs. Democracy." *Commentary*, Jan. 1993, 35–42.

Kuran, Timur. "Sparks and Prairie Fires: A Theory of Unanticipated Revolution." *Public Choice* 61, no. 1 (1989): 41–74.

Kurzman, Charles. *Democracy Denied, 1905–1915: Intellectuals and the Fate of Democracy*. Cambridge, MA: Harvard Univ. Press, 2008.

————. *The Unthinkable Revolution in Iran*. Cambridge, MA: Harvard Univ. Press, 2004.

Kux, Dennis. *India and the United States: Estranged Democracies, 1941–1991*. Washington, DC: National Defense Univ. Press, 1992.

Ladjevardi, Habib. *Khaterat-e Ali Amini: Nukhust vazir-e Iran, 1340–1341* (Memoirs of Ali Amini: Prime Minister of Iran, 1961–1962). Cambridge, MA: Iranian Oral History Project, Harvard Univ., 1995.

———. "The Origins of US Support for an Autocratic Iran." *International Journal of Middle Eastern Studies* 15, no. 2 (1983): 225–39.

Latham, Michael E. *Modernization as Ideology: American Social Science and "Nation Building" in the Kennedy Era*. Chapel Hill: Univ. of North Carolina Press, 2000.

———. *The Right Kind of Revolution: Modernization, Development, and US Foreign Policy from the Cold War to the Present*. Ithaca, NY: Cornell Univ. Press, 2011.

Leubbert, Gregory M. *Liberalism, Fascism, or Social Democracy: Social Classes and the Political Origins of Regimes in Interwar Europe*. New York: Oxford Univ. Press, 1991.

Leverett, Flynt, and Hillary Mann Leverett. *Going to Tehran: Why the United States Must Come to Terms with the Islamic Republic of Iran*. New York: Metropolitan Books, 2013.

Levinson, Jerome I., and Juan de Onis. *The Alliance That Lost Its Way: A Critical Report on the Alliance for Progress*. Chicago: Quadrangle Books, 1970.

Levitsky, Steven, and Lucan A. Way. *Competitive Authoritarianism: Hybrid Regimes after the Cold War*. Cambridge: Cambridge Univ. Press, 2010.

———. "International Linkage and Democratization." *Journal of Democracy* 16, no. 3 (2005): 20–34.

Lewis, Bernard. *What Went Wrong? Western Impact and Middle Eastern Response*. Oxford: Oxford Univ. Press, 2002.

Li, Quan, and Rafael Reuveny. "Economic Globalization and Democracy: An Empirical Analysis." *British Journal of Political Science* 33 (2003): 29–54.

Lilienthal, David E. *The Journals of David E. Lilienthal*. Vol. 5: *The Harvest Years, 1959–1963*. Edited by Helen M. Lilienthal. New York: Harper and Row, 1983.

Linz, Juan J., and Alfred C. Stepan. *Problems of Democratic Transition and Consolidation: Southern Europe, South America, and Post-Communist Europe*. Baltimore: Johns Hopkins Univ. Press, 1996.

Little, Douglas. *American Orientalism: The United States and the Middle East since 1945*. Chapel Hill: Univ. of North Carolina Press, 2002.

———. "Cold War and Covert Action: The United States and Syria, 1945–1958." *Middle East Journal* 44, no. 1 (1990): 51–76.

———. "Gideon's Band: America and the Middle East since 1945." *Diplomatic History* 18, no. 4 (1994): 513–40.

———. "Nasser Delenda Est: Lyndon Johnson, the Arabs, and the 1967 Six Day War." In *The Foreign Policies of Lyndon Johnson: Beyond Vietnam*, edited by H. W. Brands, 145–67. College Station: Texas A&M Univ. Press, 1999.

Lohbeck, Dan. *Patrick J. Hurley*. Chicago: Regnery, 1956.

Lohmann, Suzanne. "The Dynamics of International Cascades: The Monday Demonstrations in Leipzig, East Germany, 1989–1991." *World Politics* 47, no. 1 (1994): 42–101.

Looney, Robert. *Economic Origins of the Iranian Revolution*. New York: Pergamon Press, 1982.

Louis, William Roger. "Britain and the Overthrow of the Mosaddeq Government." In *Mohammad Mosaddeq and the 1953 Coup in Iran*, edited by Mark J. Gasiorowski and Malcolm Byrne, 126–77. Syracuse, NY: Syracuse Univ. Press, 2004.

———. *The British Empire in the Middle East*. Oxford: Clarendon Press, 1985.

Lytle, Mark H. *The Origins of the Iranian–American Alliance, 1941–1953*. New York: Holmes and Meier, 1987.

Mafinezam, Alidad, and Aria Mehrabi. *Iran and Its Place among Nations*. Westport, CT: Praeger, 2008.

Manchester, William, and Paul Reid. *The Last Lion: Winston Spencer Churchill, Defender of the Realm, 1940–1965*. New York: Little, Brown, 2012.

Marsh, Steve. "Anglo-American Relations and the Labour Government's 'Scuttle' from Abadan: A 'Declaration of Dependence'?" *International History Review* 35, no. 4 (2013): 817–43.

———. "Continuity and Change: Reinterpreting the Policies of the Truman and Eisenhower Administrations toward Iran, 1950–1954." *Journal of Cold War Studies* 7, no. 3 (2005): 79–123.

Matini, Jalal. *Nigahi beh Karnamah-e siyasi-e Doktor Mohammad Mossadegh* (A Glance at the Political Career of Dr. Mohammad Mossadegh). Los Angeles: Ketab, 2005.

McCullough, David. *Truman*. New York: Simon and Schuster, 1992.

McGlinchey, Stephen. *US Arms Policies towards the Shah's Iran*. New York: Routledge, 2014.

McLellan, David S. *Dean Acheson: The State Department Years.* New York: Dodd, Mead, 1976.

McMaster, H. R. *Dereliction of Duty: Lyndon Johnson, Robert McNamara, the Joint Chiefs of Staff, and the Lies That Led to Vietnam.* New York: Harper Collins, 1997.

McNamara, Robert S. *In Retrospect: The Tragedy and Lessons of Vietnam.* New York: Vintage Books, 1995.

Melanson, Richard A. "The Foundations of Eisenhower's Foreign Policy." In *Reevaluating Eisenhower: American Foreign Policy in the 1950s,* edited by Richard A. Melanson and David Mayers, 31–66. Urbana: Univ. of Illinois Press, 1987.

Milani, Abbas. *Eminent Persians: The Men and Women Who Made Modern Iran, 1941–1979.* Syracuse, NY: Syracuse Univ. Press, 2008.

———. "Hurley's Dream—How FDR Almost Brought Democracy to Iran." *Hoover Digest,* July 30, 2003. At http://www.hoover.org/publications /hoover-digest/article/6280.

———. "Iran's Paradoxical Regime." *Journal of Democracy* 26, no. 2 (2015): 52–60.

———. *The Persian Sphinx: Amir Abbas Hoveyda and the Riddle of the Iranian Revolution. A Biography.* Washington, DC: Mage, 2000.

———. *The Shah.* Basingstoke, UK: Palgrave Macmillan, 2011.

———. "The Shah's Atomic Dreams." *Foreign Policy,* Dec. 29, 2010. At http://foreignpolicy.com/2010/12/29/the-shahs-atomic-dreams/.

Milani, Mohsen M. *The Making of Iran's Islamic Revolution: From Monarchy to Islamic Republic.* Boulder, CO: Westview Press, 1988.

Milne, David. *America's Rasputin: Walt Rostow and the Vietnam War.* New York: Hill and Wang, 2008.

Milward, Alan S. *The Reconstruction of Western Europe, 1945–1951.* Berkeley: Univ. of California Press, 1984.

Mirfetros, Ali. *Doktor Mohammad Mossadegh: Asib shenasi yek shekast* (Dr. Mohammad Mossadegh: Pathology of a Failure). Los Angeles: Ketab, 2008.

Miscamble, Wilson D. "Roosevelt, Truman, and the Development of Postwar Grand Strategy." *Orbis* 53, no. 4 (2009): 553–70.

Mitchell, Timothy. *Carbon Democracy: Political Power in the Age of Oil.* New York: Verso, 2011.

Mokhtari, Fariborz. "Iran's 1953 Coup Revisited: Internal Dynamics versus External Intrigue." *Middle East Journal* 62, no. 3 (2008): 457–89.

Morgan, Ted. *FDR: A Biography.* New York: Simon and Schuster, 1985.

Morgenthau, Hans. "A Political Theory of Foreign Aid." *American Political Science Review* 56, no. 2 (1962): 301–9.

Mossadegh, Mohammad. *Khaterat va ta'allomat-e Mossadegh* (Memoirs and Musings of Mossadegh). Edited by Iraj Afshar. Tehran: Elmi, 1986.

Mottahedeh, Roy. *The Mantle of the Prophet: Religion and Politics in Iran.* Oxford: Oneworld, 2004.

Moussawi, Ibrahim. *Shi'ism and the Democratization Process in Iran: With a Focus on Wilayat al-Faqih.* London: Saqi, 2011.

Munson, Henry, Jr. *Islam and Revolution in the Middle East.* New Haven, CT: Yale Univ. Press, 1988.

Najmabadi, Afsaneh. *Land Reform and Social Change in Iran.* Salt Lake City: Univ. of Utah Press, 1987.

Nasr, Vali. "Politics within the Late-Pahlavi State: The Ministry of Economy and Industrial Policy, 1963–69." *International Journal of Middle East Studies* 32, no. 1 (2000): 97–122.

Neal, Steve. *HST: Memories of the Truman Years.* Carbondale: Southern Illinois Univ., 2003.

Nemchenok, Victor V. "In Search of Stability amid Chaos: US Policy toward Iran, 1961–1963." *Cold War History* 10, no. 3 (2010): 341–69.

———. "That so Fair a Thing Should Be so Frail: The Ford Foundation and the Failure of Rural Development in Iran, 1953–1964." *Middle East Journal* 63, no. 2 (2009): 261–84.

Nichols, David A. *Eisenhower 1956: The President's Year of Crisis—Suez and the Brink of War.* New York: Simon and Schuster, 2011.

Offiler, Ben. *US Foreign Policy and the Modernization of Iran: Kennedy, Johnson, Nixon, and the Shah.* Basingstoke, UK: Palgrave Macmillan, 2015.

O'Kane, Rosemary H. T. *Paths to Democracy: Revolution and Totalitarianism.* New York: Routledge, 2004.

Olson, Lynne. *Citizens of London: The Americans Who Stood with Britain in Its Darkest, Finest Hour.* New York: Random House, 2010.

Otsuka, Tanya. "'Where Is My Vote?': Democratizing Iranian Election Law through International Legal Recourse." *Boston College International and Comparative Law Review* 33, no. 2 (2010): 339–56.

Our Documents: 100 Milestone Documents from the National Archives. Foreword by Michael Beschloss. New York: Oxford Univ. Press, 2003.

Overseas Consultants Inc. *Interim Report to the Plan Organization of the Government of Iran, May 16, 1949.* New York: Overseas Consultants Inc., 1949.

Pahlavi, Ashraf. *Faces in a Mirror: Memoirs from Exile.* Englewood Cliffs, NJ: Prentice-Hall, 1980.

Pahlavi, Mohammad Reza. *Answer to History.* New York: Stein and Day, 1980.

———. *Mission for My Country.* New York: Hutchinson, 1961.

———. "The Shah's Proclamation on Reform." *Middle East Journal* 16, no. 1 (1962): 86–88.

Palmer, Michael A. *Guardians of the Gulf: A History of America's Expanding Role in the Persian Gulf, 1883–1992.* New York: Free Press, 1992.

Papers Relating to the Foreign Relations of the United States, 1942. Vol. 4: *The Near East and Africa.* Washington, DC: US Government Printing Office, 1975.

Papers Relating to the Foreign Relations of the United States, 1943. Vol. 4: TITLE. Washington, DC: US Government Printing Office, 19XX.

Papers Relating to the Foreign Relations of the United States, 1944. Vol. 5: TITLE. Washington, DC: US Government Printing Office, 19XX.

Papers Relating to the Foreign Relations of the United States, 1945. Vol. 8: *The Near East and Africa.* Washington, DC: US Government Printing Office, 1969.

Papers Relating to the Foreign Relations of the United States, 1946. Vol. 7: *The Near East and Africa.* Washington, DC: US Government Printing Office, 1969.

Papers Relating to the Foreign Relations of the United States, 1947. Vol. 5: *The Near East and Africa.* Washington, DC: US Government Printing Office, 1971.

Papers Relating to the Foreign Relations of the United States, 1948. Vol. 5, part 1: *The Near East, South Asia, and Africa.* Washington, DC: US Government Printing Office, 1976.

Papers Relating to the Foreign Relations of the United States, 1948. Vol. 6: TITLE. Washington, DC: US Government Printing Office, 19XX.

Papers Relating to the Foreign Relations of the United States, 1949. Vol. 6: *The Near East, South Asia, and Africa.* Washington, DC: US Government Printing Office, 1977.

Papers Relating to the Foreign Relations of the United States, 1950. Vol. 5: *The Near East, South Asia, and Africa.* Washington, DC: US Government Printing Office, 1978.

Papers Relating to the Foreign Relations of the United States, 1952–1954. Vol. 10: *United States Department of State / Iran, 1952–1954.* Washington, DC: US Government Printing Office, 1989.

Papers Relating to the Foreign Relations of the United States, 1955–1957. vol. 6: *American Republics: Multilateral, Mexico, Caribbean.* Washington, DC: US Government Printing Office, 1987.

Papers Relating to the Foreign Relations of the United States, 1955–57. Vol. 12: *Near East, Iran, Iraq.* Washington, DC: US Government Printing Office, 1991.

Papers Relating to the Foreign Relations of the United States, 1958–1960. Vol. 12: *Near East Region, Iraq, Iran, Arabian Peninsula.* Washington, DC: US Government Printing Office, 1993.

Papers Relating to the Foreign Relations of the United States, 1961–1963. Vol. 17: *Near East.* Washington, DC: US Government Printing Office, 1994.

Papers Relating to the Foreign Relations of the United States, 1961–1963. Vol. 18: *Near East, 1962–1963.* Washington, DC: US Government Printing Office, 1995.

Papers Relating to the Foreign Relations of the United States, 1964–1968. Vol. 22: *Iran.* Washington, DC: US Government Printing Office, 1999.

Papers Relating to the Foreign Relations of the United States, 1965. Vol. 5: *The Near East, South Asia, and Africa, the Far East.* Washington, DC: US Government Printing Office, 19XX.

Papers Relating to the Foreign Relations of the United States, 1969–1976. Vol. 1: *Foundations of Foreign Policy, 1969–1972.* Washington, DC: US Government Printing Office, 2003.

Papers Relating to the Foreign Relations of the United States, 1969–1976. Vol. 24: *Middle East Region and Arabian Peninsula, 1969–1972.* Washington, DC: US Government Printing Office, 2008.

Papers Relating to the Foreign Relations of the United States, 1969–1976. Vol. E-4: *Documents on Iran and Iraq, 1969–1972.* Washington, DC: US Government Printing Office, 2006.

Papers Relating to the Foreign Relations of the United States: Diplomatic Papers, the Conferences at Cairo and Tehran, 1943. Washington, DC: US Government Printing Office, 1961.

Parsi, Trita. *A Single Role of the Dice: Obama's Diplomacy with Iran.* New Haven, CT: Yale Univ. Press, 2012.

———. *Treacherous Alliance: The Secret Dealings of Israel, Iran, and the United States.* New Haven, CT: Yale Univ. Press, 2007.

Parsons, Anthony. *The Pride and the Fall: Iran, 1974–1979.* London: J. Cape, 1984.

Pearson, Ivan L. G. *In the Name of Oil: Anglo-American Relations in the Middle East, 1950–1958.* Eastbourne, UK: Sussex Academic Press, 2010.

Pfau, Richard. "The Legal Status of American Forces in Iran." *Middle East Journal* 28, no. 2 (1974): 141–53.

Pike, Otis. *CIA: The Pike Report.* Nottingham, UK: Spokesman Books, 1977.

Pollack, Kenneth M. *The Persian Puzzle: The Conflict between Iran and America.* New York: Random House, 2004.

Popp, Roland. "An Application of Modernization Theory during the Cold War? The Case of Pahlavi Iran." *International History Review* 30, no. 1 (2008): 76–98.

Prados, John. *Safe for Democracy: The Secret Wars of the CIA.* Chicago: Ivan R. Dee, 2006.

Pridham, Geoffrey. *The Dynamics of Democratization: A Comparative Approach.* New York: Continuum, 2000.

Pruessen, Ronald W. *John Foster Dulles: The Road to Power.* New York: Free Press, 1982.

Qaimmaqami, Linda Wills. "The Catalyst of Nationalism: Max Thornburg and the Failure of Private Sector Development in Iran, 1947–1951." *Diplomatic History* 19, no. 1 (1995): 1–31.

Rabe, Stephen G. *John F. Kennedy: World Leader.* Washington, DC: Potomac Books, 2010.

Rafizadeh, Mansur. *Witness: From the Shah to the Secret Arms Deal—An Insider's Account of U.S. Involvement in Iran.* New York: Morrow, 1987.

Rahnema, Ali. "Overthrowing Mosaddeq in Iran: 28 Mordad/19 August 1953." *Iranian Studies* 45, no. 5 (2012): 661–68.

Rakove, Robert B. *Kennedy, Johnson, and the Nonaligned World.* Cambridge: Cambridge Univ. Press, 2013.

Ratcliffe, Susan, ed. *Concise Oxford Dictionary of Quotations.* New York: Oxford Univ. Press, 2011.

Raviv, Dan, and Yossi Melman. *Spies against Armageddon: Inside Israel's Secret Wars.* New York: Levant Books, 2014.

Razi, G. Hossein. "Democratic–Authoritarian Attitudes and Social Background in a Non-Western Society." *Comparative Politics* 14, no. 1 (1981): 53–74.

Roosevelt, Kermit. *Countercoup: The Struggle for the Control of Iran.* New York: McGraw-Hill, 1979.

Rostow, Walt W. *Diffusion of Power: An Essay in Recent History.* New York: Macmillan, 1972.

———. *Eisenhower, Kennedy, and Foreign Aid.* Austin: Univ. of Texas Press, 1985.

———. *The Stages of Economic Growth: A Non-Communist Manifesto.* Cambridge: Cambridge Univ. Press, 1960.

Rostow, Walt W., and Max F. Millikan. *A Proposal: Key to an Effective Foreign Policy.* New York: Harper and Bros., 1957.

Rubin, Barry M. *Paved with Good Intentions: The American Experience in Iran.* New York: Oxford Univ. Press, 1980.

Safire, William. *Before the Fall: An Inside View of the Pre-Watergate White House.* New Brunswick, NJ: Transaction, 2005.

Saikal, Amin. *The Rise and Fall of the Shah.* Princeton, NJ: Princeton Univ. Press, 1980.

Sale, Richard. "Carter and Iran: From Idealism to Disaster." *Washington Quarterly* 3, no. 4 (1980): 75–87.

Samii, Abbas William. "Iran's Guardian Council as an Obstacle to Democracy." *Middle East Journal* 55, no. 4 (2001): 643–62.

———. "The Role of SAVAK in the 1978–1979 Iranian Revolution." PhD diss., Univ. of Cambridge, 1994.

Sampson, Anthony. *The Seven Sisters: The Great Oil Companies and the World They Shaped.* New York: Viking Press, 1975.

Sayeed, K. B. "Pakistan's Basic Democracy." *Middle East Journal* 15, no. 3 (1961): 249–63.

Scheman, L. Ronald, ed. *The Alliance for Progress: A Retrospective*. New York: Praeger, 1988.

Schlesinger, Arthur M., Jr. *The Imperial Presidency*. Boston: Houghton Mifflin, 1973.

———. *A Thousand Days: John F. Kennedy in the White House*. Boston: Houghton Mifflin, 2003.

Secor, Laura. *Children of Paradise: The Struggle for the Soul of Iran*. New York: Riverhead Books, 2016.

Shuster, W. Morgan. *The Strangling of Persia: Story of the European Diplomacy and Oriental Intrigue That Resulted in the Denationalization of Twelve Million Mohammedans, a Personal Narrative*. Washington, DC: Mage, 2006.

Sick, Gary. *All Fall Down: America's Tragic Encounter with Iran*. New York: Penguin, 1988.

———. "Iran: A View from the White House." *World Affairs* 149, no. 4 (1987): 209–13.

Skocpol, Theda. "Rentier State and Shi'a Islam in the Iranian Revolution." *Theory and Society* 11, no. 3 (1982): 265–83.

Slavin, Barbara. *Bitter Friends, Bosom Enemies: Iran, the US, and the Twisted Path to Confrontation*. New York: St. Martin's Press, 2007.

Smith, Jean Edward. *Eisenhower in War and Peace*. New York: Random House, 2012.

Smith, Tony. *America's Mission: The United States and the Worldwide Struggle for Democracy in the Twentieth Century*. Princeton, NJ: Princeton Univ. Press, 1994.

Sneh, Ira Nartzizenfield. *The Future Almost Arrived: How Jimmy Carter Failed to Change US Foreign Policy*. New York: Peter Lang, 2008.

Snow, Edgar. *The Other Side of the River: Red China Today*. New York: Random House, 1962.

Soroush, Abdolkarim. *Reason, Freedom, and Democracy in Islam: Essential Writings of Abdolkarim Soroush*. Translated by Mahmoud Sadri and Ahmad Sadri. New York: Oxford Univ. Press, 2000.

Stalin, Joseph. *Speeches Delivered at Meetings of Voters of the Stalin Electoral District, Moscow, December 11, 1937 and February 9, 1946*. Moscow: Foreign Language Publishing House, 1950.

Stempel, John D. *Inside the Iranian Revolution*. Bloomington: Indiana Univ. Press, 1981.

Stewart, Richard A. *Sunrise at Abadan: The British and Soviet Invasion of Iran, 1941.* New York: Praeger, 1988.

Strober, Deborah H., and Gerald S. Strober. *The Kennedy Presidency: An Oral History of the Era.* Washington, DC: Brassey's, 2003.

Stueck, William. "Reassessing US Strategy in the Aftermath of the Korean War." *Orbis* 53, no. 4 (2009): 571–90.

Sullivan, William H. *Mission to Iran.* New York: Norton, 1981.

Summitt, April. "For a White Revolution: John F. Kennedy and the Shah of Iran." *Middle East Journal* 58, no. 4 (2004): 560–75.

Taffet, Jeffrey F. *Foreign Aid as Foreign Policy: The Alliance for Progress in Latin America.* New York: Routledge, 2007.

Tanzer, Lester. *The Kennedy Circle.* Washington, DC: Luce, 1961.

Taubman, William. *Khruschev: The Man and His Era.* New York: Norton, 2003.

Thorpe, James A. "Truman's Ultimatum to Stalin on the 1946 Azerbaijan Crisis: The Making of a Myth." *Journal of Politics* 40, no. 1 (1978): 188–95.

Trenta, Luca. "The Champion of Human Rights Meets the King of Kings: Jimmy Carter, the Shah, and Iranian Illusions and Rage." *Diplomacy and Statecraft* 24, no. 3 (2013): 476–98.

Valkenier, Elizabeth Kridl. *The Soviet Union and the Third World: An Economic Bind.* New York: Praeger, 1983.

Vance, Cyrus R. *Hard Choices: Critical Years in America's Foreign Policy.* New York: Simon and Schuster, 1983.

Ward, Steven R. *Immortal: A Military History of Iran and Its Armed Forces.* Washington, DC: Georgetown Univ. Press, 2009.

Wawro, Geoffrey. *Quicksand: America's Pursuit of Power in the Middle East.* New York: Penguin, 2010.

Weiner, Tim. *Legacy of Ashes: The History of the CIA.* New York: Doubleday, 2007.

Westad, Odd Arne. *The Global Cold War: Third World Interventions and the Making of Our Time.* Cambridge: Cambridge Univ. Press, 2005.

Westwood, Andrew F. "Elections and Politics in Iran." *Middle East Journal* 15, no. 2 (1961): 153–64.

Wiarda, Howard J. *New Directions in Comparative Politics.* Boulder, CO: Westview Press, 2002.

Wise, David. "Scholars of the Nuclear Age." In *The Kennedy Circle*, edited by Lester Tanzer, 20–41. Washington DC: Luce, 1961.

Yaqub, Salim. *Containing Arab Nationalism: The Eisenhower Doctrine and the Middle East.* Chapel Hill: Univ. of North Carolina Press, 2004.

Yergin, Daniel. *Shattered Peace: The Origins of the Cold War and the National Security State.* Boston: Houghton Mifflin, 1977.

Zabih, Sepehr. *The Communist Movement in Iran.* Berkeley: Univ. of California Press, 1966.

———. *The Mossadegh Era: Roots of the Iranian Revolution.* Chicago: Lake View Press, 1982.

Zabir, Sepehr. *Iran since the Revolution.* London: Routledge, 2011.

Zahrani, Mostafa T. "The Coup That Changed the Middle East: Mossadegh v. the CIA in Perspective." *World Policy Journal* 19, no. 2 (2002): 93–99.

Zonis, Marvin. *The Political Elite of Iran.* Princeton, NJ: Princeton Univ. Press, 1971.

Index

Photograph by Shireen Sarraf.

David R. Collier is a research consultant and an adjunct professor in Boston University's Washington, DC, program.